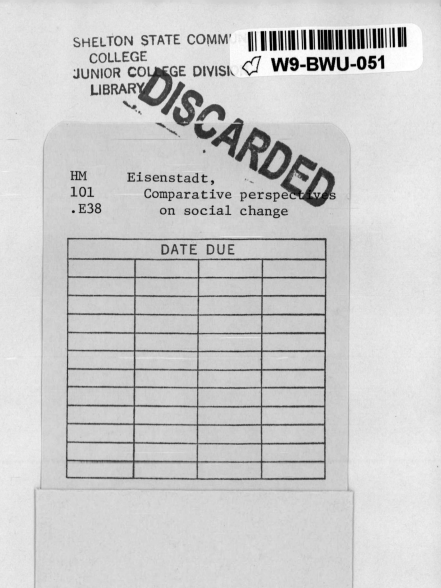

DATE DUE			

COMPARATIVE PERSPECTIVES ON

SOCIAL
CHANGE

Edited by

S. N. EISENSTADT

LITTLE, BROWN AND COMPANY Boston

LIBRARY OF CONGRESS CATALOG CARD NO. 68-11090

SECOND PRINTING

Published simultaneously in Canada by
Little, Brown & Company (Canada) Limited

PRINTED IN THE UNITED STATES OF AMERICA

ACKNOWLEDGMENTS

I would like to take this opportunity to thank all those whose encouragement and help have enabled me to put this volume together: Professor A. Inkeles, who has taken the initiative in suggesting this book, and whose criticism of the introduction and table of contents was very helpful; the authors and the original publishers of the works included in this anthology for their contributions to the field and for their consent to have them published here; to Mrs. R. Shacko and Mrs. P. Gurevitz who have greatly helped in the various steps of the preparation of the manuscript; and to the staff of Little, Brown and Company for their helpful cooperation in the editing of the work and seeing it through the various stages of publishing.

The Hebrew University   S. N. Eisenstadt
Jerusalem, Israel

TABLE OF CONTENTS

vii

Introduction

I. MAJOR THEMES IN THE SOCIOLOGICAL ANALYSIS OF SOCIAL CHANGE

The analysis of social change has constituted one of the major foci of inquiry and research from the beginning of modern sociology. Rooted as the development of sociology was in the emergence of modern, industrial society from traditional or premodern societies, it dealt, implicitly or explicitly, with change. Sociology's central concern with the nature of modern society (which has built into itself the propensity to change continuously) has emphasized even more this interest. Recent studies of so-called underdeveloped or developing societies have greatly strengthened this interest in social change.

Several recurring themes can be distinguished among the major theories of social change. One theme was the discernment of general trends in the development of society as a whole.

Some early attempts in this direction can be found in the great evolutionary theories developed by Comte, Spencer, Hobhouse in sociology, and Tylor and Westermarck in anthropology.[1]

Their major assumption—somewhat simplified—is that all societies, in all spheres of social life, pass through similar stages of development (unless arrested), moving from simpler, less complex, less differentiated to more

---

[1]For a general description and discussion of these various theories, see P.A. Sorokin, *Contemporary Sociological Theories*. New York: Harper & Brothers, 1928.

complex and differentiated stages — culminating in the modern industrial, secular society.

Side by side with those who emphasize unilinear schemes of development are those theorists who — following such thinkers of early times as the Roman historian Polybius or the famous medieval Arabian philosopher Ibn Khaldun — describe the laws of development of any single society in terms of cycles of "birth," "growth" and "decline." The two Italian sociologists Pareto and Mosca are perhaps the best known among the theorists of the classical age of sociology.[2]

This theme can also be found in the work of the contemporary sociologist Pitirim Sorokin, who in addition, however, emphasizes the differences among various civilizations, which he distinguished according to their major value orientations.[3]

Contrasted with the themes of general development are those which are primarily concerned with the trend of development of one particular type of society — usually that of Western (that is, European and North American) society.

The best examples of this approach are: de Tocqueville,[4] with his emphasis on the breakdown of various intermediary bodies (such as modern voluntary associations) and the possible development of an atomized mass-society; Marx,[5] who predicted the transition of modern society from capitalism through socialism to communism; Max Weber,[6] with his concern about the growing rationalization, bureaucratization, and "demystification" of life in modern societies; and Karl Mannheim,[7] who attempted to diagnose the specific social situation of the Western World in the late 1930's and 1940's in terms derived from Marx and Weber.

Although these theorists (with the obvious exception of Max Weber with his well-known broad comparative scope of inquiry) were mostly concerned with the development of Western (European or American)

[2] James H. Meisel (ed.), *Pareto and Mosca*. Englewood Cliffs, N.J.: Prentice Hall, 1965.

[3] P. Sorokin, *Social and Cultural Dynamics*. New York: American Book Company, 1937.

[4] A. de Tocqueville, *The Old Régime and the French Revolution* (translated by Stuart Gilbert). Garden City: Doubleday, 1955; and *Democracy in America* (translated by Henry Reeve). New York: Colonial Press, 1900.

[5] Karl Marx, *Early Writings* (translated and edited by Thomas B. Bottomore). London: C.A. Watts, 1963.

[6] Max Weber, *The Theory of Social and Economic Organization* (translated and edited by Talcott Parsons and A.M. Henderson). New York: Oxford University Press, 1947); and *Essays in Sociology* (translated and edited by H.H. Gerth and W.C. Mills). London: Kegan Paul, Trench, Trubner & Co., 1947.

[7] Karl Mannheim, *Freedom, Power and Democratic Planning*. London: Routledge and Kegan Paul, 1951.

society, their very attempts to explain these trends of development made them emphasize some specific systemic characteristics of social systems or some specific social mechanisms as the prime movers of social change which, presumably, are valid for all human societies. For example, Marx postulated that the relations among the elements of production and the concomitant crystallization of class struggle constitute the focal point of the nature of societies in general and that they are the prime movers of social change. Weber, by contrast, found the push of charismatic person-alities or groups to be one of the prime forces of change in all the major spheres of social life — in religion, in politics, and even in economics (as illustrated by his famous Protestant Ethic thesis which connected the development of modern capitalism with Calvinism and Puritanism).[8]

A somewhat different approach to the dynamics of change in societies can be found in the work of Pareto and Mosca (both mentioned earlier). They emphasized the circulation of élites — the change from one type of élite to another and the weakening of the existing élite through dissipation and its replacement by new, more vigorous ones — as the prime mover of social change. They were close to Weber in their emphasis on the roles of special, selected groups of entrepreneurs and close to Marx in their emphasis on the importance of relations of dominance for the processes of change.

In the 1920's and 1930's the search for "factors" of change often led to the choice of technology and technological innovations as the most important of such factors. Perhaps one of the best-known illustrations of this approach can be found in the recent sociological research of W.F. Ogburn. In a series of penetrating analyses, he has demonstrated the importance of technological innovation as one of the most common im-petuses for change and has shown how other spheres of social and cultural life tend to lag behind such innovation.[9]

A third theme, closely related to the second, is concern with the differ-ent impact of such factors for change on different parts of a society and concern with the differences in the nature of the impetus to change which come from different parts of a social order. This theme is illustrated by the work of R.M. MacIver, who, following the German tradition, analyzed the ways in which the social, cultural, and technological spheres tend to develop different modes of change, how they have different impacts on

[8] See on this the forthcoming selection of Max Weber's work to be published in the Heritage of Sociology series of the University of Chicago Press and the editors' introduction: S.N. Eisenstadt, "Charisma, Institution Building and Social Transformation — Max Weber and Modern Sociology."

[9] See O. Dudley Duncan (ed.), *William Ogburn on Culture and Social Change*, selected papers in The Heritage of Sociology Series. Chicago: University of Chicago Press, 1966.

other spheres, and how the different factors of change and the different responses of these spheres to them, converge in different concrete constellations.[10]

II. ANALYSIS OF SOCIAL CHANGE ON
CLASSICAL AND CONTEMPORARY SOCIOLOGY

The classical sociologists' concern with different themes of social change converged with two other aspects of inquiry — the comparative study of different societies and civilizations, and the analysis of whole societies.

For instance, Ferguson and Montesquieu in the earliest phases of modern sociology in the 18th century. Marx and de Tocqueville in the mid 19th century, and Weber and Durkheim in the late 19th and early 20th centuries, were each concerned with processes of change of various total societies or "civilizations."[11]

In early sociology the combination of three foci of inquiry — analysis of change, comparative method, and study of whole societies — culminated in the evolutionary theories which dominated social thought in the late 19th century. Because of this emphasis, most of the scholars (Comte, Spencer, Hobhouse, Tylor, and Westermarck) dealt more with the general development of society and less with the systemic characteristics and internal dynamics of any single society or social system.

With the breakdown of the evolutionary synthesis, the combination of the three foci of interest disintegrated. The analysis of total societies became the most neglected subject in sociological inquiries. Different traditions of sociological research developed which were oriented toward the study of more restricted, micro-sociological phenomena: individual behavior, small groups, family, stratification, or different types of communities.

But even in most of this work there remained an emphasis on change and, to a smaller extent, an emphasis on comparative perspective. The more recent renewal of interest in both comparative studies and in the analysis of total societies has shown that these restricted studies added many new insights to the analytical and the comparative dimensions of the analysis of social change. Moreover, the renewal of interest enabled the development of new attempts which combine the detailed analysis of single social systems with more general, comparative, and even evolutionary analyses.[12]

The growth of interest in non-European societies after World War II and the increase in the number of studies of underdeveloped societies and

[10] R.M. MacIver, *Social Causation*. Boston: Ginn & Co., 1942.
[11] See P. Sorokin, *Contemporary Sociological Theories, op. cit.*
[12] See T. Parsons, *Societies: Evolutionary and Comparative Perspectives.* Englewood-Cliffs, N.J.: Prentice-Hall, 1966. S.N. Eisenstadt, *The Political System of Empires.* New York: The Free Press, 1963.

New States also greatly facilitated the development of analyses which combined the analysis of single societies with more general, comparative and even evolutionary analyses.[13]

III. THE CENTRAL PROBLEMS IN THE COMPARATIVE ANALYSIS OF SOCIAL CHANGE

However great the differences in the various approaches to social change, some common problems can be discerned in most of them. It is these problems which sociological theory and research face today.

Perhaps the most basic of these problems are:

1. To what extent is change imminent in the nature of societies?
2. What are the general characteristics of social change?
3. To what extent and in what ways are processes of change comparable in different societies, and which aspects of change are most amenable to comparison? Is it most valuable to compare the general development of total societies in the course of human history, or is it best to compare the processes of change of one type of social organization — the family, the community, or types of economic organization — in relatively similar cultural areas?
4. What are the interrelations between the processes of change in different parts of one society and what are the interrelations in different societies?

These general problems are analyzed briefly in this introduction. In the following selections they are illustrated in detail as they bear on different types of social groups, organizations, and total societies.

IV. CHANGE AND STABILITY IN SOCIAL LIFE: THE INSTITUTIONAL FOCUS

Change is by definition contrasted with stability; but stability, and especially stability in social life, is never to be equated with rigidity or inflexibility. When we say that a certain social group or institution has been stable for a certain period of time, we do not mean that no changes have occurred within it. By the very nature of social life, any group or organization which has some temporal dimension has experienced some change in personnel. Such changes, caused by broad demographic generational trends, are part of the very nature of total societies. Therefore, all social organizations and systems, whether small or large, develop special mechanisms by which new personnel are socialized into active membership.

In addition to changes in membership, many other types of change — changes in norms, in the concrete structure of roles, and in some of the

[13] See C. Geertz (ed.), *Old Societies and New States*. New York: The Free Press, 1963.

details of organization — may take place within an institution which nevertheless is seen as stable. Thus, to take an extreme, but important example, if we talk about the stability and continuity of the Chinese Imperial System for a period of more than two thousand years, we do not mean that there were no changes in dynasties, patterns of land distribution, conquests, territorial boundaries, the relative importance of different regions or of rural as against urban centers, or that there was no innovation in art, philosophy, or religious thought. All these did indeed take place in this long period of time, as they did also in the shorter periods of existence of other imperial systems, such as the Roman, the Byzantine, or the Sassanid in Iran.

Such stability only means that certain basic institutional patterns — for example, in China, the focal position of the Emperor, the preponderance of the gentry, the unique position of the class of bureaucratic *literati,* and the cultural dominance of Confucianism — persisted throughout a period and provided for a continuous collective identity.[14]

Similarly, if we say that a given hospital has remained the same throughout a certain period of time, we do not mean that there are no changes in its personnel, in the therapeutic methods used, or in the relative status of general practitioners compared with specialists. We only mean that in some way, which perhaps is not adequately defined, this hospital may seem relatively stable in its most central features, in its basic goals and structure, and in providing a common focus of collective identity for those participating in it and using its services or for the community at large.

In these illustrations we have been talking about the behavior and interaction of individuals in organizational patterns and social roles in some types of institutional organizations such as communities, special professional or kinship groups, institutional spheres of a society (the family, the economy, the political system or the system of stratification), or in total societies.

All institutional frameworks require the creation and continuity of organizational patterns directed toward upholding certain collective goals or patterns of behavior and dealing with some of the perennial and universal problems of social life.

These institutionalizing "activities" (i.e., attempts to establish and uphold such symbols, goals, organizations, and activities) are undertaken by people placed in strategic positions in the social structure who aspire to crystallize new types of institutional and symbolic orders and who succeed in competition with other such people or groups.

Establishing institutional frameworks involves the creation and definition of norms that regulate the major units of social behavior and organi-

[14] See E. Balazs, *Chinese Civilization and Bureaucracy.* New Haven: Yale University Press, 1964, especially chapters 1, 2. S.N. Eisenstadt, *The Political Systems of Empires, op. cit.,* especially Chapter XII.

zation of the criteria that control the flow of resources between the different individuals and social units that interact in any such situation, and of the sanctions that insure that the appropriate norms are upheld.

These sanctions and norms are required for the maintenance of the specific boundaries of any given system: the identity of the units that constitute it, its relations with outside systems and the symbols that delineate its specific characteristics.

It is in such ways that groups, collectivities and institutional systems (economic, political, etc.) with some basic common identity are established as relatively distinct units, for the maintenance of which people may be committed to different degrees.

V. INSTITUTIONALIZATION AND CHANGE

Although the attempts by institutional entrepreneurs to establish and legitimize common goals and norms in terms of common values and symbols are successful to varying degrees, the goals and norms are probably never fully accepted by the entire group, organization, or society. Most sub-groups exhibit some autonomy in their attitudes toward these norms and in their willingness or ability to provide the resources demanded by the given institutionalized system. For very long periods of time a great majority of the members of a given group, organization, or society may be identified to some degree with its values and norms and be willing to provide it with the resources it needs. However, other tendencies may also develop.

Some groups may be greatly opposed to the very premises of the institutionalization of a given system, may share its values only to a very small extent, and may accept these norms as the least among evils and as binding on them only in a very limited sense. Others may share these values and accept the norms to a greater degree but may look on themselves as the more truthful repositories of these same values. They may oppose the concrete levels at which the norms are institutionalized by the élite in power and may attempt to interpret them in different ways; that is, they may attempt to establish different bargaining positions and different norms of exchange. Others may develop new interpretations of existing values and strive for a change in the very bases of the institutional order. Hence, any institutional system is never fully "homogeneous" in the sense of being fully accepted or accepted to the same degree by all those participating in it. These different orientations may become the foci of conflict and of potential institutional change.

Even more important from the point of view of our analysis is that the initial attitudes of any group to the basic premises of the institutional system may change greatly after the initial institutionalization of the system. Institutionalization necessarily requires efforts to maintain the boundaries of the system by continuous attempts to mobilize resources from different groups and individuals and efforts to maintain the legitimacy of its values, symbols, and norms. But continuous implementation of these policies may affect the positions of various groups in the society and give rise to continuous shifts both in the balance of power among them and in their orientations to the existing institutional system.

Moreover, the institutionalization of any group, organization, institutional sphere, or total society creates new subgroups, collectivities, and organizations. The new organizations develop their own needs, interests, and orientations which may impinge on various other groups and institutional spheres, thus changing the attitudes of the various other groups toward the premises of the system. Similarly, changes in the balance of forces within the system also facilitate the development and maturation of certain inherent tendencies in the structure and orientation of key groups and élites. For example, some religious groups establish wider, more universalistic, orientations and membership units which may then develop beyond the basic premises of their institutional system.

Changes in the balance of forces may be intensified by the systemic relations between any given group or institutional sphere and other groups within the given groups or society. Whatever the degree of integration of any group or total society, systemic relations between different institutional spheres — for example, the political and the economic or the political and the kinship systems — are inherent in any ongoing society. Differences always exist in the basic or predominant orientations and norms of the different parts of a wider system. Hence the occupants of the major positions within the different subgroups or institutional spheres of a society may attempt to maintain their autonomy and secure the necessary resources by making contradictory demands on different groups. Each may look for support from different parts of the society, thus exacerbating potential conflicts among the various groups, changing their relative strengths, and possibly undermining the premises of the broader unit.

Thus, the very nature of establishing institutional systems creates the possibility that "anti-systems" will develop within them, although they may vary between different institutional systems (for example, religious and political) and between different types of each; and while the anti-systems may often remain latent for very long periods of time, they may also constitute important foci of change under propitious conditions.

The existence of contradictions or conflicts among the different institutional spheres and among different groups does not, of course, preclude the possibility that any system will maintain its boundaries more or less continuously and achieve accommodations or partial insulation from different subsystems and that a definite order and stable relations among the system's parts will persist. But the possibility of conflict and potential change is always present, rooted in the very process of crystallization and maintenance of institutional systems; and the direction and occurrence of change depend heavily on the nature of this process.

Just as the propensity to change is necessarily built into any institutional system, so the direction and scope of change are not random. The direction and scope of change depend on the nature of the conflict generating the change; on the system's values, norms, and organizations; on the various internal forces operating within the system; and on the external forces to which the system is especially sensitive because of its systemic properties. These various forces naturally differ among different institutional spheres and among different societies, but the sensitivity to these forces and the tendency to change are inherent in all institutional systems.

VI. THE SOURCES OF AND IMPETUS TO CHANGE

From the preceding analysis it can be easily understood that the impetus to change can come in all social systems from both internal and external sources and especially from the interrelations between the two.

The impact of this impetus becomes especially acute when it disturbs — on any given level of social organization — the existing equilibrium among the aspirations and goals of individuals, the roles they are expected to perform, and the resources at their disposal for the performance of these roles and for the implementation of the most important institutional and collective goals.

Thus, for instance, ecological, technological, and demographic changes and the interrelations among them have been recognized in sociological research and analysis as some of the most important "causes" of social change. Each causes changes in the balance between the distribution of manpower available and resources necessary for the performance of social roles and for the implementation of institutional goals.

If the demographic and technological trends upset the balance between the aspirations of people and institutions from the point of view of the availability and distribution of resources, other forces change the aspirations and goals of the people participating in any given system.

Here of special importance are changes in the spheres of culture and values, within which the creativity of human spirit and the unfolding of its potentialities attain their fullest manifestations and may influence the course of subsequent history, and in the sphere of the family, within which the potentialities for creativity are first nurtured, developed, and the products of creativity transmitted from generation to generation.

It is therefore no surprise that demographic, technological, and cultural forces have sometimes been singled out as the "sole" causes of social change in general or of the change of some given system in particular.

Yet it is obvious that the impetus to change can also arise from other parts of any social system, from changes within its political organization, from development of new political leaders and movements, from the impetus of new professional organizations, or from changes in the composition of major élites and social strata. But whatever the sources of change, their initial impact becomes effective as they impinge on and undermine the major institutional arrangements — collective goals, roles, groups, institutional structures, or total societies — and as they open up new possibilities for the participants in these systems.

By undermining the major institutional arrangements, the forces of change call for the reorganization of the individual's patterns of behavior and social participation and of the relevant organizational, institutional, and symbolic frameworks.

On the individual level they pose the problem of insuring an individual's basic social identity as a human being, as a member of a society, and as bearer of a cultural tradition. On the structural organizational level they question the ability to organize new patterns of roles, groups, and institutional frameworks. On the cultural level they raise the question of developing some symbols and traditions which interpret and give meaning to an individual's life and social activities and guide him in the choice of his social participation in changing circumstances.

In any given situation of change there can be no assurance of a successful response to these problems. Even if successful responses do develop, they may indeed be of different kinds. Moreover, on all levels of social organization there exists the possibility of failure to develop new institutional patterns as well as failure to develop a great variety of such patterns.

VII. THE COMPARATIVE ANALYSIS OF CHANGE: THE STUDY OF CHANGES OF TRADITIONAL COMMUNITIES

In each process of change we may distinguish among: (1) the initial impetus to change and its locus in the given groups or society or in its environment; (2) the extent to which it undermines any given institutional pattern; (3) the new possibilities which are opened up by the impetus to change; and (4) the extent to which there develops within each group some ability to reorganize its social and cultural life.

The exact nature and impact of all these various factors of change necessarily differ greatly among different types of social systems. For instance, it is obvious that the exact amount of demographic, technological, or "cultural" change which affects the continuity of any social unit differs greatly among different types of groups and social systems. The degree of change in the composition of a population which may be crucial for the continuity of a small village may barely affect the broad political system of an empire or the basic contours of an economic system. Similarly, the amount of demographic, cultural, or structural-social change which may prove critical for the continuity of a relatively traditional system, of a primitive tribe, or of a patrimonial state, might be easily taken in stride in a more differentiated imperial or modern society. Any factor of change becomes operative, as we have seen above, when it impinges on the systemic properties and prerequisites of any social organization or group, or opens up possibilities of some new alternative arrangements for its members.

This concept is illustrated in the following discussion, which also emphasizes the comparative dimension of analysis. One very frequent focus of studies of change is the change and possible disintegration of traditional communities in situations of change in general and of modernization and industrialization in particular.

Change and disorganization are usually affected by the combined influence of various forces. Demographic changes — changes in the numbers, longevity, and the age and sex distribution of the population — affect the supply of available manpower and of aspirants for various social positions, increase or decrease the competition between generations, and alter the relationships between the sexes. Technological and economic change may introduce new modes and units of production, and change the bases of property holding among different groups (landowners, peasants, merchants). Political changes — establishment of new patterns of political participation or development of new political categories — usually undermine the existing patterns of authority and of political participation; broader cultural changes (e.g., educational or ideological) may have similar effects.

The impingement of these various forces on communities has, on the whole, similar results around the world: the older pattern of closed communities tends to disintegrate, giving rise to various processes of social disorganization and crises of personal identity. At the same time there arise possibilities for the crystallization of new, more differentiated and less cohesive patterns of ecological organization, and the possibility of their incorporation into new, broader social frameworks in modern class systems, new political units (the modern nation state), or new economic systems (the industrial system).

The relative similarity of these outcomes and the ability to compare the processes of change in greatly differing places in a meaningful way result from the fact that various traditional communities share some common systemic characteristics and needs: the maintenance of close social control by a small traditional group over resources and positions; the relatively small range of choice available to individuals; or the relatively fixed norms which regulate the behavior of individuals. Hence communities may react in somewhat similar ways to the impact of forces which tend to undermine these prerequisites. But the exact nature of the outcomes of these changes depends not only on the extent to which external forces undermine the existing arrangements, but also on the nature of the new opportunities made available to the members of traditional communities. The new opportunities might be in the occupational field, in the field of family relations, of education, or of political participation. In most studies these new opportunities were found to be derived from similar new social orders or systems — industrial in the economic sphere, "democratic" or "mass" in the political sphere.

Each of these new, potentially emerging systems often has its own systemic prerequisites. Industrialism needs manpower with different levels of skill, certain educational standards, and organizational abilities; a modern political system needs more active participants and political organizers; the new opportunities which open up to the members of traditional communities are usually very much in line with these systemic needs of the new types of political or economic orders.

The recognition of the existence of similarity in the nature of traditional communities on the one hand and of the demands made on them when they are put into new, modern industrial systems on the other, does not assume that all such communities are entirely identical. Communities may differ greatly with regard to most, if not all, of their individual systemic properties and prerequisites: in the degree to which they are dependent on certain economic and human resources, in the degree to which they generate forces of change which in turn impinge on their settings and undermine them, and in the degree to which the new social organizations and institutional frameworks are opened up before them. Hence, it is possible and necessary to compare different communities on all these points, and it is exactly the combination of similarity and difference which makes possible the comparative analysis of social change.

The value of the comparative analysis of processes of change in traditional communities can be illustrated by noting that this analysis need not limit itself to the study of changes under the impact of a modern political or industrial system. Processes of change in traditional communities might also be studied in other settings, for example, when the creation of a large-scale traditional empire impinges on these communities through the break-up of small or tribal groups, or patrimonial or feudal units.

The analysis of the extent to which the processes of traditional communities in historical settings are similar to or different from those in modern settings would add another dimension to comparative analysis of such communities.

VIII. THE VARIETY OF RESPONSES TO CHANGE

Comparative problems in other areas of social life are presented in the following selections. In the section on demography, an analysis of the differential impacts of changes in population on different parts of the Western hemisphere shows how relatively similar processes may have different effects according to the nature of the societies on which they impinge.

Correspondingly many studies of family life under the impact of industrialization show how this change undermines some aspects of the older, traditional types of family life, how some families can adjust themselves (often very creatively) to such new circumstances, and how such adjustments may vary greatly according to the internal structure of the family — its solidarity, the pattern of intergenerational relations, and the characteristics of the new setting into which it is thrust. For example, in Japan at least two factors existed which facilitated the transposition of many patterns of traditional family life into urban and industrial settings, and which enabled many "traditional" families to provide modern economic, political, and administrative entrepreneurs. The first factor was the ethos of the new modernizing élite, which encouraged the maintenance of many traditional loyalties; and second, the existence within many families of a very strong orientation to the attainment of status which is sanctioned by the political center. Other similar problems of the comparative analysis of change presented in the selections concern social stratification, development of economic structures, patterns of communication, and different types of "total" societies.

The comparative study of change does not consider only the nature of the impetus to change, the extent to which it undermines an existing social group, and the nature of the new opportunities opened before its members. It also stresses the great variety of personal and institutional responses to the processes of change which may develop. Responses to the problems created by the process of change may take one of several forms. The most extreme outcome is failure to develop an adequate institutional solution to the new problems. Aside from biological extinction, the consequence of such failure may be total or partial disintegration of the system, a semi-parasitic existence at the margin of another group or society, or total submersion within another society.

A less extreme response leads to "regression," the institutionalization of less differentiated systems. Examples on the level of total society would be the establishment of small patrimonial or semi-feudal chiefdoms on the ruins of an empire. On the level of community life, regressive response may take the form of withdrawal from participation in any wider setting; in the economic sphere, it may take the form of development or maintenance of traditional backward, nonefficient enterprises.

Beyond a regressive response there may also develop a very great variety of different, new, institutional responses, and the study of such varieties and of the conditions under which they develop constitutes a central concern of comparative research.

In the analysis of change in all these spheres the question is raised about the extent to which the development of an adequate response to problems of change is dependent on the availability of entrepreneurs who have the vision to respond to the problems and needs in such situations of change and the ability to mobilize the resources necessary for building new institutional frameworks. It may well be that in some situations, or in some social spheres, such responses can result from the cumulative effect of various small ad hoc arrangements undertaken by many people acting in similar organizations or groups within a given social sphere. This whole area and the conditions which produce such entrepreneurs have yet to be fully explored in sociological research.

IX. THE MUTUAL IMPINGEMENT OF PROCESSES OF CHANGE ON DIFFERENT PARTS OF SOCIETY: THE CHANGES OF TOTAL SOCIETIES

Most of the preceding considerations about the systemic characteristics of social change and their comparative implications apply with equal force to different levels of social life, be they small groups and organizations, institutional (family, economic-political) systems or "total" societies. All of these types or levels of social organization evince some *relative* autonomy with regard to processes of change. The processes of change which develop within a small group or a traditional community, or which impinge on them and which may be of great importance for their continuity may not yet greatly or directly affect the broader institutional spheres. From the point of view of the broader institutional sphere, or of the central framework of a society, such processes of change may be of only marginal importance.

The relative autonomy of different groups and spheres in a society explains to a very large extent the possibility and the necessity of comparative analysis of change in each type of social organization — family life, economic institutions, different types of small groups, or different types of communities. But this autonomy is only relative, even though it may indeed be very real in terms of the stability or continuity of any group or organization. The systemic nature of social life implies that all such groups are to some extent interdependent and that the changes in any one of them may, at certain points, impinge on others, undermining the resources which are necessary for the groups' functioning and for the opening up of new perspectives for their members.

One of the important problems in the comparative study of social change is analyzing the interrelations among different types of social organizations: for instance, how and under what conditions changes in the family may or may not impinge on the structure of an economic system and facilitate the development of such a system.

Mutual impingement of the processes of change in different spheres of social life takes place to some degree among most of the different parts or subgroups of any society. But naturally this mutual impingement becomes especially acute when it converges on the central institutional core of a society, on the level of the total society.

Any far-reaching changes which impinge on the structure of total societies usually cause very grave personal, structural, and symbolic problems. It is on the level of the total society that the close relationship between personal identity and collective identities becomes especially articulate. It is therefore on this level that the quest for the concomitant reorganization of all these fields becomes especially acute.

The quest is especially evident in the nature of one of the most common responses to processes of change of total societies. It is in relation to this quest that the more "global" types of social movements, which aim at the transformation of the total society, tend to appear, very often led by charismatic personalities who attempt to create new symbols of social, institutional, and cultural order.

It is here also that the greater variety of response to change — ranging from total extinction, through regression, up to a great variety of institutional processes — becomes much more evident.

It would not be possible within the limits of this essay and the selections presented here to analyze, or even illustrate, the problems of the comparative study of the processes of change of various groups, institutional spheres, and total societies on a broad comparative canvas ranging from primitive through historical up to modern societies. We shall, therefore, confine our discussion in the next part of the introduction to some of the problems related to the processes of change of total societies under conditions of modernization. Most of the selections, and the special introductions to the selections, will deal with parallel problems on different levels of social organization and in different institutional spheres.

X. THE BASIC CHARACTERISTICS AND PROBLEMS OF MODERNIZATION

The broad demographic and structural changes attendant on modernity have by now been more or less adequately identified in the literature. The most important among them are a high level of structural differentiation and of so-called "social mobilization," and a relatively large-scale, unified, and centralized institutional framework.[15]

The development of these various characteristics, different as it may be in various modern or modernizing societies, implies a much more far-reaching undermining of the existing social structures on all levels of social organization than has ever occurred in the history of mankind.

[15] See S.N. Eisenstadt, *Modernization, Protest and Change.* Englewood Cliffs, N.J.: Prentice-Hall, 1966.

It also implies that the new vistas which open up are much more varied and differentiated in all social spheres. Of special importance here are the growing tendencies of broad groups and strata to participate in the more central spheres of the society, in the shaping of the new emerging social and political order.[16]

It is the combination of the above factors that makes the intensity and scope of the changes which develop in situations of modernization greater than in any previous period in history, and the shocks or problems which these changes engender are correspondingly also much greater — especially since modern societies are characterized by the possibility that there will develop within them continuous processes of change.

Hence, in situations of transition to modernity there usually develop many far-reaching and extensive attempts either to transform the former social order or to construct a new one, and to create a viable institutional framework capable of absorbing continuous change. The many social, national, or religious movements which develop in these historical situations are the most important and the best known of these attempts.

Yet the establishment of such growth-sustaining structures is not assured by the mere development of the various structural characteristics of modernity. Truly enough, much of the research, which has attempted to explain the conditions under which a modern society develops and is capable of continuous growth, has assumed that the more developed a society is according to any of these indices and structural characteristics, i.e., the more differentiated it is, the more growth-sustaining it is. However, by now we know that these conditions in themselves are not enough to ensure continuous growth. Structural characteristics are not to be regarded as simple indices of successful modernization, and their development does not necessarily insure the development and continuity of modernization. Rather, they are necessary, but not sufficient, conditions for the development and continuity of a modern institutional structure capable of dealing with continuously changing problems to ensure sustained growth.

It is obvious that modern or modernizing societies have evinced great differences in the extent to which they were able to absorb these changes and to transform their structures into viable, new, growth-sustaining, modern structures.

Throughout the history of modernity there have been unsuccessful attempts at transformations of so-called breakdowns of modernization (the inability to maintain viable modern institutional structures which could absorb continuous changes and deal with new problems). Argentina since the 1930's, several contemporary Asian States, and Weimar Germany are among the most important illustrations of such breakdowns.[17]

---

[16] See S.N. Eisenstadt, *Modernization, Protest and Change, op. cit.*
[17] See S.N. Eisenstadt, *Modernization, Protest and Change, op. cit.*

XI. CONDITIONS OF SUCCESSFUL MODERNIZATION: STRONG CENTERS, STRUCTURAL AUTONOMY, AND FLEXIBILITY OF SOCIAL STRATA

What are the reasons for the differences in the respective capacities of different societies for such transformation into viable modern societies? What are the conditions which are conducive to such successful transformation? Comparative research indicates that among the conditions of special importance are: the combination of viable, flexible, and yet effective symbolic and organizational centers; a high degree of autonomy in the various basic institutional spheres (political, religious, or ideological), social organization, and stratification; and the relative openness and flexibility of broader social groups and strata.

These conditions were found to be crucial to the transformative capacities of various premodern societies — especially European, Asian and American — which either were among the initiators of modernization or were the societies on which modernization impinged from the outside. They have greatly facilitated the initial modernization and helped make the new modern central institutions and frameworks work efficiently.

Thus, for instance, the analysis of Asian societies given below[18] has shown that their internal transformation has been greatly assisted by the autonomy of social, cultural, and political institutions. In the cultural order, autonomy has facilitated the development of new symbols that support and legitimize central institution building. In the sphere of social organization, autonomy has aided the crystallization of viable new organizational nuclei without disrupting the whole pre-existing order, thus enabling the new order to rely to some extent on the forces of the old one. The relatively strong internal cohesion of family groups and broader social strata, with some status autonomy and openness toward the institutional or modern center, has helped to develop positive orientations to the new centers and to provide the necessary support and resources.

Conversely, when autonomy was absent and when the social, cultural, and political orders were intertwined or closely identified with one another, the development of viable modern structures was greatly impeded. When the broader social groups were closed, with few orientations to the centers of society or culture, they were likely to undermine the new institutional centers by withholding resources or by making intensive and unregulated demands on them.

Similarly, whenever the existing societal and cultural centers were weak — as in Latin America and to an even greater extent in Africa — they were on the whole rather ineffective in creating new, strong, viable institutional

[18]See the article by H. Benda in this book.

frameworks even though many intensive social and national movements may have developed.

XII. CONDITIONS OF SUCCESSFUL MODERNIZATION: THE STRUCTURE AND ORIENTATION OF MODERNIZING ELITES AND MOVEMENTS

With regard to great Asian societies as well as with regard to the initial cases of modernization in Europe, structural flexibility and strength of centers was not in itself enough to insure the development and continuity of modern institutional frameworks. Flexibility or the autonomy of different institutional orders created the conditions under which more active groups, movements, and élites could attempt to institute new principles of cultural direction and social integration. But the mere existence of structural flexibility neither insured that such groups would appear nor indicated the type of orientations they would develop.

It is therefore important to analyze the nature of those more active movements and élite groups (the so-called modernizing élites) and to see which of them are indeed capable of bringing about a transformation in the society.

Comparative research on modernization — from the initial modernization of Europe to the contemporary modernization of the New Nations — has provided us with some insights into the characteristics of modernizing élites which may influence their ability to effect the successful transformation of their societies.

It may be useful to distinguish between two types of social élites: (1) those which, while creating new symbols and political frameworks, were not able to effect any structural transformation to facilitate continuous growth within their respective societies (e.g., many of those of Eastern Europe between the two world wars and many of the contemporary élites in the New States); and (2) those which were relatively more successful, although in greatly different ways, in effecting changes and transformations (the élites of Mexico, Russia, Turkey, Japan, Israel, and the first modernizing élites of Western Europe).

The latter tended to be more cohesive and at the same time tried to effect an internal value transformation within the broader groups and strata. In the ideological and value spheres they aimed at the development of a set of symbols which would give meaning to the processes of change.

The successful social élites aimed at the development of a flexible set of symbols and a collective identity which, while not negating the existing traditions, could incorporate them into the new symbolic frameworks. They aimed at the transformation of the internal values of wider social groups and strata and at the development among these groups of new and more flexible orientations. They developed simultaneous orientations to the ideological transformation of collective symbols and to the concrete tasks and problems in different "practical" fields. The successful élites perceived their own legitimation not only in terms of wider changes but also in terms of providing various immediate benefits to different social groups, although they hoped ultimately the new political system would also bring marked improvements in the standard of living of the broader groups and strata of the population.

Contrasted with these orientations are the élites which showed little capacity for transformation[19] a certain "closeness," a ritual emphasis on specific and very limited types of status symbols. These symbols usually did not contain any "transcendental" or broad universalistic orientations. The élites with little transformative capacity viewed the national collectivity in terms of exclusive and limited values and symbols of status which often were derived from the preceding social structure. As a result, these élites limited their own field of perception and the scope of their own activities; hence their internal transformative power was relatively small. Their modernizing orientations were focused more on the political than on the economic sphere. Often they were focused less on the cultural sphere, in the sense of redefinition and reformation of their own basic internal value orientation. Consequently they were not able to establish a strong internal cohesiveness or strong solidarity and ideological connections with other groups and strata which also had the potential to modernize.

These two types of modernizing élites also evinced some distinct social characteristics. The élites with little transformative capacity were relatively noncohesive groups of intellectuals alienated from other élites and from the broader groups and strata of society. They were either very distant from the existing center or succeeded in totally monopolizing it to the exclusion of other groups and élites. This group of élites had very few internal social and ideological contacts or identifications (even if ambivalent ones) with either the bearers of pre-existing traditions or with the wider groups of the society.

However great the differences among them, the élites in Turkey, Israel, Japan, Mexico, and some of the more cohesive élites in countries in later stages of modernization had some contrary characteristics in common. Usually they were not only composed of intellectual groups entirely alienated from the pre-existing élites and from some of the broader groups of the society, but also were composed, to some extent, of persons who held secondary élite positions in the preceding structure and had somewhat closer relations with many active, broader groups.

The interplay between various broader structural characteristics on the one hand and the characteristics and orientations of the more active élites

[19] See the article by H. Benda in this book.

on the other is in part the reason for the great diversity in responses of groups and societies in situations of change. This is true in situations of modernization as well as in situations of change in historical societies, and not only of macro-societal change but also of change in smaller social units. The analysis of such interplay provides therefore one of the major foci of the comparative study of social change.

COMPARATIVE PERSPECTIVES ON

SOCIAL
CHANGE

SECTION ONE

Processes of Change
in the Major Spheres
of Society

Each of the articles presented in this section deals with the impact and processes of change in one major sphere of society — in the demographic and technological spheres, in the economic sphere, in the sphere of family or of social stratification, in community structure and in patterns of communication. The articles all deal with processes of change in modern societies, but emphasize different types and impacts of such processes in different modern or modernizing settings. These varied vantage points create a broad, comparative perspective.

The Impact of
Demographic Changes

In the following article, Kingsley Davis contrasts the patterns of demographic changes found in this century in the United States and Canada with those of Latin America. In doing so, he analyzes some of the general results of population increase and the different effects these results have on broader institutional patterns, especially ecological and economic patterns. Davis follows a trend of demographic analysis which attempts to relate demographic changes to different types of social settings. This trend started with studies of the population problem in the Industrial Revolution and has continued with more modern analyses of different demographic patterns in the world. Davis' own analyses are major contributions to this field of study.

1   KINGSLEY DAVIS

Recent Population Trends in the
New World: An Over-all View

The Western Hemisphere, perhaps because of its extreme contrasts, has seldom been treated demographically as a single region. Yet without wasting words to define a mythical "true region," we can say that the Americas have more in common than is ordinarily stated and that their differences are in many ways complementary and interdependent. Each American nation is nearer to several other American countries than to any non-American country, and each has peculiarities that give it specialization within the diversified economy of the entire hemisphere. The foreign trade of these countries is predominantly within the region. Recently, for example, 55 per cent of the exports of twelve Latin American states went to, and 62 per cent of the imports came from, other American countries; in 1956 the United States exports going to the rest of the Americas represented 41.5 per cent of the total value, and the imports coming from the Americas represented 54.3 per cent of the total. Foreign travel is also heavily within the hemisphere, as is foreign investment. In 1955 the value of United States direct investment in Canada and the Latin American republics (excluding dependencies) was estimated to be 68 per cent of all this country's foreign direct investment. In general, barriers are lower for intra-American commerce and for intra-American migration than for external movements of goods and people.

This interdependence would be less if it were not for at least two broad bases of similarity which, in addition to geographical contiguity, the Americas possess in common: first, the dominant institutional structure and intellectual outlook derive from Europe; second, these elements have everywhere been modified by New World conditions. Sharp cultural differences exist — some growing out of the divergent regions of Europe itself and some out of the persistence of indigenous cultures or the stage of economic development — but the common European background and common

Reprinted from *The Annals of The American Academy of Political and Social Science*, Vol. 316, 1958, pp. 1–10, with the permission of the author and the publisher. Footnotes abridged for this printing. Original reference numbers have been retained.

transplantation into a new region have given the peoples of this part of the world a broadly similar outlook. They share a sense of being part of a new and expanding region with enormous potentialities. They share a sense of freedom from some of the constrictions and historical antagonisms of Europe. They are less divided by linguistic diversity than any major region of the world.

The Western Hemisphere is by no means self-contained, and its unity rests as much upon profound but complementary differences as it does upon similarities. It may not therefore be a "region" by some definitions, but precisely because its demographic characteristics bear a systematic relation to both its diversities and its resemblance, it is a fruitful area for the study and interpretation of population trends. The present volume of THE ANNALS attempts to utilize the natural laboratory that the hemisphere thus provides. The several authors give not only the salient demographic facts, but also their views as to how these facts bear upon or derive from the economic and sociological evolution of the Americas. The purpose of this first essay is to provide an over-all view as an introduction to the more specialized contributions that follow.

THE WORLD'S FASTEST GROWING POPULATIONS

Demographically speaking, the outstanding fact concerning the Western Hemisphere in recent decades can be briefly stated. During a period when the earth's population has been increasing faster than it ever did before, our half of the world has exceeded the world rate. Furthermore, that part of the hemisphere which lies south of the United States — that is, the Caribbean islands, Middle America, and South America — has exhibited the most rapid human increase of any major region of the world. This all-time record in sheer multiplication deserves close attention.

As for the entire hemisphere, in 1940 it contained approximately 277 million people; in 1955, about 366 million — an increase of something like 89 million (or 32 per cent) in fifteen years. The average increase per decade since 1920 has been 17.5 per cent or half again as fast as the average shown by the rest of the world taken as a whole. Like the rest of the world, however, the rate of growth in our hemisphere has tended to accelerate, as the following figures show:

	Percentage Increase per Decade[1]			
Location	1920–30	1930–40	1940–50	1950–60
Western Hemisphere	17.3	11.4	19.5	21.7
Rest of World	10.4	11.3	8.9	17.3

[1] Calculated from populations given in the United Nations *Demographic Yearbook* 1956, p. 151, and 1960 projections on medium assumptions given in . . . United Nations publication, "Population Estimates for World Regions, 1955–1975 and 1975–2000."

The first step in understanding the rate of increase in the whole hemisphere is to recall that the various subregions do not contribute equally to it. The biggest dividing line is that between the highly industrial part comprising Canada and the United States and the less industrial part to the south. If for the sake of convenience rather than strict accuracy we designate all of the area south of the United States as "Latin America," we find that this section expanded its population from 90 million in 1920 to 183 million in 1955 — an increase of 100 per cent in 35 years. Northern America — Canada, United States, Alaska, Greenland, Bermuda, St. Pierre, and Miquelon — also reached 183 million in 1955; since, however, it had started with 117 rather than 90 million in 1920, its increase over the entire period was only 56 per cent or a little more than half the rate of increase for "Latin America."

The fact that the United States and Canada have been lagging behind the other American countries does not mean that, by ordinary standards, their populations are growing slowly. Their performance must be judged in comparison to other industrial countries. Taking the industrial countries of the world as a whole, we find that since about the time of World War I, in contrast to earlier periods, they have been exhibiting a slower rate of population growth than the underdeveloped countries as a whole. But among the industrial countries, Canada and the United States have rates of increase that are among the highest. Since 1920, in fact, their average growth rate is about three times that of the industrial countries of northwest and central Europe.

Rates of Increase. Among the less developed nations of the world where population increase has generally reached unprecedented proportions, the countries and territories of Latin America are far and away in the lead. The high rate of population growth in the entire hemisphere is thus a function of both the fast rate of increase in Canada and the United States compared to other industrial nations and the extraordinarily fast rate in Latin America compared to other underindustrialized areas. This can be seen by classifying the world's regions and computing their rates of increase.

Regions	Percentage Gain 1920–1960[2]	Regions	Percentage Gain 1920–1960[2]
Underdeveloped Regions	70.5	*Developed Regions*	41.1
Latin America	126.3	Australia-New Zealand	92.4
Asia (excluding Japan)	68.4	Japan	71.7
Africa	67.6	Northern America	68.4
Pacific Islands	63.6	U.S.S.R.	36.1
Southern Europe	42.6	Northwest and Central Europe	23.3

[2] Source same as in footnote 1.

One should note that Northern America does not show the fastest growth among the industrial areas; since, however, most of the world's industrial population is still found in Europe, the United States and Canada are above average for this type of region.

As for the future, there is scant reason to expect that rapid population growth in the Americas will soon cease. Recent projections by the Population Branch of the United Nations show, on the basis of medium and rather conservative assumptions, what may be reasonably expected. According to these figures, contained in Table 1, the entire hemisphere will grow from 403 million in 1960 to 905 million in 2000 representing a gain of 125 per cent in 40 years, second only to Asia in rate of increase. Latin America, however, will gain faster than any other major region, primarily because of the extraordinary multiplication in those parts lying in the tropical latitudes.

TABLE 1. MEDIUM ESTIMATES OF FUTURE
POPULATIONS IN MAJOR REGIONS[a]

Country	Population (in Millions)			Percentage Gain
	1960	1975	2000	1960 to 2000
Northern America	197	240	312	58.4
Latin America	205.8	304.1	592.8	188.0
Central America	46.3	72.3	150	224.0
Caribbean	19.6	27.1	48	144.9
Tropical South America	107	163	339	216.8
Temperate South America	32.9	41.7	55.8	69.6
Africa	235	303	517	120.0
Asia	1,620	2,210	3,870	138.9
Europe	424	476	568	34.0
Oceania	16.3	21.0	29.3	79.8
USSR	215	275	379	76.3
World	2,910	3,830	6,270	115.5

[a] From Population Branch, United Nations, "Population Estimates for World Regions, 1955–1975 and 1975–2000." These are estimates based on medium assumptions. Since at the moment of writing they have not been published, they are of course subject to revision. Columns do not add to world total because of rounding.

Necessarily, no responsible demographer pretends to "predict" future populations, and the Population Branch of the United Nations certainly does not do so. The population of the American hemisphere in the year 2000 may actually turn out to be only a few million, or more than a billion, depending on what happens between now and then. The projections given here are simply estimates made systematically on the basis of recent population dynamics. They are reasonable deductions as to the future implications of recent developments. On the whole, the Population Branch considers its projections for 1975 more likely to prove true than those for 2000, and it believes that its "medium" estimates are conservative. The "high" estimate for the Western Hemisphere in 2000 runs to 976 million, the "low" estimate to 719 million. The general assumption in all of the projections is that there will be an orderly pattern of population change, that no unprecedented world calamity or completely new development will intervene to destroy the pattern. One should regard the projections, therefore, as simply rough indications of the order of magnitude implicit in present dynamics if they continue their general evolutionary pattern.

Demographically speaking, the main reason for the hemisphere's fast population growth is the widening spread between birth and death rates. This widening breach is recently common to the entire region, but its magnitude has been greater in Latin America; also, the direction and relative influence of the two variables — fertility and mortality — have been different in Northern and Latin America.

The secondary reason for the population growth is continued immigration. This factor has had greatest influence in Canada, less in the United States, and still less in much of Latin America; but it should not be ignored.

DEMOGRAPHIC CAUSES IN CANADA AND THE UNITED STATES

Let us look more closely at the differences between Northern and Latin America in the way fertility and mortality have behaved. As is well known, Canada and the United States underwent a long decline in birth rates beginning far back in the nineteenth century and extending to the 1930's. After 1940, however, they sustained a marked *rise* in births. The United States crude birth rate, for example, in 1951–1956 reached the level it had shown in 1925 (though never equaling any year prior to 1925). Average rates by five-year periods were as follows:

ANNUAL BIRTHS PER 1000 POPULATION

Year	United States[4]	Canada
1920–24	26.8	27.4
1925–29	23.2	24.1
1930–34	19.7	22.2
1935–39	18.8	20.3
1940–44	21.2	23.0
1945–49	24.1	26.9
1950–56	24.9	27.9

[4] The United States figures are corrected for underregistration except for 1955 and 1956, when the error from this source would be small.

Although crude rates, because they are influenced by the age structure, are defective indices of fertility, the figures nevertheless indicate a substantial reproductive recovery in both countries.

If, now, we look at the United States-Canadian death rates, we find that they apparently declined during the entire time from at least the middle of the nineteenth century onward. In the United States the drop in the death rate was on the whole slower than the drop in the birth rate up until the late 1930's, and for this reason, despite very substantial immigration, the rate of population growth declined steadily. In Canada the picture is not so clear, but it appears that the drop in the death rate was at least no faster than the decline in fertility, for there was no upward trend in population growth even with immigration. Table 2 shows that the rate of increase in the United States population fell regularly from 1860 to 1940, while the rate in the Canadian population fell regularly from 1910 to 1940.

TABLE 2. GROWTH RATE OF UNITED STATES
AND CANADIAN POPULATIONS

Year	Per Cent Increase per Decade	
	United States	*Canada[a]*
1850–60	35.6	32.6
1860–70	26.6	14.2
1870–80	26.0	17.2
1880–90	25.5	11.8
1890–1900	20.7	11.1
1900–10	21.0	34.2
1910–20	14.9	21.9
1920–30	16.1	18.1
1930–40	7.2	10.9
1940–50	14.5	18.6
1950–60	18.4[b]	28.4[b]

[a] In the case of Canada the census is taken one year after the turn of the decade. The last figure, however, is based on the 1950 population.

[b] Estimates from the United Nations, Population Branch, "Future Population Estimates for World Regions." . . .

When the birth rate rose in these two countries after 1940, thus reversing the long downward trend, the death rate continued its steady decline. As a result, the spread between the two rates widened markedly and, as Table 2 makes clear, the rate of population growth rose sharply. The change in the birth rate, upward this time, was however again much faster than the change in the death rate, which continued downward. It can be calculated that in the United States the rise in the birth rate since 1940 has been more than four times as important in producing the increased population growth as was the decline of the death rate; and in Canada it has been more than five times as important.

Postwar immigration into both Canada and the United States, as Helen Eckerson shows in the present volume, has been substantial. The United States, still the world's greatest immigrant-receiving country, has accepted a larger number than Canada, but not in relation to population. Immigration has consequently made a bigger contribution to Canada's postwar upsurge in population than it has to the United States rise.

In sum, it is the changes in fertility that provide the main explanation of rising or falling rates of population growth in industrial Northern America. The unpredicted population growth since the war has been due principally to an increased birth rate and only secondarily to lower mortality and enhanced immigration. A rough assessment of the relative contribution of each demographic variable to the postwar spurt in growth yields the following:

Country	Rise in Birth Rate	Fall in Death Rate	Increased Immigration
United States	74%	18%	8%
Canada	58%	12%	30%

THE PATTERN OF DEMOGRAPHIC CHANGE IN LATIN AMERICA

In most of the countries to the South, the pattern of change is different from that just described for Canada and the United States. With respect to fertility, for example, there has been no long decline in the birth rate except in Argentina and perhaps in Uruguay. Instead the birth rate has tended to persist at a high level, usually between 40 and 50 per thousand when registration is reasonably accurate. Thus no low point was reached in births during the depression, nor has there been much of a rise since then. The acceleration of population growth in Latin America is clearly not due to a rise in fertility.

Nor is the acceleration due particularly to increased immigration. The majority of immigrants to the New World have been going, as in the past, to Northern America; and in Latin America itself, as Richard Robbins points out, only three countries have received a substantial influx since the war.

We are left, then, with a decline in mortality as the predominant demographic factor causing the rise in the growth rate of Latin American populations. Whereas the Canadian-United States death rates showed a continued but gradual drop from what was in 1920 already a low level, the rates in most of the other American countries have fallen precipitously from very high levels, the rate of decline tending to increase. Unfortunately, the data on mortality in Latin America are generally poor; but I have taken eleven countries which have the better death registration systems and have computed the average percentage decline in the crude death rate by five-year intervals with the following results:

Years	Average Percentage Decline in Annual Death Rate[6]
From 1920–24 to 1925–29	6.0
From 1925–29 to 1930–34	7.7
From 1930–34 to 1935–39	8.1
From 1935–39 to 1940–44	7.8
From 1940–44 to 1945–49	16.2
From 1945–49 to 1950–54	17.1

Since crude death rates reflect changes in the age structure and in the accuracy of registration, the declines noted here may either overstate or understate the actual trend; but there can be no doubt about the unprecedented speed and recent acceleration of the fall in the death rate. A similar precipitous decline has been occurring in most of the other less-industrial parts of the world.

In Latin America, therefore, it is the tumbling of the death rate, rather than a rise of fertility as in Canada and the United States, that explains the phenomenal increase in population growth since 1940. At the present time the human tide in Latin America appears to be ascending about 36 per cent faster than in Northern America. Mexico, for example, has more than doubled its population since 1925, reaching 30½ million by 1956. The Mexican birth rate for 1955 is recorded as 46, nearly twice that of the United States, and the death rate as only 13, having dropped 43 per cent since 1940. It looks as though Mexico's population (already augmented by about a million each year) will soon be growing at a rate of 3½ per cent per year. At this rate it will double every twenty years and increase tenfold in 67 years. Other countries in the area are also approaching this situation, including El Salvador, Venezuela, Guatemala, Honduras, Panama, and the Dominican Republic.

During the next two or three decades the growth-rate difference between

---

[6] The percentage decline in the annual death rate between each pair of successive quinquenia was computed for *each* country. This percentage was then averaged for the group of countries, each country counting as one. The eleven countries involved in the comparison had a combined population of over 70 million in 1955. They were: Argentina, Barbados, Chile, Costa Rica, El Salvador, Jamaica, Mexico, Panama, Puerto Rico, Trinidad and Tobago, and Venezuela. Lack of suitable data for Puerto Rico prior to 1930 prevented that country's inclusion in the first two comparisons.

Northern America and most of the other countries is likely to expand. The main factor supporting higher growth rates in Canada and the United States — the postwar rise in fertility — is apparently leveling off, while the main factor in Latin America — mortality decline — is continuing. Birth rates in Latin America show little sign of receding from their customarily high level, although Argentina's — and probably Uruguay's — rate has behaved more like that of the United States than like that of Mexico; and Puerto Rico's rate has declined since 1947. It seems likely that the first broad area of Latin America to achieve a modern birth level will be the temperate and more industrial southern part of South America, and this is the reason the United Nations estimates a lower future population growth for that region.

BEHIND THE DEMOGRAPHIC PATTERN

If we ask why; among the world's underdeveloped areas, Latin America leads in population growth, and why the United States and Canada are close to the lead among the industrial nations, a full answer is too complex to be given here. However, it is helpful to recall two features of the Western Hemisphere already mentioned — first, that it is still a "new" region of the world, and, second, that it is a region in which European culture is everywhere dominant.

Significantly, Latin America is the only major part of the world which is peopled by colonizing Europeans and yet is preponderantly agrarian and non-industrial. All other underdeveloped areas, aside from parts of Europe itself, are non-European in race and culture. Among the less industrial regions of the earth, therefore, the Latin Americans have the advantage of both a European background and a new and relatively empty territory. This fact helps to explain why it has been easier to transmit to them the modern techniques of death control than it has been in most other underdeveloped areas. It also helps to explain the expansionist attitude. Although parts of the Caribbean and Central America are crowded, the region as a whole has a comparatively low population density in relation to resources. South America, in fact, is still an empty shell, fully peopled near the coasts but almost empty in the interior. With 16 per cent of the world's inhabitable land area and, as of 1955, only 6.8 per cent of the world's people, Latin America as a whole still feels that its opportunities are abundant. This translates itself into the belief that an increased population is a good thing, that high birth rates and brisk immigration should be favored.

In Northern America the social order brought by the colonists was not the more feudal and stratified type found in southern Europe, but the more competitive and industrialized type found in northwest Europe. This order thrived in the New World, with the result that until about 1920, its population grew faster than that of Latin America. However, the demographic effects of mature industrialism kept slowing the rate of increase by depressing fertility. When a rebound came in the 1940's and 1950's, it was destined to be greater and to last longer than the similar rebound in industrial Europe because the United States and Canada are still new countries in which the restraints in fertility do not derive mainly from lack of economic opportunities.

It will be noticed from figures given earlier that the only industrial countries exceeding Northern America in rate of population growth between 1920 and 1960 are Australia and New Zealand. (Japan, which was slightly ahead, is a special case of late industrialization, too far afield to treat here.) The reason is that both Australia and New Zealand are "newer." [7] Their period of fast numerical increase therefore came later than that of Canada and the United States, and their rebound after the depression was at least equal if not greater.

Australia, New Zealand, Canada, and the United States are not likely to repeat the very rapid human increase they exhibited earlier. Remarkable as their postwar upsurge has been, it has not enabled them to match the underdeveloped areas, especially Latin America, because their rise in births has not equaled the latter's fall in deaths.

SOME FUTURE IMPLICATIONS

One likely consequence of the trends so far described is a radical shift in the numerical balance within the hemisphere. Whereas in 1920 the ratio of the United States-Canadian population to that in the rest of the hemisphere was 1.3 to 1, it will probably be reduced to 0.8 to 1 by 1975, and to 0.5 to 1 by the end of the century. Heretofore, the United States has been the demographic giant of the region. In 1920 it had more people than the rest of the two continents combined; at present its ratio is down to 0.8 to 1. It will probably retain its position as the largest nation up to at least the end of the century, but its ratio to the second and third will decline (see Table 3). The first six nations seem destined to retain their 1920 ranks,

TABLE 3. RELATIVE SIZE OF UNITED STATES POPULATION

Countries	Ratios: U. S. ÷ Other Unit			
	1920	1960	1975	2000
United States ÷ Second Country (Brazil)	3.9	2.7	2.1	1.3
United States ÷ Next Five Countries	1.6	1.2	1.0	.6
United States ÷ Rest of Hemisphere	1.1	.8	.7	.5

[7] In 1861 only 27,000 Europeans inhabited New Zealand, and in 1841 only 221,000 inhabited Australia.

though not their relative ratios, through 1975; but if the United Nations projections hold true beyond that date, Peru and Colombia will both eclipse Canada, and Colombia will eclipse Argentina.

One should not assume that political positions will shift correspondingly. National strength does not rest solely on population size, particularly as science and economic efficiency take precedence over sheer manpower. However, when other things are roughly equal, sheer numbers count heavily. If Canada and the United States are to keep their positions of leadership, they will have to rely increasingly upon human capacities rather than upon human numbers.

If rapid population growth intensifies economic problems, it may weaken rather than strengthen a nation. Such a prospect, if found anywhere in our hemisphere, is to be found in Latin America where the population growth is greater and the economies weaker. The question of whether population expansion in this region is impeding the rate of economic gain really turns on the extent to which the swift drop in mortality is due to economic advance itself or to external factors. If it is mainly due to the former, there is no necessary economic disadvantage (whatever other disadvantages there may be) in population growth. If, on the other hand, the drop in deaths is chiefly the result of other factors, the chances are that it is reducing *per capita* income below what it would otherwise be. George Stolnitz presents reasons for crediting much of the mortality reduction in Latin America to extra economic factors. These reasons seem convincing to me, especially since there are signs of population pressure in many of the Latin American economies.

Any adverse economic effects, however, are hard to see because they are partially masked by the wave of postwar prosperity characterizing this region. Should this wave continue until the economies are transformed into modern industrial systems, the birth rate would ultimately turn downward and the rate of population increase would drop. There is no guarantee, however, that the rise in national incomes will continue uninterruptedly. To the extent that mortality control is coming from external sources — foreign science, personnel, and funds — a halt in economic growth would not stop it. Instead, the death rate would continue downward, the birth rate would probably remain high, and the population expansion would continue until the unfavorable effects of poverty on mortality more than matched the favorable effects of outside influence.

Characteristics of Latin American Economy. Some of the danger signals in the present Latin American economic situation are these: [8] (1) Although the rise in *per capita* gross product was rapid during 1945–1955, averaging 2.3 per cent per annum, the increase was greater in the first half

[8] These points are summarized from the excellent survey in the United Nations *Economic Bulletin for Latin America,* Vol. 2 (Feb. 1957).

than in the latter half of the period. (2) *Per capita* agricultural production for export fell in 1956 to the lowest level in 15 years, due partly to increased domestic needs as well as to bad weather and bad markets. (3) Despite the rapid urbanization and heavy rural-urban migration which Mr. Browning describes in the present volume, the increase of the rural population has not diminished during 1925 to 1955. Thus the tendency of the agricultural population to cease to grow, so characteristic of advancing economies,[9] is not occurring except in a few countries such as Chile, Cuba, Uruguay, Venezuela, and, over a long period, Argentina. (4) Partly because of the shortage of land in some countries and lack of opportunity in others, there is widespread underemployment of males in the agricultural sector. (5) Although industrial output has risen, the proportion of the labor force employed in manufacturing has tended to remain stationary. At the same time the proportion employed in services has increased rapidly; in 1950 it embraced 25.3 per cent of the labor force as compared to 18.1 per cent in industry (only half of which was in manufacturing proper as opposed to handicraft). The ratio of services to industry, which normally moves downward instead of upward in the middle stages of industrial development, is so high as to appear excessive. (6) Within the manufacturing sector the production of capital goods and of intermediate products is not commensurate with the emphasis on final consumer goods.

These characteristics of the Latin American economy point to serious imbalances that must be overcome if the current boom is to continue uninterruptedly. Some of them suggest that excessive population growth may be a factor. Whether it is or not at the present time, the current human increase seems to be too fast to be sustained over the long pull. Either the economy will eventually fail to move ahead, in which case the death rate will ultimately be pushed up; or the economy will continue to gain, in which case fertility will eventually be depressed. We know that at the present time the number of living children in each family is greater than it ever was before, with greater strain on the resources of parents. We know too that the movement of millions of people to the towns and cities increases the costs and inconvenience of children. The effect of present trends is therefore such as to cause those trends eventually to subside. Accordingly, the important question is not whether the amazing population growth of today can be sustained indefinitely, but when it is likely to cease. We can agree with Harrison Brown that a billion people in the hemisphere can be supported fairly well (and agree with him also that the prospect of that many is unpleasant), but maintain at the same time that half a billion could be supported just as well or perhaps far better.

[9] The decline in the growth-rate of the U. S. rural population started in 1810, long before it set in for the total population. In Canada the decline started in 1851, at the latest. The U. S. farm population fell in absolute numbers after 1910.

Notes for
Further Reading

For a more general view of population trends and of their broad impacts on social change, see:

Cipolla, C.M., *The Economic History of World Population*. Harmondworth: Penguin Books, 1962.

Some of the relevant studies on the relation of population growth to the Industrial Revolution are:

Ashton, T.S., *The Industrial Revolution 1760–1830*. London: Oxford University Press, 1948.

Marshall, T.H., "The Population Problem during the Industrial Revolution," in E.M. Carus Wilson (ed.), *Essays in Economic History*. London: Edward Arnold, 1954.

Marshall, T.H., *et al.*, *The Population Problem, The Experts and the Public*. London: G. Allen & Unwin, 1938.

Among the articles by Kingsley Davis which deal with comparative effects of modern demographic changes, we would like to mention:

Davis, K., "The Origin and Growth of Urbanization in the World," *American Journal of Sociology*, Vol. 60, 1955, pp. 429–437.

——————— "Population," *Scientific American*, Vol. 209, Sept., 1963, pp. 62–71.

——————— "Population and the Further Spread of Industrial Society," *Proceedings of the American Philosophical Society*, Vol. 95, 1951, pp. 8–19.

II

The Impact of
Technological Changes

Studies of the impact of broad technological changes on society and studies of the relations among technology, ecology, and social change have constituted, as we noted in the general introduction, one of the major foci of sociological inquiry. The importance of technological change for the larger society has been studied in many settings — for example, situations of initial modernization, or the industrialization of primitive or traditional societies. Most of these studies, by their very nature, have dealt with relatively broad developments and changes.

There are, however, fewer studies of the direct effects of technological changes on more specific segments of society — the impact of technological innovation in a modern factory, railroad, or other industrial setting, for example. Faunce's article presented here is such a study. Its major interest lies in its very detailed analysis of changes brought by automation.

2   WILLIAM A. FAUNCE

Automation in the Automobile Industry:
Some Consequences for In-Plant
Social Structure

Although study of the work group has always been one of the important
concerns of industrial sociologists, the effect of changing production technology upon work groups has received relatively little attention. The currently accelerated rate of technological innovation in American industry
provides some unique opportunities for research in this area. This paper
reports an attempt to discover the effects of the introduction of automatic
transfer machines upon interaction patterns in an automobile engine plant.
The findings of the study are summarized and their implications for some
recurrent themes in industrial sociology are considered.

The research upon which the paper is based involved interviews with
125 workers selected randomly from four large machining departments of
one of the most highly automated automobile engine plants in Detroit. All
of these workers had been transferred to the automated plant from older
plants of the same company and about 80 per cent of them were working
in the same job classification in the new as in the older plants. Comparisons could be made therefore between interaction patterns among workers who had performed essentially the same functions under the two kinds
of conditions. The workers interviewed had an average of almost 20 years
seniority and had been on their automated jobs an average of 15.4 months
at the time of the interviews, so it is presumed that they had sufficient
experience with both kinds of jobs on which to base such comparisons.

The respondents were asked to compare their *last* previous job in the
non-automated plants with their present job with relation to the following areas: (1) size of work group, defined as the number of other workers
the respondent thought of as "being in the group that works around you";
(2) size of interaction group, defined as the number of other workers the
respondent "talked with most often on the job"; (3) frequency of interaction on the job; (4) the nature of this interaction; and (5) number of

Reprinted from *American Sociological Review*, Vol. 23, Aug., 1958, pp. 401–7,
with permission of the author and the American Sociological Association.

jobs involving teamwork, that is, jobs where two or more workers were required to perform the particular operations on the job.

One apparent factor determining the size of interaction groups and the frequency of interaction within these groups in the factory setting is the way in which work stations are spaced along the production line. In the older, non-automated plants in which the respondents had previously worked, machines were spaced on either side of a moving conveyor usually with a worker at each machine. Where the worker was responsible for more than one machine operation, these operations were performed in a circle or "dial" in front of the worker. The average distance between work stations in these plants was somewhat under ten feet. The average size of the work group was about ten employees, with interaction occurring most frequently among the four or five working most closely nearby or directly across from each other on the line. The patterns of interaction were similar to those reported by Walker and Guest, who found interaction occurring most frequently among the two to five workers next to and across from each other on the line and within a series of overlapping groups along the assembly line.[1] While there were some differences between the findings of this study and those reported by Walker and Guest, resulting primarily from the differences between assembly and machining operations, it seems probable that there are some general characteristics of on-the-job social interaction which are common to mass production industries using conventional assembly or machining procedures.

Work stations being relatively adjacent and many jobs not requiring close and constant attention, social interaction was frequent in the old plants. In response to the question, "Were you able to talk very often to the men around you while you were working?" over 80 per cent of the workers interviewed answered affirmatively. Over 60 per cent of the social contacts reported on these jobs occurred as frequently as once or twice an hour. Interaction was especially frequent on those jobs where more than one worker was required to perform the particular operation and, although a majority of jobs in both the old and the new automated plants did not involve teamwork, there were significantly more such jobs in the old plants (P < .001).

Another characteristic of the old jobs which provided opportunity for frequent social interaction was control of work pace by the machine operator. If the worker is able to vary work pace, he is able to create opportunities for social intercourse with others around him on the job. Interaction occurred significantly more frequently among workers who were able

---

[1] Charles R. Walker and Robert H. Guest, *The Man on the Assembly Line,* Cambridge: Harvard University Press, 1952, pp. 67–72. For a more recent study of an automated plant, see Charles R. Walker, *Toward the Automatic Factory: A Case Study of Men and Machines,* New Haven: Yale University Press, 1957.

to vary work pace and to take a break in both the old non-automated plants and among those workers in the new plant who controlled work pace.

The variables proposed here as having an important effect upon the frequency and nature of social interaction on the job include: (1) amount of attention required by the job, (2) distance between work stations, (3) extent of control of work pace, (4) machine noise, and (5) number of jobs involving team work. The earlier discussion suggests that the combination of these variables characteristic of production departments using conventional machining techniques permitted frequent social interaction. As a result of the changes in production techniques in the automated plant, this combination of variables changed considerably. Workers reported that automated jobs required much closer and more constant attention than non-automated jobs (P $<.02$). A significantly greater distance between work stations was reported in the new plant, with the average distance between workers being just under twenty feet (P $<.001$). There were fewer jobs in the automated plant where work pace was controlled by the machine operator (P $<.001$). A slightly larger proportion of workers indicated that the automated machines were noisier than non-automated machinery.[2] Finally, as previously noted, there were significantly fewer jobs involving team work in the automated plant (P $<.001$).

TABLE 1. SOCIAL INTERACTION ON THE JOB

	Automated Job (N = 123)	Non-Automated Job (N = 124)
Able to interact often	46.3%	80.6%
Unable to interact often	53.7	19.4
	Chi square = 31.42	
	P $<.001$	

If the variables considered above are important in the structuring of interaction groups in these plants, the possibility follows that there would be less frequent social interaction within smaller groups of workers in the automated plant. The data support this hypothesis. In response to the question, "Are you able to talk very often to the men around you while you are working?" over 80 per cent of the interviewees answered affirmatively with regard to their old job while only about 45 per cent answered affirmatively with reference to their present job in the automated plant.

[2] While the difference here between the proportions was small, if it represents any increase in machine noise it should be noted that even a slight rise in volume of noise becomes an increasingly effective barrier to communication as the distance between work stations increases.

TABLE 2. FREQUENCY OF SOCIAL INTERACTION ON THE JOB

	Automated Job (N = 117)	Non-Automated Job (N = 119)
Every few minutes or so	18.5%	43.6%
Once or twice an hour	12.6	18.8
Four or five times a day	24.4	23.9
Once a day or less	44.5	13.7
	Chi square = 32.39	
	P < .001	

There were also significantly fewer social contacts per day reported, with only 18 per cent occurring "every few minutes or so" on automated jobs while over 40 per cent of reported interaction was this frequent on non-automated jobs.

When the data in Table 2 are broken down in terms of size of interaction groups at each level of frequency of interaction, the mean-square contingency coefficient is increased, suggesting that interaction is not only less frequent in the automated plant but occurs among fewer workers. Further evidence that interaction groups are significantly smaller in automated plants is presented in Table 3.

Relationship patterns within these groups also differed in the automated plant. In the old plants each worker along the line characteristically belonged to a somewhat different interaction group than the worker next to him. In the new plant, however, work groups were structured so that the men on each transfer line tended to form a separate and isolated group. In spite of this fact and although there was some interdependence of function among the workers on each transfer line, no feeling of teamwork is suggested by the data.[3] One explanation for the failure of workers to

TABLE 3. SIZE OF INTERACTION GROUPS

	Automated Job (N = 120)	Non-Automated Job (N = 115)
Four or fewer in group	79.2%	54.8%
Five or more in group	20.8	45.2%
	Chi square = 15.81	
	P < .001	

[3] It is apparently possible in some automated plants to develop teamwork on the job. Friedmann cites the increasing use of production teams in French automated plants to foster cooperation and joint responsibility. G. Friedmann, "Où va le Travail Humain?" *Human Organization*, 13 (1955), pp. 29–33.

perceive these groups as "teams," as might be expected under other conditions, is the difficulty in communication within the groups on the job. Because of the impossibility of verbal communication in some sections of automated departments, an elaborate system of sign language had been developed. These hand signals were used primarily for necessary communications about the job, but there were also signs indicating such messages as the time of day and the approach of the foreman or other supervisors, as well as some descriptive gestures used as expressions of opinion of various kinds. Much of the infrequent verbal communication which was reported in the automated departments of the new plant also dealt with the job or with topics necessary for the performance of the job. There was very little of the free interchange regarding non-work matters which appears to have been characteristic of interaction in the older, non-automated plants.

In general, the data suggest that many workers are virtually isolated socially on automated production lines. Under such conditions, it might be expected that fewer close relationships or friendships would develop on the job. Several questions were included in the interview schedule dealing with the number of friendships formed in the automated and non-automated plants. In response to the question, "Would you say you had made more friends on your present job or on your old job?", only 13 per cent of the respondents answered in the affirmative, while 47 per cent reported making more friends on their previous, non-automated job. Of the remaining 40 per cent, who noted no difference between the two jobs in answering this question, a majority responded either that they had "no difficulty making friends any place" or that they were working with the same people in the new plant as on their previous jobs. In response to another question, almost two and one-half times as many workers reported that they used to get together socially off the job more often with friends from the old plant than they do now with friends from the new plant. Approximately half of the respondents, however, reported no difference between automated and non-automated jobs in this respect, with most of these indicating that they did not get together socially after working hours with friends from either job. Most workers having been on their last previous, non-automated job for a somewhat longer period and in some instances being co-workers of the same people on their present job as on their previous job, these data should not be interpreted, of course, as evidence that fewer close relationships necessarily develop among workers on automated production lines. The size of the observed differences, however, suggests that further research might show this to be the case.

In addition to alterations in social interaction among workers, automation has produced some shifts in the relations between workers and supervision. The source of these shifts can be traced to changes in the nature of the job of the machine operator. The worker on the automated line is responsible for a larger share of the production process. The job requires more constant and careful attention. The results of failure to attend closely to the job are more costly and, because of the increased complexity of the transfer machinery and the fact that it has only recently been introduced into the automobile industry, machine breakdowns are more frequent in automated departments. These factors play a major role in increasing the amount of supervision of workers on automated jobs. This growth in supervision is accompanied by a reduction in the number of workers per foreman in the new plant as well as an increase in the amount of time spent by the foreman in direct supervision on the line. Both general foremen and superintendents also give more time in the production departments on the line in the automated plant. Tables 4 and 5 show that workers reported significantly more frequent contacts with foremen, general foremen, and superintendents on their present jobs than occurred in the old, non-automated plants.

TABLE 4. FREQUENCY OF CONTACT WITH FOREMAN

	Automated Job (N = 122)	Non-Automated Job (N = 121)
Very often	40.2%	25.0%
Often	31.1	32.5
Once in awhile, seldom or never	28.7	42.5
	Chi square = 7.60	
	P < .05	

The data suggest further that there has been a change not only in amount of supervision but in the nature of the relationship between workers and first line supervisors. In response to the question, "Would you say

TABLE 5. FREQUENCY OF CONTACT WITH GENERAL FOREMAN OR SUPERINTENDENT

	Automated Job (N = 119)	Non-Automated Job (N = 119)
Often	57.2%	36.1%
Once in awhile	27.7	35.3
Seldom or never	15.1	28.6
	Chi square = 11.64	
	P < .01	

it is easier to get along with the foreman on your present job or on your old job?", a larger proportion of workers reported that the relationship had been better on the old job. Moreover, of those who said that they got along better with their foreman in the new, automated plant, 50 per cent listed personal characteristics of the foreman as the principal reason, while fewer than nine per cent cited personal characteristics as a reason for preferring relations with foremen on the old job. In most instances, however, the foremen in the new plant had also been foremen in the old; therefore, this shift in worker-foremen relations is not attributable to personality differences but to a change in the *role* of the foreman in the automated plant.

Most of the foremen in this plant had at one time been machine operators using conventional machining techniques. Most of them also had been foremen for relatively long periods of time. For these reasons, in the non-automated plants, they were apparently able to supervise the older, experienced workers, who comprised the majority of the work force in such plants, with a minimal use of the authority vested in the foremanship. With the increasing pressures upon the foremen resulting from the change to automated production techniques, however, there has been a change in this pattern of interaction between foremen and workers. The following quotations from interviews suggest the nature of this change:

> We have 100 men in the [automated] department and we have five foremen. Before, we had 134 men and one foreman and one assistant. It was better on the old job. Nobody breathing down your neck. Over here it's altogether different, just push, push, push all the time.
> They never say hello . . . treat you like a machine. They used to be friendly. Now they seem to be under a strain.
> The foremen at the new plant have too much to do and too much responsibility and they get tired and cranky. They'll die of a heart attack yet.

Although no foremen were interviewed in connection with this study, there are indications in the material of some reasons for the increasing pressure upon the foreman on the automated line which may account for the changes in his relationship with workers. The general assignment of the foreman is to see that production schedules are met in the section for which he is responsible. In the older plants, the foreman accomplished this task by making sure that each worker was performing his share of the operation at the required speed and by seeing that machine breakdowns were promptly repaired. On automated lines, however, whatever skill in the exercise of authority a foreman may have acquired is of little avail since the worker does not control the pace of the transfer machine and the production rate is not varied by either the intensity with which the operator watches the machine or the vigor with which he pushes the button. Furthermore, when a machine breakdown occurred in the older, non-automated plants it generally involved only one machine, the line itself usually continued, and repairs could often be made by either the operator or the foreman. When a breakdown occurs on the automatic transfer machines in the new plant, often the whole line stops, as much as a million dollars worth of machinery may be idled while the repairs are made, and neither the foreman nor the operator has the requisite skills to make many of the necessary repairs. Thus the foreman in the automated plant is faced with meeting increased production schedules without being able to utilize effectively either his acquired "human relations" skills or the knowledge he has accumulated about conventional machining processes. The resulting tensions have, it seems, produced changes in his relations with workers. Although further research would be necessary to document the specific nature of these changes, the data suggest that there have been significant changes in the role of the foreman on the automated line.

Before considering the implications of these findings for common themes in industrial sociology, certain analytic problems posed by the nature of the research design of this study should be noted. The respondents were asked to compare past with present experiences; therefore there is the possibility of distortions of recall. This paper is concerned, however, not primarily with the attitudes of workers toward the change, but with the nature of the change itself. Thus less selectivity of recall might be expected. It may be added that there were less than two years in each instance since the workers' last experience with non-automated jobs and that there was little noticeable difficulty in recall in responding to questions about these jobs.

The fact that all of the workers had previously been employed in non-automated plants might be expected to affect the findings of the study, although this result is perhaps less the case when a description rather than an evaluation of change is requested. The larger study from which this paper is taken, however, analyzes not only the nature of the change but individual and organizational adjustments to changes in production technology as well; hence the necessity here to consider workers who had experienced the shift from the older type of plant to automation.[4]

The possibility that some of the differences associated with automation may be attributed to the relative newness of the technology rather than the pattern of technology as such should be recognized. For example, the workers' failure to identify with specific work groups and their perception of changes in supervisory style of foremen may be the result of the dis-

[4] See William A. Faunce, "Automation in the Automobile Industry: Some Consequences for In-Plant and Union-Management Relationships," Ph.D. dissertation, Wayne State University, 1957.

ruption of established patterns not as yet replaced. While the variation in amount of experience with automation was limited among workers in the study, no appreciable differences were found between the responses of workers who had been in the new plant throughout the two year period during which it had been in operation and of those who had more recently transferred to the plant. The question of which of the specific changes in the social structure of the new plant can be attributed to automatic technology and which to the "disequilibrium" in the situation during the period of change can be best answered through further research.[5]

If the changes in social structure in this plant are at all representative of the effects of automation elsewhere and if the current rate of introduction of automated machinery into American industry increases, the findings reported here may have important implications for certain recurrent themes in industrial sociology. One of these is illustrated by the persistent effort to relate diverse social and psychological variables to the productivity of work groups. For example, there have been numerous attempts in studies of human relations in industry to establish interconnections between work group morale and its productivity. Apart from the questionable assumption that increasing output is necessarily a goal of industrial work groups,[6] the findings of the present investigation raise the additional question of the applicability of such studies to automated industries. The "morale" of the operator who pushes a button that starts the operation of a transfer machine has no effect whatsoever upon the rate of production of that machine. Where work pace is no longer controlled by the worker, man-hour productivity becomes a meaningless measure of achievement of group goals even where cohesive work groups exist and where they are identified with the organization to the degree that output is accepted as a goal of such groups.

Study of the effects of style of leadership upon cohesiveness of work groups and upon output constitutes another recurrent theme in industrial sociology. While "output" of machine repairmen, bench hands or other workers not directly involved in the production process may be affected by style of leadership, for the majority of workers in the automated plant, who do not control work pace, the manner of leadership does not affect productivity. In situations where the nature of the machine process effec-

---

[5] A second study of this plane is planned in connection with the Automation Research Project of the Labor and Industrial Relations Center at Michigan State University.

[6] Some studies have demonstrated that group cohesiveness and morale may also be effective in subverting management objectives and restricting output. See, e.g., D. Roy, "Quota Restriction and Goldbricking in a Machine Shop," *American Journal of Sociology*, 57 (1952), pp. 427–442; D. Collins, M. Dalton, and D. Roy, "Restriction of Output and Social Cleavage in Industry," *Applied Anthropology*, 5 (1946), pp. 1–14.

tively prevents social interaction, moreover, variations in leadership style cannot be regarded as a significant factor affecting cohesiveness of work groups. In most studies of effects of leadership upon informal social structure, type of leadership has been treated as an independent variable. In the analysis of the foreman's relationship with the work group or groups for which he is responsible, however, the question of the effect of the nature of group structure upon the role of the foreman may be equally important. The situation which characterized the pre-automation plants in this study, where the foreman was apparently integrated into cohesive work groups, may make appropriate a style of leadership which is neither possible nor appropriate in the automated plant, given changes in informal social structure of the kind described above. Further study of the changing role of the foreman in automated industries is needed, and such research should include analysis of the extent to which changes in *group structure* affect leadership style.

A series of related studies in industrial sociology rest upon the assumption of relatively cohesive work groups. It is assumed, for example, that primary relations are more likely to develop in smaller groups in investigations of the effect of size of work group upon job satisfaction, regular attendance, or industrial peace. Similarly, the study of the degree of identification of work group members with the larger organization and its goals assumes such identification to be a group product. A third illustration is the analysis of the extent of diffusion of authority in an organization where there is concern for work group participation in decision-making, for autonomy of work groups, or for "self-determination" by work groups. The conception of the work group in these and similar studies incorporates the view that active involvement of the members of the group in group processes, identification with a particular group, and opportunity for frequent interaction within the group are present. While such a conception may be appropriate in some industrial settings, it is clearly inappropriate when applied to the automated automobile engine plant. The workers in this plant were able to identify a certain number of people with whom they worked, but the work group thus identified was defined almost exclusively in terms of spatial proximity or similarity of function. Where groups are conceived in this way and not as interaction systems, the assumption that morale, determination of goals, or decision-making in general will emerge as *group* products is a tenuous one.

Sometimes the term work group has been loosely applied in industrial sociology to any small functionally interdependent collectivity of workers. Changes in informal social structure resulting from automation point to the necessity for a more rigorous definition of the work group concept and to the need for caution in the application of the concept in analysis of the consequences of group activity. Many of the working concepts in industrial sociology have been developed in the study of "human relations in industry" and are oriented to interactional patterns in the "small group." The effects of automation upon social structure in the workplace suggest that a broader conceptualization of industrial social systems may be required.

Notes for
Further Reading

Among the more general works on the impact of technology on society, see:

Forde, D., *Habitat Economy and Society*. London: Methuen Co., 1929.

Ginsberg, E., *Technology and Social Change*. New York: Columbia University Press, 1964.

Ogburn, W.F., "On Culture and Social Change," selected papers edited and with an introduction by O. Dudley Duncan, The Heritage of Sociology Series. Chicago: University of Chicago Press, 1966.

Sahlins, M.D., "Culture and Environment: The Study of Cultural Ecology," in Sol Tax (ed.), *Horizons of Anthropology*. Chicago: Aldine Publishing Company, 1964, pp. 132–147.

For more detailed analyses of the impact of technological changes on traditional societies, see:

Epstein, A.L., *Politics in an African Community*. Manchester: Manchester University Press, 1958.

Epstein, Scarlett T., *Economic Development and Social Change in South India*. Manchester: Manchester University Press, 1962.

Forde, D. (ed.), *Social Implications of Industrialisation and Urbanisation in Africa South of the Sahara*. Unesco, 1956.

Nash, M., *Machine Age Maya: The Industrialization of a Guatemalan Community*. Glencoe, Ill.: The Free Press, 1958.

More detailed analyses of the impact of technology in modern industry in general and of automation in particular can be found in:

Cottrell, F. "Technology and Social Change on American Railroads," in George K. Zollschan and Walter Hirsch (eds.), *Social Change*. Boston: Houghton Mifflin Co., 1954, pp. 699–727.

Dahmén, E. "Technology, Innovation and International Industrial Transformation," *International Social Science Bulletin*, Vol. 4, No. 2, 1954, pp. 246–252.

Diebold, J., "Automation as a Challenge to Management," *International Social Science Bulletin*, Vol. 10, No. 1, 1958, pp. 37–44.

Faunce, W.A., "Automation and the Automobile Worker," *Social Problems*, Vol. VII, Fall 1959, pp. 125–132.

Killingsworth, C.C., "Industrial Relations and Automation," *The Annals of the American Academy of Political and Social Science*, Vol. 340, 1962, pp. 69–87.

III

Patterns of Economic Change

The following excerpts from an article by Habakkuk deal with the conditions of modern economic change and industrialization. He brings together relatively detailed analyses of specific economic factors (for example, the development of the labor force, the structure of capital, and technological innovation) and analyses of the convergence of these factors during the initial stages of industrialization in Western Europe. On the basis of these analyses he draws some general comparative indications about the conditions necessary for modern economic growth. His article is one of the best examples of the vast literature on economic development which has been published during the last two decades.

3   H. J. HABAKKUK

The Historical Experience on the Basic
Conditions of Economic Progress

The historical experience I propose to consider is primarily that of Western Europe (including England), the U.S.A., Russia and Japan before 1914, i.e., the group of countries which there is some reason to believe experienced a marked acceleration in the trend of their output at some period in the preceding 100 or 150 years. I shall take it for granted — though it might well be debated — that the main stimulus to growth came from changes in industry, and that the advance in agriculture can most plausibly be regarded as a response to such changes. I know of no reason why industry should necessarily make the pace, and indeed Adam Smith thought that "the cultivation and improvement of the country . . . must necessarily be prior to the increase of the town"; but it seems in fact to have done so. This essay is therefore primarily an enquiry into the conditions which, in these areas, favored industrialization. It would be possible to shed light on this subject by considering the reasons for the absence of economic progress during most of human history over most of the world. But here I am concerned with the different questions of why growth did occur in certain areas.

At the present stage of knowledge it is possible to explain, though only in a rough and ready fashion, the economic fortunes of any single economy, but the conditions favorable to growth are so varied, and combine in so many different ways, that it is not possible to give a list of essential requisites that is more than a string of platitudes. And since some of the conditions cannot be quantitatively conceived, and many which can be so conceived cannot, because of the deficiency of our sources, be measured, it may very well be that we shall never be able to make generalized statements about them.

It is probable that the most important of the conditions which made Europe the cradle of economic advance originated very far back in her

Reprinted from *Economic Progress: Papers and Proceedings of a Round Table Held by the International Economic Association*, ed. Leon H. Dupriez (1955) (pp. 149–169, with omissions), by permission of the author and of The International Economic Association.

history. Since early medieval times, parts of Europe exhibited economic progress of a kind which so far as we know did not take place in other continents — progress which was slow by the standards of the last 200 years, which affected only a small sector of the economy, which was for long periods retarded or reversed, but which is evidence of favorable conditions absent elsewhere. Thus, by the early eighteenth century many parts of Europe already had in some measure many of the facilities, the absence of which is often supposed to account for the failure of the backward areas of the present day to generate economic progress; credit, distribution and transport facilities, supplies of relatively skilled labor, acquisitive attitudes were already to be found in certain parts of Britain, Germany, the Low Countries and Italy. However deficient these facilities were, entrepreneurs did not have to provide them *ab initio* as they would in the undeveloped areas of today.

Adam Smith's explanation of the mechanism by which this type of economic advance was achieved is still the most reasonable. Given initial differences in aptitude or equipment, man's propensity to trade would extend the market and promote a greater division of labor; this increased the efficiency of labor directly, and also facilitated the invention and improvement of machines. To this must be added two other elements of explanation: (a) As society by this means became wealthier it was able to afford an increasing amount of those types of long-lived equipment whose capital content was heavy in relation to its annual yield; in the societies under discussion this meant primarily improved transport facilities. (b) The increase in total demand and/or the shifts in demand brought out and identified those branches of production in which improvement was possible, and sometimes created stringencies in the supply of particular commodities which stimulated the search for new methods. Most of the economically important inventions of the Industrial Revolution-period can more plausibly be ascribed to the pressure of increasing demand rather than to the random operation of the human instinct of contrivance, changes in factor prices, or the Schumpeterian innovator (who became an important agent of advance only at a relatively late stage).

Though its working would be accelerated by changes in religious belief which enhanced the value of material success, or by accessions of scientific knowledge the mechanism was autonomous, and, in the absence of destructive wars and natural disasters and so long as the supply of labor and capital was elastic, the advance tended to be sustained though of course not necessarily uniform. The progress depended on the extent of the market but itself promoted the extension of the market; each advance created the conditions for a further advance and indeed positively stimulated it; each successful solution of a production problem contributed to the general body of experience and knowledge which could be drawn on for the solution of further problems. In the process, skills and attitudes favorable to economic growth were developed.

This seems to me, at this very low level of generalization, the model which most corresponds with what happened in Europe up to the eighteenth century. In this sort of slow cumulative growth, many of the problems which face contemporary undeveloped countries in their attempt to industrialize did not arise. Advances took place gradually in many parts of the economy — it is striking in how many fields of activity in eighteenth century England new methods were being adopted — and so they tended to provide their own markets. The complementarity of different industries which new industrializing countries attempt to establish by policy was here product of spontaneous growth.

The generative power was provided by trade, and the ultimate explanation of the progressive economic history of Europe compared with other continents is that the simple facts of geography — river systems, proximity to the sea, great differences of natural advantage in a relatively small area — were exceptionally favorable to trade and a progressive extension of the market; and there is a good deal to be said for the old view that the acceleration of economic changes in the late eighteenth century was primarily the result of the great expansion of overseas trade in the two preceding centuries.

THE CONDITIONS OF ENGLAND'S INDUSTRIAL LEADERSHIP

I now turn to attempt a more detailed explanation of this acceleration of economic advance, which is associated with changes in the iron and cotton textiles industries and with the development of steam power. These changes were not made simultaneously in the parts of Europe in which they were ultimately adopted; they were made within small areas of a single country, England, and then diffused. Why?

English trade, both internal and external, was exceptionally favored by geography, and less impeded by destructive wars, disorder and political instability than that of continental countries: and this may well be the crucial reason why the mechanism worked more effectively in England than elsewhere, and why the momentum of her economy in the century before the great industrial changes was on balance greater than elsewhere.

Then again the barriers presented by state policy and by social institutions to the exploitations of any given range of economic opportunities were much smaller in England.

(a) In almost every continental country the state attempted in its own interests to maintain detailed regulation of economic life — regulation which, since it was designed mainly to preserve the existing structure, was unfavorable to spontaneous change. In this scheme of things, advance was to come from state-promoted and state-aided concerns exempted from the regulations. For a variety of reasons this did not prove a successful method of promoting industrial growth — political considerations determined the choice of the men to whom the concessions were granted, and they were protected by their privileged position from the stimulus of competition. A system in many ways similar existed in England in the sixteenth and early seventeenth centuries and was destroyed by the Civil War. Compared with the continent therefore, the English state did not exert its power to prevent the discarding of old types of activity in favor of those which yielded a higher return.

(b) Social mobility was very much greater in England. In many parts of the continent the peasants were still subject to various forms of serfdom, and the guilds were still key institutions. Large numbers of the population were tied to the soil, and entry into trades was not free. For both these reasons the scope for men of relatively obscure origin with bright ideas and enterprising temperament was very much greater in England.

The factors which were in some sense, external to the mechanism were exceptionally favorable to its operation in England. The size and nature of the market, on which more than on anything else the working of the mechanism depended, were also exceptionally favorable. The geographical size of the market available to English manufacturers was wide — transport costs were lower, marketing facilities better, internal tariffs, tolls, etc., such as existed in most continental countries, were absent.

The nature of the market, i.e., the purchasing power and tastes of the individuals who composed it, was more favorable; and this was of crucial importance when transport costs severely restricted the geographical market for many products. Japan, in the 1890's, could, by producing at low prices, rapidly acquire a very wide market; eighteenth century industrial areas could not.

(a) In the first place average per capita incomes were higher than on the continent. There were large numbers of people with a reasonable margin above subsistence for the consumption of manufactured goods. The inducement to expand an individual industry was not therefore impeded by the very inelastic demand which faces an industry in the poorer countries of the modern world.

(b) Moreover, the English consuming public were more likely to make use of any increase in their command over goods, rather than hoard, or take it out in increased leisure. A large eighteenth century literature was devoted to the factors which, by frustrating the flow of new demands for goods, would deprive the mechanism of its stimulus. The brake most commonly feared was laziness: instead of using their increased productive power to purchase more of the old goods and/or new goods, thus stimulating further advance, people would just take more time off, and the advance would consequently lose momentum. This undoubtedly happened in England, and it has happened in most countries in the early stages of industrialization. But the sector of English society characterized by a high preference for leisure was probably smaller than elsewhere. There was a large sector of English society which was willing to work harder to acquire the increasing range of goods available.

Both these features of the English market were primarily due to the importance of the middle group incomes. English society at the end of the seventeenth century was distinguished from the societies of the continent by the large part of the national income which accrued to people with moderate sized incomes — according to Gregory King, as much as half. The relatively great importance of this middle group is due, in turn, partly to social causes of long standing, and partly to differences of tax systems. The middle-income groups were relatively large in England for the same reason as they were large in all the great trading centers of the pre-industrial age. Secondly, taxation on the continent was not only heavier, but was highly regressive and taxed the mass of the population for the benefit of a very small class.

(c) Moreover, this large middle market was a market for solid substantial goods as opposed to fine quality goods, i.e., for just the sort of goods suitable for machine production.

It is easy to see that the mechanism we have outlined might in favorable conditions produce a leap in economic activity, and this is what seems to have happened in the late eighteenth century. Both in the primary iron industry and in cotton there were exceptionally strong stimuli to the invention and adoption of new methods: in the former, the shortage of timber and the consequent dependence on foreign supplies for a large part of a munition of war, wrought iron; in the latter, the lack of balance between the spinning and weaving sections. The solutions to the problems so created made possible very much larger production at lower costs and the whole momentum of economic advance was thereby accelerated.

These seem to me the main reasons why the Industrial Revolution happened in England rather than in, for example, France. Except in so far as it may have had some part in directing investment into transport facilities, I do not think that the English priority can be attributed to greater availability of capital, and even transport facilities were primarily a response to prior industrial development, and — there is every reason to suppose — would have been built sooner or later, even if capital had been scarcer. Even more obviously, the economic advance of this period was not due to superior supplies of labor. The extent to which once economic advance had acquired momentum, it was not held up by inelasticities of labor and capital is a point I shall consider later.

THE CONDITIONS OF SUCCESSFUL "IMITATION"

There were broadly two reactions to the English Industrial Revolution.

1. In some countries there was direct imitation stimulated in varying degrees by the competition of English exports. The new technology was predominantly, though by no means exclusively, an English product and the first stages in the industrialization of other countries generally consisted in taking over this technology.

2. There were other countries whose economic growth was stimulated by increased British demand for imports. Since this was a demand for primary products the economic growth did not, for the most part, take the form of rapid industrialization. In some countries the increased demand may very well have retarded industrialization; in Sweden, possibly, where, until the last quarter of the century, growth primarily took the form of the expansion of her traditional timber and iron production. On the other hand, the increase in the home market which the growth made possible helped to create a basis for possible industrialization.

I propose to confine myself to the imitators. There are certain general observations to be made.

(a) Their problem differed from that of England in that there was a large stock of new techniques they could take over. But the difference in this respect is not one of principle. The commonest pattern of industrialization is for a country to take over the techniques already employed elsewhere, start to produce goods hitherto imported and win its home market. The English industrialization conforms in several respects to this pattern. It starts with the establishment in England of industries and techniques long established elsewhere.

(b) The period of absorption of foreign techniques was very long in England, but the adoption of English techniques by continental countries was nowhere rapid by modern standards. Compared with the sort of industrializations of underdeveloped areas which are contemplated at the present day, the industrialization of Germany, Japan and the United States was slow.

(c) The areas in which the new techniques were successfully adopted all possessed, at the start, supplies of skilled craftsman labor, and a nucleus of initiative and organizing ability; they were all rich in natural resources in relation to their populations; even Russia had a level of income per head very much above that of modern India. Most of them had textile and primary iron industries not widely dissimilar in organization and level of development to the corresponding English industries before their advance in the later eighteenth century. Except for Russia the level of skill was sufficiently high to present few technical difficulties in the way to imitation, and any gap in cultural standards was small. For this reason, nineteenth century experience is of doubtful relevance to the industrialization of undeveloped areas in the modern world.

I now propose to consider why some countries imitated with more success than others. The attempt confronts a major difficulty, for while it is possible to say that certain minima of economic achievement and technical skill were basic conditions of economic growth it is difficult to assess the importance, in determining the relative rates of growth, of differences above these minima.

THE FACTOR EQUIPMENT OF THE IMITATORS

One source of difference was the difference of return which the introduction of new techniques offered in the various countries. The most important of the new methods relied heavily on coal, and where coal was dear and charcoal cheap, as was the case in France, the scope for cost-reduction by the introduction of the new methods may very well have been small. The consequences of dear coal can be traced throughout the French economy. Because coke was slow to replace charcoal in the primary iron industry, this industry failed to achieve the opportunities for increased specialisation which geographical concentration might have afforded. Because of this lack of industrial concentration the incentive to build was less. The slow introduction of steam power was partly responsible for the deficiencies of the French metal working and machine industries. A more rapid introduction of the methods would clearly have been to the advantage of the French economy as a whole, but it is not clear that it would have yielded returns to the industry introducing them in the period ahead which it is reasonable for entrepreneurs to consider. There is no way of assessing precisely the responsibility of dear coal but it has still to be demonstrated that the French adoption of the new technique was slower than was warranted by her natural economic advantages. Similarly, over wide areas of the continent efficiency wages were so low that it is not at all clear that it would have paid entrepreneurs to introduce the new methods, a main advantage of which was that they economised labor. The common assumption, however, which I accept for the purposes of this argument is that the most important disparities cannot be explained in this way.

THE STRENGTH OF THE INITIATIVE

There were obvious social conditions, as essential to industrialization as the new techniques, which, except in the U.S.A., did not exist, and which could only be established by state action. The state power in each of these countries was sufficiently strong to undertake the necessary drastic reconstructions of the social structure (e.g., abolition of serfdom in Prussia, of serfdom and the mir in Russia). This was in some sense a basic condition. Then there had to be a large number of potential native entrepreneurs. Though in Russia, Japan and Germany the state took the initiative in developing certain industries, and though the initial impetus so given was important, it is very doubtful whether the resources of any state in the 19th century would have been sufficient to carry through an industrial revolution. Moreover, though English enterprise played a significant part in the early phases of French, German and Russian industrialization, there is no case before 1914 of a major industrialization being carried far on the basis of foreign enterprise. The international mobility of enterprise seems to have been low. Some native source of initiative therefore was a basic condition, and it is often argued that some countries had more venturesome entrepreneurs for such reasons as national character, cultural background and institutions; political and social attitudes, i.e., for non-economic reasons. Thus, the rapid industrialization of Japan compared with that of India and China is often attributed (where it is not attributed to the existence in Japan of a state prepared to initiate economic change) to the Samurai, "a ruling class which possessed prestige and self-confidence," but which "was not rigidly demarcated from the rest of the population nor . . . conservative in its outlook." The contrast of Japan with India is certainly one which requires explanation, since India had many of the basic conditions of industrialization — a merchant class, banking, and transport facilities, considerable production for the market — and perhaps in this case difference in character and quality of the native entrepreneurs was the decisive factor.

The slow growth of the French economy in the nineteenth century has been attributed to the social attitudes of the French entrepreneurs. The characteristic firm was the exclusive family firm; the motive of the family was not to maximize wealth, but to maintain a position, and even the most progressive firms exhibited this attitude. The argument is sometimes supported by the assertion that the army and the administration attracted a large amount of entrepreneurial ability, in contrast to Germany where, because of the exclusive tendency of the Prussian military and political system, the loss of potential entrepreneurs was smaller. It is also suggested that, for reasons which have nothing to do with the economic endowments of the two countries, the typical German entrepreneur was better educated, and therefore had wider horizons than his French counterpart.

It is extraordinarily difficult to know how much weight to attach to this factor since it is impossible to test entrepreneurial ability except by achievement and this begs the question. There is no *a priori* reason why it should not sometimes have been the major factor. But in the French case, the one that has been argued in most detail, it looks as if the character of enterprise was primarily a product of the economic environment rather than the reverse. For foreign concerns of France behaved in much the same way as the French, and the great corporations behaved in much the same way as the family. Moreover, the family firm was a common feature of nineteenth century capitalism, and elsewhere proved not only not incompatible with rapid progress but its main agent.

THE NATURE OF THE MARKET

There were important differences in the internal market conditions in respect of (a) the type of goods demanded, (b) the degree of homogeneity of the market, and (c) the character of its response to the availability of new goods. In the U.S.A. conditions under all three heads were exceptionally favorable.

    (a) Primarily because the new land was opened up in ways favorable to a wide distribution of landownership, there was a large market for substantial simple goods of a sort which lent themselves to standardized machine production. (In South America a large class of medium-sized property owners did not develop because, at an early stage, the land was occupied by great estates, and this is one reason why areas not deficient in natural resources failed to exhibit economic growth.)

    (b) There was an absence of deeply grained traditional tastes, regional and social, which, in Europe, impeded the process whereby the competition of the more efficient firms forced the adoption of new methods and equipment throughout the economy.

    (c) There was little desire to hoard, and a low value was placed on leisure.

All the European continental countries had suffered in the 18th century from social and fiscal arrangements which made their agricultural populations poor markets for substantial simple goods, and which deflected industry towards meeting the luxury demands of a small upper class market. Arrangements of this sort persisted in Russia far into the 19th century, and even in France, where they had been destroyed by the Revolution, they left their mark on industry — the differential advantages of French industry tended to be in the luxury lines. It seems however that, except perhaps in Russia, average per capita income was by the middle of the century sufficiently high in these countries to provide a market for substantial industries goods. Industrialists were not faced with the highly inelastic demand which results from extreme poverty.

They were however unhomogeneous markets with deeply rooted regional and social tastes. It was these forces of market imperfection, I am inclined to think, which were mainly responsible for the very slow diffusion in most countries on the continent of the new techniques, particularly in textiles, and for the failure of those firms which did adopt them to make more rapid progress; this rather than the ability of the workers in the old forms of industry to endure increasing misery. (Similarly, the stability and rigidness of tastes, the conservative attitude to new tastes, throughout the East and particularly in China — witness the difficulty of Western traders in finding exports, other than bullion and opium, acceptable to these markets — was a factor in limiting the growth of their industries.)

The characteristic of the market they served was primarily responsible for the sort of oligopolistic structure of French industry Mr. Landes has described. Why market imperfections were — as appears to have been the case — a less important impediment in Germany, also a predominantly peasant country, is a question to which I have no satisfactory answer. Possibly something is to be attributed to the fact that the French industrial structure had got set in an oligopolistic pattern *before* the building of the French railways, and was strong enough to resist the pressures set up by falling transport costs; whereas in Germany, where industrial development was later and the railways earlier, the pattern had less chance to establish itself. It is clear that hoarding was more prevalent in the peasant societies of the continent than in either England or the U.S.A., and it is possible that, in the early stages of industrialization, the elasticity of demand for goods in terms of effort was lower. And in so far as these two conditions prevailed, the market for manufactured goods in these countries failed to expand as rapidly as their natural resources and technical potentialities warranted. But I know of no evidence which would enable one to compare the various continental countries on this point.

A further market condition may be considered. Industrialization was accompanied by a rapid increase in population, and, in the early stages, the increase in national income was predominantly an increase in the number of individual incomes rather than in income per head; there was a widening rather than a deepening of consumption. This, though not a basic condition of growth, certainly made the task of entrepreneurs easier.

CAPITAL SUPPLIES

How far was the momentum of economic progress retarded by shortage of capital and finance? It is a striking fact that, though all these countries at the start of the process had very small savings, the process of capital accumulation does not appear to have involved a reduction in consumption. Though for the period under review there are no reliable figures, the extent to which this was due to borrowing from abroad was probably small. The borrowing of France, Germany and Japan in relation to their total capital formation was quite modest. The reasons for this — not of course equally important in all countries — were: (a) all these countries possessed before industrialization a substantial industry of the domestic type, (b) the initial stages of industrialization were gradual.

These countries were able, therefore, to provide a very large part of their own capital equipment, and also meet out of their own resources the additional demand resulting from the income created by the investment. They did not, that is to say, need large foreign loans to cover deficits in their current account. (In the case of Japan, the need for foreign loans was further reduced by an increase, which in this context was fortuitous, of her exports of raw silk.) There is an obvious contrast with the development of the regions of recent settlement, most of which in the early stages were incapable of producing their own capital equipment, depended very heavily on imports for their consumer goods, and were developed very rapidly. Most of these latter drew heavily on foreign capital — Canada, for example, in the decade 1900–1910 drew almost half its aggregate net investment from abroad — but this is not true of the pre-1914 industrializations, except for Russia, where 80–90% of the capital in iron and steel and oil was foreign-owned.

Probably the main reason why capital formation did not involve a reduction in consumption levels is that there were, at the start of the process, reserves of unused capacity which could be brought into use with relatively little additional capital, land not exploited well below the level of existing techniques, disguised agricultural unemployment. Because of these reserves, the resources for capital investment were provided not only out of the products of that investment, but also out of the increase in output (primarily agricultural output) stimulated by the increase in demand. This argument does not of course hold to the extent to which the employment of these unused resources involved capital outlay; but it appears that considerable increase in yields per acre and in effective acreage could be achieved with very little additional capital.

The speed and size of the response depended, not only on the extent of the unused resources available, but on the agrarian structure, the existing transport and marketing facilities etc. The U.S.A. was exceptionally well placed, not only because of her large supplies of land, but because these had been developed in the first place to meet the needs of the market, and her agriculture, therefore, responded rapidly to any increase in demand. Among European countries, England was best placed, less because of her ratio of men to land than because of her system of land tenure; the landlord/tenant-farmer system is much better adapted than peasant agriculture to change the character and increase the output of its agriculture. Peasant systems are relatively unresponsive, and partly for this reason industrialization has often involved the attempted destruction of the peasantry. Where the response was slow, but the forces of expansion were strong, we should expect inflations to have occurred, and possibly for conditions to be less favorable to growth; and it is conceivable that further investigation will show that differences in response did influence the speed of growth in these countries. My impression, however, is that with the possible exception of Russia the response was sufficient for the rate of growth permitted by the other limiting factors.

Where the additional output was entirely absorbed by an increase in population, there would, of course, have been nothing available to contribute to capital investment, and it is clear that in some societies this is what happened. In the Balkans, indeed, it appears that increase in demand, though it stimulated an increase in agricultural output, stimulated a proportionately greater increase of population, and a consequent fall in income per head. But in none of the Western European industrializing countries did this happen, though in Germany something like it might have happened but for emigration.

Once the early stages had been passed, the rapid rise of real income itself provided the capital; mid-Victorian England, Germany after 1890, Japan in the inter-war period all proved capable of very high rates of saving.

My conclusion is that, for these reasons, the rate of capital investment actually achieved did not involve a fall in consumption. This, however, does not dispose of the question — was this rate retarded by shortage of finance? Were there a large number of projects which entrepreneurs actively wanted to undertake but which they were prevented from undertaking by the nature of the terms on which they could obtain funds? This is a question which it is not possible to answer with precision. Entrepreneurs completely frustrated by lack of funds leave no trace, and though many cases can be cited of well-known industrial figures who at one time or another faced finance difficulties, it is difficult to say how important these cases were. Moreover though the rates of interest on first-class securities can be compared country by country, it is extremely difficult to obtain information about the structure of rates in the different countries. The differences in the first-class security rate from area to area were not sufficiently great, one would have supposed to have had much influence on the level of investment, but there may very well have been great and influential differences, as between the various areas, in lenders' assessment of the riskiness of industrial borrowers. My general impression, however, is that finance was not a major influence on the rate of growth. My reasons for believing this are

(I) It was relatively easy for an entrepreneur in the early stages of industrialization to start a project with his private savings and those of his friends and relations, and to finance subsequent growth by ploughing back profits. Two conditions of his ability to do this were

> (a) The state of existing techniques of production. The means of production required for the smallest unit of investment which was technically and economically feasible, were small in relation

to the savings of the potential entrepreneur. This was obviously
more true of the initiating country than of the imitators, who had
the opportunity of taking over in a single step projects which in
the initiating country had taken several stages. But I should be
inclined to argue that none of the European nineteenth century
imitators lagged behind the initiator in techniques sufficiently far
to make a very significant difference. I except Russia and Japan
from this generalization.

(b) A high rate of profit. It has been argued that a condition of rapid
accumulation from plowed-back profits was the stickiness of
wages when prices were rising. Possibly, too, it had something to
do with the slow entry, for reasons not connected with availability
of capital, of new firms, which allowed the leaders a period of
exceptionally high profits. For these two reasons, the need of
entrepreneurs to obtain funds from outside sources was limited.
But

(c) in all these areas, except Russia, there were loan markets, im-
perfect, of course, compared with those of the late nineteenth
century, but highly developed compared with those of modern
India and the Middle East. A borrower who could offer good
security could borrow at a rate which was approximately uniform
over a wide area; and for reasons given in (a) and (b) above, it
was fairly easy for entrepreneurs to accumulate the assets which
would enable them, when plowed-back profits were inadequate,
to offer good security for a loan.

There was one project characteristic of the early stages of industrialization, where, in certain countries, these sources of finance were clearly inadequate — the railway — and here the state intervened and either built
the railways, providing the finance partly out of taxation, or guaranteed
the interest on loans issued by private entrepreneurs. Some states took
the necessary action earlier than others, and the differences of timing
obviously had a powerful effect on the rate of economic growth (viz. the
importance of the fact that Germany had her railway system a decade
before France); but if lack of finance influenced the government, it was
usually to accelerate rather than retard state intervention.

(II) In the later stages of industrialization, there was some tendency,
the strength of which varied widely of course from industry to industry,
for the smallest practicable unit to become large in relation to the funds
available to a single industrialist from the sources we have discussed.
And, in so far as this happened, the possibility increases that fruitful
developments may have been retarded or frustrated by shortage of finance.
The fact that the self-financing family firm continued to prevail over so
much of European industry — including some of the most rapidly growing industries — can be used in evidence both for and against rating this
possibility high, it may be taken as a sign either of the adequacy of the

older sources of finance, or of the inadequacy of any alternative. A less ambiguous piece of evidence is the great resourcefulness and ingenuity shown where there was a marked shortage of funds in relation to available opportunities, in adapting or devising institutions to provide entrepreneurs with funds; witness the invention of the preference share, the developments in banking (particularly the German industrial banks), the adaptation of forms of joint-stock organization, and the role of the Zaibatzu in Japan. There may, of course, have been a considerable time-lag between these developments and the needs to which they were a response, the fact that these adaptations were made in the end is no proof that there was not a long period in which economic growth was retarded for the lack of them. But on the whole what impresses is the speed of the adaptation.

The suggestions which for purposes of discussion I wish to make are therefore, that so far as the nineteenth century industrializations are concerned (1) societies in which other conditions were favorable were usually capable of devising adequate financial institutions; (2) where the agricultural sector was responsive to an increase in demand, the real resources devoted to investment did not involve a contraction of consumption.

LABOR SUPPLIES

To what extent and in what ways was the momentum of economic progress affected by availability of labor? Can a certain sort of labor market be said to have been a "basic condition" of economic progress? In the classical version of things, the rising real wages of labor were the major internal force tending to halt accumulation, and the argument depended mainly on the unresponsiveness of food supply. There are really two quite distinct questions.

(1) How responsive was population to an increase in demand? This is partly a question of how favourable natural resources were to an expansion of food production — a question we have already discussed; it is partly a question of social structure, nature of crops, inheritance laws, etc.

(2) On what terms was the increase made available to industry? which is mainly a question of the legal and social impediments to movement.

In all these countries, except France, industrialization was accompanied by rapid natural increase. It is in dispute how far, in each case, this was due to (a) the effect of medical improvements on death rates, (b) the effect of higher living standards on birth rates, (c) the effect of increased demand for labor (working mainly through marriage rates) on birth rates. But there might be general agreement that the increase was primarily a response to industrialization, rather than vice-versa, and that, in the period before labor became geographically mobile, some population-response was a basic condition of industrialization. (There is no contradiction between this and the belief that shortage of labor was a stimulus to labor-saving inventions in early 18th century England and to the installation of labor-saving machinery in 19th century U.S.A.)

The population-response varied widely, according not only to the elasticity of food supplies, but to general cultural patterns, age at marriage, inheritance customs, etc. The increase was exceptionally rapid in the U.S.A. It was weak only in France, where wide distribution of property coupled with equal division of inheritance provided strong inducement to postpone marriage. This seems, therefore, to have been a basic condition that was easily satisfied.

Much more important were the variations in the strength of the institutional impediments to the movement of population. The wide distribution of property rights in continental Europe made labor everywhere rather immobile. This was less of an impediment in Germany, where the emancipation of the serfs east of the Elbe was carried out in such a way as to create a substantial proletariat. The impediment to movement was greatest in Russia, where, even after the abolition of serfdom, the communal ownership of land and communal responsibility for taxation which survived almost until 1914, made permanent movements of labor exceptionally difficult. Probably the main influence of this immobility in the early stages of industrialization was on the gap between the terms on which labor was available to the factory and to domestic industry. In both Russia and France, but particularly in the former, the relatively high cost of attracting permanent labor into the industrial areas was one of the main factors depriving the factory of the power to compete the older forms of industry out of existence, but I know of no evidence sufficient to determine the importance of this factor as compared with the market imperfections already discussed.

To what extent was skilled labor a basic condition? The most intractable shortage was of the skill to construct and service the new machines, but there was also a shortage of the semi-skilled labor required to operate them. Though all these countries, except Russia had many skilled craftsmen of the locksmith type, a very high premium on skill persisted throughout the early stages of industrialization. The problem was met in part by direct attempts to train labor (in Germany the adaptation of gild apprenticeship rules, the various forms of technical education), and partly by adjusting the machinery to suit the capacity of the labor force (the early development of fool-proof mass-production machinery in the U.S.A., which was less well supplied with craft skills). There appear to be no significant differences on this point between initiator and imitators. The later mechanizations were more rapid and therefore the demand for skilled labor larger; but, for the same reason, the skilled craftsmen were more easily uprooted for work in the factory. Furthermore the imitators drew on the supplies of skilled English labor to alleviate exceptionally severe shortages. The nineteenth century industrializations experienced great difficulties not only in training skill, but in adapting labor to the exigencies of work in the factory. From its very nature, the acquisition of skills and of new attitudes to work was a slow process, and the deficiencies of labor were a more important retarding factor than shortage of finance.

Notes for Further Reading

For general works dealing with comparative analysis of economic development, see:

Gershenkron, A., *Economic Backwardness in Historical Perspective*. Cambridge, Mass.: Harvard University Press, 1962.

Hoselitz, B.F., *Sociological Aspects of Economic Growth*. Glencoe, Ill.: The Free Press, 1960.

Kerr, C., et al., *Industrialism and Industrial Man*. Cambridge, Mass.: Harvard University Press, 1960.

Kuznets, S., *Economic Change*. New York: W.W. Norton, 1953.

For more detailed studies of economic development in different settings, see:

Abegglen, J.C., *The Japanese Factory*. Glencoe, Ill.: Free Press of Glencoe, Inc., 1958.

Epstein, T.S., *Economic Development and Social Change in South India*. Manchester: The University Press, 1962.

Kuznets, S., W.E. Moore, et al. (eds.), *Economic Growth: Brazil, India, Japan*. Durham: Duke University Press, 1955.

Lockwood, W.W., *The Economic Development of Japan*. Princeton: Princeton University Press, 1954.

——————— (ed.), *The State and Economic Enterprise in Japan*, Princeton: Princeton University Press, 1965.

Supple, B.E. (ed.), *The Experience of Economic Growth*. N.Y.: Random House, 1963.

For a broad comparative-historical analysis of the relations between economic and political changes, see:

Polanyi, K., et al. (eds.), *Trade and Market in the Early Empire*. Glencoe, Ill.: The Free Press and the Falcon's Wing Press, 1957.

Weber, M., *General Economic History*. New York: Collier Macmillan, 1961.

IV

Changes in the Family

These excerpts from one of Goode's many studies on industrialization and the family examine in detail the "fit" between a definite type of family structure and the industrial system. He questions the common assumption that a traditional or extended type of family is incompatible with industrialization. By showing that this assumption does not hold, that a relatively wide variety of family type is compatible with industrialization, and that industrialization need not always result in the deterioration of the families' traditional bases and orientations, Goode illustrates that change is relatively autonomous in different parts of the social structure.

Industrialization and Family Change

THE CONJUGAL FAMILY AS AN IDEAL TYPE

World changes in family patterns suggest that industrialization must indeed contain the prime social variables, since, wherever any movement toward industrialization occurs, the family system moves toward some kind of "conjugal" pattern — i.e., few kinship ties with distant relatives, and an emphasis on the nuclear family unit of husband and wife with their children. Most analysts, confronted with this phenomenon, have succumbed to the temptation to assume that industrialization is the independent variable and that family change is the dependent one. Let us, before yielding to this temptation, examine the problem more closely.

Both the *degrees* and the *types* of these family changes have not yet been charted adequately. The *processes* by which they occur have not been revealed. The detailed facts necessary for the first task, and the rigorous theory necessary for the second, are as yet insufficient. I have been engaged in trying to summarize many of the facts; but space forbids their presentation here,[8] though, later in this paper, I shall describe a few of these trends. At this point, let us consider the theoretical problem.

We must remember that, in current family theory, "conjugal family" (sometimes, "nuclear family") is used to refer to three very different notions.[9] Most commonly, it is technically an idle type, in the Weberian sense.[10] Second, it is an *ideal*, since attitude or value surveys would show

Reprinted from "Industrialization and Family Change," in B. F. Hoselitz and W. E. Moore (eds.), *Industrialization and Society*. Paris: UNESCO-Mouton, 1963. Pp. 239–255, with permission of the author and United Nations Educational, Scientific and Cultural Organization. Article abridged for this printing. Original footnote numbers have been retained.

[8] They will be published in my *World Changes in Family Patterns* (Glencoe, Ill., forthcoming).

[9] I shall use the term "conjugal," since "nuclear" should refer to a structural unit made up of father, mother, and children, which may exist relatively independently (conjugal), or be bound up with other such units to form extended family systems (polygyny, through a common father; polyandry, through a common mother), or various lineages through certain blood relatives.

[10] Max Weber, " 'Objectivity' in Social Science and Social Policy," in *The Methodology of the Social Sciences*, trans. Edward A. Shils and Henry A. Finch

that a substantial (but unknown) percentage of American, or European, or other populations would view certain of its characteristics as legitimate, proper, or good. Third, some percentage (at present unknown) of families in the Western culture complex and elsewhere, do, in *fact* and behavior, conform to the structurally defining characteristics of this family type.

It is crucial, however, to understand that the conjugal family, as commonly described, is not a summary derived from empirical studies of the family. Usually, it is a theoretical construction, in which several central variables have been combined to make a hypothetical structural harmony, and other characteristics have then been "derived" from them sociologically.

The most important characteristic of the ideal-type conjugal family is that it excludes a wide range of affinal and blood relatives from its everyday affairs — there is no great *extension* of the kin network.[11] Most of its other characteristics can be inferred from this complex trait. Omitting the derivation itself, we can list them as follows:

(1) The couple cannot count on a large number of kinfolk for help, just as these cannot call on the couple for services.

(2) Neither couple nor kinfolk have many *rights* with respect to one another; thus their reciprocal obligations are few.

(3) Necessarily, then, they have few moral (or other) controls over one another.

(4) Kinfolk do not choose the couple's residence location — which is, therefore, "neolocal," and reinforces the couple's independence (by lowering its rate of social interaction with kin).

(5) The couple's choice of one another as mate was dependent on them, not based on the rights or interests of the kin; in turn, marital adjustment is primarily between husband and wife.

(6) When this system emerges, the age at marriage will change; but theory does not permit a prediction of its direction — youngsters must be old enough to take care of themselves.

(7) Fertility is based on the needs of the couple, and may be high (frontier) or low (urban industry).

(8) The system is omnilineal;[12] neither kin line has great weight.

(9) The small nuclear unit is the chief place where the emotional input-

---

(Glencoe, Ill., 1949), pp. 89 ff. See also the brief summary in William J. Goode, "Note on the Ideal Type," American Sociological Review, XII (August, 1947), 473–75.

[11] For additional variables important in comparing family systems, see Goode, "Horizons in Family Theory," 178–91.

[12] The term is Max Gluckman's.

output balance of the individual spouses must be maintained, since there is nowhere else to go.

(10) Consequently, the divorce rate will be high — though again, we cannot predict whether it will fall or rise when such a system emerges.

(11) Remarriage, after the death of one's spouse or after divorce, is highly probable.

Such an ideal-type construct should be compared with family behavior and ideals in various cultures where approximations to the conjugal system are thought to exist. To my knowledge, no such comparison has been made. We do know that, in both England and the United States, the lower-class family — presumably the least extended of families — does recognize and interact with a range of kin other than those contained in the nuclear unit.[13]

The ideal-type construct fails to fit both reality and social theory in one important respect. The family system *cannot* be limited to the nuclear unit without the application of political force. Grandparent-grandchild ties are strong; sibling ties are strong; and, therefore, parents-in-law interact relatively frequently with their children-in-law, and married people interact frequently with their siblings-in-law. The most common kind of "visiting" and "social occasions," even in the United States, remains that of seeing relatives. They are inextricably linked to the nuclear unit, since they cannot be rejected without their rejection simultaneously hurting or angering a member of *one's own* nuclear family — e.g., the child cannot ignore his uncle without hurting one of his own parents. This theoretical and empirical point is important in assessing the relations between industrialization and social change, since it (a) emphasizes some of the *limits* of the family's adjustment to outside pressures, and (b) raises the problem of how the industrialization process — as in Russia, Israel, and China — must adjust *to* the family.

The "Fit" Between the Conjugal Family and the Industrial System. We can ignore the theoretically empty argument about whether political and economic variables determine family patterns, or the reverse. Our concern is to discover *any* determinate relations among any particular family variables and those of other institutional orders. However, we can investigate the theoretical "harmony" or "fit" between the ideal-type con-

---

[13] See, for example, Raymond Firth (ed.), *Two Studies of Kinship in London* (London, 1956); Michael Young and Peter Wilmott, *Family and Kinship in East London* (London, 1957); Elizabeth Bott, *Family and Social Network* (London, 1957). Unpublished research by both Morris Zelditch and Eugene Litwak have shown the importance of many kin links in the United States. See Eugene Litwak, "Occupational Mobility and Extended Family Cohesion," *American Sociological Review*, XXV (February, 1960), 9–21.

struct and industrialization. A second, equally important, task is to determine their empirical harmony or discord with one another. Third, we must eventually see *how* or through which processes each affects (or has affected) the other.

The second task has been attacked primarily by those who are interested in labor supply in primitive or peasant societies. In general, some investigators have noted that family systems *other* than the conjugal usually do not always yield an adequate labor pool — though they may do so if the existing economic or family system is under stress.[14] Head taxes were used to separate men from their families in Africa. Men's objections to women's leaving home for outside jobs still limit the female labor supply in various parts of Islam. On the other hand, certain primitive societies, like Palau and Manus, have willingly supplied labor to the new system.[15] In our own system, the strains between the conjugal family and the industrial system have not been empirically measured — though this matter is the subject of innumerable sermonizing essays by moralists both literary and religious.

It will be relevant to our subsequent consideration of an important point if we examine the demands of industrialization pertinent for family change. Bureaucratization can occur without industrialization (T'ang China, for example), and so can urbanization (Dahomey, Tokugawa Japan), However, neither occurs without a rise in the technological level of the society; and the modern system of industry never emerges without both bureaucratization and urbanization. The social characteristics traditionally used in analyses of both these processes also apply to industrialization.

The prime social trait of modern industrial enterprise is that — ideally, and to a considerable extent empirically — the individual obtains a position on the basis of his achievement, relative to the demands of the job. His achievement is measured universalistically — i.e., the same standards apply to all job-holders of the same status. His link with the job is functionally specific: the enterprise may not dictate his behavior except in so far as it is directly relevant to getting the job done.

Structurally, such a system is necessarily open-class; it requires both geographical and social mobility. These characteristics are intensified, under industrialization, by the smaller percentage of jobs based on land (and thus on inheritance).

[14] A good analysis from field data is made in Wilbert E. Moore's study of traditional family patterns and industrial demands in Mexico, *Industrialization and Labor* (Ithaca, N.Y., 1951), especially chaps. ix–xi. See also Herbert Blumer, "Early Industrialization and the Laboring Class," *Sociological Quarterly*, I (January, 1960), 5–14.

[15] Both were, it should be remembered, "primitive capitalisms." See Margaret Mead, *New Lives for Old* (New York, 1956); and H. G. Barnett, *Being a Palauan* (New York, 1960).

Various analysts have derived certain relations, some of them intuitive, between industrialization and the conjugal family. These, familiar to the social scientist, may be summarized as follows:

(1) The neolocality of the conjugal system frees the individual from specific geographical ties.

(2) An individual with a limited kin network is facilitated in selecting the industrial job best suited to his skill. He can invest only in himself, not in his kin. He can change his style of life more easily.

(3) Family can be separated from enterprise, so that the achievement, universalistic, and functionally specific criteria of the latter are free to operate without interference from the ascriptive, particularistic, and emotionally diffuse criteria of the former.

(4) The necessarily individual ownership in a conjugal system permits mobility of capital for investment.

(5) Limiting the kin networks prevents them from interlocking to form a set of closed class strata.

(6) The unremitting discipline or — in the upper-level professional, managerial, and creative positions — overly demanding requirements of modern technology are psychologically burdensome. The emotionality of the conjugal family helps to restore a psychological balance — at least, the technical system has no moral responsibility for it.

(7) Omnilineal in pattern, this system maintains no lineage and does not concentrate a family's land or wealth in the hands of one son or daughter.

(8) The talents of both sexes are given greater scope for development to fit the manifold demands of a complex technology.

(9) The small size of the family unit, and its emotional diffuseness, preclude much specification of the status obligations of each member. As a result, more individual variation in conforming to role obligations is permitted, and each individual is better able to fit the range of possible industrial demands.

(10) Since youngsters choose their own spouses and should be economically independent, a long period of family dependence is legitimated. This enables each individual to find a niche appropriate to his talents in the industrial system.

We must emphasize that these "harmonies" do not explain either why industrializing countries seem to move toward some form of the conjugal system, or through which pressures they do so. Before examining this point further, we shall note some "disharmonies" and class variations.

Non-adjustment Between Industrial and Familial Demands. The fact that disharmonies exist suggests again the independence of the two sets of variables. For example, child care is typically given over to one person, the wife; as a rule, there are no additional female kin who might free the young woman for work in the industrial system. Second, the substantial development of labor-saving devices interacts with the specialization of a *highly* industrialized system; the consequence is that the modern American mother is overburdened — to use the case which is so often cited to prove the opposite. These devices for the most part save no labor at all; they merely raise the standards of cleanliness, repairs, freedom from germs, etc. — an ironic confirmation of Marx's gloss on Mill's nineteenth-century doubt about whether mechanical inventions had lightened man's toil. These inventions had, Marx asserted, no such *aim* in the modern system.[16] Among modern inventions, I think, not even detergents and the dish-washing machine "save" any labor for the housewife. The housewife must spend most of her time in creating time-and-place utility — i.e., acting as chauffeur, purchaser, administrator, etc.

In consequence, American women have not become much more "career-minded" over the past half-century. Polling data indicate that the same is true of women in Western Europe.[17] Except for those teaching in colleges, the proportion of women in the established professions in the United States did not change greatly from 1910 to 1950; doubtless the percentage of college-educated women who have gone into these professions has actually dropped.

Furthermore, the amount of housework is great, and husbands and wives are presumably equal — so, generally, the husband has to help with it after his working hours. This diverts much of his energy from his occupation.

The strains between industrialization and the family system which it is thought to fit are discernible in certain class differences. By definition, the middle and upper strata are more "successful" in the industrial system but, in fact, their kin pattern is *less* close to the conjugal pattern than the kin pattern of the lower strata. Upper strata recognize the widest extension of kin, maintain most control over the courtship and marriage choices of their young, and give and receive help from one another most often.

Consequently, the "freedom" that the lower strata have from their kin is like their freedom to sell their labor in an open industrial market. They are less encumbered by the weight of kin when they are *able* to move upward in the occupational system; but they also get less help from their kin when they *try* to move. Like the English peasants who, from late

[16] Numerous studies over the past generation have shown that mothers work extremely long hours. See Mirra Komarovsky, *Women in the Modern World* (Boston, 1953), chap. iv; also, Marx, *Capital* (New York, 1936), 405.

[17] See Theodore M. Caplow, *The Sociology of Work* (Minneapolis, Minn., 1954), chap. xv. For France and Belgium, see *Sociologie comparée de la famille contemporaine* (Paris, 1955), p. 68; and *La condition sociale de la femme* (Brussels, 1956, pp. 53 ff.

medieval times through the early nineteenth century,[18] were "freed" from the land by the various enclosure movements, or the nineteenth-century workers who were "freed from their tools" by machinery, the lower strata have fewer family ties and less family stability, and enjoy less family-based economic and material security.

To that degree, the "integration" of the lower-class family pattern — i.e., the most conjugal — is greatest, primarily in the sense that the individual is forced to enter the labor market with far less family support. He may move where the system needs him — hopefully, where his best opportunity lies — but he *must* fit its demands, since no extended-kin network will interest itself in his fate. His job moves him about and pays him little, so that he cannot keep his kin ties active; on the other hand, since his kin are *also* in the lower strata, his loss from relinquishing them is not great.

A further inference may be drawn. The middle and upper strata have (a) more *resources*, in any system, with which to resist the undermining pressures of the industrialization process (e.g., capital with which to support their youngsters through long professional training); and (b) to considerable *interest* in holding their family system intact against those pressures (because their existing kin network is more active and useful). We assume, then, that, in an industrializing process, both the peasant and primitive proletarians are forced to adjust their family patterns more swiftly to the industrial system, and find at least more immediate opportunities in it. By contrast, the middle and upper strata can utilize these new opportunities best by loosening their kin ties more slowly. Thus, changes in middle- and upper-strata family systems are more likely to occur later in the process.

We must express one important caution. The inference last made applies, only if a non-conjugal, or extended, family pattern actually existed in the lower strata *before* industrialization. I am inclined to believe that the conjugal system will be found, *empirically*, to be more widespread than has been supposed in the lower strata of Japan, China, India, and the Arab world.

    Occupational Merit and Family. We deliberately made our list of apparent harmonies general, to open the possibility of additional examples beyond the Western culture complex.

---

[18] The enclosure movements were different in kind; and the degree to which they were important in creating a labor pool is debatable. However, from the fifteenth century on, there was a floating labor supply. The late eighteenth century (when the agricultural revolution displaced many agricultural workers) was a period of war, colonial emigration, and urban migration — i.e., it was characterized by loose ties to family and locality. See G. R. Elton, *England under the Tudors* (London, 1955), pp. 78–81, 201–07, 230–33; and T.S. Ashton, *An Economic History of England: The Eighteenth Century* (London, 1955), pp. 36–47.

In the Western world there have been several periods — to my knowledge, not yet examined in this context — during which there was relatively high class mobility, based to a substantial extent on achievement. One of the most striking examples occurred during the twelfth and thirteenth centuries in Europe. These centuries constituted an era of marked economic expansion and increased trade. During the era, numerous buildings were constructed, and hundreds of convents, churches, and monasteries were founded. All these enterprises called for a range of administrative and even philosophic talent. Then, as in all epochs, a large proportion of the high-ranking clerical jobs went to the members of the privileged classes; but the expansion of job opportunities, and certain Church policies, engendered a considerable amount of class mobility. However, during that period, there is no evidence to indicate there was any remarkable change in the family systems of Europe; without question, there was no real movement toward a conjugal system. On the other hand, to the extent that the Church succeeded in its recurrent, and ultimately successful, effort to eliminate the family from its clergy, that group was marked by some steps toward the ultimate system of pure merit — the system in which each individual ideally stands alone, without a family; the system whose first eloquent prophet was Plato.

A second case, too complex to analyze here in detail, has obvious relevance. The data about Chinese class mobility are more reliable than those about the High Middle Ages in Europe, because each Chinese dynasty accepted the task of compiling the biographies of important men in the preceding epoch. Knowing the historiographic customs of China, we know that these biographies were formalized; but they do contain enough data to enable us to make rough guesses about the various dynasties from the T'ang through the Ch'ing. Each study has shown that one-third to three-quarters of the men of high position in any given generation were "new men," with no apparent family base in the upper stratum. Hsu, using local district biographies, found that only one-fifth of the men had three generations of higher-class position behind them.[19] The Chinese laid great stress, ideologically, and in fact, on achievement. They had, compared to Europe, a relatively high level of technological and industrial development, at least until the beginning of the nineteenth century; but they did not move toward the conjugal system.

[19] By now, the data on this point are extensive. Robert M. Marsh, in *The Mandarins* (Glencoe, Ill., 1961), has summarized these data. In the Ch'ing Dynasty, the amount of mobility was somewhat less than that in the United States, according to certain criteria. P'an Kuang-tan and Fei Hsiao-t'ung restricted themselves to the examination system alone, and decided that it was not a significant mobility ladder. Cf. the analysis in Robert M. Marsh, "Bureaucratic Constraints on Nepotism in the Ch'ing Period," *Journal of Asian Studies*, XIX (February, 1960), 117–19.

Ideology of Family and Industrialization. There is an ideology of "economic progress" and industrialization, and an ideology of the conjugal family; spokesmen for both appear in non-Western countries before any great changes are discernible in either industrial or familial behavior.

Although elders may deplore them, both appeal to the intellectuals, to the young, to women, and to the disadvantaged generally. The ideology of the conjugal family, I suggest, is critically important in the current family changes taking place in the world. It is a radical philosophy — it is destructive of the older traditions, while having its roots in more general radical principles which arouse its adherents *politically*. It asserts equality, against class, caste, or sex barriers. It advocates the individual's right to choose his or her spouse or place to live, and his right to select which kin obligations he will respect, independent of the decisions of kin. It asserts the worth of the individual, against the kinship-controlled elements of wealth or ethnic group. It even encourages love as a right, opposing the marriage prearranged among kin. It proclaims one's right to change one's family life if it is unpleasant.[20]

Of course, no conjugal family system actually lives up to its principles. However, these express values which, at some levels of consciousness and in many strata, *arouse* peoples the world over — even when they are not yet ready to accept these notions fully. Everywhere, men and women have some resentments against their family system, to which this pattern offers a beguiling alternative.

The ideology enters the society through some spokesmen *before* industrialization; I shall suggest below that it prepares individuals somewhat for their adjustment to industrialization. Its first proponents are usually from the elite. But the debate spreads; and changes in court decisions and laws implement both the political and the family ideology. Most of the major family legislation in the past two decades has moved toward a conjugal pattern. Such legal actions shape both custom and the terms of the ideological debate, whether in Africa or China.[21]

Family as an Independent Causal Element in Industrialization. Progress toward a conjugal system may facilitate industrialization in non-Western countries, and may have been instrumental in Western industrial-

[20] William L. Kolb has argued that those who inveigh against romantic love as a foundation for marriage often use anti-democratic principles in "Sociologically Established Family Norms and Democratic Values," *Social Forces*, XXVI (May, 1948), 451–56. See also my "The Theoretical Importance of Love," *American Sociological Review*, XXIV (February, 1959), 38–47.

[21] Arthur Phillips has written a useful summary of the influence of Western ideology on family decisions in native law; see "Marriage Laws in Africa," chap. ii, Arthur Phillips (ed.), *Survey of African Marriage and Family Life* (London, 1953). Revisions of Chinese codes after 1911 were especially influenced by the Swiss Code.

ization. Let us entertain this thesis a moment, since it seems to have no champion at present.

We cannot view non-Western family systems as basically like the Western systems of some undefined earlier historical phase just before industrialization. The evolutionary model may be in error. For the past thousand years, the family systems of the West have been very different from those of China, India, Japan, Africa, or Islam. There has been no clan system or lineage system in the West. No ancestor worship has existed; and individuals, not families, have been held responsible for crimes. Elders have arranged marriages — but youngsters have had a greater voice in the final choice, partly because (except, perhaps, for the Latin upper strata at divers times and places) young women have not been segregated from young men, even when kept under the scrutiny of a chaperone. Child marriages have never been the ideal or the statistical average. There has been an ideal (still held, but never strong) that a large kin group should live under one roof; but the dominant pattern — which caused marriage among farmers to occur late, on the average — has been that a young couple should have land enough to support themselves independently before marrying. No regularized concubinage or polygyny has been known. The leader of the family has not been even ideally the eldest male, however much deference he was paid.[22]

Moreover, the Protestant Reformation sharpened these differences. It seems more than fortuitous that Henry VIII's break with Rome was precipitated by his insistence that he had the right to make an individual choice about his marital future; and it seems not merely a matter of chance that, a century later, it was a Puritan who made the first serious modern plea for the right to divorce. Our ample documentation of the extraordinary role which ascetic Protestants played in the early development of science, industry, and capitalism should not obscure their less direct, but perhaps not less weighty, influence on an emerging philosophy of anti-traditionalism, freedom of speech, egalitarianism, political liberty, and individualism. Their contribution to the ideology of the conjugal family, a transformation of that philosophy, seems equally important; but historical inquiry has not yet delved into it.[23]

[22] For relevant, though not conclusive, data on certain of these points, see George C. Homans, *English Villagers of the Thirteenth Century* (Cambridge, 1941); Josiah C. Russell, *British Medieval Population* (Albuquerque, New Mexico, 1948), chaps. vii–viii; K. H. Connell, *The Population of Ireland 1750–1845* (Oxford, 1950), chaps. ii–iii; Louis Henry, *Anciennes familles genevoises* (Paris, 1956); Regine Pernoud, "La vie de famille du Moyen Age à l'ancien regime," in Robert Prigent (ed.), *Renouveau des idées sur la famille* (Paris, 1954), pp. 27–32; and G. G. Coulton, *Medieval Panorama* (New York, 1955), chaps. xxv, xlv, xlvi.

[23] For a good analysis of the Puritan family, see Edmund S. Morgan, *The Puritan Family* (Boston, 1944). Milton's "The Doctrine and Discipline of Divorce" was first published in 1643.

The Puritans conceived of the husband-wife relationship as a loving one. This concept emphasized much less the partner's place as merely a link in a kin network. Even during the early period of colonial settlement in the United States, the Puritans' children began to insist on free marriage choice. In his religion, as in his work philosophy, the Puritan was responsible for himself as an individual; he was not merely an ascriptive part of a kin group. His family attitudes fitted him for the opportunities of a new industrialism and capitalism.

Even if this general notion cannot be demonstrated, it is at least indicative of family differences that English workers did not resist factory mechanization because they ranked the values, roles, and enterprises of the extended family higher than the opportunities of the new era. When they did resist, it was on very different grounds — such as wage levels and threats of unemployment. In contrast to the situations reported in some less industrialized countries today, English factory owners rarely had any problem of labor supply. Some investigators have claimed that most of the English opposition to mechanization actually came after it was well under way, and that it was due to the impact of mechanization on the internal structure of the individual family unit, not its impact on the kin network.[24]

It seems, then, that it might be fruitful to inquire whether, in the early phases of Western industrialization, some changes in family patterns had already occurred that prepared certain strata for the new system.

An interesting modern case in point is the Communist attempt to undermine the old Chinese family, and to go *beyond* the conjugal family, in order to accelerate industrialization. If our earlier theoretical analysis has been correct, some variant of a "communal family" pattern would answer the demands of industrialism better than a conjugal family could. Plato's variant was more radical than the Chinese blueprint; but in both, as in the kibbutz, the goal is to weaken kinship obligations, whether between parent and child or between spouses.

Western criticism of China, like earlier attacks on parallel systems in Russia, has largely ignored the possible industrial efficiency of a communal family system. The appraisal has been focused on the totalitarian control over the young, on indoctrination. However, when the objective is rapid industrialization, the older Chinese family (in its post-Manchu form as well) is a definite hindrance; and even the Western conjugal family is not so efficient a structure for permitting individuals to take jobs where they are needed, on the basis of individual achievement. Allocation by achievement violates the family values of all other systems, for it is ultimately *individual* in character — talents and skills are individual, not

[24] Neil J. Smelser, *Social Change in the Industrial Revolution* (Chicago, 1959), chaps. ix–x.

family, traits. Rapid industrialization, as an all-embracing goal, would, therefore, require family ties to be reduced as much as possible.

We are not denying the costs of such a system. Had Plato established his Republic, the competitive atmosphere would have been at least as psychologically destructive as that of, say, New York. No such system has ever evolved naturally, without political direction and revolutionary fervor; both Israel and Russia have retreated somewhat from the ideal; and the Chinese have had to de-emphasize certain elements in their campaign (e.g., by reassuring the young Chinese they still owed their parents some care)[25] — these facts suggest that industrial and technological criteria are not entirely prepotent, and that the amount of energy required for a family pattern which is even less binding than the conjugal may be excessive.

SOME WORLD CHANGES IN FAMILY PATTERNS

If family variables are indeed independent (and they may be overridden, even though independent, under certain circumstances), we can assume that the *direction* of change for *specific* family traits, such as rate of divorce or age at marriage, might be very different from one industrializing system to another — though all of them might be generally moving toward a conjugal pattern. For example, in the broad matrilineal belt of Central African societies, the power of the father is increasing, in contrast to the movement toward female egalitarianism and weakening patriliny in most of the world. However, in the same area, the divorce rate is probably not changing (it has always been high) and will doubtless eventually drop somewhat, in contrast to China, Europe, India, or much of the rest of Africa. In Japan, the divorce rate has been dropping since the turn of the century, in contrast to the other great industrializing areas; and it has also been dropping among the Algerian Moslems.

Lengthy explication of each of these trends would be necessary for adequate exposition. However, we may succinctly, if cryptically, say that each high or low rate in the pre-industrializing or early industrializing phase was the product of specific family patterns. These earlier patterns begin to move toward some conjugal family variant; and thus the rates fall or rise, according to their previous level. In much of Africa, for instance, it seems highly likely that, as the family systems approximate a conjugal form, the marital fertility rates will *increase*, the age of females

---

[25] Feng Ting, "Love and Support of Parents Also a Necessary Virtue of the Socialist Society," in *Chung Kuo Ch'ing Nien* (*China Youth*) XXIV (December, 1956); translated and reprinted in *Extracts from China Mainland Magazines*, LXV (January, 1957), 17–20; and Yuan Po, "What Attitudes Should One Take Toward One's Parents," *Chung Kuo Ch'ing Nien* (December, 1954), translated and reprinted in *Survey of China Mainland Press*, CMLXXIII (January, 1955), 30–32.

at first marriage will rise, and the age of males will not change greatly. We cannot make any predictions, without prior empirical observations, about which elements will resist these pressures more or less. And, since no accepted classification of *forms* of industrialization exists, we cannot yet predict how different forms will affect different family systems.

It might be worthwhile to omit the consideration of the theoretical and empirical bases of many of these changes, and merely list some of the major ones.

(1) Freedom of marital choice, with the following concomitant changes.
  (a) Marital bargaining is taken from the hands of elders;
  (b) The young couple must be economically independent;
  (c) The age of females at marriage is likely to drop in Japan, but to rise slightly in China and substantially in Arab countries and India; the age of males depends on several additional variables; at a minimum, there develops the notion of a "proper maturity at marriage" for both;
  (d) The pattern of class homogamy does not change greatly;
  (e) In cultures where there was nearly universal marriage (India, Japan, China), there may be a slight diminution in the percentage ever married; and
  (f) Age-discrepant marriages, i.e., between spouses of very different ages, diminish.

(2) Marriages between close kin (e.g., between cousins) decrease.

(3) The dowry or bride price begins to disappear.[26]

(4) Illegitimacy rates increase in systems where most marriages have been consummated between children (e.g., India — but *not* China and Japan). Since most civilizations seem to have various forms of marital unions which are not fully legitimate, the movement toward a conjugal system may (as in Japan) actually reduce the illegitimacy rate.

(5) Concubinage and polygamy decline.

(6) Theory cannot predict whether fertility in a conjugal system will be high or low — but fertility will be controlled in the interests of the couple, and not of the kin group. Under industrialization, of course, the rate usually falls. And any movement toward a conjugal system reduces the *size of household* — even in Africa, where possibly the marital fertility ratio may be increasing.

(7) Infanticide decreases — though we have no firm numerical data with which to measure its past rate in those countries where it allegedly once existed (India, Japan, China, and the Arab world).

(8) Matriliny weakens — although here our Western bias may exag-

---

[26] Its persistence even in urban Africa is based primarily on the lack of an accepted ceremonial substitute for the validation of a marriage.

gerate changes in lower-caste Indian or Central African systems; i.e., because the system seems strange, we are more alert to changes in it.[27]

(9) The divorce rate will be high, but the *trend* in any given culture will depend on its prior level. It may drop if the rate was already high and the new system yields some new elements of stability (e.g., the removal of the Japanese parents-in-law's right to send the bride to her parents).

(10) Remarriage after divorce or the death of one's spouse becomes common in areas where it was rare. Here, stereotypes confuse somewhat, since divorce was certainly more common in some countries (e.g., China) than commonly supposed, as was remarriage of the widow or widower (as in China and Japan).

CONCLUSION

Rejecting evolutionism in its nineteenth-century form, we have created no theory of social change of comparable scope. However, we have returned to a more sober appraisal of the detailed facts of social change. We are both aided and hindered by the nearly universal pressure of industrialization upon human societies in this era. The visible presence of industrialization often obscures the independent effect of other ranges of variables upon the total process — or, indeed, upon industrialization.

The analysis of family change is especially difficult, since reliable descriptions of systems of even a few generations ago are so rare. The classical family of Western nostalgia is a myth — a myth which perhaps has its mythical counterparts in most civilizations — and to measure change by that base line usually leads to error.

In addition, theoretical analysis must take account of the fact that the conjugal family, toward which industrialization is thought to be pressing all family systems, is primarily an ideal-type construct. It is, second, a set of ideals; and, third, it is an observable pattern of behavior. We must examine each facet independently if we are to understand changes in the modern world.

In general, the ideal type of the conjugal family demonstrably does fit the central demands of an industrial system. On the other hand, there are necessary strains between the two, and there are theoretical and empirical limits on the adjustment between them. Moreover, we can not neglect the question, "To what extent does industrialization meet the needs of the

[27] A matrilineage is in any event somewhat difficult to maintain. See the excellent analysis of its structural peculiarities in David M. Schneider, "The Distinctive Features of Matrilineal Descent Groups" (Mimeographed. Berkeley, California, 1959); also (with Kathleen Gough), *Matrilineal Kinship*, Berkeley, University of California, 1961.

conjugal family?" A number of differences in the adjustments of various class strata to the patterns of industrialization suggest the independence of family variables and the strains between two great sets of processes.

In addition, we clearly do not yet know just *how* — i.e., through which processes — the two interact. The achievement or merit occupational systems, in China, and in Europe during the High Middle Ages, imply that variables we have not yet distinguished may be operative.

In the contemporary world, there is an important set of forces in the ideology of the conjugal family, which is structurally similar to that of economic progress. Both have important radical roots and appeal to the disadvantaged, to women, to the young, and to intellectuals — even when they do not fully accept the ideology or are unable to conform to it in action. The ideology enters into political and legal debate and into court decisions, thus furthering a number of changes toward a conjugal pattern.

It would be worthwhile to investigate whether the Western family systems, for many centuries, have been better organized than others, to take advantage of industrial opportunities; and whether shifts in family attitudes may be attributed particularly to the Puritans, whose ties with industrialization are well documented. The independent importance of this adjustment is discernible in the campaign of the Chinese to go "beyond" the conjugal family to a communal system which would be even better suited to the needs of industrialization. Although such a system would create new strains — some of which have already been observed — it would solve some of the problems of strain between the conjugal system and industrialization.

Family and industrial variables are independent though interacting. Hence, even when most family systems move toward some conjugal form, specific indexes of change will move in different directions, depending on the state of things at the inception of the new era. We have presented a number of examples of such differing trends. In addition, we outlined a list of many of the major trends characteristic of most of the world's population. How far they will go, or how rapidly, we cannot ascertain as yet.

Notes for
Further Reading

For a more general analysis of this area see:

Goode, W. J., *World Revolution and Family Patterns*. New York: The Free Press of Glencoe, 1963.

Nimkoff, M.F. (ed.), *Comparative Family Systems*. Boston: Houghton Mifflin Company, 1965.

For the analysis of specific types of families in their encounter with modern settings, see:

Levy, M., Jr., *The Family Revolution in Modern China*. Cambridge, Mass.: Harvard University Press, 1946.

Marris, P., *Family and Social Change in an African City* (A Study of Rehousing in Lagos). London: Routledge and Kegan Paul, 1961.

Willmott, P. and M. Young, *Family and Class in a London Suburb*. London: Routledge and Kegan Paul, 1960.

Yang, C.K., *The Chinese Family in the Communist Revolution*. Cambridge, Mass.: Harvard University Press, 1959.

V

Changes in Class Structure

The two articles on changes in class structure in modern societies illustrate two different, yet complementary, aspects of analysis of changes in stratification.

The study by van Doorn, "The Changed Position of Unskilled Workers in the Social Structure of the Netherlands," presents an analysis of the changes in the status of one social group and stratum, in this case one of the lowest, in a modern industrial setting under the impact of two interconnected forces — changes in technology in the broader economic settings on the one hand, and in political structure on the other. These two forces tend to work in contrary directions; the changes in technology make the situation of this group worse, while the democratization of the social structure puts in their hands new weapons, political power, and the power of the vote, through which they may, to some extent, improve their social status.

But such forces imply not only change in the concrete standing of any given group but also change in the relative importance of the basic criteria of social status — power, wealth, and prestige.

It is perhaps from the point of view of the relative importance of such criteria that the second article, that of Feldmesser on stratification in Soviet Russia, is very instructive. The Russian (Soviet) society, according to its basic conception and ideology, should have been classless — whatever distinctions and status differences it had were supposed to be regulated by political criteria and considerations, and not by occupation and wealth. Similarly, among the rewards that were allocated to its members the income differences were initially considered least important and most contrary to the basic premises of the revolutionary ideology. But, as this article shows, the actual situation is rather different for two interconnected reasons. One is that the very predominance of power creates its own system of differentiation; the other is that the encounter between those initial orientations of the Soviet élite and the exigencies of a modern industrial society necessarily creates another series of processes of differentiation based on education and skills. This is to some extent common to all industrial societies, but at the same time differs according to the basic orientations of each regime.

5   JACQUES A. A. VAN DOORN

The Changed Position of Unskilled Workers
in the Social Structure of the Netherlands

I. INTRODUCTION

The aim of this study is to indicate the relation between the recent development of Dutch social structure on the one hand and changes in the social status of the unskilled worker on the other. Since at this stage knowledge of this subject is not very well advanced, it is impossible to do more than just indicate such relations. The present attempt to tackle this problem may be justified by the following considerations. In the first place, although the unskilled workers constitute a numerically very important group in every industrialised country, their status has not been given much attention. Secondly, a study of the historical background as well as the present situation of this occupational category throws an interesting light on the development and structure of the society as a whole.

Reprinted from *Transactions of the Third World Congress of Sociology*. London: International Sociological Association, 1956, Vol. 3, pp. 113–124, with permission of the International Sociological Association.

A third consideration is that this group, seen from the viewpoint of social policy, is often regarded as a "problem group." [1]

It should be pointed out, that in this article the term "unskilled worker" stands for the industrial worker without special occupational training. That the borderline between this category and that of the skilled worker will thus remain rather vague, will prove to be of little consequence for a study of this kind.

Although the unskilled worker is found in practically all important branches of industry in the world, his history and status in North-West Europe shows a number of special characteristics. This is to some extent due to factors of a very factual kind, such as the relatively early industrialisation of these countries. In part however, it is connected with the ideological — in this case the Marxist-socialistic interpretation of the social status of the industrial worker. This specifically historical and ideological context makes it inevitable to connect his former and present social position with the well-worn problems of the "proletariat," "capitalism" and "class struggle." Even though the discussion around this subject is in itself no longer up-to-date, it is worthwhile to become acquainted with it since it clarifies the present situation of the unskilled worker.

It is clear that the Dutch social system, though showing affinities with the general N.W.-European system, possesses a number of specific characteristics, due among other things to the fact that industrialisation came relatively late in comparison with neighbouring countries. A generalisation from the Dutch situation however, is by no means impossible. As a starting point and at the same time as a general vein of this study, we may consider the inadequacy of modern, largely American-influenced, industrial sociology. This branch of knowledge had, apart from its many merits, too much the character of a "factory sociology" to be able to do full justice to the European system of relations which is so strongly connected with historical-ideological factors. The standpoint of the old German "Betriebssoziologie" (Weber, Briefs, Geck, De Man, Herkner, Bernays) with its emphasis on the relation between social structure and industrial development was in this respect more fertile. To a certain extent its tradition has been continued by the French school of Friedmann.

Also in the Netherlands, the antithesis between the more limited and the broader standpoint has been the subject of much argument. The

---

[1] This is evident from the book of J. Haveman, *De ongeschoolde arbeider* (1952), also from a few postwar, government-sponsored studies, dealing with the problem of so-called "mass-youth," a category sought mainly in the environment of unskilled workers. See: *Maatschappelijke verwildering der jeugd*. Rapport betreffende het onderzoek naar de geestesgesteldheid van de massajeugd. Den Haag 1952; *Bronnenboek*, bevattende gegevens ten grondslag liggend aan Rapport Maatschappelijke verwildering der jeugd. Den Haag 1953; *Moderne jeugd op haar weg naar volwassenheid*. Den Haag 1953.

"bedrijfssociologie" (industrial sociology) introduced after 1945 (Olden-dorff, Ydo, Horringa)[2] leaned strongly towards the Mayo-Roethlisberger-school, whereas Kuylaars[3] even wanted to attach the problem of unskilled work in the first instance to the nature of the work, thereby focusing on its effect on the personality structure and via this concept on the whole society. Haveman[4] on the other hand, studied the unskilled worker as a special social type with a clearly determinable social environment of its own and its own subculture. The generalisation of this viewpoint was sharply criticised.[5]

The study of the unskilled worker should necessarily be based on a study of the development of the industrial work-process, to which the unskilled worker, in fact, owes his name. The central problem is, how-ever, whether this kind of work is carried out by a category of individuals occupying an exceptional position in a social as well as in a cultural sense. In other words: does the unskilled worker constitute not only an indus-trial type, but also a social type?

In the following line of argument, the status of the unskilled worker will be considered in connection with the evolution of a number of struc-tural elements in Dutch society during the last 70 to 80 years.

II. THE UNSKILLED WORKER AS AN INDUSTRIAL TYPE

Unskilled labour is as old as humanity, but the unskilled worker in our sense is a product of industrial development in the last centuries, and is therefore a relatively recent occupational type.

In the 19th century there was in fact no clear type of unskilled indus-trial worker in evidence in the Netherlands. Even the factory worker be-longed to a heterogeneous category since industrial production took place more often in workshops than in factories. This implies, that there existed a great deal of work differentiation: the unskilled worker was an ap-prentice, that is, he was temporarily "unskilled," but he would later have the function of skilled workman, either master or foreman.[6]

---

[2] A. Oldendorff, De betekenis van de bedrijfssociologie voor de sociale weten-schappen, in Sociologisch Jaarboek, VII, 1953; M. G. Ydo, Plezier in het werk, 1947; D. Horringa, Mens en groep in het moderne bedrijf, 2d ed. 1953.

[3] A. M. Kuylaars, Het verband tussen werk en leven van de industriele loonar-beider als object van een sociale ondernemingspolitiek, 1951.

[4] Haveman, op. cit.

[5] J. A. A. van Doorn, De proletarische achterhoede. Een sociologische critiek, 1954.

[6] A. Touraine, Veranderingen in de beroepsstructuur der Franse mechanische industrie, in Mens en Maatschappij, XXVIII, 1, 15 Jan. 1953, pp. 20, 21. Com-pare: I. J. Brugmans, De arbeidende klasse in Nederland in de 19e eeuw, 2d ed. 1929, pp. 75 ff.

All through the 19th century home industries and crafts remained important. Only when the Taylor system gained the upper hand, a process of "unlearning" began to take place, a process which Kuylaars calls "drainage" of work. It was this development which brought into being the large category of workers who can be termed "unskilled workers." Knowledge and initiative, training and insight are now to a considerable degree delegated to those who are their superiors in the industrial hierarchy: the representatives of the "Thinking Department." [7]

Further industrial development leads to further differentiation of labour. Linework, teamwork, shift-work, casual work, assistant's work as well as a very large differentiation according to the technical nature of the work, are the results. All this tends to obscure the borderline between skilled and unskilled work. The shift from professional training to a sense of responsibility as pointed out by Touraine,[8] has also been found in a few large industries in the Netherlands — for instance at the Hoogovens (blast furnaces) at Velsen[9] — but this is still exceptional.

It can, however, be said that the relation between the unskilled worker and the industrial concern has been subjected to important changes. The social policy of the government, the influence of the trade-unions and the viewpoints current in employer's circles have increasingly tended to change this relation in favour of the worker. In the main, however, workers who perform exclusively unskilled work and who draw their maximum wages in about their 20th year of age, still constitute a very large part of the industrial labour force.

III. THE UNSKILLED WORKER A SOCIAL TYPE?

The origin of the unskilled worker as an *industrial* type lies in the modern factory organization of the production process, as a social type he originates from the 19th century proletariat. By "proletariat" in this context is meant the category of wage-labourers in industry, who are compelled to sell their labour in the economic market and who derive the main part of their subsistence from this source.[10] Briefs has drawn attention to the fact that this category of wage-labourers, seen from an historical angle, started out by gradually detaching itself from the masses of the poor. Only some time after Marx "stösst die Arbeiterfrage das eigentliche Armeleute-Problem von sich ab." [11]

[7] Touraine, 22, 23.
[8] P. 20 ff.
[9] W. J. Bruyn, Rapport betreffende het onderzoek, etc., in: *Sociologisch Bulletin,* VI, 1, 1952.
[10] G. Briefs, Das gewerbliche Proletariat in: *Grundriss der Sozialökonomik,* IX, 1, 1926, p. 150.
[11] Briefs, 143.

In the Netherlands in the middle of the last century factory workers
were drawn from the mass of paupers to such an extent that they were
indistinguishable from this group and were heaped together as "the
poor." [12] Industrial work, for that matter, had a clearly philanthropic
character and was in part carried on in workhouses. The position of this
proletariat was here, as in neighbouring countries, far from attractive:
classed as the lowest stratum of society, badly paid, compelled to keep
very long working-hours and having very little social security, their situation was indeed truly "proletarian." [13]

The unskilled worker was in every respect part of this proletariat. Although on the one hand some mention is made of specialized workers —
mostly foreigners — who occupied a more favourable position, there was
no separate category of unskilled workers. Much more accentuated than
the difference between skilled and unskilled was the differentiation as to
type of work and work-conditions found in industry and factory work,
the various branches of industry and the various regions of the country.[14]
Also important was the difference in position between "permanent" and
"casual" workers.[15]

In the last fifty years unskilled labour has become a phenomenon of
more and more gigantic dimensions. Large numbers of unskilled workers
are at the moment crowding the Dutch industrial concerns. The question
whether this has made the unskilled worker into a clearly delimited *social*
type, can only be answered by an analysis of the historical evolution of
the industrial proletariat.

The changes in the situation of the proletariat appear to be quite considerable. Among them the following will be mentioned:

(*a*) the change from "situational class into mentality class," [16] that is, a
growing consciousness of one's own value and strength, and concomi-
tantly the struggle to improve one's living conditions; (*b*) the enormous
rise in prosperity, in which wage labourers had an important share; (*c*)
the social democratization and in connection therewith the social integration of large parts of the formerly more isolated working-class into the
society; (*d*) the cultural democratization and the tendency among a large

[12] Brugmans, 77 ff.
[13] Particularly Brugmans, chapters II, III and IV ; summary in L. J. G. Verberne,
De Nederlandsche arbeidersbeweging in de negentiende eeuw, 1940, chapter II.
[14] Brugmans, 136 f. and *passim* in chapter II.
[15] Particularly where irregular work demands a large number of casual labourers,
as for instance at the docks. Cf. for example, P. J. Bouman and W. H. Bouman,
De groei van de grote werkstad. Een studie over de bevolking van Rotterdam, 2d ed.,
1955, 47 ff.
[16] Terms introduced by Van Heek following Kruyt's example of analogous concepts. F. Van Heek, *Klassen- en standenstructuur als sociologische begrippen*, 1948,
pp. 12, 33.

part of the proletariat to acquire bourgeois characteristics; (*e*) political deradicalization taking place in the last decades.

Evidently this development has not proceeded in every part of the country to the same degree — Holland too has what are called its "ontwikkelingsgebiden" (development-regions), which can be compared with the underdeveloped regions elsewhere. In the main, however, the effect of the processes mentioned above cannot be denied. The questions which now have to be answered, are:

(1) has the proletariat in all its sections, experienced equally important changes of position and if not, which groups are in any way lagging behind?

(2) Is it true, as might be expected and as has been contended,[17] that it is the unskilled worker who has lagged behind in this evolution, even, in the opinion of some authors, to such an extent that his position gravitates towards a social and cultural isolation?

(3) In what fields has such a lag shown itself or does it become manifest in all fields?

(4) How can the lag at certain points and with certain groups be explained?

(5) What does such an explanation tell us about the future development of the position of the unskilled worker?

IV. THE UNSKILLED WORKER AND CHANGES IN SOCIAL STRATIFICATION

The social structure of the Netherlands in the 19th century possessed all the characteristics of a mixed estate and class structure.[18] Next to the old patriciate and large groups of citizens and craftsmen with strong status characteristics, fast growing new groups of entrepreneurs and industrial workers had appeared. But though the structure was extremely differentiated, it was clearly based on a number of large strata, which, in relation to one another, occupied a rather stable, hierarchical position.

The socio-economic and cultural development which took place after-

[17] Haveman's book entirely concentrates on the thesis that there exists a fundamental dichotomy between the unskilled and "others" (p. 187), that these unskilled are clearly living in isolation and possess a separate subculture (e.g. p. 203).

[18] Following Van Heek's definition (1948): "A society has an 'estate'-structure if it consists of a vertical ranking of socially unequal groups which are mutually distinguishable by a difference in the degree of social prestige, a different style of living and an unequal distribution of rights and obligations" (p. 7); "a society has a class structure if it consists mainly of groups which in a system of predominantly individual property, are socially unequal since in the market of goods and services, where they have opposite interests, they occupy market-positions of different power" (p. 12).

wards radically changed this relatively simple structure. The units of the estate — and class structure broke down as the result of a growing importance of occupation in determining the status of the individual, while at the same time occupation detached itself from the estate and class structure. The macrostratification of estates and classes receded into the background as occupational stratification grew in importance.[19]

In the last decades this occupational stratification has become more and more functional, that is, more organized in vast, aim-directed associations such as big industrial concerns, government services, and army. This accentuates the formal character of labour and it brings the persons carrying various occupational functions into strictly hierarchical positions.[20] This development implies for the unskilled worker that his social position becomes sharper in outline, while it is moreover fixed at the bottom of the occupational ladder. The process of internal differentiation to skilled, trained and unskilled, as already indicated by Briefs and Herkner[21] goes in this development of organizational functionalism, in the direction of further elaboration and refinement. Such concepts as job analysis and work classification, which are now coming to the forefront, are logical consequences of this development.

In the first place, the various types of unskilled labour can now be more sharply defined. This increases on the one hand the differences in distance between the unskilled workers and between them and the skilled, who occupy a higher status; on the other hand there is the fact that the unskilled has been formally accepted in organizational groups, which give him status and fulfil his need of security and safety.

A second point is that social mobility becomes more connected with function. A new type of mobility[22] arises which for the unskilled worker is sometimes more unfavourable since it refers in the first instance to job qualifications — but which at other times offers increased possibilities for mobility, since an ability to carry out functions will smooth the way to higher status. Particularly in big enterprises much attention is paid to an increase of these possibilities for climbing. The facts prove that — contrary to what was expected — social climbing is far from being a rare phenomenon among the unskilled, also in the second generation.[23] It is

[19] Van Heek, *Stijging en daling op de maatschappelijke ladder* (1945), 43 ff, 50 ff.

[20] Cf. J. A. A. van Doorn, Het probleem van de beroepsstratificatie, in: *Sociologische Gids*, II, 6 Juni, 1955.

[21] Briefs, 218, 220.

[22] Cf. the "old" and "new" type of mobility in S. M. Lipset and R. Bendix, "Social Mobility and Occupational Career Patterns" in: *Class Status and Power, a reader in social stratification*, London 1954, pp. 457 ff.

[23] This refers to investigations carried out by Van Heek, Buurma, Tobi and Luyckx, and Bordewijk. A summary of the results in: J. A. A. van Doorn, *Prole-*

also remarkable that the division made in industrial enterprises between the skilled and the unskilled has in many cases not created obstacles to social contacts outside the work situation.[24]

It is not denied, that there are groups of unskilled workers, who lead a rather isolated existence and who live at the periphery of the society, often in the social environment of problem-cases and asocial persons.[25] They live in pauperized neighbourhoods where social norms are accepted which are rejected by other labourers. These more or less socially isolated groups of the unskilled are residual groups which are only incidentally, partly, and with some difficulty, integrated with society. They consist of casual workers, recipients of relief, hawkers and other independents with small means, among whom this peripherous group of unskilled factory workers has found a place. They move in the social milieu of the under-dogs, from which it appears to be difficult to escape, while the existing education-patterns also block the road to escape for their children.

V. THE UNSKILLED WORKER AND THE CHANGES IN INCOME LEVEL

One of the most important socio-economic phenomena of the last fifty years is the deproletarization of the majority of the industrial workers. It can be stated that they have often surpassed the small independents in economic position. This goes in the first place for the skilled worker, but it is equally true for many unskilled ones.[26] Moreover, the income of the unskilled does not differ a great deal from that of the skilled,[27] though within the group of workers, the former naturally form the weaker party. Up to a point the unskilled worker is still a "proletarian," as he has nothing to offer but his physical force, while he cannot refer to specialistic abilities. Nevertheless, his position in the economic structure is not that of the lowest group. Below him is the category consisting of costermongers, seasonal workers, casual workers and recipients of poor relief, small independents and pensioners. About the year 1938 these groups were

---

tarische achterhoede, 43 ff. 57 ff. Also G. Kuiper, *Mobiliteit in de sociale en beroepshierarchie,* 1953, chapter XIII.

[24] This refers to investigations carried out by Van Heek, Buurma, Kuiper, and others.

[25] Haveman, 42 ff.; H. P. M. Litjens, *Onmaatschappelijke gezinnen,* 1953, *passim,* particularly p. 156 ff.

[26] L. F. Jens, *Criminaliteit te Utrecht in verband met familie en wijk,* 1940, 32; H. Verwey-Jonker, *Lage inkomens,* 1943, 77 ff. 168.

[27] Thus, for instance, in Nov. 1948 the average wages of an unskilled worker were f0·95 per hour (weekly wages: f47·05), of a trained worker f1·— (weekly wages f49·06) and of a skilled worker f1·08 (weekly wages f53·38). Quoted from Kuylaars, p. 160.

estimated to comprise about 10% of the Dutch population. The unskilled factory worker does not, as a rule, belong to this lowest stratum.[28]

His economic position however remains precarious. If other factors come into play, he may be expected to sink to the lowest prosperity-level — the rearguard in the army of the economically emancipated.

VI. THE UNSKILLED WORKER AND THE CHANGES IN CULTURAL PATTERN

Hendrik de Man has in his writings[29] drawn attention to the fact that the "Proletkult," propagated by early socialism, was a failure. In the Netherlands one finds until the thirties, though decreasingly, attempts to establish "socialist" or "labour" culture, namely in the style of the youth movement. At present, however, the middle-class character of the working class can no longer be denied. The unskilled worker in the Netherlands, like the rest of the population, has adopted the cultural patterns of the middle class and lower middle class and he cultivates these patterns to the best of his ability. This is expressed in dress, food, furniture, education and leisure, as well as in manners and forms of address.[30]

This does not mean that the diffusion of bourgeois-patterns has spread over the whole group of the unskilled. Some less superficial elements of culture such as aspirations for further education, intellectual interests[31] and the like, are certainly less accepted in working class than in middle-class circles and less among the unskilled than among the skilled. It is probable that on these points the gap between working class and middle class (non-manual workers of higher social status) is wider than between the skilled and the unskilled, although this differs according to the cultural elements concerned.[32] It is certain that part of the workers largely but not exclusively the unskilled, have remained more or less outside the process of adoption and assimilation of middle-class values. These workers are part of the cultural bottom layer of the society, a stratum to which also belongs the socially maladjusted. In the main they lack middle-class desires, while their cultural luggage consists of a mixture of middle-class

[28] Verwey-Jonker passim.

[29] Particularly in his *Psychologie van het socialisme*, 2d ed. 1929, among other places: chapter IX: Proletarische cultuur of verburgerlijking? (p. 171 ff.).

[30] It would be interesting to study the introduction of the words: "heer," "dame" and "mevrouw" (respectively: gentlemen, lady, madam), used in the post-war press to indicate every labourer('s wife), contrary to the situation previously. As regards the spending of leisure time, see: the report of the Central Bureau for Statistics, *Radio en vrijetijdsbesteding*, 1954, 57 f. and other places.

[31] J. P. Kruyt, *Arbeiders en nieuwe middenstand*, 1947, 13, Van Doorn, *Proletarische achterhoede*, 42 ff.

[32] Central Bureau for Statistics, *Radio*, 57 f.

"gesunkenes Kulturgut" and traces of folk culture. In these old working-class communities in particular, such old cultural forms appear to have maintained themselves longest as a separate subculture.[33]

VII. THE UNSKILLED WORKER AND CHANGES IN POLITICAL ORGANIZATION

As happened in other European countries, the growing self-consciousness of the proletariat led in the last half of the past century to a political radicalization in the direction of socialism. The pioneers of this movement, largely originating from the group of the skilled, have since 1894 (the foundation of the Social-Democratic Labour Party)[34] led socialism into reformative channels. Industrialization which, contrary to the situation in countries like Great-Britian and Belgium, started late and could therefore avoid the worst excesses, promoted, together with the Dutch sense of moderation, the speedy decline of a chiliastic anarchism (Domela Nieuwenhuis).

After a few conflicts between both wars (danger of a revolution in 1918; mutiny on the man-of-war "Zeven Provinciën"; unemployment-riots in the thirties), the political labour party became "settled," a process which was actually completed after 1945. The S.D.A.P., which in that year was rechristened: "Partij van de Arbeid" (Labour Party) aims at becoming a national party (the so-called break-through towards the confessional groups).

It seems plausible that the existing political radicalism, as expressed for instance in communism, has to be found mainly in the group of unskilled workers. When comparing the number of the unskilled (25% of the total working population, while another 45% is semi-skilled) with the number of those who voted for the communists (in recent years always under 10% of the total number of votes), it appears however, that the preference for communism is only found among a minority of the unskilled. It also becomes apparent, that the regional distribution of communists is determined by socio-cultural factors, to such an extent, that at present there is no evident general relationship between unskilled workers and leftist radicalism, since there are cultural, social and religious factors crosscutting such a relationship. The steady decrease of communist influence since 1945 adds to the impression that it was not the status of unskilled worker which gave political radicalism its support, but an interplay of local and historical factors among which this status was only one.

[33] Van Doorn, *Proletarische achterhoede*, 13–23; cf. *Enige aspecten van sociale wijkopbouw*, 1955, 20 ff.
[34] Verberne, 127.

VIII. THE UNSKILLED WORKER AND
CHANGES IN THE LOCAL COMMUNITY

Dutch urban life of the working classes was in the 19th century still strongly determined by the neighbourhood environment. Such *working class neighbourhoods* can be defined as limited local units, established a long time ago and usually situated in the old part of the town, units which are characterized by a specific cultural style and a sense of social cohesion. They are socially, but not socio-economically homogeneous. The pauper as well as the priest, the casual worker as well as the shopkeeper, they all "belong." [35] Examples of neighbourhoods, which have long (till a few decades ago) retained this character, are the "Jordaan" (Amsterdam) and "Wijk C" (Utrecht).[36] In a sense such neighbourhoods are the characteristic territorial substructures of a society of which the lowest stratum consists of a working class which is functionally little differentiated.

Around 1900 these working-class neighbourhoods became involved in a process of disintegration. The most energetic inhabitants — as a rule industrial workers — left these districts for the newly-built quarters at the urban periphery. Although the formation of a mentality class of industrial workers, promotes the disintegration of working class neighbourhoods, the modern workers' *residential districts* can on the other hand be seen as a visible symbol of the emancipation of the proletariat. The inhabitants all have a relatively similar socio-economic status; they are for the most part factory workers, whether predominantly skilled or predominantly unskilled.

The working-class neighbourhoods, drained by this process, sink to a very low level. They become the districts of the casual workers, spivs, hawkers, mixed with mainly unskilled workers, who are unable or unwilling to give up the neighbourhood relations. Where the process of pauperization has progressed far, the unskilled also often leave the neighbourhood.[37] His outlook on work and his work rhythm, his social aspirations and economic position, induce him to select a different place of residence.

These migration-processes took place mainly before and after the first world-war, and in older industrial towns had already started in 1870.[38] After 1945 this process has started anew, now covering a larger area. The present mass housing projects, which in the big towns (Amsterdam, Rotterdam and the Hague) have resulted in the building of residential

[35] Van Doorn, *Proletarische achterhoede*, 16 ff.
[36] Van Doorn, 16 ff.; on Rotterdam: Bouman and Bouman, 53.
[37] Van Doorn, *Proletarische achterhoede*, 17 f. and the authors quoted there: Jens, De Vooys, and others; I. E. van Hulten, *Stijging en daling in een modern grootbedrijf*, 1954, 42.
[38] P. de Jong, Hoogvliet, de groeiende satellietstad onder de rook van Rotterdam, in: *Sociologisch Bulletin*, VII, 4, 1953, 31 ff.

quarters for tens of thousands, have effected an unprecedented mixing of social groups. The unskilled workers have shared in this process and have for the first time to a considerable extent taken up their residence amidst other occupational groups. It is at present impossible to forecast, to what extent this social mixing will continue also after the housing shortage has disappeared. It is certainly true that skilled and in part also unskilled workers have learned to accept co-residence with traditionally middle class groups.

IX. THE RECRUITMENT OF THE UNSKILLED WORKER AND THE PERIOD OF INDUSTRIALIZATION

A very important factor is finally the effect of the period of industrialization on the status and attitudes of the unskilled worker. It makes a considerable difference whether the recruitment of factory workers started about 1850 or about 1950. In the former case, recruitment often led to proletarization and pauperization of the people concerned, whereas in the latter case the social policy of government and industrial concerns aimed at mitigating the disintegrating effects of industrialization and at meeting them half-way. The transition to the industrial labour process therefore proceeded without great shocks or tensions.

Even to this day, the historical background of the industrialization process can still clearly be discerned in the social situation of the unskilled worker. The existence of political radicalism and a traditional class opposition in the large towns and in some old industrial districts can in part be traced back to an early industrialization.[39] The rather high degree of pauperization of a large number of the unskilled in old industrial towns like Maastricht and Den Bosch has had its influence on the present high percentage of socially maladjusted persons.[40]

On the other hand, the labourers who were drawn into industrial work for the first time with the present intensive industrialization of the rural regions were much less subjected to processes of political radicalization and social isolation. From the agrarian sphere they landed in an industrial environment, which led them straight on the road towards cultural bourgeoisie and social integration. (South-east Drenthe).[41]

Other factors such as the socially integrative power of active religious politics (the mining district of South-Limburg) are also indicative of the importance of the period when the unskilled worker made his appearance as an industrial type. This factor cuts through the general tendencies in

[39] F. van Heek, Twee richtingen in de bedrijfssociologie, in: *Mens en Maatschappij*, XXVIII, 1, Jan. 1953, 13.
[40] Litjens, 95, 96.
[41] Haveman, 129 ff.

the status-development of the unskilled worker, and it explains regional differences in status as differences in the phase of industrialization.

X. CONCLUSIONS

In the years since 1860–1870 the Dutch social system has developed in the direction of functional integration, economic progress, middle class cultural norms, political deradicalization and disintegration of the old ties based on local residence. This development has spread to the majority of the members of the former industrial proletariat.

In spite of the fact that these processes take place at different rates of speed while various parts of the country are in different stages of development, it is possible to indicate the formation of a number of residual groups, the members of which show a serious lag compared with the "normal" tendencies in the society. Although the unskilled take part in most of the processes mentioned, they often occupy also in the residual groups a numerically strong position.

As it seems likely that this development is still going on, a further drainage of the residual groups can be expected. That the processes of social and cultural integration seem to get increasingly less hold of the residual groups, indicates that the drainage has had the effect of a negative selection. It is to be feared that the resistance against integration will increase as the isolated position of these groups will more and more be connected with mental deficiency, maladjustments, asocial attitudes, criminality, etc. If then from these residual groups there are still individuals who offer their services as unskilled workers, it may well appear that they do not meet the minimal demands made by the industrial production process. The separation between unskilled workers and proletarian rearguard will then be complete.

A final conclusion is, that "the" unskilled worker does not, at the moment at any rate, constitute a homogeneous social type. This category is too much "in transition," too much involved in a number of rapid changes in the society, to be, so far as the Netherlands are concerned, a useful concept in the sociological analysis of social structure.

This also implies that it is dangerous to approach — as is sometimes done by industrial sociology — the problems of the industrial worker from the viewpoint of industrial categories. It is not the industrial concern which mainly determines the structure of society, but the structure of the industrial concern results from the totality of social processes going on in the society at a certain point of time.

Toward the Classless Society?

A great deal has been written on the emergence of gross inequalities of wealth, privilege, and official honor in Soviet society. The process, fully described and documented, may be said to have begun with a famous speech by Stalin in 1931, in which he denounced "equality-mongering" in the wage structure and called for a new attitude of "solicitude" toward the intelligentsia; it manifested itself in highly differentiated incomes, in a change in the composition of the Communist Party, in the establishment of tuition fees and other more subtle obstacles to higher education, in elegant uniforms and elaborate titles, and in a host of other ways. By the end of World War II, and particularly during the last years of Stalin's life, the trend was clear: the Soviet Union was well advanced along a seemingly irreversible course toward a rigid system of social stratification, in which the upper classes would remain upper, the lower classes lower, and the twain would rarely meet.

Yet the irreversible has now been reversed. With that breathtaking facility which so often startles us, the Soviet leadership has launched a series of measures calculated to reduce the degree and rigidity of differentiation in Soviet society to a very considerable extent. Many observers have not yet fully apprehended this turn of events, if only because all its component parts had not been assembled in one place: to do so is one objective of the present study. But partly, too, the lack of comprehension is due to a reluctance to credit Soviet leaders with the desire or ability to achieve so "virtuous" an aim as social equality — or rather, it is due to a failure to appreciate the *meaning* of equality in the Soviet system. A second objective here is to define that meaning.

THE "REVIVAL OF DEMOCRACY"

[He] began to trample crudely on the methods of collectivity in leadership . . . to order people around and push aside the personnel of Soviet and economic organizations. . . . [He] decided questions great and small by himself, completely ignoring the opinions of others.

Reprinted from *Problems of Communism*, a publication of the United States Information Agency, No. 2, March–April, Vol. 9 (1960), pp. 31–39, by permission of the United States Information Agency. Article abridged for this printing.

[He] flattered himself with the belief that all [improvements] were due only to his own merits. The more successfully things went, the more conceited he became, the more airs he gave himself.

. . . you get the impression that everything other people do is bad, and only the things [he] does are good.

These scathing remarks could well have been taken from Khrushchev's secret speech to the 20th Congress of the CPSU exposing the incredible extremes to which Stalin's method of one-man rule had gone. A common reaction to this speech abroad was to see in it a confirmation of the trend toward inequality. The intelligentsia, or the "state bourgeoisie," [1] despite their privileges vis-à-vis other elements of the population, had long resented the Stalinist tyranny. Now, as a result of their increasing power in an industrialized and militarized state, they had reached the point where they could force Khrushchev to confess that they had been unjustly treated, to promise them the freedom of decision-making, and to guarantee the security of their status.

Subsequent comments in the Soviet press have belied this interpretation. The quotations do not come from the secret speech; they are attacks on, respectively, a raion party secretary, the chairman of a city soviet executive committee, and a factory director.[2] For, as it now appears, the secret speech was directed not only at the one big Stalin, but also at all the other little Stalins who had grown up in his image. It has been followed up not with praise for Soviet administrators, but with denunciations of "administrirovanie" — the high-handed, arrogant ways of officials who have exercised "petty tutelage" over their subordinates; who have glossed over shortcomings, suppressed criticism, and persecuted their critics; who have been "inattentive to the workers and their needs"; who have, in short, violated the letter of Soviet law and the spirit of "Communist morality."

Denunciations of this sort are not, of course, a new phenomenon; but what is interesting today is not only the frequency and vehemence of such attacks but the implicit admission that the inspiration for bad administrative habits came from very high up. Accordingly, Khrushchev's own behavior, so sharply at variance with Stalin's, has been held up as an example for others to follow: Soviet officials have been urged to get closer to the people, to pay more attention to them, and not to rely exclusively on existing channels of authority. Sessions of local soviets are being held more frequently; there have been occasional reports of ministers and de-

[1] The term is Hugh Seton-Watson's, in an article presenting this interpretation: "The Soviet Ruling Class," Problems of Communism, No. 3 (May–June), 1956.
[2] Respectively in Pravda, Nov. 23, 1957, and Izvestia, Jan. 16, 1958, and June 13, 1959. These are samples from a plethora of similar articles.

partment heads being subjected to questioning by deputies; in some instances, agendas of meetings have been posted and public hearings held on the items under discussion. The number of deputies in local soviets has been increased by 1,800,000, and unpaid activists have been taking on tasks formerly performed by the executive staff — as if housewives were indeed to run the state.[3] Along the same lines, there has been a large-scale effort to reinvigorate the system of worker and peasant correspondents, to protect them from reprisals by the targets of their criticism, and to have them do more of the newspapers' work in place of the professional journalistic staff.[4] A party journal has told *raion* newspapers that they were not limited to criticizing "only rank-and-file workers and 'second-rank' officials of *raion* organizations." [5]

The appeal for "popular participation" to reform the deeply ingrained bureaucratic habits of Soviet officialdom has even been extended to the party-controlled trade unions, which have been urged to shake off their submissiveness to factory executives and to offer vigorous opposition when necessary.[6] Instances of rambunctious local trade-union committees have been held up for emulation, and workers enjoined to criticize "without being afraid that it will upset some director or other," and without having their remarks "prepared" or "cleared" by higher authorities.[7]

Another indication of the new spirit antedating the 20th Congress, has been the abolishment of the uniforms, insignia of rank, and titles which had been authorized for many civilian occupations during and after the war.[8] There has been an appeal for more informal relations and less social distance between those of high rank and those of low, and for an end to such practices in the armed forces as separate dining rooms for the several ranks.[9]

In general, the party seems to have been going out of its way to assert its respect for "ordinary" workers and peasants, a development reminiscent, as are many aspects of this campaign, of the attitude prevailing during the first decade after the October Revolution. Reversing a trend of more than 20 years' duration, the party has made a deliberate attempt to

[3] See especially the editorial in *Sovetskoe Gosudarstvo i Pravo*, No. 3 (May), 1956, pp. 3–14; *Izvestia*, May 22 and 23, Oct. 12, and Nov. 24, 1957; Aug. 1, 1958; and May 24, 1959.

[4] *Pravda*, June 8, 1959, and many earlier sources. This matter as well as the treatment of readers' letters were the subjects of Central Committee resolutions: *Pravda*, Aug. 26, 1958, and *Izvestia*, Oct. 11, 1958.

[5] *Partiinaia Zhizn*, No. 14 (July), 1959, p. 55.

[6] Report to the 20th Congress, *Pravda*, Feb. 15, 1956.

[7] *Pravda*, July 11, 1959; see also *Izvestia*, June 25, 1957.

[8] Decree of July 12, 1954, in *Sbornik Zakonov SSSR i Ukazov Prezidiuma Verkhovnovo Soveta SSSR*, Moscow, 1959, pp. 411–13.

[9] *Krasnaia Zvezda*, Aug. 21, 1957.

recruit more workers and peasants into its ranks: so much so, that Khrushchev was able to report at the 21st Congress that two-thirds of current admissions were in those categories, a figure which he accurately called a "considerable increase." [10] In addition, the Soviet press has published numerous editorials, articles, and letters passionately proclaiming the honor and worth of manual labor in a socialist society, filled with glowing words about citizens who are not afraid of soiling their hands, who are "creating material values for the people," rather than "sitting in offices and filing papers." This is not a new line, either, though it had lain dormant for some time. In recent speeches and articles, the third member has often been missing from the traditional trinity of "workers, collective farm peasants, and intelligentsia."

The rights and privileges mentioned thus far may seem to be only honorific. To be sure, they do not signify any real diffusion of the locus of power in Soviet society. Nevertheless, their importance should not be underrated: they do, after all, attempt to raise the ordinary worker's self-respect, and to imbue him with the consciousness — denied to him under Stalin — of his own contribution to the country's industrial progress. Having for years been exposed to harassment, incessant exhortations, and an attitude on the part of the authorities bordering on contempt, he is not likely to scorn even this — however mild — token of recognition and respect.

ADJUSTMENTS IN THE INCOME STRUCTURE

In any event, more tangible rewards have also resulted from the new policy. Although we need not take too literally all of the promises made by Khrushchev — and by Malenkov before him — to increase the output of consumers' goods, there is every indication that the lowest paid Soviet workers and peasants have been placed in a better competitive position to buy whatever is available.

On the one hand, minimum wages were raised in 1956, and two more increases scheduled in the current plan will bring the wage floor up to 500–600 rubles a month by 1965 — hardly a level of luxury, but approximately twice what it is now; raises have also been promised to "medium-paid workers and employees." [11] Old-age and disability pensions have been increased, too. Income taxes have been revised in favor of the lowest income brackets.[12]

On the other hand, there has been a good deal of talk, and some action,

[10] *Pravda,* Jan. 28, 1959. See also T. H. Rigby, "Social Orientation of Recruitment and Distribution of Membership in the Communist Party of the Soviet Union," *American Slavic and East European Review,* No. 3 (October), 1957.

[11] *Pravda,* Sept. 9, 1956, and Nov. 14, 1958.

[12] *Sbornik Zakonov . . . ,* pp. 505–506.

aimed at reducing the incomes of managerial and scientific personnel. In particular, the awarding of lavish bonuses to administrative, party, and other officials has been repeatedly attacked, and it is almost certain that the worst abuses are being corrected, "voluntarily" if not otherwise. A decree of the Council of Ministers has warned against excessive expense accounts on *komandirovki* (business trips) — another common source of added income for economic staffs.[13] Sputniks notwithstanding, the scientists have come in for their share of criticism, too, for holding multiple jobs and for receiving high income "merely" because they have higher degrees.[14]

The range of differentiation is being contracted not only between manual and non-manual workers, but within the manual group as well. Wages in a number of industries have been sporadically revised over the past five years, the guiding principle being "a rise in the proportion of basic wage rates in workers' earnings." Although the primary motives seemed to be economic and bookkeeping concerns — to restrain inflationary forces and restore simplicity to the wage structure — it was implied that many of the premiums and increments which had permitted the rise of an inner aristocracy among the workers would be curtailed or eliminated. It has now been authoritatively stated that greater equality of wages is a deliberate intention. A. Volkov, who succeeded Kaganovich as head of the Committee on Labor and Wages, has declared that, "with the aim of decreasing the gap between maximum and minimum wage rates," such measures as these are to be undertaken: a reduction in the number of skill categories and in the ratio between the highest and lowest rates to "no more than" two to one; a "sharp" decrease in the use of progressive piece-work rates; and a replacement of individual bonuses by collective bonuses, spreading the benefits of a single worker's accomplishment to his whole work team.[15]

RURAL REMEDIES

Even more striking have been the changes in the agricultural sector. Adjustments in crop-purchase prices and agricultural taxes and other steps taken since 1953 have raised the income of collective farmers in general while diminishing the range of earnings among and within the collective.[16] On several occasions, Khrushchev has referred to the "excessively high

---

[13] *Izvestia*, April 4 and June 6, 1959.

[14] *Kosomolskaia Pravda*, March 20 and April 6, 1956; *Pravda*, July 2, 1959.

[15] *Pravda*, Nov. 25, 1958. At the 21st Congress, Khrushchev remarked that it was also time to eliminate the differential paid for work in remote places: *Pravda*, Feb. 1, 1959. Premiums evidently will be preserved for hot or underground jobs and hard physical labor.

[16] Lazar Volin, "Reform in Agriculture," *Problems of Communism*, No. 1 (Jan.–Feb.), 1959.

incomes" of some collective farms (as he has to the "unjustifiably high incomes" of some workers). One remedy, analogous to the industrial wage reform, has been the establishment of a uniform pricing system for agricultural purchases, without bonuses for exceeding the purchase plan, with the result, according to Khrushchev, that "many collective farms will undoubtedly get more, while the leading collective farms will receive . . . somewhat less than now. And this," he added, "will be entirely fair."[17] Especially interesting is his implicit denial of the principle laid down by Stalin in 1931: that wide income differentials were needed as incentives to raise production. Khrushchev, on the contrary, has asserted that the farms with low income due to poor production are discouraged from increasing their output:

> . . . collective farms that did not achieve the planned harvest . . . were penalized, as it were. . . . This, of course, did not spur them on. . . . The goal here must be a more correct determination of pay . . . in order to provide incentive not only to the leading but to all collective farms.[18]

In connection with the shift, now apparently under way, from payment by workdays to guaranteed cash payments, the whole problem of income differentiation in agriculture was recently discussed in three articles in the Soviet Union's leading economic journal. Among situations they cited as "unjustifiable" are: income differentials among collective farms due to varying locations, soil fertility, or crops; those between peasants and farm executives, due to the closer linking of peasant earnings to the volume of output; and those among the peasants themselves, due to too many pay-rate categories with too steep increases, and to inequitable discrepancies in output norms. The remedies are fairly obvious, and cases are cited in which they are already being applied.[19]

REFORM IN EDUCATION

The school system initiated in the 1930's was one of the major props of social differentiation. Its salient features, for present purposes, were these: seven years of education were nominally compulsory, although it has been revealed that as late as 1958 only 80 per cent of the young people were completing the course.[20] After the seven-year school, a youngster might: (1) go to work in a job requiring little or no skill; (2) be drafted into

[17] *Pravda*, June 21, 1958.
[18] *Ibid.*
[19] *Voprosy Ekonomiki*, No. 2 (Feb.), 1959, pp. 80–88, 113–22, 143–49. In addition, see *Izvestia*, Nov. 30, 1958, in which a collective farm chairman reports that his own earnings now vary according to the volume of output, but are not to exceed 1500 rubles a month.
[20] *Literaturnaia Gazeta*, July 3, 1958. Khrushchev has used this figure on several occasions.

a labor-reserves school, providing training of up to two years for occupations of moderate skill; (3) enter a *teknikum*, a three- or four-year school for highly skilled manual and some non-manual occupations; or (4) proceed to the upper grades of a ten-year school for essentially "academic" training, preparatory in almost all cases to matriculation at a higher educational institution (*vuz*). Tuition fees were charged in the *vuzes*, ten-year schools and *teknikums*. Scholarships were available at *teknikums*, while room, board, and uniforms were free in the labor-reserves schools, but no such aids were offered to pupils of the ten-year school. For both material and "cultural" reasons, therefore, the tendency was for children from lower-status families to attend the vocational schools and enter the same sort of occupations already held by their parents, while children of the "elite" were more likely to take the academic sequence preparing them for professional and administrative positions. The greater informal influence which highly placed parents could exercise on those responsible for *vuz* admission strengthened this tendency. The schools thus contributed to the cleavage between manual and nonmanual groups.

The decision, adopted at the 19th Congress and re-affirmed at the 20th, to implement universal ten-year education wreaked havoc with this arrangement. Since ten-year schooling was to be compulsory, tuition fees made little sense, and they were accordingly abolished.[21] On the other hand *vuz* enrollments were not expanded; most of the ten-year graduates were expected to go directly to work, or into *teknikums* or other vocational schools.[22] This meant, in turn, a revision of the ten-year-school curriculum: physical education, music, art, mechanical drawing and other "practical studies," were increased at the expense of academic courses, and the latter were simplified in content, with fewer examinations and less homework. The effect of these changes — again in part intended — was to make school more accessible and more comfortable for the children of workers and peasants, improving their chances for scholastic success; and to blur the distinction between education for the manual worker and education for his occupational and social superior.

New Problems and a New Program. But the reform proved unsatisfactory in important respects. In particular, graduates of the ten-year schools clung to the idea that they were entitled to a higher education. Many of them resented going either to work or to a vocational school, preferring to wait until they could gain admission to a *vuz* — and this in the face of an imminent labor shortage caused by the birth deficiencies of the war years. One attempt at solving this problem was the campaign, re-

[21] *Izvestia*, June 10, 1956.
[22] Nicholas DeWitt, "Upheaval in Education," *Problems of Communism*, No. 1 (Jan.–Feb.), 1959.

ferred to above, stressing anew the dignity of manual labor; but it proved futile. Khrushchev then struck boldly: rejecting the ten-year principle, he declared that eight years of education were all that was necessary, and that such training should be "close to life" — i.e., primarily vocational. He proclaimed a "sacred slogan": "All students must prepare for useful work" and take a full-time job upon completion of the eighth grade.

> This . . . will be democratic since more equal conditions will be created for all citizens: neither the position nor the pleas of parents will exempt anyone, whoever he may be, from productive labor. . . .[23]

This program met two related goals: a labor force would be trained, in a minimum amount of time, for the kind of work that would be the lot of most;[24] and the notion of an automatic transition from secondary school to higher education would be dispelled. The purpose and atmosphere of the new type of school are suggested by the fact that pupils will combine their studies with productive work and with such chores as cleaning classrooms, tending shrubbery, and preparing and serving lunches. After the educational overhaul is completed, in three to five years, all students who wish to receive full secondary schooling (now to be of eleven years' duration)[25] will do so by correspondence of in evening or off-season schools, without taking time away from their jobs. Although there was much discussion of schools for the "gifted," which would not require students to work while studying, it is significant that no provision was made for them (except in the areas of music and dance) in the reform as it was finally enacted. The labor-reserves system as such now seems to be a dead letter, though it might be more accurate to say that in effect it has been extended to embrace all schools and all young people.

Regulation of Vuz Admissions. At the same time, changes have been effected to improve the chances of workers' and peasants' children competing for entrance to higher educational institutions. Khrushchev and others had repeatedly deplored the handicaps faced by children of lower-status families, scoring in particular the fact that the "competition of parents" with influence was as important in determining *vuz* admissions as was the competition in entrance examinations.[26] In Moscow's

[23] Memorandum to the Central Committee, *Pravda*, Sept. 21, 1958.

[24] Khrushchev estimated an annual increment of 2 to 3.5 million youths in the labor force two years earlier than under the old program (*ibid.*); this gain is exclusive of the part-time work to be performed by pupils in most grades.

[25] It should be pointed out that the eight-year school is not a condensation of the ten-year curriculum but an expansion of the seven-year school — again indicative of the relaxation of academic rigor.

[26] See especially Khrushchev's speech to the 13th Congress of the Kemsomol, *Pravda*, April 19, 1958, and his memorandum to the Central Committee, *ibid.*, Sept. 21, 1958.

higher schools, said Khrushchev, children of workers and collective farmers made up only 30 to 40 per cent of the enrollment. The abolition of
tuition fees in the *vuzes*, along with those in the secondary schools, was
one move calculated to alter this situation. It is particularly revealing that
this step was taken at a time when pressure for admission to higher education from the growing ranks of ten-year graduates was reaching its peak
— that is, when selectivity in admissions was becoming most necessary. If
there were truth in the hypothesis of growing class stratification under
pressure from a powerful "state bourgeoisie," just the opposite might have
been expected — i.e., a rise in the tuition fees as a convenient way of
shutting out low-income applicants.

Very different rules of competition were instead set up. A rising proportion (currently, 80 per cent) of *vuz* admissions was reserved for applicants with at least two years of work experience or military service;[27]
presumably, this will become a universal requirement when the secondary-
school reform is complete. Meanwhile, honor graduates of the ten-year
schools and the *teknikums* are now obliged to compete in entrance examinations along with everybody else — and, for the sake of "objectivity,"
the written part of the examinations is turned in under a pseudonym.[28] In
most fields, the first two or three years of higher education are to be combined with full-time work, in order both to weed out the less serious students and to impress the future *vuz* graduates with the "glorious traditions of our working class and collective-farm peasantry" — i.e., to blunt
the forces making for social separateness.[29] The method of awarding
scholarships has been revised to take more account of the material needs
of the student, and somewhat less of his grades; special courses are being
organized to help *vuz* applicants who have not completed secondary education, or who have been out of school for a while; and all applicants
must present recommendations from places of work and also from party,
Komsomol, or trade-union organizations, whose representatives in addition sit on admissions boards[30] — all of which recall the days when the
official aim was to "proletarianize" the higher schools. Given the recent
Soviet willingness to publish more figures (so long as they "look good"),

[27] *Ibid.*, June 4, 1958.

[28] *Ibid.*, June 4 and Nov. 12, 1958; *Izvestia*, April 4, 1959. Since honor graduates formerly were admitted without entrance examinations, high-status parents
(according to Khrushchev) often put pressure on secondary-school teachers to give
their children good grades (*Pravda*, Sept. 21, 1958).

[29] See Khrushchev's memorandum, *Pravda*, Sept. 21, 1958, and the Central
Committee resolution on school reform, *ibid.*, Nov. 14, 1958; also Minister of
Higher Education Yelyutin's discussions of the problem, *ibid.*, Sept. 17, 1958, and
Izvestia, Dec. 24, 1958.

[30] See *Komsomolskaia Pravda*, Aug. 16, 1956; *Vestnik Vysshei Shkoly*, No. 9
(Sept.), 1957, pp. 3–5; *Pravda*, June 4, 1958; and *Izvestia*, Dec. 24, 1958, and
April 4, 1959.

it may be predicted that we shall soon have, for the first time since 1938, comprehensive data on the social origins of students in higher education.[31]

The subject of educational reform cannot be passed over without taking notice of the boarding schools. When Khrushchev first broached the topic at the 20th Congress, observers assumed (as in the case of the secret speech) that his proposal demonstrated the influence of the elite and that the new schools — despite his protestation to the contrary — would be exclusive institutions for the privileged.

The reality of the boarding school has been a far cry from these suppositions. Priority in admission has gone — as, after all, Khrushchev said it should — to children from large or low-income families, and to others from disadvantaged environments. Fees are charged, but they have been waived for those who could not afford them — again in accord with Khrushchev's original suggestion. Moreover, the curriculum has been strictly polytechnical, providing training for such occupations as lathe operators, electricians, farm machine operators, stenographers, typists, etc. — hardly pursuits becoming to an aristocratic caste.[32]

IS THE CLASSLESS SOCIETY COMING?

The scope and force of the trend away from extreme differentiation are unmistakable. There are many clues other than those which have already been cited: criticism of the practice of assigning chauffeured cars to officials; a pervasive, if still partial, change in the method of awarding medals and orders; a demand that the Soviet fashion journal concern itself less with evening gowns and furs and more with "everyday" clothes. To dismiss all this evidence as mere window-dressing, as ritual obeisance to an ideology, explains nothing: for why is it happening *now*? Why should Khrushchev feel compelled to renew rituals that Stalin has long neglected, rituals that offend the sensibilities of the "elite"? What, then, does account for the change? Is one facet of the "transition to communism" to be the end of class distinctions?

[31] Another prediction which might be ventured is the resurrection of intelligence and aptitude tests, abolished in the 1930's on the grounds that they emphasized inherited rather than acquired traits and discriminated against children of workers and peasants. In effect, the criteria of "ability" became instead school examinations, grades, and *vuz* entrance examinations, which actually discriminate more heavily against low-status students in terms of the motivational or "cultural" influences in their lives. Intelligence-test scores are now considered less immutable than was once thought to be the case, and Khrushchev may "discover" that IQ tests are a more "objective" (i.e., less class-biased) measure of ability than achievement tests.

[32] On the schools, see *Pravda*, Feb. 15 and July 1, 1956; *Uchitelskaia Gazeta*, June 27, 1956; *Trud*, July 27, 1956; *Pravda*, Oct. 9, 1958. It might be noted that many, if not most, of the boarding schools have been converted from former seven- or ten-year schools, probably due to insufficient construction funds.

Stalin, it seems clear, had felt that a high degree of differentiation was necessary to achieve his overriding goal — a very rapid process of industrialization subject to his absolute control. This meant, in the first place, that a group of loyal and competent administrators and other brain-workers had to be created, and quickly. It also meant that large segments of the population would have to be deprived, at least "temporarily," of material returns from their labor, in order that greater proportions of production could be applied to the expansion of industrial capacity. The consequently depressed condition of the workers and peasants Stalin sought to turn to good purpose, by offering them great rewards for joining the administrative and technical corps — hence the wealth, privilege, and prestige which came to define the upper end of the occupational hierarchy. The need for upward mobility to escape a life of privation would induce people to strive for educational training and vocational achievement, and would encourage obedience to Stalin's dictates, while the chance for upward mobility would serve as a substitute for the more prosaic benefits of a slow and moderate rise in the general standard of living.

The gap thus generated between the higher statuses and the lower ably served Stalin's purposes in some respects. Those in high position came to live a different kind of life, free from the material anxieties of those over whom they stood. They became, in short, "insulated" from the less fortunate: blind or indifferent to the needs and wishes of the masses. For they learned that success was to be had by winning the favor not of those below them but of those above them, which was exactly what Stalin wanted them to learn. Now that the policy has come under fire, the attitude which it engendered has been amply described in the Soviet press, for example in this criticism of the "self-willed" official as a type:

> Tell such an official that he has disturbed his subordinate's state of mind, and he will probably be amazed: "His state of mind? Brother, we're having trouble meeting our plan here, and I have no time to look into all sorts of cases of melancholia."[33]

THE PROBLEMS OF STALINIST POLICY

Nevertheless, extreme social differentiation had its less desirable aspects, too. For one thing, it "over-motivated" the population: anything less than a higher education, and the higher occupation it brought, was regarded as a disgrace for an upper-status child and as a sad fate for a lower-status child — hence, the intense pressure exerted on the educational institutions, the reluctance of youths to commit themselves to factory jobs. For another

[33] *Izvestia,* Jan. 18, 1958.

and more important thing, it interfered with the operation of the impersonal selection system necessary to an efficient economy and to the reward-function of upward mobility. Those in higher and better-paid positions were able to use their influence and their money to assure similar places for their children, at the expense of potentially more capable or more loyal children from less-favored families. Perhaps even worse, some children from well-to-do families neither studied nor worked, but lived off their parents' income — an idle existence which not only meant a loss to the labor force but also, if the Soviet press is to be believed, led in many cases to alcoholism, crime, or even to the acceptance of "bourgeois ideology." [34]

This excessive measure of status security perverted adults as well as children. Once a man was granted local power, he was able to suppress or punish, if not ignore, criticism from his inferiors, and he cooperated with his colleagues to evade the regime's cross-checks on him. This had been intermittently acknowedged in the Soviet Union under the label of *semeistvennost* ("family-ness"), but the full dimensions of the problem are only now being revealed. Among many instances, one may be cited concerning the chairman of a city soviet executive committee who "forbade his assistants and the heads of the city executive committee departments to appeal to party organs without his consent." [35] Thus, higher authorities were precluded from receiving the information they needed to keep tabs on their own subordinates. Or, if the party did manage to find out about and remove some incompetent or dishonest official, he often reappeared in another responsible position — partly, at least, as the result of friendships formed and mutual obligations exacted. Indeed, an integral part of the pattern has been the concern of officials to find places in the *apparat* for friends and relatives who could reciprocally provide a haven if necessary.

All of this was simply the obverse side of the arbitrary power delegated to local officials, for the sake of allowing them to carry out their instructions from above without interference from below. But it was ironically self-defeating: by being freed of criticism from below, administrators were able to free themselves of supervision from above. This threatened to contravene the cardinal dogma of the Soviet system, which has come to be known as Stalinism though it could as well be called Leninism or Khrushchevism: that ultimate power belongs exclusively to the party — or more accurately, to the head of the party. Whenever any group jeopardizes that principle, it must be struck down, and that is what Khrushchev is

[34] Mark G. Field, "Drink and Delinquency in the U.S.S.R.," *Problems of Communism*, No. 3 (May–June), 1955; Allen Kassof, "Youth vs. The Regime: Conflict in Values," *ibid.*, No. 3 (May–June), 1957.
[35] *Izvestia*, Jan. 16, 1958.

doing. Stalin, in other words, forgot his Stalinism; and Khrushchev is not repudiating Stalinism, he is, if anything, reinstating it.

KHRUSHCHEV'S TWO-SIDED TASK

No doubt, the Soviet press, in characteristic fashion, has exaggerated the threat. Stalin was not a complete fool, and when all is said and done, he does seem to have kept things pretty well under control. If the group whose growth he fostered was an "elite," then surely no elite has ever proved so utterly helpless in preventing actions which, like those at present, so adversely affect it. The danger was a distant cloud — but a good Bolshevik tries not to wait until the storm has swept away his fortifications. Khrushchev's task, then, is to rid the "state bourgeoisie" of its cockiness, to disabuse it of the notion that it is safe whatever it does, to infuse into it fresh blood, personnel more responsive to orders. Just because of the kinds of positions these people occupy, the task will not be easy, and the plan may be "underfulfilled." But given the Soviet political structure, the odds are on Khrushchev's side.

The nature of the targets at which Khrushchev has taken aim makes his crusade sound like an echo of earlier revolutionary periods; but in actuality, the development does not connote a return to the situation that prevailed in the early 1920's, for Khrushchev has learned something from Soviet history. The extremes of high and low incomes are to be moderated — but "equality-mongering" is still wrong. Mass participation and criticism from below are to be permitted — but not "violations of state discipline" or "slander of the party and its leaders." Executives should be more humble, more attentive to their subordinates — but the principle of "one-man management" is to be preserved. "The struggle against the cult of the individual does not at all mean a belittling of the significance of leadership and leaders. . . . The party does not advocate the denial of authorities." [36] Moreover, Khrushchev has expressly defended the nonmanual pursuits — "those who work in offices are not at all bureaucrats, they are the creative people who originate that which is new . . ." — and he has strongly implied that, even under communism, there will still be the bosses and the bossed: communist society will be "highly organized." [37] Complete equality is not just around the corner, nor even being contemplated.

"CLASSLESSNESS" DEFINED

Nevertheless, Khrushchev *is* seeking a classless society, in the proper sense of the term. If an "upper class," for example, means anything, it means a group of people who share fairly distinctive values and advantages which

[36] *Partiinaia Zhizn*, No. 7 (April), 1956, p. 5.
[37] *Pravda*, July 2, 1959; also Khrushchev's report to the 21st Congress, *Pravda*, Jan. 28, 1959.

they are able to hold on to for some length of time, even against the resistance of others. Yet in the totalitarian scheme of things, it is essential to the preservation of party supremacy that no group become so entrenched in positions of strength as to become insulated against further demands from the party. An "upper class," or any other "class," is no more admissible than an autonomous trade union or ethnic group. Hence the party must insist — in the long run — that every man be individually and continuously on trial, that status and rewards remain contingent and ephemeral. The greatest threat to the party is the development of a sense of identification or solidarity within a group — or class — and this is precisely what was happening to the Soviet elite. Khrushchev's war against the bourgeoisie is, in fact, only an extension of the battle with the bureaucrats which has long been a part of Soviet policy, even if it was sometimes muted. In short, "classlessness" is essentially a corollary of Stalinism.

Khrushchev, however, believes himself to be in a better position to attain it than Stalin ever was. The creation of a substantial industrial base has relieved him of the urgency which Stalin so acutely felt. Automation, as he has frequently pointed out, really has diminished the differences between mental workers and manual. The spread of education has freed him from dependence on a relatively small group as the only source of administrative and intellectual personnel; workers and peasants can now be brought into the *vuzes* with less risk of lowering the quality of education (as happened in the 1920's). Finally, he evidently presumes that a long period of enforced political homogeneity has led to the withering away of deviant values among Soviet citizens. Criticism from below would thus be less dangerous, since it is more likely to accord with what the party wants. The only agency left which has enabled Soviet man to maintain and transmit both "hostile" values and favored positions, with even a small degree of success, is the family — whence the significance of the boarding schools (and other attempts to loosen family bonds). For the boarding schools are destined to be not elite institutions, but universal ones: the instrument by which the regime hopes finally to achieve control over the last remaining semi-autonomous activity, the rearing of children.[38] This, too, is an objective which will be familiar to students of Soviet history, but unlike the situation earlier, Soviet leaders may well feel that they now have, or can produce, the material facilities with which to realize it.

Yet it is unlikely that the regime has solved, once and for all, the problem of inequality. Power corrupts — even delegated power. Workers and

---

[38] "The sooner we provide nurseries, kindergartens, and boarding schools for all children, the sooner and the more successfully will the task of the Communist upbringing of the growing generation be accomplished": Khrushchev's theses on the Seven-Year Plan, *Pravda*, Nov. 14, 1958. See also the decree on the boarding schools in *Pravda*, May 26, 1959.

peasants, no less than intelligentsia, will sooner or later try to put their privileges to uses which, so far as the party is concerned, are "selfish." They may, for example, try to develop a monopoly of their own on higher education, or act "prematurely" to increase the production of consumers' goods or raise wages, in a kind of latter-day "workers' opposition." Or, once terror is removed, they may turn out not to have lost all their hostile values, after all. When that happens, they will once more be put back in the inferior position they knew up to Stalin's death. No end is in sight to this ancient practice of playing one off against the other, this alternate granting of status privilege within a basically classless framework, as the Soviet system struggles with its perennial and fundamental problem: the need to control the controllers.

Notes for
Further Reading

Many of the general and comparative materials on stratification have been put together in:

Lipset, S.M. and R. Bendix (eds.), *Class, Status and Power*. Glencoe, Ill.: The Free Press, 1966, second edition. *Comparative Studies in Society and History*, Vol. 5, 1963, pp. 285–303.

For analyses of stratification in modernizing societies, see:

Abegglen, J.C. and H. Mannari, "Leaders of Modern Japan: Social Origins and Mobility," *Economic Development and Cultural Change*, Vol. 9, No. 1, Part II, 1960, pp. 109–134.

Bailey, F.G., "Closed Social Stratification," *European Journal of Sociology*, Vol. 4, 1963, pp. 107–129.

Beteille, A., *Caste, Class and Power: Changing Patterns of Stratification in a Tangore Village*. Berkeley: University of California Press, 1966.

Fei, H., *Peasant Life in China*. London: K. Paul, Trench, Trubner, 1947.

Tiryakian, E., "Occupational Stratification and Aspiration in an Underdeveloped Country: The Philippines," *Economic Development and Cultural Change*, Vol. 7, 1959, pp. 431–444.

For general analysis of one crucial aspect of stratification in modern society, social mobility, see:

Lipset, S.M. and R. Bendix, *Social Mobility in Industrial Society*. Berkeley: University of California Press, 1959.

For specific analyses of changes in patterns of stratification in modern societies, see:

Helmos, R. (ed.), *The Development of Industrial Societies*, Sociological Review Monograph 9, Keele, 1964.

Inkeles, A. and K. Geiger (eds.), *Soviet Society: A Book of Readings*. Boston: Houghton Mifflin, 1961, esp. Chapter V.

Kahl, J.A., *The American Class Structure*. New York: Rinehart & Co., 1957.

Mills, C.W., *The Power Elite*. New York: Oxford University Press, 1951.

Transactions of the Second World Congress of Sociology. London: International Sociology Association, 1954, Vol. II.

Transactions of the Third World Congress of Sociology. London: International Sociological Association, 1956, Vol. III.

VI

Changes in Community
Structure and Life

The two articles presented here provide different approaches to the analysis of the impact of processes of change on community life.

The first article, excerpts from a study by Geertz, describes in a very perceptive way the impact of change on an Indonesian village, concentrating on one aspect of village life — that of ritual as manifested in funeral rites. But Geertz deals not only with changes in the contents of such ritual. He also relates ritual to the problem of change in social organization, individual life, and cultural meanings alike — showing not only their close interrelation, but also the autonomy of the processes of change and of reactions to them on each of these levels.

The second article, by Wilkening, provides us with a general analysis of the different types and impacts of change on rural communities.

7   CLIFFORD GEERTZ

Ritual and Social Change: A Javanese Example

I shall try to show how an approach which does not distinguish the "logico-meaningful" cultural aspects of the ritual pattern from the "causal-functional" social structural aspects is unable to account adequately for this ritual failure, and how an approach which does so distinguish them is able to analyze more explicitly the cause of the trouble. It will further be argued that such an approach is able to avoid the simplistic view of the functional role of religion in society which sees that role merely as structure-conserving, and to substitute for it a more complex conception of the relations between religious belief and practice and secular social life. Historical materials can be fitted into such a conception, and the functional analysis of religion can therefore be widened to deal more adequately with processes of change.

THE SETTING

The case to be described is that of a funeral held in Modjokuto, a small town in eastern Central Java. A young boy, about ten years of age, who was living with his uncle and aunt, died very suddenly but his death, instead of being followed by the usual hurried, subdued, yet methodically efficient, Javanese funeral ceremony and burial routine, brought on an extended period of pronounced social strain and severe psychological tension. The complex of beliefs and rituals which had for generations brought countless Javanese safely through the difficult post-mortem period suddenly failed to work with its accustomed effectiveness. To understand why it failed demands knowledge and understanding of a whole range of social and cultural changes which have taken place in Java since the first decades of this century. This disrupted funeral was in fact but a microcosmic example of the broader conflicts, structural dissolutions, and

From *American Anthropologist*, Vol. 59, No. 1, February, 1957, pp. 34–38; 40–54. Reprinted with the permission of the author and the American Anthropological Association. Article abridged for this printing. Original footnote numbers have been retained.

attempted reintegrations which, in one form or another, are characteristic of contemporary Indonesian society.

The religious tradition of Java, particularly of the peasantry, is a composite of Indian, Islamic, and indigenous Southeast Asian elements (Landon 1949). The rise of large, militaristic kingdoms in the inland rice basins in the early centuries of the Christian era was associated with the diffusion of Hinduist and Buddhist culture patterns to the island; the expansion of international maritime trade in the port cities of the northern coast in the fifteenth and sixteenth centuries was associated with the diffusion of Islamic patterns. Working their way into the peasant mass, these two world religions became fused with the underlying animistic traditions characteristic of the whole Malaysian culture area. The result was a balanced syncretism of myth and ritual in which Hindu gods and goddesses, Moslem prophets and saints, and local place spirits and demons all found a proper place.

The central ritual form in this syncretism is a communal feast, called the *slametan*. Slametans, which are given with only slight variations in form and content on almost all occasions of religious significance — at passage points in the life cycle, on calendrical holidays, at certain stages of the crop cycle, on changing one's residence, etc. — are intended to be both offerings to the spirits and commensal mechanisms of social integration for the living. The meal, which consists of specially prepared dishes, each symbolic of a particular religious concept, is cooked by the female members of one nuclear family household and set out on mats in the middle of the living-room. The male head of the household invites the male heads of the eight or ten contiguous households to attend; no close neighbor is ignored in favor of one farther away. After a speech by the host explaining the spiritual purpose of the feast and a short Arabic chant, each man takes a few hurried, almost furtive, gulps of food, wraps the remainder of the meal in a banana-leaf basket, and returns home to share it with his family. It is said that the spirits draw their sustenance from the odor of the food, the incense which is burned, and the Moslem prayer; the human participants draw theirs from the material substance of the food and from their social interaction. The result of this quiet, undramatic little ritual is twofold: the spirits are appeased and neighborhood solidarity is strengthened.

The ordinary canons of functional theory are quite adequate for the analysis of such a pattern. It can rather easily be shown that the slametan is well designed both to "tune-up the ultimate value attitudes" necessary to the effective integration of a territorially based social structure, and to fulfill the psychological needs for intellectual coherence and emotional stability characteristic of a peasant population. The Javanese village (once or twice a year, village-wide slametans are held) is essentially a set of geographically contiguous, but rather self-consciously autonomous, nuclear family households whose economic and political interdependence is of roughly the same circumscribed and explicitly defined sort as that demonstrated in the slametan. The demands of the labor-intensive rice and dry-crop agricultural process require the perpetuation of specific modes of technical co-operation and enforce a sense of community on the otherwise rather self-contained families — a sense of community which the slametan clearly reinforces. And when we consider the manner in which various conceptual and behavioral elements from Hindu-Buddhism, Islam, and "animism" are reinterpreted and balanced to form a distinctive and nearly homogeneous religious style, the close functional adjustment between the communal feast pattern and the conditions of Javanese rural life is even more readily apparent.

But the fact is that in all but the most isolated parts of Java, both the simple territorial basis of village social integration and the syncretic basis of its cultural homogeneity have been progressively undermined over the past fifty years. Population growth, urbanization, monetization, occupational differentiation, and the like, have combined to weaken the traditional ties of peasant social structure; and the winds of doctrine which have accompanied the appearance of these structural changes have disturbed the simple uniformity of religious belief and practice characteristic of an earlier period. The rise of nationalism, Marxism, and Islamic reform as ideologies, which resulted in part from the increasing complexity of Javanese society, has affected not only the large cities where these creeds first appeared and have always had their greatest strength, but has had a heavy impact on the smaller towns and villages as well. In fact, much of recent Javanese social change is perhaps most aptly characterized as a shift from a situation in which the primary integrative ties between individuals (or between families) are phrased in terms of geographical proximity to one in which they are phrased in terms of ideological like-mindedness.

In the villages and small towns these major ideological changes appeared largely in the guise of a widening split between those who emphasized the Islamic aspects of the indigenous religious syncretism and those who emphasized the Hinduist and animistic elements. It is true that some difference between these variant subtraditions has been present since the arrival of Islam; some individuals have always been particularly skilled in Arabic chanting or particularly learned in Moslem law, while others have been adept at more Hinduistic mystical practices or specialists in local curing techniques. But these contrasts were softened by the easy tolerance of the Javanese for a wide range of religious concepts, so long as basic ritual patterns — i.e., slametans — were faithfully supported;

whatever social divisiveness they stimulated was largely obscured by the over-riding commonalities of rural and small-town life.

However, the appearance after 1910 of Islamic modernism (as well as vigorous conservative reactions against it) and religious nationalism among the economically and politically sophisticated trading classes of the larger cities strengthened the feeling for Islam as an exclusivist, anti-syncretic creed among the more orthodox element of the mass of the population. Similarly, secular nationalism and Marxism, appearing among the civil servants and the expanding proletariat of these cities, strengthened the pre-Islamic (i.e., Hinduist-animist) elements of the syncretic pattern, which these groups tended to prize as a counterweight to puristic Islam and which some of them adopted as a general religious framework in which to set their more specifically political ideas. On the one hand, there arose a more self-conscious Moslem, basing his religious beliefs and practices more explicitly on the international and universalistic doctrines of Mohammed; on the other hand there arose a more self-conscious "nativist," attempting to evolve a generalized religious system out of the material — muting the more Islamic elements — of his inherited religious tradition. And the contrast between the first kind of man, called a *santri,* and the second, called an *abangan,* grew steadily more acute, until today it forms the major cultural distinction in the whole of the Modjokuto area.[3]

It is especially in the town that this contrast has come to play a crucial role. The absence of pressures toward interfamilial co-operation exerted by the technical requirements of wet-rice growing, as well as lessened effectiveness of the traditional forms of village government in the face of the complexities of urban living, severely weaken the social supports of the syncretic village pattern. When each man makes his living — as chauffeur, trader, clerk, or laborer — more or less independently of how his neighbors make theirs, his sense of the importance of the neighborhood community naturally diminishes. A more differentiated class system, more bureaucratic and impersonal forms of government, greater heterogeneity of social background, all tend to lead to the same result: the de-emphasis of strictly geographical ties in favor of diffusely ideological ones. For the townsman, the distinction between santri and abangan becomes even sharper, for it emerges as his primary point of social reference; it becomes a symbol of his social identity, rather than a mere contrast in belief. The sort of friends he will have, the sort of organizations he will join, the

[3] For a description of the role of the santri-abangan distinction in the rural areas of Modjokuto, see Jay 1956. A third religious variant which I have discriminated elsewhere (Geertz 1956, and in press), the *prijaji,* is mainly confined to upper-class civil servants, teachers, and clerks, and so will not be dealt with here.

sort of political leadership he will follow, the sort of person he or his
son will marry, will all be strongly influenced by the side of this ideological bifurcation which he adopts as his own.

There is thus emerging in the town — though not only in the town — a
new pattern of social living organized in terms of an altered framework
of cultural classification. Among the elite this new pattern has already
become rather highly developed, but among the mass of the townspeople
it is still in the process of formation. Particularly in the *kampongs*, the
off-the-street neighborhoods in which the common Javanese townsmen
live crowded together in a helter-skelter profusion of little bamboo
houses, one finds a transitional society in which the traditional forms of
rural living are being steadily dissolved and new forms steadily reconstructed. In these enclaves of peasants-come-to-town (or of sons and
grandsons of peasants-come-to-town), Redfield's folk culture is being
constantly converted into his urban culture, though this latter is not accurately characterized by such negative and residual terms as "secular,"
"individualized," and "culturally disorganized." What is occurring in the
kampongs is not so much a destruction of traditional ways of life, as a
construction of a new one; the sharp social conflict characteristic of these
lower-class neighborhoods is not simply indicative of a loss of cultural
consensus, but rather indicative of a search, not yet entirely successful, for
new, more generalized, and flexible patterns of belief and value.

In Modjokuto, as in most of Indonesia, this search is taking place largely
within the social context of the mass political parties, as well as in the
women's clubs, youth organizations, labor unions, and other sodalities
formally or informally linked with them. There are several of these parties
(though the recent general election severely reduced their number), each
led by educated urban elites — civil servants, teachers, traders, students,
and the like — and each competing with the others for the political
allegiance of both the half rural, half urban kampong dwellers and of
the mass of the peasantry. And almost without exception, they appeal to
one or another side of the santri-abangan split. Of this complex of political parties and sodalities, only two are of immediate concern to us here:
Masjumi, a huge, Islam-based political party; and Permai, a vigorously
anti-Moslem politico-religious cult. . . .

THE FUNERAL

The mood of a Javanese funeral is not one of hysterical bereavement, unrestrained sobbing, or even of formalized cries of grief for the deceased's
departure. Rather, it is a calm, undemonstrative, almost languid letting go,
a brief ritualized relinquishment of a relationship no longer possible.
Tears are not approved of and certainly not encouraged; the effort is to
get the job done, not to linger over the pleasures of grief. The detailed

busy-work of the funeral, the politely formal social intercourse with the neighbors pressing in from all sides, the series of commemorative slametans stretched out at intervals for almost three years — the whole momentum of the Javanese ritual system is supposed to carry out through grief without severe emotional disturbance. For the mourner, the funeral and postfuneral ritual is said to produce a feeling of *iklas*, a kind of willed affectlessness, a detached and static state of "not caring"; for the neighborhood group it is said to produce *rukun*, "communal harmony."

The actual service is in essence simply another version of the slametan, adapted to the special requirements of interment. When the news of a death is broadcast through the area, everyone in the neighborhood must drop what he is doing and go immediately to the home of the survivors. The women bring bowls of rice, which is cooked up into a slametan; the men begin to cut wooden grave markers and to dig a grave. Soon the Modin arrives and begins to direct activities. The corpse is washed in ceremonially prepared water by the relatives (who unflinchingly hold the body on their laps to demonstrate their affection for the deceased as well as their self-control); then it is wrapped in muslin. About a dozen santris, under the leadership of the Modin, chant Arabic prayers over the body for five or ten minutes; after this it is carried, amid various ritual acts, in a ceremonial procession to the graveyard, where it is interred in prescribed ways. The Modin reads a graveside speech to the deceased, reminding him of his duties as a believing Moslem; and the funeral is over, usually only two or three hours after death. The funeral proper is followed by commemorative slametans in the home of the survivors at three, seven, forty, and one hundred days after death; on the first and second anniversary of death; and, finally, on the thousandth day, when the corpse is considered to have turned to dust and the gap between the living and the dead to have become absolute.

This was the ritual pattern which was called into play when Paidjan died. As soon as dawn broke (death occurred in the early hours of the morning), Karman, the uncle, dispatched a telegram to the boy's parents in a nearby city, telling them in characteristic Javanese fashion that their son was ill. This evasion was intended to soften the impact of death by allowing them to become aware of it more gradually. Javanese feel that emotional damage results not from the severity of a frustration but from the suddenness with which it comes, the degree to which it "surprises" one unprepared for it. It is "shock," not suffering itself, which is feared. Next, in the expectation that the parents would arrive within a few hours, Karman sent for the Modin to begin the ceremony. This was done on the theory that by the time the parents had come little would be left to do but inter the body, and they would thus once more be spared unnecessary stress. By ten o'clock at the very latest it should all be over; a saddening incident, but a ritually muted one.

But when the Modin, as he later told me, arrived at Karman's house and saw the poster displaying Permai's political symbol, he told Karman that he could not perform the ritual. After all, Karman belonged to "another religion" and he, the Modin, did not know the correct burial rituals for it; all he knew was Islam. "I don't want to insult your religion," he said piously, "on the contrary, I hold it in the utmost regard, for there is no intolerance in Islam. But I don't know your ritual. The Christians have their own ritual and their own specialist (the local preacher), but what does Permai do? Do they burn the corpse or what?" (This is a sly allusion to Hindu burial practices; evidently the Modin enjoyed himself hugely in this interchange.) Karman was, the Modin told me, rather upset at all this and evidently surprised, for although he was an active member of Permai, he was a fairly unsophisticated one. It had evidently never occurred to him that the anti-Moslem-funeral agitation of the party would ever appear as a concrete problem, or that the Modin would actually refuse to officiate. Karman was actually not a bad fellow, the Modin concluded; he was but a dupe of his leaders.

After leaving the now highly agitated Karman, the Modin went directly to the subdistrict officer to ask if he had acted properly. The officer was morally bound to say that he had, and thus fortified the Modin returned home to find Karman and the village policeman, to whom he had gone in desperation, waiting for him. The policeman, a personal friend of Karman's, told the Modin that according to time-honored custom he was supposed to bury everyone with impartiality, never mind whether he happened to agree with their politics. But the Modin, having now been personally supported by the subdistrict officer, insisted that it was no longer his responsibility. However, he suggested, if Karman wished, he could go to the village chief's office and sign a public statement, sealed with the Government stamp and countersigned by the village chief in the presence of two witnesses, declaring that he, Karman, was a true believing Moslem and that he wished the Modin to bury the boy according to Islamic custom. At this suggestion that he officially abandon his religious beliefs, Karman exploded into a rage and stormed from the house, rather uncharacteristic behavior for a Javanese. By the time he arrived home again, at his wit's end about what to do next, he found to his dismay that the news of the boy's death had been broadcast and the entire neighborhood was already gathering for the ceremony.

Like most of the kampongs in the town of Modjokuto, the one in which I lived consisted both of pious santris and ardent abangans (as well as a number of less intense adherents of either side), mixed together in a more or less random manner. In the town, people are forced to live where they can and take whomever they find for neighbors, in contrast to the rural areas where whole neighborhoods, even whole villages, still tend to be made up almost entirely of either abangans or santris. The majority of the santris in the kampong were members of Masjumi and most of the abangans were followers of Permai, and in daily life, social interaction between the two groups was minimal. The abangans, most of whom were either petty artisans or manual laborers, gathered each late afternoon at Karman's roadside coffee shop for the idle twilight conversations which are typical of small town and village life in Java; the santris — tailors, traders and store-keepers for the most part — usually gathered in one or another of the santri-run shops for the same purpose. But despite this lack of close social ties, the demonstration of territorial unity at a funeral was still felt by both groups to be an unavoidable duty; of all the Javanese rituals, the funeral probably carries the greatest obligation on attendance. Everyone who lives within a certain roughly defined radius of the survivors' home is expected to come to the ceremony; and on this occasion everyone did.

With this as background, it is not surprising that when I arrived at Karman's house about eight o'clock, I found two separate clusters of sullen men squatting disconsolately on either side of the yard, a nervous group of whispering women sitting idly inside the house near the still clothed body, and a general air of doubt and uneasiness in place of the usual quiet busyness of slametan preparing, body washing and guest greeting. The abangans were grouped near the house where Karman was crouched, staring blankly off into space, and where Sudjoko and Sastro, the town Chairman and Secretary of Permai (the only nonresidents of the kampong present) sat on chairs, looking vaguely out of place. The santris were crowded together under the narrow shadow of a coconut palm about thirty yards away, chatting quietly to one another about everything but the problem at hand. The almost motionless scene suggested an unlooked-for intermission in a familiar drama, as when a motion picture stops in the mid-action.

After a half hour or so, a few of the abangans began to chip halfheartedly away at pieces of wood to make grave markers and a few women began to construct small flower offerings for want of anything better to do; but it was clear that the ritual was arrested and that no one quite knew what to do next. Tension slowly rose. People nervously watched the sun rise higher and higher in the sky, or glanced at the impassive Karman. Mutterings about the sorry state of affairs began to appear ("everything these days is a political problem," an old, traditionalistic man of about eighty grumbled to me, "you can't even die any more but what it becomes a political problem"). Finally, about 9:30, a young santri tailor named Abu decided to try to do something about the situation before it deteriorated entirely: he stood up and gestured to Karman, the first serious instrumental act which had occurred all morning. And Karman, roused from his meditation, crossed the no-man's-land to talk to him.

As a matter of fact, Abu occupied a rather special position in the kampong. Although he was a pious santri and a loyal Masjumi member, he had more contact with the Permai group because his tailor shop was located directly behind Karman's coffee shop. Though Abu, who stuck to his sewing machine night and day, was not properly a member of this group, he would often exchange comments with them from his work bench about twenty feet away. True, a certain amount of tension existed between him and the Permai people over religious issues. Once, when I was inquiring about their eschatological beliefs, they referred me sarcastically to Abu, saying he was an expert, and they teased him quite openly about what they considered the wholly ridiculous Islamic theories of the after life. Nevertheless, he had something of a social bond with them, and it was perhaps reasonable that he should be the one to try to break the deadlock.

"It is already nearly noon," Abu said, "things can't go straight on like this." He suggested that he send Umar, another of the santris, to see if the Modin could now be induced to come; perhaps things were cooler with him now. Meanwhile, he could get the washing and wrapping of the corpse started himself. Karman replied that he would think about it, and returned to the other side of the yard for a discussion with the two Permai leaders. After a few minutes of vigorous gesturing and nodding, Karman returned and said simply, "All right, that way." "I know how you feel," Abu said, "I'll just do what is absolutely necessary and keep the Islam out as much as possible." He gathered the santris together and they entered the house.

The first requisite was stripping the corpse (which was still lying on the floor, because no one could bring himself to move it). But by now the body was rigid, making it necessary to cut the clothes off with a knife, an unusual procedure which deeply disturbed everyone, especially the women clustered around. The santris finally managed to get the body outside and set up the bathing enclosure. Abu asked for volunteers for the washing; he reminded them that God would consider such an act a good work. But the relatives, who normally would be expected to undertake this task, were by now so deeply shaken and confused that they were unable to bring themselves to hold the boy on their laps in the customary fashion. There was another wait while people looked hopelessly at each other. Finally, Pak Sura, a member of Karman's group but no relative, took the boy on his lap, although he was clearly frightened and kept whispering a protective spell. One reason the Javanese give for their custom of rapid burial is that it is dangerous to have the spirit of the deceased hovering around the house.

Before the washing could begin, however, someone raised the question as to whether one person was enough — wasn't it usually three? No one was quite sure, including Abu; some thought that although it was customary to have three people it was not obligatory, and some thought three a necessary number. After about ten minutes of anxious discussion, a male cousin of the boy and a carpenter, unrelated to him, managed to work up the courage to join Pak Sura. Abu, attempting to act the Modin's role as best he could, sprinkled a few drops of water on the corpse and then it was washed, rather haphazardly and in unsacralized water. When this was finished, however, the procedure was again stalled, for no one knew exactly how to arrange the small cotton pads which, under Moslem law, should plug the body orifices. Karman's wife, sister of the deceased's mother, could evidently take no more, for she broke into a loud, unrestrained wailing, the only demonstration of this sort I witnessed among the dozen or so Javanese funerals I attended. Everyone was further upset ·by this development, and most of the kampong women made a frantic but unavailing effort to comfort her. Most of the men remained seated in the yard, outwardly calm and inexpressive, but the embarrassed uneasiness which had been present since the beginning seemed to be turning toward fearful desperation. "It is not nice for her to cry that way," several men said to me, "it isn't proper." At this point, the Modin arrived.

However, he was still adamant. Further, he warned Abu that he was courting eternal damnation by his actions. "You will have to answer to God on Judgment Day," he said, "if you make mistakes in the ritual. It will be your responsibility. For a Moslem, burial is a serious matter and must be carried out according to the Law by someone who knows what the Law is, not according to the will of the individual." He then suggested to Sudjoko and Sastro, the Permai leaders, that they take charge of the funeral, for as party "intellectuals" they must certainly know what kind of funeral customs Permai followed. The two leaders, who had not moved from their chairs, considered this as everyone watched expectantly, but they finally refused, with some chagrin, saying they really did not know how to go about it. The Modin shrugged and turned away. One of the bystanders, a friend of Karman's, then suggested that they just take the body out and bury it and forget about the whole ritual; it was extremely dangerous to leave things as they were much longer. I don't know whether this remarkable suggestion would have been followed, for at this juncture the mother and father of the dead child entered the kampong.

They seemed quite composed. They were not unaware of the death, for the father later told me he had suspected as much when he got the telegram; he and ·his wife had prepared themselves for the worst and were more or less resigned by the time they arrived. When they approached the kampong and saw the whole neighborhood gathered, they knew that their fears were well founded. When Karman's wife, whose weeping had subsided slightly, saw the dead boy's mother come into the yard, she burst free of those who were comforting her and with a shriek rushed to embrace her sister. In what seemed a split second, both women had dissolved into wild hysterics and the crowd had rushed in and pulled them apart, dragging them to houses at opposite sides of the kampong. Their wailing continued in undiminished volume, and nervous comments arose to the effect that they ought to get on with the burial in one fashion or another, before the boy's spirit possessed someone.

But the mother now insisted on seeing the body of her child before it was wrapped. The father at first forbade it, angrily ordering her to stop crying — didn't she know that such behavior would darken the boy's pathway to the other world? But she persisted and so they brought her, stumbling, to where he lay in Karman's house. The women tried to keep her from drawing too close, but she broke loose and began to kiss the boy about the genitals. She was snatched away almost immediately by her husband and the women, though she screamed that she had not yet finished; and they pulled her into the back room where she subsided into a daze. After awhile — the body was finally being wrapped, the Modin having unbent enough to point out where the cotton pads went — she seemed to lose her bearings entirely and began to move about the yard shaking hands with everyone, all strangers to her, and saying "forgive me my faults, forgive me my faults." Again she was forcibly restrained; people said, "calm yourself, think of your other children — do you want to follow your son to the grave?"

The corpse was now wrapped and new suggestions were made that it be taken off immediately to the graveyard. At this point, Abu approached the father, who, he evidently felt, had now displaced Karman as the man legally responsible for the proceedings. Abu explained that the Modin, being a Government official, did not feel free to approach the father himself, but he would like to know: how did he wish the boy to be buried — the Islamic way or what? The father, somewhat bewildered, said, "Of course, the Islamic way. I don't have much of any religion, but I'm not a Christian, and when it comes to death the burial should be the Islamic way. Completely Islamic." Abu explained again that the Modin could not approach the father directly, but that he, being "free," could do as he pleased. He said that he had tried to help as best he could but that he had been careful to do nothing Islamic before the father came. It was too bad, he apologized, about all the tension that was in the air, that political differences had to make so much trouble. But after all, everything had to be "clear" and "legal" about the funeral. It was important for the boy's soul. The santris, somewhat gleefully, now chanted their prayers over the corpse, and it was carried to the grave and buried in the usual manner. The Modin gave the usual graveyard speech, as amended for children, and the funeral was finally completed. None of the relatives or the women went to the graveyard; but when we returned to the house — it was now well after noon — the slametan was finally served, and Paidjan's spirit presumably left the kampong to begin its journey to the other world.

Three days later, in the evening, the first of the commemorative slametans was held, but it turned out that not only were no santris present but that it was as much a Permai political and religious cult meeting as a mourning ritual. Karman started off in the traditional fashion by announcing in high Javanese that this was a slametan in remembrance of the death of Paidjan. Sudjoko, the Permai leader, immediately burst in saying, "No, no, that is wrong. At a third day slametan you just eat and give a long Islamic chant for the dead, and we are certainly not going to do that." He then launched into a long, rambling speech. Everyone, he said, must know the philosophical-religious basis of the country. "Suppose this American (he pointed to me; he was not at all pleased by my presence) came up and asked you: what is the spiritual basis of the country? and you didn't know — wouldn't you be ashamed?"

He went on in this vein, building up a whole rationale for the present national political structure on the basis of a mystical interpretation of President Sukarno's "Five Points" (Monotheism, Social Justice, Humanitarianism, Democracy, and Nationalism[5]) which are the official ideological foundation of the new republic. Aided by Karman and others, he worked out a micromacrocosm correspondence theory in which the individual is seen to be but a small replica of the state, and the state but an enlarged image of the individual. If the state is to be ordered, then the individual must also be ordered; each implies the other. As the President's Five Points are at the basis of the state, so the five senses are at the basis of an individual. The process of harmonizing both are the same, and it is this we must be sure we know. The discussion continued for nearly half an hour, ranging widely through religious, philosophical, and political issues (including, evidently for my benefit, a discussion of the Rosenbergs' execution).

We paused for coffee and as Sudjoko was about to begin again, Paidjan's father, who had been sitting quietly and expressionless, began suddenly to talk, softly and with a curiously mechanical tonelessness, almost as if he were reasoning with himself but without much hope of success. "I am sorry for my rough city accent," he said, "but I very much want to say something." He hoped they would forgive him; they could continue

[5] For a fuller discussion of President Sukarno's *pantjasila* ideology and his attempt to root it in general Indonesian values, see Kahin 1952:122–127.

their discussion in a moment. "I have been trying to be iklas ("detached," "resigned") about Paidjan's death. I'm convinced that everything that could have been done for him was done and that his death was just an event which simply happened." He said he was still in Modjokuto because he could not yet face the people where he lived, couldn't face having to tell each one of them what had occurred. His wife, he said, was a little more iklas now too. It was hard, though. He kept telling himself it was just the will of God, but it was so hard, for nowadays people didn't agree on things any more; one person tells you one thing and others tell you another. It's hard to know which is right, to know what to believe. He said he appreciated all the Modjokuto people coming to the funeral, and he was sorry it had been all mixed up. "I'm not very religious myself. I'm not Masjumi and I'm not Permai. But I wanted the boy to be buried in the old way. I hope no one's feelings were hurt." He said again he was trying to be iklas, to tell himself it was just the will of God, but it was hard, for things were so confused these days. It was hard to see why the boy should have died.

This sort of public expression of one's feelings is extremely unusual — in my experience unique — among Javanese, and in the formalized traditional slametan pattern there is simply no place for it (nor for philosophical or political discussion). Everyone present was rather shaken by the father's talk, and there was a painful silence. Sudjoko finally began to talk again, but this time he described in detail the boy's death. How Paidjan had first gotten a fever and Karman had called him, Sudjoko, to come and say a Permai spell. But the boy did not respond. They finally took him to a male nurse in the hospital, where he was given an injection. But still he worsened. He vomited blood and went into convulsions, which Sudjoko described rather graphically, and then he died. "I don't know why the Permai spell didn't work," he said, "it has worked before. This time it didn't. I don't know why; that sort of thing can't be explained no matter how much you think about it. Sometimes it just works and sometimes it just doesn't." There was another silence and then, after about ten minutes more of political discussion, we disbanded. The father returned the next day to his home and I was not invited to any of the later slametans. When I left the field about four months later, Karman's wife had still not entirely recovered from the experience, the tension between the santris and the abangans in the kampong had increased, and everyone wondered what would happen the next time a death occurred in a Permai family.

ANALYSIS

"Of all the sources of religion," wrote Malinowski, "the supreme and final crisis of life — death — is of the greatest importance" (1948:29). Death,

he argued, provokes in the survivors a dual response of love and loath-
ing, a deepgoing emotional ambivalence of fascination and fear which
threatens both the psychological and social foundations of human existence. The survivors are drawn toward the deceased by their affection for
him, repelled from him by the dreadful transformation wrought by death.
Funeral rites, and the mourning practices which follow them, focus
around this paradoxical desire both to maintain the tie in the face of
death and to break the bond immediately and utterly, and to insure the
domination of the will to live over the tendency to despair. Mortuary
rituals maintain the continuity of human life by preventing the survivors
from yielding either to the impulse to flee panic-stricken from the scene
or to the contrary impulse to follow the deceased into the grave:

> "And here into this play of emotional forces, into this supreme dilemma
> of life and final death, religion steps in, selecting the positive creed, the
> comforting view, the culturally valuable belief in immortality, in the
> spirit independent of the body, and in the continuance of life after
> death. In the various ceremonies at death, in commemoration and com-
> munion with the departed, and worship of ancestral ghosts, religion
> gives body and form to the saving beliefs . . . Exactly the same function
> it fulfills also with regard to the whole group. The ceremonial of death
> which ties the survivors to the body and rivets them to the place of
> death, the beliefs in the existence of the spirit, in its beneficent influ-
> ences or malevolent intentions, in the duties of a series of commemo-
> rative or sacrificial ceremonies — in all this religion counteracts the
> centrifugal forces of fear, dismay, demoralization, and provides the most
> powerful means of reintegration of the group's shaken solidarity and of
> the re-establishment of its morale. In short, religion here assures the
> victory of tradition over the mere negative response of thwarted instinct"
> (ibid.: 33–35).

To this sort of theory, a case such as that described above clearly poses
some difficult problems. Not only was the victory of tradition and culture
over "thwarted instinct" a narrow one at best, but it seemed as if the
ritual were tearing the society apart rather than integrating it, were disorganizing personalities rather than healing them. To this the functionalist has a ready answer, which takes one of two forms depending upon
whether he follows the Durkheim or the Malinowski tradition: social disintegration or cultural demoralization. Rapid social change has disrupted
Javanese society and this is reflected in a disintegrated culture; as the
unified state of traditional village society was mirrored in the unified
slametan, so the broken society of the kampong is mirrored in the broken
slametan of the funeral ritual we have just witnessed. Or, in the alternate
phraseology, cultural decay has led to social fragmentation; loss of a
vigorous folk tradition has weakened the moral ties between individuals.

It seems to me that there are two things wrong with this argument, no matter in which of the two vocabularies it is stated: it identifies social (or cultural) conflict with social (or cultural) disintegration; it denies independent roles to both culture and social structure, regarding one of the two as a mere epiphenomenon of the other.

In the first place, kampong life is not simply anomic. Though it is marked by vigorous social conflicts, as is our own society, it nevertheless proceeds fairly effectively in most areas. If governmental, economic, familial, stratificatory, and social control institutions functioned as poorly as did Paidjan's funeral, a kampong would indeed be an uncomfortable place in which to live. But though some of the typical symptoms of urban upheaval — such as increased gambling, petty thievery, and prostitution — are to some degree present, kampong social life is clearly not on the verge of collapse; everyday social interaction does not limp along with the suppressed bitterness and deep uncertainty we have seen focused around burial. For most of its members most of the time, a semiurban neighborhood in Modjokuto offers a viable way of life, despite its material disadvantages and its transitional character; and for all the sentimentality which has been lavished on descriptions of rural life in Java, this is probably as much as one could say for the village. As a matter of fact, it is around religious beliefs and practices — slametans, holidays, curing, sorcery, cult groups, etc. — that the most seriously disruptive events seem to cluster. Religion here is somehow the center and source of stress, not merely the reflection of stress elsewhere in the society.[6]

Yet it is not a source of stress because commitment to the inherited patterns of belief and ritual has been weakened. The conflict around Paidjan's death took place simply because all the kampong residents did share a common, highly integrated, cultural tradition concerning funerals. There was no argument over whether the slametan pattern was the correct ritual, whether the neighbors were obligated to attend, or whether the supernatural concepts upon which the ritual is based were valid ones. For both santris and abangans in the kampongs, the slametan maintains its force as a genuine sacred symbol; it still provides a meaningful framework for facing death — for most people the only meaningful framework. We cannot attribute the failure of the ritual to secularization, to a growth in skepticism, or to a disinterest in the traditional "saving beliefs," any more than we can attribute it to anomie.

We must rather, I think, ascribe it to a discontinuity between the form of integration existing in the social structural ("causal-functional") dimension and the form of integration existing in the cultural ("logico-

[6] For a description of a somewhat disrupted celebration of the end of the Fast holiday, Hari Raya (îd al-fitr) in Modjokuto, which shows many formal similarities to Paidjan's funeral, see Geertz, in press.

meaningful") dimension — a discontinuity which leads not to social and cultural disintegration, but to social and cultural conflict. In more concrete, if somewhat aphoristic terms, the difficulty lies in the fact that socially kampong people are urbanites, while culturally they are still folk.

I have already pointed out that the Javanese kampong represents a transitional sort of society, that its members stand "in between" the more or less fully urbanized elite and the more or less traditionally organized peasantry. The social structural forms in which they participate are for the most part urban ones. The emergence of a highly differentiated occupational structure in place of the almost entirely agricultural one of the countryside; the virtual disappearance of the semihereditary, traditional village government as a personalistic buffer between the individual and the rationalized central government bureaucracy, and its replacement by the more flexible forms of modern parliamentary democracy; the evolution of a multiclass society in which the kampong, unlike the village, is not even a potentially self-sufficient entity, but is only one dependent subpart — all this means that the kampong man lives in a very urban world. Socially, his is a *Gesellschaft* existence.

But on the cultural level — the level of meaning — there is much less of a contrast between the kampong dweller and the villager; much more between him and a member of the urban elite. The patterns of belief, expression, and value to which the kampong man is committed — his world-view, ethos, ethic, or whatever — differ only slightly from those followed by the villager. Amid a radically more complex social environment, he clings noticeably to the symbols which guided him or his parents through life in rural society. And it is this fact which gave rise to the psychological and social tension surrounding Paidjan's funeral.

The disorganization of the ritual resulted from a basic ambiguity in the meaning of the rite for those who participated in it. Most simply stated, this ambiguity lay in the fact that the symbols which compose the slametan had both religious and political significance, were charged with both sacred and profane import. The people who came into Karman's yard, including Karman himself, were not sure whether they were engaged in a sacralized consideration of first and last things or in a secular struggle for power. This is why the old man (he was a graveyard keeper, as a matter of fact) complained to me that dying was nowadays a political problem; why the village policeman accused the Modin not of religious but of political bias for refusing to bury Paidjan; why the unsophisticated Karman was astonished when his ideological commitments suddenly loomed as obstacles to his religious practices; why Abu was torn between his willingness to submerge political differences in the interest of a harmonious funeral and his unwillingness to trifle with his religious beliefs in the interest of his own salvation; why the commemorative rite oscillated between political diatribe and a poignant search for an adequate explanation of what had happened — why, in sum, the slametan religious pattern stumbled when it attempted to "step in" with the "positive creed" and "the culturally valuable belief."

As emphasized earlier, the present severity of the contrast between santri and abangan is in great part due to the rise of nationalist social movements in twentieth-century Indonesia. In the larger cities where these movements were born, they were originally of various sorts: tradesmen's societies to fight Chinese competition; unions of workers to resist plantation exploitation; religious groups trying to redefine ultimate concepts; philosophical discussion clubs attempting to clarify Indonesian metaphysical and moral notions; school associations striving to revivify Indonesian education; co-operative societies trying to work out new forms of economic organization; cultural groups moving toward a renaissance of Indonesian artistic life; and, of course, political parties working to build up effective opposition to Dutch rule. As time wore on, however, the struggle for independence absorbed more and more the energies of all these essentially elite groups. Whatever the distinctive aim of each of them — economic reconstruction, religious reform, artistic renaissance — it became submerged in a diffuse political ideology; all the groups were increasingly concerned with one end as the prerequisite of all further social and cultural progress — freedom. By the time the revolution began in 1945, reformulation of ideas outside the political sphere had noticeably slackened and most aspects of life had become intensly ideologized, a tendency which has continued into the post-war period.

In the villages and small town kampongs, the early, specific phase of nationalism had only a minor effect. But as the movement unified and moved toward eventual triumph, the masses too began to be affected and, as I have pointed out, mainly through the medium of religious symbols. The highly urbanized elite forged their bonds to the peasantry not in terms of complex political and economic theory, which would have had little meaning in a rural context, but in terms of concepts and values already present there. As the major line of demarcation among the elite was between those who took Islamic doctrine as the overall basis of their mass appeal and those who took a generalized philosophical refinement of the indigenous syncretic tradition as such a basis, so in the countryside santri and abangan soon became not simply religious but political categories, denoting the followers of these two diffuse approaches to the organization of the emerging independent society. When the achievement of political freedom strengthened the importance of factional politics in parliamentary government, the santri-abangan distinction became, on the local level at least, one of the primary ideological axes around which the process of party maneuvering took place.

The effect of this development has been to cause political debate and religious propitiation to be carried out in the same vocabulary. A koranic chant becomes an affirmation of political allegiance as well as a paean to God; a burning of incense expresses one's secular ideology as well as one's sacred beliefs. Slametans now tend to be marked by anxious discussions of the various elements in the ritual, of what their "real" significance is; by arguments as to whether a particular practice is essential or optional; by abangan uneasiness when santris lift their eyes to pray and santri uneasiness when abangans recite a protective spell. At death, as we have seen, the traditional symbols tend both to solidify individuals in the face of social loss and to remind them of their differences; to emphasize the broadly human themes of mortality and undeserved suffering and the narrowly social ones of factional opposition and party struggle; to strengthen the values the participants hold in common and to "tune up" their animosities and suspicions. The rituals themselves become matters of political conflict; forms for the sacralization of marriage and death are transformed into important party issues. In such an equivocal cultural setting, the average kampong Javanese finds it increasingly difficult to determine the proper attitude toward a particular event, to choose the meaning of a given symbol appropriate to a given social context.

The corollary of this interference of political meanings with religious meanings also occurs: the interference of religious meanings with political ones. Because the same symbols are used in both political and religious contexts, people often regard party struggle as involving not merely the usual ebb and flow of parliamentary maneuver, the necessary factional give-and-take of democratic government, but involving as well decisions on basic values and ultimates. Kampong people in particular tend to see the open struggle for power explicitly institutionalized in the new republican forms of government as a struggle for the right to establish different brands of essentially religious principles as official: "if the abangans get in, the koranic teachers will be forbidden to hold classes"; "if the santris get in, we shall all have to pray five times a day." The normal conflict involved in electoral striving for office is heightened by the idea that literally everything is at stake: the "if we win, it is our country" idea that the group which gains power has a right, as one man said, "to put his own foundation under the state." Politics thus takes on a kind of sacralized bitterness; and one village election in a suburban Modjokuto village actually had to be held twice because of the intense pressures generated in this way.

The kampong man is, so to speak, caught between his ultimate and his proximate concepts. Because he is forced to formulate his essentially metaphysical ideas, his response to such basic "problems" as fate, suffering, and evil, in the same terms as he states his claims to secular power, his political rights and aspirations, he experiences difficulty in enacting either a socially and psychologically efficient funeral or a smoothly running election.

But a ritual is not just a pattern of meaning; it is also a form of social interaction. Thus, in addition to creating cultural ambiguity, the attempt to bring a religious pattern from a relatively less differentiated rural background into an urban context also gives rise to social conflict, simply because the kind of social integration demonstrated by the pattern is not congruent with the major patterns of integration in the society generally. The way kampong people go about maintaining solidarity in everyday life is quite different from the way the slametan insists that they should go about maintaining it.

As emphasized earlier, the slametan is essentially a territorially based ritual; it assumes the primary tie between families to be that of residential propinquity. One set of neighbors is considered a significant social unit (politically, religiously, economically) as against another set of neighbors; one village as against another village; one village-cluster as against another village-cluster. In the town, this pattern has in large part changed. Significant social groups are defined by a plurality of factors — class, political commitment, occupation, ethnicity, regional origins, religious preference, age, and sex, as well as residence. The new urban form of organization consists of a careful balance of conflicting forces arising out of diverse contexts: class differences are softened by ideological similarities; ethic conflicts by common economic interests; political opposition, as we have been, by residential intimacy. But in the midst of all this pluralistic checking and balancing, the slametan remains unchanged, blind to the major lines of social and cultural demarcation in urban life. For it, the primary classifying characteristic of an individual is where he lives.

Thus when an occasion arises demanding sacralization — a life-cycle transition, a holiday, a serious illness — the religious form which must be employed acts not with but against the grain of social equilibrium. The slametan ignores those recently devised mechanisms of social insulation which in daily life keep group conflict within fixed bounds, as it also ignores the newly evolved patterns of social integration among opposed groups which balance contradictory tensions in a reasonably effective fashion. People are pressed into an intimacy they would as soon avoid; where the incongruity between the social assumptions of the ritual ("we are all culturally homogeneous peasants together") and what is in fact the case ("we are several different kinds of people who must perforce live together despite our serious value disagreements") leads to a deep uneasiness of which Paidjan's funeral was but an extreme example. In the kampong, the holding of a slametan increasingly serves to remind people that the neighborhood bonds they are strengthening through a dramatic enactment are no longer the bonds which most emphatically hold them together. These latter are ideological, class, occupation, and political bonds, divergent ties which are no longer adequately summed up in territorial relationships.

In sum, the disruption of Paidjan's funeral may be traced to a single source: an incongruity between the cultural framework of meaning and the patterning of social interaction, an incongruity due to the persistence in an urban environment of a religious symbol system adjusted to peasant social structure. Static functionalsim, of either the sociological or social psychological sort, is unable to isolate this kind of incongruity because it fails to discriminate between logico-meaningful integration and causal-functional integration; because it fails to realize that cultural structure and social structure are not mere reflexes of one another but independent, yet interdependent, variables. The driving forces in social change can be clearly formulated only by a more dynamic form of functionalist theory, one which takes into account the fact that man's need to live in a world to which he can attribute some significance, whose essential import he feels he can grasp, often diverges from his concurrent need to maintain a functioning social organism. A diffuse concept of culture as "learned behavior," a static view of social structure as an equilibrated pattern of interaction, and a stated or unstated assumption that the two must somehow (save in "disorganized" situations) be simpler mirror images of one another, is rather too primitive a conceptual apparatus with which to attack such problems as those raised by Paidjan's unfortunate but instructive funeral.

References Cited

LANDON, K.
 1949   Southeast Asia, crossroad of religions. Chicago.
MALINOWSKI, BRONISLAW
 1948   Magic, science and religion and other essays. Glencoe, Illinois, and Boston, Massachusetts.

8   E. A. WILKENING

Some Perspectives on
Change in Rural Societies

The problem of change has been of continuing interest to rural sociologists. However, most of the concern for change has been directed toward specific topics such as family living, farm technology, rural institutions, and industrialization. There has been little attempt to relate change in these specific areas to general theories of social change. This has probably been due no less to failings on the part of the students of rural life than to the inadequacy of existing theories of change.

In a recent article, Wilbert Moore, whom you will hear tomorrow night, attempts to show that social change is a respectable topic of concern for sociologists.[3] He would move the chapters on social change from the end to a more central position in textbooks of sociology. Talcott Parsons, after dealing with the structural aspects of society, has become more concerned with its dynamic aspects.[4] He is now teaching a seminar on "Societal Evolution," which is certainly an innovation in the curricula of sociology. These and many other efforts indicate a growing concern for the study of change on the part of sociologists.[5]

Anthropologists have continued to pursue the problem of change by means of studies of primitive and peasant societies.[6] Raymond Firth and

Reprinted from *Rural Sociology*, Vol. 29, March 1964, pp. 1–17, with permission of the author and the Rural Sociological Society. Footnotes abridged for this printing. Original reference numbers have been retained.

[3] Wilbert E. Moore, "A Reconsideration of Theories of Social Change," *American Sociological Review*, 25 (December, 1960), pp. 810–818.

[4] Talcott Parsons, "Some Considerations in the Theory of Social Change," *Rural Sociology*, 26 (September, 1961), pp. 219–239.

[5] For earlier contributors to the field, we are particularly indebted to: Emile Durkheim, *The Division of Labor in Society*, tr. from the French by George Simpson, Glencoe, Ill.: The Free Press, 1952; Pitirim Sorokin, *Society, Culture, and Personality*, New York: Harper & Brothers, 1947, p. 699; Moore, *op. cit.*; and W. F. Ogburn, *Social Change*, New York: Huebsch & Co., 1922.

[6] Ralph Linton, *The Study of Man*, New York: D. Appleton-Century Company, Inc., 1936; Bronislaw Malinowski, *The Dynamics of Cultural Change*, New Haven; Yale University Press, 1945; John Gillin, *The Ways of Man*, New York: Appleton-Century-Crofts, 1948; and Margaret Mead, *Cultural Patterns and Technical Change*, New York: Columbia University Press (A UNESCO Publication), 1953.

Homer Barnett have added new insights to the understanding of change as a function of the interaction of the individual with the group and its culture.[7] Biologists have also become interested in the applicability of certain principles of evolution to human society.[8]

At first there appears to be little in common with the different approaches to the study of change. This is in part due to differences in the conceptual and methodological tools used and in part to the different types of changes considered. It is the purpose of this paper to show that there are certain societal processes which provide a common framework for studying change. These processes pertain to changes in the structure and functions of social systems and to the relationship of social systems to other systems, including the physical and biological.

The processes are *specialization, integration,* and *adaptation.* They are felt to be most essential in understanding change at the level of the social system. Other processes such as diffusion, acculturation, learning, and problem solving, commonly discussed in connection with change, operate primarily at the individual or at the cultural level rather than at the level of the social system. While these processes are equally important, the development of a theory of change requires the consideration of what change is and how it occurs at the level of the social system before individual and cultural processes can be more fully understood.

THE NATURE AND DIRECTION OF CHANGE

Underlying most of the discussion of change is the assumption that change has direction. All agents and agencies of change make some judgment about what kind of change is "good" and what kind is "bad." But what is "good" for one society may be "bad" for another. Advanced societies have more material goods, live longer, and appear to gain more satisfaction with less toil than do the less advanced ones. As Moore indicates, the contributions of science and technology to the solution of human problems are accepted in the long run over less efficient solutions.[9] But, then, are technology and science the main criteria by which change is to be judged?

We can observe the direction of change by contrasting peasant society with modern rural society. Peasant society is characterized by self-sufficiency, a family-centered social structure, and limited participation in the world outside the village or locality. The time and effort spent per unit

[7] Raymond Firth, *Elements of Social Organization,* London: Watts & Co., 1951; and H. B. Barnett, *Innovation,* New York: McGraw-Hill Book Co., 1953.

[8] A. E. Emerson, "The Evolution of Adaptation in Population Systems" in *Evolution after Darwin,* vol. 1 of *The Evolution of Life,* edited by Sol Tax, Chicago: The University of Chicago Press, 1960, pp. 307–343.

[9] Moore, *op. cit.,* pp. 813.

of production is high, leaving little to exchange in the market for other goods and services. Because of constant threats to his family, to his crops, and to his way of life, the peasant is oriented toward security rather than toward innovation. He is motivated more by the desire to maintain and keep what he has than by the desire to expand and to improve his lot. As Heilbroner says:

> Indeed, a very large percentage of the human race today lives in . . . small virtually self-contained peasant communities which provide for their own survival with a minimum of contact with the outside world. This large majority of mankind suffers great poverty, but it also knows a certain economic independence. If it did not, it would have been wiped out centuries ago.[10]

Contrast this picture of the peasant with the modern commercial farmer. His production is specialized and oriented to market demands; he is dependent upon many specialized services; he makes frequent trips to urban centers; his children go to schools integrated with towns and cities; and only one out of five or less of his sons remains on the farm. While he may put in long hours of work, he produces enough to feed 20 to 25 families off the land. He has much greater opportunity than the peasant farmer to satisfy his material and nonmaterial wants. For example, an Australian farmer said that he would take on any new idea that would make more money but would not interfere with his golf. It is a mark of advancement that he can choose between making more money and enjoying his leisure time.

While we are concerned with change, we should keep in mind that most of man's effort and activity goes into maintenance of existing patterns of life rather than into changing those patterns. Most activities of the individual and of the social system perform a conserving rather than an innovating function. When farmers in a Brazilian community were asked with whom they discussed new practices, there was little response, since the concept of "new practices" was not a part of their thinking. Change is a luxury which many individuals and groups cannot afford because of the risks involved. The institutionalization of change, present in advanced societies, is the result of a long process of evolution itself.

STRUCTURAL DIFFERENTIATION AND FUNCTIONAL SPECIALIZATION

The process of specialization accompanied by a differentiation of social structure leads to the production of more goods and services with less effort. Hence, through specialization and division of labor, the self-sufficient

[10] Robert L. Heilbroner, *The Making of Economic Society*, Englewood Cliffs, N.J.: Prentice-Hall, Inc., 1962, p. 3.

peasant society is transformed into one in which there are many occupations, and whose products and services are exchanged through a barter or a money economy. In the traditional peasant society, farm and family are inseparable. Each is geared to the other in such a way that production and consumption activities are closely integrated. This is what makes peasant society so persistent and impregnable. But, this very close interdependence of family and farm in which one is limited by the other also makes for inflexibility and inefficiency in the attainment of individual and group goals. While the division of labor by sex and age, or even by caste, as in India, may be highly developed, there is little allowance for specialization according to the interests and abilities of individuals or of groups. Specialization leads to change when resources can be obtained from outside the family, and there is specialization in production among farmers as well as between farmers and other occupations.

This process is a condition of increasing specialization, but how does this process work? An Indian farmer was asked why he didn't use an additional irrigated plot which was available to him. He replied that he was producing enough rice for his family on his present plot, so why should he grow more? Apparently, using additional land would upset the delicate equilibrium of production and consumption involving the relationship between family members and other villagers. The shift to a market economy is a major "breakthrough" for this type of peasant society. Economic risk and social pressure await the person who attempts to expand his production for the market. But, as Firth indicates, with the provision of new alternatives and the freedom to choose them, changes will occur in the structure of the society.[11]

The market economy requires a shift from one enterprise to another on the part of those already marketing some of their products. This requires specialization over a period of time. Sanders relates the problem of shifting enterprises among Greek peasants.[12]

> When a farmer shifts from wheat to cotton or to rice, he makes more than an economic decision; he also determines much about family relationships in his home. Growing wheat calls for very different participation of the woman than does the cultivation of rice in irrigated fields . . . or if the family shifts from sheep raising to settled farming, the fate of the children is also apt to be different.

The introduction of commercial crops in many African societies is welcomed by those who need money to acquire goods observed in the cities. But, the introduction of cattle or tractor power for the cultivation of

[11] Firth, *op. cit.*, p. 40.
[12] Irwin T. Sanders, *Rainbow in the Rock: The People of Rural Greece*, Cambridge, Mass.: Harvard University Press, 1962, p. 298.

crops means a change in the roles of man and woman. Traditionally the woman has tended the crops. Also, in less differentiated societies, material items and services have a social as well as an economic value.[13] Firth relates the conflict on the part of the Maori farmer who has adopted European methods of agriculture, yet is expected to take the time off to attend the ceremonies and perform the rituals of the native group, thereby neglecting his farm.[14] In many developing societies change proceeds by the meshing of traditional customs with the requirements of a more specialized and differentiated society.

Now, considering the advanced countries, specialization is also occurring in many areas of rural life. There is evidence that specialized commodity organizations are becoming more important than the general farm organizations. Too many conflicts of interest develop within the general farm organizations to be effective in formulating agricultural policy. The shift from the one-room to the consolidated school, the closing of open-country churches to become part of larger parishes, the replacement of the general store in the hamlet or village with specialized stores in the larger towns are all a part of this process. The current concern for the small town in this country is a symptom of this process of specialization in educational, recreational, religious, and economic activities. With better means of transportation there is access to larger centers providing a better selection of goods and services. This problem is accentuated by the fact that there are fewer farmers and the size of their families is smaller.

The late Professor Kolb was among the contributors to the understanding of the process of specialization in rural life.[15] In his study of Walworth County, Wisconsin, he found that the trade centers, which at the time of C. J. Galpin's classical study provided all the essential services for the trade center community, had begun to specialize in certain services. Hence, as aspirations and the opportunities for their satisfaction expand, activities become more specialized within an expanded population base.

Another aspect of specialization is the provision of technical and professional services. Whether these are provided by the government or not, the problem is much the same. Among peasant societies the professionals are not likely to be agents of change. Even the "new elites," while motivated to promote change, find themselves a part of bureaucracies which have been geared to control and to serve functions and not to change or

[13] Indifference curves used by economists are based upon assumptions as to psychological elements of utility which are largely unknown.
    Firth, *op. cit.*, p. 128.
[14] Firth, *op. cit.*, p. 119.
[15] John H. Kolb, *Emerging Rural Communities*, Madison: The University of Wisconsin Press, 1959, pp. 158–184.

innovation functions.[16] Furthermore, specialization of the professional may not enable him to deal effectively with problems which have many ramifications. Specialized training is likely to result in greater difficulty in developing reciprocal relationships in societies not accustomed to specialized services. In order to be most effective, specialization of the change agent must proceed with specialization in the demands for services. This has implications for the recruitment, training, and definition of the role of the professional worker. Although this problem cannot be dealt with here, a statement by Arthur Lewis is appropriate. He states that the professional in poor countries must learn more social science than in the rich countries, since change is occurring more rapidly in the poor countries.[17] I would add that not only are changes occurring more rapidly but that changes in techniques are much more likely to involve social change in a peasant society than in an industrial society. The technician who does not take into account the social consequences of his innovations is likely to be surprised, frustrated, or even kicked out.

Specialization has been demonstrated in studies pertaining to the communication of information about innovations in agriculture. Farmers seek information about different problems from different sources.[18] There is also a distinction between the "instrumental" and the "integrative" or "expressive" leader. The innovator or instrumental leader in agriculture is usually not the same person as the leader in religious, educational, or public services. As farming becomes specialized, the informants and influentials also become specialized. This is in contrast to the less advanced agricultural community in which the local influential may be the source for all types of information.

Still another type of specialization to which considerable attention has been given in farm practice adoption research is the utilization of different sources of information at different stages in the process of adopting and innovation. Where the mass media are accessible for most farmers, these media tend to be the initial source for most new ideas in farming; other

[16] Richard F. Behrendt, "The Emergence of New Elites and New Political Integration Forms and Their Influence on Economic Development" in *Transactions of the Fifth World Congress of Sociology*, vol. 11 of *The Sociology of Development*, Louvain, France: International Sociological Association.

[17] W. Arthur Lewis, "Education for Scientific Professions in the Poor Countries," *Daedalus*, Proceedings of the American Academy of Arts and Sciences, 91 (Spring, 1962), p. 313.

[18] E. A. Wilkening, Joan Tully, and Hartley Presser, "Communication and the Acceptance of Recommended Farm Practices Among Dairy Farmers of Northern Victoria," *Rural Sociology*, 27 (June, 1962), pp. 116–197; and Snell Putney and Gladys Putney, "Radical Innovation and Prestige," *American Sociological Review*, 27 (August, 1962), pp. 548–551.

farmers are usually sought before deciding whether to adopt innovations; and experts or commercial dealers are frequently the source for specific and technical information about how to implement innovations.[19] While the sources utilized depend upon their accessibility and upon the type of innovation, the important point is that there is a specialization of communication channels in the process of technological as well as in other types of change. The recognition of this principle is likely to add to greater efficiency in the use of resources in promoting change.

THE PROCESS OF INTEGRATION

Specialization is of little value without the integration of the specialized functions into a larger social system. This is an aspect of change frequently not recognized by the promoters of change. Fals-Borda gave attention to this problem of integration in socio-cultural change in his study of Saucio, Colombia.[20] As Steward and Shimkin state, "Above all, the perpetuation of innovations is greatly influenced not only by their intrinsic merits and capabilities with the culture, but also by their relationship to the status, communication and educational systems of the society." [21] This suggests that the acceptance of innovations requires their integration into patterns with respect to time and space, with respect to status and role, and with respect to the symbolic and value systems of the society.

The type of the integrative mechanisms will vary with the level of development of the society. Here Durkheim's distinction between "mechanical" and "organic" solidarity is relevant. Mechanical solidarity is based upon the homogeneity of the members of the group, while organic solidarity is based upon the division of labor found in industrialized societies.[22] The first type depends upon a common heritage, norms, and activities; while the latter depends upon complementary roles and activities.

Rural sociologists have perhaps tended to give more attention to the integration of groups based upon similarities of interests and attitudes and less to integration of the "organic" type. This may have occurred because of the tendency to identify with the interests of the rural segment

[19] James H. Copp, M. L. Sill, and Emory Brown, "The Function of Information Sources in the Farm Practice Adoption Process," Rural Sociology, 23 (June, 1958), pp. 146–157; Everett M. Rogers and George M. Beal, "The Importance of Personal Influence in the Adoption of Technological Changes," Social Forces, 36 (May, 1958); and E. A. Wilkening, "Roles of Communicating Agents in Technological Change in Agriculture," Social Forces, 34 (May, 1956), pp. 361–367.

[20] Orlando Fals-Borda, Facts and Theory of Sociological Change in a Rural Social System, Bogota: Universidad Nacional de Colombia, Departmento de Sociologia, Monografias Sociologica, No. 2, 1960, p. 25.

[21] Julian Steward and Demitri B. Shimkin, "Some Mechanisms of Sociocultural Evolution," Daedalus, Proceedings of the Academy of Arts and Sciences, 90 (Summer, 1961), pp. 477–497.

[22] Durkheim, op. cit.

of society, its institutions and organizations. In our interest to elevate the level of one segment of society we have emphasized the values of rural life to offset unfavorable comparisons with urban life. This identification with one segment of society tended perhaps to keep us from taking a broader perspective upon the problems with which we are concerned.

The solidarity of peasant society is based upon a patriarchal, village-centered structure in which ownership and attachment to land is a central focus. With technology, transportation, and opportunities for urban employment the kinship-centered structure gives way to a class type of structure.

The process is documented in Hofstee's account of Dutch rural society.[23] Up to 50 years ago the relationship of farmer to farm laborer was a very personal one, with the laborer frequently living in a house on the farmer's property. The laborer regarded the farmer with respect and took a personal interest in the farm. Due to more opportunities for work off the farm and a desire for a more favored position in society, the relationships of farmer and farm laborer became strained. The present relationship is more that of employee-employer, and the laborer usually lives in town rather than on the farm. The changes in economic relationships have been accompanied by changes in the political alignments of the farm laborers and the secession of the "Reformed" Churches from the Dutch Reformed Church. The result is that the Dutch village has changed from one in which there was only one set of norms, opinions, and interests to one in which there are several.

The development from a family and locality basis of integration to a class society is one of the most important aspects of social change in this country. One of the earliest studies of this development was that by Walter Goldschmidt of the two communities in California.[24] In the large commercial farm community with the owners living in town and the farm workers living in the community there were cleavages between the two groups in social, political, and religious activities. In the family-farm community this cleavage did not exist.

In "Plainville," Gallaher finds that economic achievement rather than residence and lineage has become the most important factor in the assignment of status which is in conformity with the basis of social rank in the larger society. However, he did not find a well-established system of social classes as had been indicated by West in his study of the same community 15 years earlier.[25] Vidich and Bensman refer to "class" as an important

[23] E. W. Hofstee, *Rural Life and Welfare in the Netherlands*, The Hague: Government Printing and Publishing Office, 1957, p. 331.

[24] Walter Goldschmidt, *As You Sow*, New York: Harcourt, Brace and Company, 1947.

[25] Art Gallaher, Jr., *Plainville Fifteen Years Later*, New York and London: Columbia University Press, 1961, p. 197.

aspect of social structure in a New York community, but state that consumption patterns rather than production patterns are becoming the
determinants of class, again in keeping with the tendency in the larger
society.[26] Perhaps this development is characteristic of an affluent society
in which ceilings are placed upon economic status and styles of life become more important than one's contribution to the economic system. This
suggests that in the future social class based upon position in the productive system may become less important than at the present time.

In addition to the development of a class structure based upon similar
social and economic interests, there are other integrating structures accompanying change. For example, certain societies in Africa with centralized authority have adopted lasting changes more rapidly than have
those with more local autonomy.[27] All societies use the authority of the
state to a greater or lesser degree to bring about change. The question is
one of how much pressure centralized government can or should exert in
the form of rewards and punishment for integrating the specialized activities needed to foster change. It should be clear that authority without
legitimation by the people is not the issue. The issue is one of the role
of local, state, and/or national governments as well as of private institutions in regulating the exchange of goods and services among the various
segments of society. If societies are to obtain the products of the outside
world, they must contribute to the goods and services demanded by the
larger society, and abide by certain rules for their exchange.

One of the most extensive experiments in the use of external force and
incentives of shift from a self-sufficient peasant economy to an advanced
economy is China. According to Yang, "Regardless of whether the peasants' thoughts and attitudes underwent genuine transformation, there was
little doubt that a whole range of new social and political concepts on the
national level were being pressed into their consciousness, thus broadening the peasant mind from the narrow confines of the village world to
the national political order." [28] Yang observes, as of a few years ago, that
the transition is far from accomplished. While the peasants attempted to
conform to the expectations of the collectives or cooperatives, they returned to the deeply rooted family system when the cooperatives failed to
function. The condition of the well-kept subsistence plots was a clear contrast to the poorly operated cooperatives.

[26] Arthur J. Vidich and Joseph Bensman, *Small Town in Mass Society*, Princeton, N.J.: Princeton University Press, 1958, p. 78.
[27] Ethel M. Albert, "Socio-political Organization and Receptivity to Change:
Some Differences Between Ruanda and Urundi," *Southwestern Journal of Anthropology*, 16 (Spring, 1960).
[28] C. K. A. Yang, *A Chinese Village in Early Communist Transition*, Cambridge:
Massachusetts Institute of Technology Press, 1959, p. 75.

As rural society becomes an integral part of the economic, political, and social functioning of the larger society, greater attention needs to be given to the problem of integration. Schwarzweller and Brown have noted how the high school in eastern Kentucky has provided the most important linkage of the local community with the larger society.[29] While economic, political, and religious activities provide ties with the outside world, the effect of the high school with its middle-class, urban-trained teachers and its emphasis upon generalized knowledge has a greater integrating effect than other institutions.

Sports also provide integration by providing an outlet of expressive behavior and by providing for identification by the specialized groups within the larger community. Hofstee indicates that change after the War in Holland was accompanied by the organization of football clubs.[30] He observed that those slow to adopt football clubs were also slow to adopt other new ideas including membership in farm organizations and attendance at agricultural schools. Benvenuti also found that those farmers who participated in musical and other cultural affairs in Holland were the most progressive.[31] In Australia sports for farmers and townsmen alike are an "obsession," as an Australian put it. All types of sports — tennis, bowling, football, cricket, and golf — are followed by farmers, their wives, and children. These sports activities cut across town and country, party and class. It is somewhat surprising that the influence of sports and other recreational activities has only recently become the subject of study by sociologists in this country. Perhaps this is due, in part, to the low value of recreation in American rural life which stems from our puritanical tradition.

The problem of integration of rural and urban interests is one with which many rural sociologists have been concerned. Numerous studies have confirmed the inadequacy of local government and existing institutions and organizations to cope with these problems involving both town and country. The reluctance of local governmental units to become a part of integrated governmental structures and regional commissions has hindered progress in the handling of the problems of education, health, recreation, and the many other services needed in these areas. The extent to which resistance to such integration rests upon the unwillingness to give up local power and positions, upon a real conflict of interests among occupational and residential groups, or upon uncertainties and a lack of

---

[29] Harry Schwarzweller and James S. Brown, "Education as a Cultural Bridge Between Eastern Kentucky and the Great Society," *Rural Sociology*, 27 (December, 1962), pp. 357–373.

[30] Hofstee, *op. cit.*, p. 311.

[31] Bruno Benvenuti, *Farming and Cultural Change*, Netherlands: Van Gorcum, 1962.

knowledge of the problems and the means for their solution certainly needs further study.

The current Rural Areas Development program is the most recent attempt on the part of the federal government to provide a unified attack upon problems in rural areas. Several significant studies have already been made in connection with this program. Yet, more has been done on the nature and cause of the problems than on the structure and process of their solution.[32] One study has compared the structure and speed of organizing various watersheds in Kansas. The findings suggest that the integration of leadership and the presence of formal associations are among the characteristics which distinguish one of two areas which organized most rapidly.[33] It is my feeling that we know relatively little about the structure and process of integrating the many diverse local interests as well as the roles of the many specialized agencies in attacking area problems.

This seems to be the heart of the problem of community development the world over. Reports of the failure of community development programs, which appear to be as frequent as reports of their success, suggest that the problems of integrating local and national interests, levels of administration, and specialized services are major problems. The problem of planned change in rural areas is just as much, if not more, a problem of the integration of the many local and professional interests at all levels than of knowing what changes should be made or of having the facilities for making them. Until the problem of integration is solved, special interests, factions, and agency disputes will block the progress of the best intended programs.

The rational organization of a society must also be accompanied by the acceptance of the values supporting the new structure. Old values may be incorporated within the new structure, but in any event members of subordinate groups must see their own goals and interests being supported by the larger group. An anthropologist has observed how religious pursuits have changed in Ceylon to support a more universalistic approach to religious worship.[34] To the new intelligentsia, Buddha is perceived as a person who attained esteem by hard work and striving rather than as a god to be worshipped.

Religious systems play a central role in the integration process. In most societies the priest, minister, or other functionary is concerned with the

[32] Jon A. Doerflinger and D. G. Marshall, *The Story of Price County, Wisconsin*, Madison: Wisconsin Agr. Exp. Sta., Res. Bull. 220, June, 1960.

[33] Ralph E. Dakin, "Variations in Power Structures and Organizing Efficiency: A Comparative Study of Farm Areas," *Sociological Quarterly*, 3 (July, 1962), pp. 228–250.

[34] Michael Ames, "Ideological Systems and Social Change in Ceylon," *Human Organization*, 22 (Spring, 1963), pp. 45–53.

definition, interpretation, and alleviation of the anxieties of people. Changes in technology and in social relationships tend to increase these anxieties due to the breakdown of existing norms and values. Religious leaders frequently play an important role in the redefinition of norms and values in keeping with their integration into larger systems as was the case in Ceylon. The Calvinist ethic of salvation through the individual's own effort is one example of the role of religious dogma in the social and economic realm. The efforts of the priests and ministers to support social and economic reforms in Latin America appear to be quite significant. It would contribute greatly to our knowledge of the integrative mechanisms as a part of social change to know what type of religious activities provide integration in support of the changing social order and what types retard change. The function of religion in social change is probably related to the structure of the religious system as well as to its content. The growth of new religious sects in a changing society represents a differentiation process within religious bodies, while denominations, on the other hand, are integrating into unified bodies. But, perhaps the integration among religious groups is not as significant as the role which these bodies, separately or combined, play in the integration of changes in the physical, biological, economic, social, and political realms into the ideological, ethical, and value systems.

THE PROCESS OF ADAPTATION

The third process relating to change is that of adaptation. Adaptation is used by biologists to refer to the process whereby the individual, the species, and the community of plant and animal individuals and species adapt to each other and to their environment. This adaptation involves mechanisms for the regulation and control of the environment and for the self-regulation of the individual species as the units or subsystems of the larger system. This process, also known as "homeostasis," is defined by biologists as the self-regulation of optimal conditions for the maintenance and continuation on the system whether it be the individual or the species or the community of species.[35] The simplest illustration as applied to the individual is temperature control. The "homeostatic" mechanism of temperature control is so finely developed in man that life is possible only within a narrow range of temperature. Yet, because of this temperature control, he is able to function in a wide range of climatic conditions. According to biologists, the evolution of subhuman species is in the direction of greater self-regulation or homeostasis.[36]

[35] W. B. Cannon, *The Wisdom of the Body*, New York: W. W. Norton and Co., 1932.
[36] A. E. Emerson, *op. cit.*

Man has developed this principle of self-regulation beyond that of any subhuman species. One of the main contributions of George H. Mead is his statement that man interprets the stimuli which he receives and acts in accordance with his perception of the meaning of these stimuli upon others with whom he interacts.[37] In short, man constantly controls his behavior in order to control his environment for the attainment of future as well as for the attainment of present goals. This is what most of technological development does. Technology enables man to increase his control over the natural resources and thereby reduce the unpredictability of production. But, just as essential as technology for this control is the social organization and the culture, which are composed of the supporting ideas, norms, and values.

Some proponents of change assume that all that is necessary for change is that man increase his control over his physical and biological environment, without his seeing the need for the regulation of his own actions in view of these resources. The best illustration of this discrepancy is the effect of the spread of medical knowledge in the underdeveloped areas of the world. The result is that population increases faster than resources can be developed to supply food. Hence, the per capita consumption of food is much less in many parts of the world now than before the introduction of health and medical techniques. This is because of our orientation to the welfare of the individual or family rather than to that of the total society over a span of time. The resulting population explosion in all parts of the world, even in the U. S., has brought to us the realization that regulation of births is also essential for the welfare of the present as well as of future generations.

Let us consider again the family farm to illustrate the process of adaptation. What are the mechanisms of self-regulation and how are they related to specialization and differentiation? In the peasant economy regulation of production is primarily through the interaction of household and the farm. The products produced are based upon family needs and interests. Interaction between the man who usually cultivates the crops and the woman who prepares the food and clothing provides the regulating mechanism. Lack of communication between husband and wife, or at least between those responsible for tending the crops and livestock and those preparing them for use, no doubt is a frequent occurrence. Yet, in a subsistence economy the adjustments are likely to be made rather quickly because of the close association of producer and consumer. This is no doubt another reason for the pervasiveness of peasant society throughout the world. The interaction of producer and consumer is direct and effective.

[37] George H. Mead, *Mind, Self and Society*, Chicago: University of Chicago Press, 1934.

The shift from a subsistence to a market economy produces a much greater problem of self-regulation. The family conference is replaced by the market as the mechanism of regulation. Money and prices enter the picture. Production is geared to the anticipated market a year or more hence. The farmer's decision is complicated by the uncertainties of weather, pests, and disease over which he has limited control. Production for the market requires additional land, capital, and management ability for what are called "economies of scale." Mechanisms for the accumulation of resources are necessary. However, such accumulation frequently takes on other significance than its contribution to production. Because land ownership also means power, prestige, and privileges of many kinds, the mechanisms for adjusting land to the demands of production are frequently limited. Land is tied to the family, political, or other noneconomic considerations.

The imposition of a central management system usually fails to produce the desired result because of the lack of flexibility of the use of resources and of the allocation of rewards to the people who must make the effort.[38] Subsistence-oriented peasants are not easily influenced by the attraction of more profits when a large share of these go to other persons. Furthermore, the demand for consumption items tends to take precedence over capital accumulation needed for increased production, not only for the household but also for the ceremonies and feasts for the clan and village. The rewards in prestige and social approval for sharing products with kin and community may be greater than that which money can buy. In this instance ritual and ceremony connected with birth, marriage, death, and other occasions are the regulating mechanisms for production and distribution of resources. It is obvious that this kind of regulating mechanism does not take into account the needs and demands of the larger society.

As the farm and the household become more distinct as institutional units, the mechanisms for regulation become more complex. The farm may produce for the market, yet the family provides the land, labor, and capital for the most part. At this point regulation of the allocation of resources between farm and family takes on a different form. The husband as farm operator confronts the wife as manager of the household. Agreement as to the priority of expenditures affects both farm and household. A study of decision making among Wisconsin farm families suggests that the wife's involvement in farm decisions is associated with the adoption of innovations on the farm only when she agrees with her husband that the farm should receive priority over the household in the expenditure of extra funds which might become available. Because of the de-

[38] Erven J. Long, "The Family Farm in Domestic and Foreign Land Tenure Policy," *Journal of Farm Economics*, 64 (May, 1962), pp. 550–559.

pendence of the household upon the farm when resources are limited, progress in the farm enterprise must ordinarily precede that of the household. The recognition on the part of the wife of this process is conducive to change on the farm.

The regulation of the farm enterprise is essentially the entrepreneurial function. It is the farmer as entrepreneur who decides what combination of resources will bring the best return in view of the market or domestic demands. This may be in the form of the recombination of existing resources or the development of new techniques for the more efficient use of resources. While both perform a similar function, they require different qualities. New techniques may be imported, but as Hagen indicates, most techniques introduced from the outside must be modified and adapted to local institutions and to the specific enterprise.[39] According to Hagen, a prerequisite of innovation is creativity as well as the motivation to create, and these qualities are rooted in the early training and socialization of the child. The need for achievement[40] and for autonomy and the quality of creative imagination grow out of the early relationships of children to their parents. When deviant behavior resulting from such qualities appears in traditional societies, it tends to be suppressed.[41] According to Hagen and McClelland, it is only when the conditions for the development of such qualities and for their freedom of expression are present that innovations flourish. Accordingly, basic changes in the structure and functioning of societies do not occur quickly but over generations.

This view of social change, however, appears to be too pessimistic. It fails to recognize the importance of the forces of change acting in systems above that of the individual and of the family. While personality affects the commitment of the individual to behavior which involves risk in an attempt to satisfy his needs, innovations are introduced and accepted through the manipulation of resources and rewards by the community, by change agents, by the market system, by the government, and by international relationships. Nevertheless, there is little doubt that the early training of the child is an important process contributing to the kind of personalities conducive to entrepreneurial functions including self-regulation necessary for innovation, growth, and economic development.

Education is another means of self-regulation within a society. In peasant society education tends to emphasize the conserving function. For example, the Greek peasant is anxious for his children to have an education. Sanders quotes a Greek informant as saying: "Education is perhaps

---

[39] Everett E. Hagen, *On the Theory of Social Change: How Economic Growth Begins*, Homewood, Ill.: The Dorsey Press, 1962, pp. 30–34.

[40] David C. McClelland, *The Achieving Society*, Princeton: D. Van Nostrand Company, Inc., 1961.

[41] Hagen, *op. cit.*, p. 179.

the most prized goal in Greece." [42] Despite this he observes that by the third or fourth grade half of those who started school drop out. Further indictment of the educational system is that while the teachers develop among their pupils a strong feeling of national identity, they focus their attention on the glories of the past and upon learning about ancient Greece with little concern for the problems of today.[43] The schools directed by state and national governments, in most countries which have a high proportion of peasants, are not agents of change in rural society. While they provide a connection with the outside world and a channel of mobility for the sons and daughters of peasants to go to the city, they have little to offer the person who is concerned with improvement in agriculture, health, and living conditions in his own village or community. There is little feedback of local needs to the centralized school system which trains the teachers, sets the curricula, and sometimes gives the examinations. Where the school performs the function of passing on the tradition of the past rather than inculcating new ideas and skills, there is little association of educational level with progressive farming. The tendency of the educational system to alienate Indian youth from the problems of the Indian village is observed by Kusum Nair in her provocative book, *Blossoms in the Dust*.[44] Even in a progressive Australian dairy farming community and in a commercial dairy farming county of Wisconsin, educational level was not associated with the adoption of improved farm practices.

The challenge of the schools in the technologically advanced countries is just as great as in peasant societies. With only about one out of five of the sons of farmers returning to the farm, there is a great need for an educational system which prepares rural children as well as urban children for the rapidly changing occupational structure. The demand for professionals, technicians, and white collar jobs continues to expand, while machines take over the unskilled and semiskilled jobs.[45] Recent studies show that farm boys and girls are at a disadvantage in the labor market because of a lack of necessary knowledge and skills. The consolidation and integration of school systems have extended the opportunities for rural children, but there is much confusion over the kind of curricula needed. For those who have the ability, preparation in science, mathematics, language, and social sciences is necessary. For others, training in the manual skills might be provided through the extension of more voca-

[42] Sanders, *op. cit.*, p. 241.

[43] *Ibid.*, p. 249.

[44] Kusum Nair, *Blossoms in the Dust*, New York: Frederick A. Praeger, Inc., 1962.

[45] *Manpower Challenge of the 1960's*, Washington, D. C.: U. S. Department of Labor, 1960.

tional type sources. But, at all levels the emphasis must be upon the kind of education which will provide maximum flexibility for the individual as the job market changes.

CONCLUSIONS

In conclusion, one of the main assumptions underlying this discussion is that we must study change not only as a matter of individual choice and action but also as a function of social systems of various types and levels. The studies of farm practice adoption point more and more to the importance of group norms, pressures, and processes as the important determinants in the acceptance of innovations. These studies need to be conceptualized, designed, and understood within the "system" frame of reference. The unit of study should include cliques, communities, organizations, institutions, and other social systems as well as individuals and families.

The relevant dimensions of these systems include (a) social and other cleavages based upon characteristics such as kinship, nationality, religious, and political distinctions; (b) the structure of power and influence; (c) the extent and nature of social contact and communication within the systems; and (d) the extent and nature of linkage and communication between systems and subsystems.[46]

Secondly, measures of the more general processes or conditions of change must be developed. While measures of specific indications of change are needed, they need to be placed within the more general concepts, such as specialization, integration, and adaptation. This will enable us to measure change on a more objective basis instead of making value assumptions upon what is "good" or "bad" for the society we are studying or in which we are working. The difficulty with the development of such measures should not keep us from making the attempt. We already use measures of specialization and integration, but these ordinarily have not been defined as a function of the larger social systems of community, village, and society. While we have been concerned with reciprocal behavior, two-way communication, etc., few sociologists have utilized the concept of "self-regulation" or "feedback" as applied to social systems.

Finally, comparative studies are needed in which the dimensions of families, farms, communities, and other systems are studied as they relate to change. While comparative studies are fraught with many difficulties, they lead to new insights and raise new questions necessary to lead to generalizations about social change and how it occurs. The real challenge is that of developing culture-free measures of structure and process nec-

---

[46] The need for studying diffusion within and between social systems is suggested by Elihu Katz and others, in "Research in the Diffusion of Innovation," *American Sociological Review*, 28 (April, 1963), p. 241.

essary for arriving at scientific generalizations pertaining to the processes, prediction, and control of change.

Notes for
Further Reading

For a general analysis of community changes, see:

Martindale, D., "The Formation and Destruction of Communities," in George K. Zollschan and Walter Hirsch (eds.), *Social Change*. Boston: Houghton Mifflin Company, 1964, pp. 61–87.

Analyses of process of changes in community life in situations of historical change and modernization, can be found in:

Bascom, W., "Urbanization among the Yoruba," in Simon and Phoebe Ottenberg (eds.), *Cultures and Societies of Africa*. New York: Random House, 1960, pp. 255–283.

Dube, S.C., *India's Changing Villages* (Human Factors in Development). London: Routledge and Kegan Paul, 1958.

Gallo, A.G., "The Transformation of the Indian Community in New Spain 1500–1800," *Journal of World History*, Vol. 2, 1955, pp. 581–608.

Geertz, C., "Social Change and Economic Modernization in Two Indonesian Towns," in Everett E. Hagen, *On the Theory of Social Change*. Homewood, Ill.: The Dorsey Press, 1962.

Sobol, A., "The French Rural Community in the 18th and 19th Centuries," *Past and Present*, No. 10, Nov., 1956, pp. 78–96.

Yoshida, T., "Cultural Integration and Change in Japanese Villages," *American Anthropologist*, Vol. 65, No. 1, 1963, pp. 102–116.

For studies of changes in community life in modern settings, see:

Axelrod, M., "Urban Structure and Social Participation," *American Sociological Review*, Vol. XXI, 1956, pp. 13–18.

Hughes, E.H., *French Canada in Transition*. Chicago: University of Chicago Press, 1942.

Lynd, R.M. and H.M., *Middletown*. New York: Meridian Books, 1957.

Willmott, P., *The Evolution of a Community: A Study of Dagenham after Forty Years*. London: Routledge and Kegan Paul, 1963.

VII

Changes in Patterns
of Communication

The following article "Towards a Communication Theory of Modernization" by D. Lerner analyzes another aspect of processes of change of
modernizing societies. One of the basic features of the institutional structure of modern societies is the possibility that the processes and media of
communication may become more autonomous, independent sources of
change, of undermining the older patterns of social life, and of the development of new motivations, expectations, and aspirations. This, however,
may not insure the achievement of a stable institutional pattern, and of
orderly behavior regulated by adherence to stable norms.

This article emphasizes that it is perhaps the conflict between changing aspirations and the ability to absorb them institutionally that causes
tensions to become especially acute and articulate in situations of modernization.

The importance of the media of communication does not belittle the
importance of less formal, face-to-face channels of communication — it
only changes the relations between the formal and informal channels. The
study of the impact of different channels of communication is one of the
important foci of the comparative study of change in modernizing societies.

Toward a Communication Theory of
Modernization: A Set of Considerations

In the city of Teheran, in 1954, there were 36 registered "film companies."
Only one of these companies had actually produced, distributed, and exhibited any films; the other 35 had yet to complete production of their
first film.

How did this odd situation come about? The sequence of events begins
at Teheran University, where the old traditions of Iranian learning and
the new demands of Iranian modernization are locked in a deadly struggle, from which there issues annually a horde of distorted and disfigured
progeny called "graduates." These are the young men who, under the
compulsion to maintain or attain an elevated social status, attended or
evaded four years of magistral lectures and passed a final examination.
They have acquired certain standard adornments — i.e., acquaintance with
Persian history and Shariya law, familiarity with the glories of Persian art
and poetry, certified by the ability to quote yards of Firdausi and appropriate stanzas of Saadi.

These young men are all dressed up — but they have no place to go. They
are much too numerous to be absorbed into the traditional social orders
represented by government, army, priesthood. Already the Iranian government periodically discovers itself unable to meet the payroll of its
swollen bureaucracy. Nor is Iran developing an adequate supply of new
occupations deemed fitting for college graduates. These graduates face
only the bleak prospect of unemployment and underemployment. Accordingly they seek to occupy themselves in ways that will be amusing if not
rewarding. A half-dozen such graduates organize themselves around a 35
millimeter camera and form a "film company." But their outlook is dismal.
Most of them will never produce a film; those who do will never be able
to market it. It is unlikely that, even if they wish to show it free ·of
charge, their film will ever be seen beyond their circle of friends. There

Reprinted from "Toward a Communication Theory of Modernization: A Set of
Considerations" in Lucian W. Pye (ed.), *Communication and Political Development*. Princeton, N.J.: Princeton University Press, 1963. Pp. 327–50, with permission of the Princeton University Press.

are few cinemas in Teheran, and they are for commercial hire. Frustration and failure thus await most young Iranians who seek to make a career in the mass media.

The key factor in this unhappy situation is the uncertain and inadequate tempo of Iranian modernization. The supply of new life-opportunities does not keep pace with — is indeed steadily outpaced by — the burgeoning demands of the new literates. In 1958 I summarized the Iranian situation in the following terms, which remain cogent in 1962:

"Incorporation of new men is no easy task in a non-growth economy. Iran develops few of those constantly growing and changing occupational holes which embody young men in the elite structure. The clergy, the military, the bureaucracy — all these are charges on the public treasury, already overburdened and scarcely capable of expansion. The teaching corps is pitifully inadequate, but unlikely to multiply opportunities until Iran develops a modernizing economy in which literacy is an essential skill. Without an expanding business sector, there is little room for the lawyer and accountant, for the specialist in industrial management or labor relations, for the insurance broker or the investment manager, for the account executive or the public relations counsel. Advertising is stillborn and the mass media abortive. Where in Iran is 'the man in the gray flannel suit'? Whatever his unpopularity among Westerners wearied by opinion brokers, in Iran he would be a more useful stimulus to modernization than the agitational intellectual in a hairshirt of vivid hue.

"Given its limited absorptive capacity, Iran suffers from an overproduction of intellectuals. In a society about 90% illiterate, several thousand young persons go through the classical routines of higher education each year. Learning no skills that can be productively employed, these collegians seek outlets in the symbol-manipulating arts toward which their humanistic studies have oriented them. Their effort supplies a poignant instance of usable training rendered useless by its social environment — newspapers without readers that last a week or a month, film companies that never produce a film. The mass media, as distinctive index of the Participant Society, flourish only where the mass has sufficient skill in literacy, sufficient motivation to share 'borrowed experience,' sufficient cash to consume the mediated product. In Iran the mass media are anemic and with them, annually, die a thousand hopes." [1]

The thousand hopes that die in Iran each year are multiplied into millions throughout the underdeveloped countries around the world that exhibit communication malfunctioning in their efforts to modernize. What

[1] Daniel Lerner, *The Passing of Traditional Society*, Glencoe, Ill., The Free Press, 1958, p. 362.

is the common mechanism underlying these numerous cases where the communication gears fail to mesh with the motor of modernization? Various formulations have been offered us in the excellent chapters in this book. Each points to essential factors in a comprehensive theoretical understanding of the interaction between communications and political development. No paper achieves such a comprehensive theoretical understanding — a statement of such force as to suffuse us with the beautiful feeling of perfect illumination — as does a Newtonian account of the solar system as a *gravitational* system or a Wienerian account of all systems as *entropic* systems. It may be prudent at this stage of our knowledge about communication systems and social systems to aim at something less than this. The present effort is only a set of considerations drawn from an incomplete theoretical base.

The theoretical base of this paper is the proposition that modernity is an interactive behavioral system. It is a "style of life" whose components are *interactive* in the sense that the efficient functioning of any one of them requires the efficient functioning of all the others. The components are *behavioral* in the sense that they operate only through the activity of individual human beings. They form a *system* in the sense that significant variation in the activity of one component will be associated with significant variation in the activity of all other components.

The terseness of these definitions should not obscure the amplitude of the proposition, which is coterminous with the basic theorem of behavioral science — namely, that the operation of a social system, or sub-system, can be accounted for by the statistical distribution of behavioral components among its members. Thus a society operates its polity as a representative democracy if a large fraction of its members are qualified to vote, and regularly do vote, in elections that actually decide which of several competing candidates shall occupy the offices authorized to make decisions on specified issues of public policy. Thus a society operates its economy under capitalism in the measure that its members are free to decide how they shall use their own savings in order to maximize their own wealth. The statistical distribution of items that form the index — i.e., components of the system — determines how we characterize a society.

There is much that remains to be clarified in the behavioral conception of society. But it does, even in its present condition, authorize systematic efforts to locate linkages between personal and aggregative behavior, to establish reciprocity between individuals and institutions, to associate samples with systems. Operating on this authorization, this paper will seek to clarify how and why it comes about that the mass media function effectively only in modern and rapidly modernizing societies. We know empirically that this is so. Here we wish to develop further the idea that media systems and social systems have "gone together so regularly because, in some historical sense, they *had to* go together." [2]

I. THE NEW REVOLUTION OF RISING FRUSTRATIONS

These considerations arise from reflection on the course of the developing areas over the past decade. It has not been a smooth course nor a consistent one. It has falsified the predictions and belied the assumptions of those who foresaw the coming of the good society to the backward areas. Among its casualties has been the assumption that if some particular input was made — i.e., investment capital, industrial plant, agricultural methods, entrepreneurial training, or any other "key factor" preferred by the analyst — then a modernization process would be generated more or less spontaneously. This is a serious casualty. As the editor of this volume has aptly written in his introduction: "Faith in spontaneity died soon after the first ex-colonial people began to experience frustrations and disappointment at becoming a modern nation."

This bitter experience is new to us and requires careful evaluation — particularly by those among us who want the defeats of the past decade to help prepare the modest victories that may still be hoped for in the next. The decade of the 1950's witnessed the spread of economic development projects around much of the world. This process of reviving cultures, emerging nations, and new states was widely characterized as a "revolution of rising expectations." People throughout the backward and impoverished areas of the world suddenly acquired the sense that a better life was possible for them. Now leaders arose who encouraged their people to believe in the immanence of progress and the fulfillment of their new, often millennial, hopes. A great forward surge of expectancy and aspiration, of desire and demand, was awakened during the past decade among peoples who for centuries had remained hopeless and inert. This forward feeling was shared by those of us whose unchanging task is to understand.

A significantly different mood characterizes our thinking about the decade before us. While rising expectations continue to spread around the underdeveloped world, those of us who retain our interest in comprehending or programming rapid growth have learned that the ways of progress are hard to find, that aspirations are more easily aroused than satisfied. There is a new concern that the 1960's may witness a radical counter-

[2] *Ibid.*, p. 438. See also Daniel Lerner, "Communication Systems and Social Systems," *Behavioral Science*, Vol. 2, No. 4, October 1957; Gabriel A. Almond and James S. Coleman, *The Politics of the Developing Areas*, Princeton, Princeton University Press, 1960, p. 536; Lucian W. Pye, *Politics, Personality, and Nation Building*, New Haven, Yale University Press, 1962, p. 15.

formation: a revolution of rising frustrations. Observers have had to temper hope with prudence, for the limits on rapid growth have become more clearly visible through our recent experience. There is a seasoned concern with maintenance of equilibrium in societies undergoing rapid change. Soberly, responsible persons now tend to look for guidance less to ideology than to theory, less to dogma than to data. A new era of systematic research into the mysteries of modernization has opened.

Any restless area presents social research with an excellent opportunity to meet the need for a theoretically sound, empirically based exposition of the process called modernization. To be sure, there are particularities in each situation. Particularities can be wedded to generalizations, however, if we focus social research in any area upon those aspects of the process which it shares with other regions of the world that are seeking to accompany rapid economic growth with rapid social change. The political function in this process is to maintain stable controls over these rapid changes — i.e., to preside over a dynamic equilibrium.

In these terms there are two main sets of problems that confront the development process everywhere: mobility and stability. By mobility we mean the problems of societal dynamism; by stability we mean the problems of societal equilibrium. Mobility is the agent of social change. Only insofar as individual persons can change their place in the world, their position in society, their own self-image does social change occur. Social change is in this sense the sum of mobilities acquired by individual persons. (In a more precise sense, as we shall see, societal equilibrium can be expressed as a ratio between individual mobility and institutional stability.)

It is fairly well established that a systematic relationship between the major forms of mobility — physical, social, and psychic — is required for a modern participant society. As to sequence and phasing, we have only the Western experience to serve as full-scale model. Historically, in the Western world mobility evolved in successive phases over many centuries. The first phase was *geographic* mobility. Man was unbound from his native soil. The age of exploration opened new worlds, the age of migration peopled them with men transplanted from their native heath. The second phase was *social* mobility. Once liberated from his native soil, man sought liberation from his native status. The transplanted man was no longer obliged to be his father's shadow, routinized in a social role conferred upon him by his birth. Instead, as he had changed his place on the earth, so he sought to change his place in society.

The third phase was *psychic* mobility. The man who had changed his native soil and native status felt obliged, finally, to change his native self. If he was no longer his father's shadow, then he had to work out for himself a personality that fitted his actual life situation. Once he had changed his ancestral home and inherited status, thereby transforming his place and his role, he had to transform himself in ways suitable to his new situation. The acquisition and diffusion of psychic mobility may well be the greatest characterological transformation in modern history, indeed since the rise and spread of the great world religions. It is in any case the most fundamental human factor that must be comprehended by all who plan rapid economic growth by means of rapid social change. For psychic mobility — what we have elsewhere called empathy — is the mechanism by which individual men transform themselves in sufficient breadth and depth to make social change self-sustaining.[3]

This Western experience is what gave us that faith in spontaneity which Professor Pye assures us died a little while ago. We assumed that in any country that was given the right amount of investment or training or whatnot empathy would rise and mobility would be accelerated — and the good society would be attained sooner or later. But the good society can only be attained later in the measure that advances are made to attain it at each stage, for in development terms the long run can only be a sequence of short runs. Hence stability is essential. The past decade has taught us that mobility, while indispensable to rapid social change, is not enough. It is a necessary but not sufficient condition of growth. Since mobility is a seeking for something better, it must be balanced by a finding — as, in equilibrium, a demand must be balanced by a supply. It is the continuing failure of many transitional societies to maintain the balance of psychic supply-and-demand that underlies the new revolution of rising frustrations.

II. THE WANT:GET RATIO

The spread of frustration in areas developing less rapidly than their people wish can be seen as the outcome of a deep imbalance between achievement and aspiration. In simple terms, this situation arises when many people in a society want far more than they can hope to get. This disparity in the want:get ratio has been studied intensively in the social science literature in terms of achievement and aspiration. The relationship we here propose for study can be expressed by the following equation (adapted from an ingenious formula of William James[4]):

$$\text{Satisfaction} = \frac{\text{Achievement}}{\text{Aspiration}}$$

This formula alerts us to the proposition that an individual's level of sat-

[3] Daniel Lerner, The Passing of Traditional Society, p. 43. Also K. Gompertz, "The Relation of Empathy to Effective Communication," Journalism Quarterly, xxxvii, Autumn 1960, pp. 533–546.

[4] William James, Psychology: Briefer Course, New York, Holt, 1923, p. 187.

isfaction is always, at any moment of his life, a ratio between what he wants and what he gets, i.e., between his aspirations and his achievements. A person with low achievement may be satisfied if his aspirations are equally low. A person with high achievement may still be dissatisfied if his aspirations far exceed his accomplishments. Relative deprivation, as has been shown, is the effective measure of satisfaction among individuals and groups.

It is a serious imbalance in this ratio that characterizes areas beset by rising frustrations. Typically in these situations the denominator increases faster than the numerator — i.e., aspiration outruns achievement so far that many people, even if they are making some progress toward their goal, are dissatisfied because they get so much less than they want. Indeed, in some developing countries aspirations have risen so high as to annul significant achievements in the society as a whole.

How does such an imbalance in the want:get ratio occur? How can it be prevented or cured? What, in short, are the social institutions that affect the level of aspiration, the level of achievement, and the ratio between them? There are six institutions which function as the principal agencies of social change (or its inhibition): the economy, the police, the family, the community, the school, the media.

About the first five we can be very brief. If the economy can be made to supply all the opportunities needed to maintain reasonable equilibrium between achievements and aspirations — if the want:get ratio can be balanced by simply supplying all that people want — then there is no problem of frustration. Everyone is happy. Similarly, if the frustrations that arise are settled simply by police methods, then also there is no problem — at least, not for social research. Social research has little to contribute in situations of over-achievement or under-aspiration. Where riches outrun wants, where coercion inhibits desires, there social research is not needed. In most transitional societies that concern us, however, neither of these conditions obtains.

A more complex agency of social change is the family. Typically in developing areas the family acts as an instrument of conservatism and the retardation of change. It acts also, however, as an instrument of balance. To the degree that mobility involves the breaking of traditional family ties (and I believe the degree is high), this is a built-in destabilizer of the modernization process. How to replace the stability of traditional family ties by other methods is a deep problem of social equilibrium under conditions of rapid change.

Similarly, the community may act as a powerful force to promote or impede balanced growth. Here the force hinges upon the individuals who function as activators and enthusiasts of modernization. Where these people emerge and prevail, communities tend to become positive agents of the purpose that modernization seeks to accomplish. Otherwise, in the absence of effective activators and enthusiasts, the coalition of adversaries and indifferents that forms within every transitional community will impede growth and disrupt equilibrium.

The schools, under conditions of modernization, are necessarily instruments of social change. They must teach what is new and modern, what is desirable and obtainable, because they have no other curriculum worth supporting. There are of course important variations in the effectiveness with which different schools produce modernizers and their products serve modernization. We shall not discuss schools further here, despite their importance, because their institutional role and behavioral function — in our model of modernization — can be handled as a variant of the mass media in the communication process.

The mass media, finally, are a major instrument of social change. They make indispensable inputs to the psycho-political life of a transitional society via the minds and hearts of its people. Theirs is the critical input to satisfaction in emerging nations and to citizenship in new states. To perceive the communication crux of modernization, we must consider deeply three propositions: (1) that the mass media bring new aspirations to people — and then, since the empathic individual imagination quickly (logarithmically it appears)[5] outruns societal achievement, it brings dissatisfaction conceived as frustration of aspiration; (2) that, despite the now-evident risks of frustration, the mass media continue to spread around the world — inexorably and unilaterally; (3) that modernization — conceived as the maximization of satisfaction — can succeed (achieve more at less cost) if, and only if, a clarifying communication theory and practice are activated.

On the first proposition I have already written so much that I shall simply incorporate in this paper conclusions which any interested reader can pursue further in my (and other) published work.[6] On the second point I have published descriptive studies of the inexorable and unilateral spread of mass media around the world, showing that no society, once it acquires a media system, does go back to an oral system of communication.[7] In the next section of this chapter I want to explore *why* this is so. Then we shall turn to the third — and crucial — proposition about communication theory and practice.

[5] This refinement of my basic theory I owe to my student Howard Rosenthal. See his "A Statistical Approach to Comparative Politics" (M.I.T. CENIS document number C/62-9, 1962)....

[6] See footnote 2.

[7] See Daniel Lerner, "Communication Systems and Social Systems."

III. HOW AND WHY THE MASS MEDIA SPREAD

If the mass media are to have some significant effect on modernization and democratic development — whether to facilitate or impede these desiderata — the first condition is that the mass media must spread. For, if the mass media do not spread, then we have no problem to discuss. We thus consider the question: what conditions determine whether the mass media spread?

One major condition is economic: the level of economic development in a country determines whether the mass media spread. All industrially developed countries produce mass media systems. No pre-industrial country produces mass media systems. Between these extremes lie the range of cases that interest us here, i.e., the developing nations. Here the general rule is that mass media spread in a direct and monotonic relationship with a rising level of industrial capacity. Where this rule applies, in general the spread of the mass media facilitates modernization. Where the rule does not apply, one may expect to find that the spreading mass media impede (or, perhaps more accurately, "deviate") modernization. Why does this simple rule have such general force as is here claimed?

The reasoning is clear if we consider information as a commodity. It is produced, distributed, and consumed like all other commodities. This brings information within the rule of the market. Notably, the supply-demand reciprocal comes into operation. This means that, to evaluate the functioning of a communication sub-system within a societal system, it is essential to consider — it may even be wise to begin with — the conditions that determine the efficient functioning of all economic processes: the capacity to produce and the capacity to consume.

We shall consider each of these briefly. Our discussion will draw its substance from the market economy model of the modern Western nations. It is in these countries, where the mass media developed in the private sector, that the mass media spread first historically, and where they remain today the most widespread in quantity of both production and consumption. Any account of this process that wishes to be relevant to happenings in the mass media around the world today must provide some reasonable explanation for the variant economic evolution of the mass media in the Communist countries and the developing countries. The Soviet system provides some especially interesting deviations from the rule of supply and demand, e.g., the political rule of enforced supply and acquiescent demand for a social commodity taken out of the economic market place. Events in the developing countries, such as India and Egypt, do not yet form a "system," but they do alert us to the possibility of new ways of handling information that differ significantly from the historic evolution in the modern West. We shall therefore try to frame our discussion in categories that *must* apply to the operation of mass media whether a country be capitalist, Communist, or neutralist.

Capacity to Produce. There must be a capacity to produce. No country — whether its ideology be Hamiltonian, Stalinist, or Gandhian — can produce in formation via mass media until it has an economic capacity to construct and maintain the physical plant of the mass media. I have made a simple checklist of the items needed to produce mass media products. This checklist is neither precise nor comprehensive. It is simply a reminder of what it has taken historically and what it takes today to produce information via the mass media. A glance will indicate how much more complex this list would become if one were considering the most efficient means of producing information according to strict considerations of economic optima. But such considerations lie far outside the present purview of developing countries. For these countries the simple checklist will do.

CAPACITY TO PRODUCE: A CHECKLIST

1. Plant: Buildings
                 Utilities (power, light, water)
                 Facilities (studios, workshops, offices)

2. Equipment: Books (linotype)
                 Newspapers (rotary)
                 Magazines (rotogravure)
                 Movies (film, camera)
                 Radio (amplifier, transmitter)
                 Television ("picture tube")
                 [Future standard equipment: satellites]

3. Personnel: Copy producers (reporters, scripters, features)
                 Copy presenters (actors, printers, "layout")
                 Managerial corps (editor, publisher, producer,
                    director)

The items required to produce information via the mass media are grouped under the three categories of plant, equipment, personnel. The three categories, as well as the items listed within them, are arranged in ascending order of complexity. They may even be construed as a scale upon which rising levels of economic capacity could be calibrated. Thus, if one thinks of the contemporary United States, it may seem too rudimentary to list the "plant." Yet efforts to spread the mass media in the developing countries have foundered, and continue to founder today, on just the three items listed in this category.

Even the item of buildings is a large hurdle and frequent stumbling-block. For one thing, buildings of adequate shape and size do not exist in most of the villages and towns and small cities of the developing countries. The mass media are perforce restricted to the capital cities for just this reason. But even such a capital city as Teheran, as we have seen, does not have enough buildings of the right shape and size to permit production or consumption of many full-length movies. The buildings in which the mass media operate must be provided with efficient utilities, such as power, light, water. How could a proper newspaper operate in Teheran without efficient telephonic communication, without regular telephone links to the great oil refineries at Abadan, to the summer and winter residences of the Shah, to other capitals of the world — not to mention the electronic equipment needed for receiving the huge volume of daily news files coming from the international press services? Yet which of us does not remember some amusing or frustrating incident connected with his use of the telephone in a rapidly developing country? Which of us has not witnessed the inhibiting, and sometimes paralyzing, restrictions placed upon the mass media in these countries by the inadequacy of their facilities? Of the thirty-six film companies in Teheran, only one had studios. This was the only company that had managed to produce a full-length feature film.

The varieties of equipment required by the mass media are manifold, complicated, and expensive. I have listed the principal media in the historic order of their evolution, which corresponds also to the complexity of the equipment they required at the time their major development occurred. Thus the book publishing industry was able to develop on the basis of the simple linotype machine. A further technological advance made possible the spread of the mass circulation daily newspaper, namely the rotary press. Illustrated magazines were a medium of elite communication because of their cost until the development of rotogravure machines made possible the cheap production of millions of copies of illustrated monthlies and weeklies. Similarly, the rapid development in our century of movies, radio, and television as industries hinged upon the capacity of American industry to produce at acceptable prices the mechanical and electronic equipment which is indispensable to the functioning of these mass media. The communication revolution of our time was technological before it became anything else. It is not implausible that in our century communication satellites will become standard equipment for the efficient functioning of mass media systems in many countries throughout the world.

The economic level of any country hinges also upon the quantity and quality of its skilled personnel. Particularly in the mass communication industries the capacity to produce hinges upon the availability of a corps of communicators, i.e., a substantial body of personnel trained in the array of special skills required for immediate production. Needed first of all are the skills that produce copy — whether it be for the news columns of a daily paper, a feature article in a weekly magazine, the script of a radio program, or the scenario of a movie or television show. Consider in passing the variety of features that fill the pages of every major daily newspaper. What a great variety of tastes, skills, and interests are needed to produce all this copy! Reflect for a moment that the man who has written a novel rarely turns out to be the man best equipped to adapt his own work for production as a movie. The man who does this may well be a person of much less creative talent but with superior specialized skill in "scripting." Consider the further array of skills needed to present copy, after it has been produced, to the consuming public. Actors do this for the spoken word, printers for the written word. But consider the extremely specialized skill required for that essential presentation function performed by the so-called "layout man." To make such large enterprises as a daily newspaper, a radio station, or a film company operate efficiently, a skilled managerial corps is also necessary. These are the editors and publishers, the producers and directors who are the kingpins of the mass communications industries. Without these many and varied persons the mass media have no capacity to produce.

If we simply reflect on the developing countries we know best in these terms, we promptly perceive that these conditions may well determine whether the mass media will spread. In reflecting further on the central question — whether the spread of the mass media will facilitate or impede modernization — we must take account of another condition: the capacity to consume.

Capacity to Consume. Three factors determine whether the capacity to consume media products spreads — and how fast — in any country: cash, literacy, motivation. There is a simple side to this matter. A person needs cash to buy a radio, a cinema ticket, a newspaper. If a newspaper costs as much as a loaf of bread, and if his ready cash is in a chronic state of short supply, then there is a diminishing probability that a person will consume newspapers. On the same simple level: only a literate person *can* read a book, paper, or magazine, and only a motivated person *wants* to read. The media flourish therefore in the measure that their society equips the individuals with cash, literacy, and motivation to consume their products.

There is a more complex sociology, however, that underlies each of these factors and their reciprocal interaction. It is no accident that the mass media developed in the monetized sector of every economy. The barter of country newspapers against farmers' produce or artisans' products was a brief and transitory phase — occasionally magnified in the sentimental memoirs of superannuated country editors. The media grew in the monetized sector because this is the distinctively modern sector of every economy. The media, as index and agent of modernization, *had* to grow in the sector where every other modern pattern of production and consumption was growing or else remain stunted.

The efficient operation of a money economy was made possible only by a great transformation in the thoughtways and life-ways of millions of people. Historically, in any society the "sense of cash" is an acquired trait. It has to be learned, often painfully, by a great many people before their society can negotiate the perilous passage from barter to exchange. Consider, for example, this sentence on the traditional Anatolian peasantry by Professor H. A. R. Gibb: "We may suppose the *re'aya* to have been animated hardly at all by any idea of gain, and to have worked their land with a minimum of effort and very little knowledge." [8]

Gain, effort, knowledge — these are huge categories of discourse. For any adequate comprehension of the personality transformation which accompanied the shift from barter to cash in contemporary Turkey we are obliged to take these large terms in their historical sense. What has been acquired in one generation among a population that had always been ignorant and indifferent is precisely the sense of gain, effort, knowledge which came over centuries to guide personal behavior in the modern participant society of the West.

Cash is an essential solvent in modern life, and the achievement of rising per capita income distribution is a major objective of modern societies. Here the political and sociological problems of the developing countries become intertwined with their economic problems. Economies long caught in the vicious circle of poverty cannot easily break through into the modern industrial system of expanding production of goods and services. This fact reflects no inherent and inevitable distaste for the good things of life among developing peoples. It reflects rather the difficult communication process — which in the West occurred over several centuries — of stimulating desires and providing means for satisfying them where neither desires nor facilities have previously existed. Westerners engaged in economic development problems have only recently recognized that, once a start is made, the reciprocity between desires and facilities tends to operate in the new nations as elsewhere.

Consumption of media products is thus an economic function, but it performs simultaneously several other functions that are sociological, psychological, and political. Literacy is a technical requirement for media consumption. But literacy, once acquired, becomes a prime mover in the modernization of every aspect of life. Literacy is indeed the basic personal skill that underlies the whole modernizing sequence. With literacy

[8] Hamilton A. R. Gibb and H. Bowen, *Islamic Society and the West*, London, Oxford University Press, 1950, Vol. 1, Part 1, p. 244.

people acquire more than the simple skill of reading. Professor Becker concludes that the written word first equipped men with a "transpersonal memory";[9] Professor Innis writes that historically "man's activities and powers were roughly extended in proportion to the increased use of written records." [10] The very act of achieving distance and control over a formal language gives people access to the world of vicarious experience and trains them to use the complicated mechanism of empathy which is needed to cope with this world. It supplies media consumers, who stimulate media production, thereby activating the reciprocal relationship whose consequences for modernization we have noted. This is why media participation, in every country we have studied, exhibits a centripetal tendency. Those who read newspapers also tend to be the heaviest consumers of movies, broadcasts, and all other media products. Throughout the Middle East illiterate respondents said of their literate compatriots: "They live in another world." Thus literacy becomes the sociological pivot in the activation of psychic mobility, the publicly shared skill which binds modern man's varied daily round into a consistent participant lifestyle.

Literacy is in this sense also a precondition for motivation. People who can read usually do read — as, indeed, they consume more of all the audio-visual products of the media (the well-known "centripetal effect") and participate more fully in all the modernizing activities of their society. What is required to motivate the isolated and illiterate peasants and tribesmen who compose the bulk of the world's population is to provide them with clues as to what the better things of life might be. Needed there is a massive growth of imaginativeness about alternatives to their present life-ways, and a simultaneous growth of institutional means for handling these alternative life-ways. There is no suggestion here that all people should learn to admire precisely the same things as people in the Western society. It is suggested, much more simply, that before any enduring transformation of the vicious circle of poverty can be started, people will have to learn about the life-ways evolved in other societies. What they subsequently accept, adapt, or reject is a matter which each man will in due course decide for himself. Whether he will have the capacity to reach a rational decision hinges, in turn, upon the fullness of his participation in the modernizing process as it works through every sector of his personal and social life. The final test comes in the arena of political participation.

Mass Media and Political Democracy. Democratic governance comes late historically and typically appears as a crowning institution of the participant society. In countries which have achieved stable growth

[9] Carl L. Becker, *Progress and Power*, Stanford, Stanford University Press, 1936.
[10] Harold Adams Innis, *Empire and Communications*, Oxford, Clarendon Press, 1950, p. 11.   •

at a high level of modernity the literate individual tends to be the newspaper reader, the cash customer, and the voter.

The media teach people participation of this sort by depicting for them new and strange situations and by familiarizing them with a range of opinions among which they can choose. Some people learn better than others, the variation reflecting their differential skill in empathy. For empathy, in the several aspects it exhibits, is the basic communication skill required of modern men. Empathy endows a person with the capacity to imagine himself as proprietor of a bigger grocery store in a city, to wear nice clothes and live in a nice house, to be interested in "what is going on in the world" and to "get out of his hole." With the spread of curiosity and imagination among a previously quietistic population come the human skills needed for social growth and economic development.

· The connection between mass media and political democracy is especially close. Both audiences and constituencies are composed of participant individuals. People participate in the public life of their country mainly by having opinions about many matters which in the isolation of traditional society did not concern them. Participant persons have opinions on a variety of issues and situations which they may never have experienced directly — such as what the government should do about irrigation, how the Algerian revolt could be settled, whether money should be sent to Jordan or armies to Israel, and so on. By having and expressing opinions on such matters a person participates in the network of public communication as well as in political decision.

The mechanism which links public opinion so intimately with political democracy is reciprocal expectation. The governed develop the habit of having opinions, and expressing them, because they expect to be heeded by their governors. The governors, who had been shaped by this expectation and share it, in turn expect the expression of *vox populi* on current issues of public policy. In this idealized formulation of the relationship, then, the spread of mass media cannot impede but can only facilitate democratic development.

But ideal types do not always match perfectly with their empirical instances. In the developed democracy of the United States, for example, the capacity to produce information via mass media is virtually unlimited. The capacity to consume media products — thanks to an abundant supply and widespread distribution of cash, literacy, motivation — is unparalleled anywhere in human history. The production-consumption reciprocal has operated efficiently on a very high level over many decades. Yet as American society presented the world with its most developed model of modernity, certain flaws in the operation of the system became apparent. I do not speak of the Great Crash of 1929 — which exhibited a merely technical flaw in management of the economic sub-system. I speak of a much deeper flaw in the participant system as a whole, i.e., the emergence

of non-voting as a political phenomenon. A generation ago Harold Gos-
nell called our attention to this danger. In recent years an alarmed David
Riesman has generalized this phenomenon to the larger menace of political apathy. If Americans were really suffering from widespread apathy
about their public life, then a cornerstone of our media-opinion system
would be crumbling — namely, in our terms, the cornerstone of motivation. (We note in passing that in the developed democracy of France only
a short while ago leading thinkers and scholars convened for solemn discussion of political apathy in France — of all places!)

If one danger to developed democracies comes from literate nonvoters,
the parallel danger to developing democracies comes from the reverse
configuration, i.e., *non-literate voters!* Can universal suffrage operate efficiently in a country like India or Egypt which is 90 per cent illiterate? Can
the wise Jeffersonian concept of a literacy test for voters be completely
ignored nowadays because we have radio? President Nasser has proffered
a counter-doctrine for the developing countries, to wit: "It is true that
most of our people are still illiterate. But politically that counts far less
than it did twenty years ago. . . . Radio has changed everything. . . .
Today people in the most remote villages hear of what is happening
everywhere and form their opinions. Leaders' cannot govern as they once
did. We live in a new world." [11]

But has radio really changed everything? When illiterate "people in the
most remote villages hear of what is happening everywhere," what do they
really hear? They hear, usually via the communal receiver at the village
square in the presence of the local elite, the news and views selected for
their ears by Egyptian State Broadcasting (ESB). Their receivers bring
no alternative news from other radio stations. Being illiterate, they can
receive no alternative news and views from newspapers and magazines
and books published anywhere.

In terms of personal achievement almost nothing happens to these
"people in the most remote villages" by way of Radio Cairo: broadcasting
now supplies them with the kind of rote learning each acquired by mem-
orizing the Koran (which he could not read) in childhood. But in terms
of personal aspiration nearly everything happened to these people when
radio came to their remote villages. For the first time in their experience
— both the experience of centuries inherited through their parents and
their own lives — these isolated villagers were invited (and by none less
than their rulers!) to participate in the public affairs of their nation.

The invitation carried with it, however, none of the enabling legislation
needed to make radio-listening an integrative agent of modernization. In
a modern society the radio listener is also the cash customer and the
voter. In the remote villages of Egypt, when the government inserted

[11] Gamal Abdul Nasser, *Egypt's Liberation*, Washington, D.C., Public Affairs
Press, 1955.

radio into the community, nothing else changed in the daily round of life
— except the structure of expectations. This is the typical situation that
over the past decade has been producing the revolution of rising frustrations. The mass media have been used to stimulate people in some sense.
It does so by raising their levels of aspiration — for the good things of
the world, for a better life. No adequate provision is made, however, for
raising the levels of achievement. Thus people are encouraged to want
more than they can possibly get, aspirations rapidly outrun achievements,
and frustrations spread. This is how the vicious circle of poverty operates
in the psychological dimension.

The impact of this psychic disequilibrium — its force as a positive impediment to modernization — has been disclosed by Major Salah Salem,
the youthful Minister of National Guidance who tried to run the Egyptian
mass media during the contest for power between Naguib and Nasser.
Major Salem, finding his problems of national guidance insoluble, finally
solved them by voluntarily locking himself in jail. There he prepared a
memoir of his own frustration in the impossible task of converting an inert
and isolated peasantry into an informed and participant citizenry by the
mass media alone. Major Salem concludes: "Personally I am convinced
that the public was wrong." [12]

In similar vein, Nasser has written retrospectively: "Before July 23rd
I had imagined that the whole nation was ready and prepared, waiting
for nothing but a vanguard to lead the charge. . . . I thought this role
would never take more than a few hours . . . — but how different is the
reality from the dream! The masses that came were disunited, divided
groups of stragglers. . . . There was a confirmed individual egotism. The
word 'I' was on every tongue. It was the solution to every difficulty, the
cure for every ill." [13]

These judgments by leaders who were frustrated in their aspiration for
quick and easy modernization reveal why transitional Egypt — in the
dozen years since its liberation — has been so deeply frustrated. Can "the
people," in Salem's sense, ever really be "wrong"? Can a social revolution ever really be accomplished in "a few hours" — or its failure attributed, in Nasser's sense, to "egotism"? Or is it, rather, that these young
enthusiasts had never learned Lasswell's lesson — that political life is
largely a question of "who gets what"? When people get involved in
politics, it is natural that they should expect to get more of whatever it
is they want. Instead of rebuffing such aspirations as egotism, the states-
man of an enlarging polity and modernizing society will rather seek to
expand opportunities for people to get what they want. He will seek
above all to maintain a tolerable balance between levels of aspiration and

[12] This memoir is quoted in D. Lerner, *The Passing of Traditional Society*, pp.
244–245.
[13] Gamal Abdul Nasser, *op. cit.*, pp. 244–245.

achievement. In guiding the society out of the vicious circle toward a growth cycle his conception of the role of public communication is likely to be crucial.

IV. FROM VICIOUS CIRCLE TO GROWTH CYCLE

"The vicious circle of poverty" is a phrase used to characterize the situation in which no sustained economic growth is possible because each specific advance is rapidly checked by some counter-tendency in the social system. The most important of such counter-tendencies is excessive population growth. Any significant economic progress tends to prolong life by reducing famine and pestilence. When death rates decrease more rapidly than birth rates — often, indeed, while birth rates are increasing — then rapid population growth occurs. In poor countries population growth tends to "lead" economic growth by setting rates of increase that must be attained so that the society can stay at its existing levels of poverty. No surpluses can be generated, hence no "leap forward" is possible. Singer has succinctly summarized "the dominant vicious circle of low production — no surpluses for economic investment — no tools and equipment — low standards of production. An underdeveloped country is poor because it has no industry; and it has no industry because it is poor." [14]

The picture looks quite different in a society which has broken out of the vicious circle and set its course toward the achievement of a growth cycle. The new situation is vividly illustrated by the following diagram: [15]

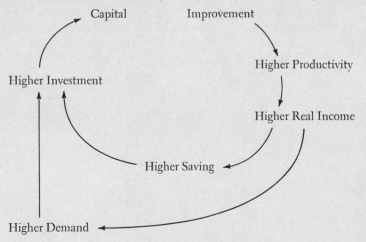

[14] Hans W. Singer "Economic Progress in Underdeveloped Countries," *Social Research*, xvi, 1, March 1949, p. 5.

[15] Gerald M. Meier and Robert E. Baldwin, *Economic Development: Theory, History, Policy*, New York, Wiley, 1957, pp. 319–320.

The story told by this diagram reaches its climax with the achievement of a significant rise in real income. Such a rise becomes significant when it enables the society simultaneously to raise both demand and saving. We have seen that otherwise, in a poor society, small increases of income tend to be consumed promptly — with nothing left over for saving, hence investment. But when income rises rapidly enough to permit higher consumption and also higher saving, then the growth cycle is initiated. Higher investment leads to capital improvement and rising productivity, which in turn raise real income enough to encourage both higher saving and demand. Thereby higher investment is again stimulated — and the growth cycle becomes self-sustaining.

Specialists on economic development appear to be generally agreed on some version of this picture of the break-out from the vicious circle. There is less consensus, however, on the economic policies that will lead most efficiently from the break-out to the self-sustaining growth cycle. Contemporary economic thinking has tended to emphasize two quite different sets of theoretical analyses — which we may characterize as "disequilibria" and "balanced growth" theories — leading to different policies and programs.

It is difficult to resolve the issues between disequilibria and balanced growth on a theoretical level. The arguments rest in both cases on factors extraneous to the economy — i.e., on the values, beliefs, and institutions of a country and, especially, on its capacity to change these psychosocial factors as may be required for sustained economic growth. For example: higher income, even if rapid and substantial, will not necessarily lead to commensurate increases of saving and investment. There are numerous cases where higher income has led only to conspicuous consumption of imported products or to savings that were invested only abroad — hence with no effect on production and growth at home.

The growth cycle, which stipulates that higher income must be coupled with both higher consumption and investment, is likely to occur only in a society where effort is associated with reward — where saving is likely to compound interest, where investment at home is likely to conjoin personal with patriotic satisfactions (rather than exploit the latter and deny the former). The association of effort with reward comes from the matrix of social institutions, psychological beliefs, political efficiency (in managing public adaptation to innovation) within which economic programs are obliged to operate.

The association of effort with reward, of aspiration with achievement, is a communication process. People must learn to make this association in their own daily lives — linking what they see with what they hear, what they want with what they do, what they do with what they get. Communication is, in this sense, the main instrument of socialization, as socialization is, in turn, the main agency of social change. To parallel the economist's model of the growth cycle, we may represent the conditions for an expanding polity and modernizing society as follows (adapting the input functions proposed by Gabriel Almond).[16]

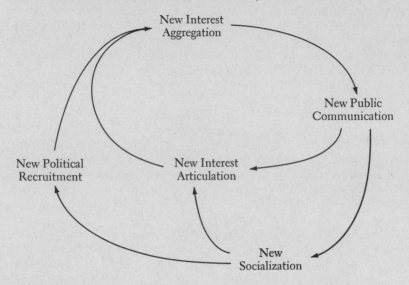

The modernization process begins with new public communication — the diffusion of new ideas and new information which stimulate people to want to behave in new ways. It stimulates the peasant to want to be a freeholding farmer, the farmer's son to want to learn reading so that he can work in the town, the farmer's wife to want to stop bearing children, the farmer's daughter to want to wear a dress and do her hair. In this way new public communication leads directly to new articulation of private interests.

Simultaneously — by analogy with the significant increase of real income that enables both saving and demand to rise simultaneously — new public communication activates new modes of socialization. If new interest-articulation parallels demand, then new socialization parallels saving — the factor that will make possible new investment and, ultimately the supply of new satisfactions for the new demands. So, while new communication is promoting new articulation of interests among the existing generation, it is also preparing a new generation who will incorporate these interests and go beyond them. The farmer's daughter who wants to show her face is likely to raise a daughter who wants to speak her mind. The

16 Gabriel A. Almond and James S. Coleman, *op. cit.*, p. 17.

farmer's son who wants literacy and a town job is likely to raise a son who wants a diploma and a white collar. Socialization thus produces, ideally, the new man with new ideas in sufficient quality and quantity to stabilize innovation over time.

In order to incorporate innovation efficiently, a society must translate it from private interests into public institutions. An essential step forward must be made from the articulation of the aggregation of private interests — which, when aggregated and accepted in the polity, become the public institutions of a society. It is also necessary that a new process of political recruitment come into operation. Among the newly socialized generation some must be recruited into political life so that the new aggregation of interests into institutions may be accomplished and sustained. So it is that, starting from a breakthrough in communication, reinforced by new ways of socialization (ideas of what one's children may be and practices designed to achieve these aspirations), a new political class is recruited that aggregates the new interests articulated within the society in such fashion as to create its new institutions — its version of modernity.

V. LOOKING AHEAD

Our set of considerations has been presented tersely. We have merely raised and related considerations that need to be explored in depth. This is a task for social scientists in the decade ahead — a task that will be the better performed in the measure that we improve our understanding of the communication crux of the modernizing process.

Our understanding begins with recognition that the revolution of rising expectations has been a major casualty of the past decade. In its place has risen a potential revolution of rising frustrations. This represents a deep danger to the growth of democratic polity in the world. People who do not aspire do not achieve; people who do not achieve do not prosper. Frustration produces aggression or regression.

Aggression in today's transitional societies expresses itself through violence based on moralistic but often inhumane ideologies. Such doctrines, albeit in prettier euphemisms, authorize fear, greed, and hate to operate as racism, xenophobia, vengeance. Regression in these societies signals the return to apathy and the narcosis of resignation. Aggression among transitional peoples victimizes others; regression victimizes themselves. Neither process is compatible with the dynamic equilibrium that promotes modernization. Hence the global spread of frustration must be checked and a tolerable ratio of aspirations to achievements must be instigated.

Communication is the crux. In the introduction of this volume it was observed that "the state of politics is a function of the communication process." The communication catastrophe in transitional societies has been their failure to discourage — often, indeed, their effort to encourage — the "insatiable expectations of politics" that lead ultimately only to frustration. Short-sighted politicians have been sowing a storm they may not be able to harvest. The policy of whipping up enthusiasm on short-run issues by creating insatiable expectations has never produced long-run payoffs.

What is needed in the years ahead is a new conception of public communication as the crucial instrument which can promote psychic mobility, political stability under conditions of societal equilibrium. The mass media can be used to mobilize the energies of living persons (without creating insatiable expectations) by the rational articulation of new interests. Flanked by the schools and community leaders, the mass media can simultaneously induce a new process of socialization among the rising generation that will, among other effects, recruit new participants into political life. These two processes — short-run mobilization and long-run socialization — can then converge, a generation later, in new aggregations of private interests which are the stuff of a democratic polity.

What we have sketched here is of course an idealized model. In the measure that it corresponds to reality the model provides clarification and guidance for those who must think and act in the transitional lands. The task for future research is to determine under what conditions the model does or does not work, so that a better model may be developed to shape a more effective communication process where it is most needed. This calls for close and continuous cooperation between men of knowledge and men of action on the most challenging social problem of our time — the modernizing of most of the world.

Notes for
Further Reading

The comparative study of communication is of relatively recent origin. For general discussions of processes of communication in their social settings, see:

Katz, E., "The Two Step Flow of Communication," *Public Opinion Quarterly*, Vol. 21, 1957, pp. 61–78.

Katz, E. and P. Lazarsfeld, *Personal Influence*. Glencoe, Ill.: The Free Press, 1955.

For comparative studies of communication in different social settings, see:

Eisenstadt, S.N., "Communication and Reference Group Behavior," in S.N. Eisenstadt, *Essays on Comparative Institutions*. New York: John Wiley & Sons, 1965, pp. 309–343.

————— "Communication Systems and Social Structure: in Exploratory Comparative Study," *ibid.*, pp. 344–358.

Marriot, McKim, "Changing Channels of Cultural Transmission in Indian Civilization," *Proceedings of the American Ethnological Society,* 1959, pp. 66–74.

For analysis of processes of communication as related especially to modernization, see:

Hyman, H., "Mass Media and Political Socialization, the Role of Patterns of Communication," in Lucian W. Pye (ed.), *Communication and Political Development.* Princeton: Princeton University Press, 1963, pp. 128–149.

Pye, L.W. "Communications Patterns and the Problems of Representative Government in Non-Western Societies," *Public Opinion Quarterly,* Vol. 20, Spring 1956, pp. 24–57.

Shils, E., "Demagogues and Cadres in the Political Development of the New States," in Pye, *op. cit.,* pp. 64–78.

SECTION TWO

Responses to Change: Personal Level and Social Movements

In the preceding chapters we have been concerned mostly with the structure of change in different institutional spheres during modernization, and only to a minimal extent with different responses to change. The chapters in this section present in greater detail some analyses of the effect of the processes of change on different aspects of social life, especially on community life in its various aspects, and different types of responses to these impacts. These responses are analyzed first on the personal level, and second on the level of wider movements of change.

VIII

The Personal Dimensions
of Change

The following article discusses change, and responses to it, on the personal level. It deals with the effect of changes in the total society on an individual's identity: his feelings of insecurity, his conception of himself and of the relations between his personal identity and the collective symbols of the total society.

Lifton's article presents an analysis mostly in terms of modal personality types in their orientations to the basic dimension of historical change of their complex society — of their past and present and of their evaluation of these changes in terms of their own personal identity. Different views of their changing society are based on their perception of their cultural heritage, on the traditions from which responses to change are drawn, and on their perception of the problems of the new collective identity which becomes crystallized in periods of change.

The article by Lifton is necessarily confined to one country. It does, however, contain very important general analytical concepts for the analysis of the personal response in situations of change — concepts which can be applied to a broader, comparative analysis.

Individual Patterns in Historical Change:
Imagery of Japanese Youth

Man not only lives within history; he is changed by it, and he causes it to change. This interplay between individual lives and wider historical forces is many-sided, erratic, seemingly contradictory, charged as it is by capricious human emotions. Yet there are common patterns — shared images and styles of imagery — which men call forth in their efforts to deal with the threat and promise of a changing outer and inner world. These patterns can sometimes be seen most clearly in cultures outside of one's own, and I have found them to be extremely vivid in present-day Japan.

In recent work with Japanese youth I have attempted to study the living experience of historical change through intensive series of interviews with more than fifty young men and women between the ages of 18 and 25. I was thus able to observe, for periods of from several months to two years, intellectual and emotional fluctuations in a group particularly sensitive to historical change. Their sensitivity derived first, from their age group, since as young adults they were at a stage of life characterized by an urge to experiment with the ideologies and technologies which motor historical change; second, from their selection, as they were mostly undergraduates at leading universities in Tokyo and Kyoto, outstanding in their intellectual, organizational, or creative abilities; and third, from their modern heritage — since recent generations of Japanese students and intellectuals have been unique in the impressive combination of eagerness, quick mastery, and inner resistance, with which they have embraced outside influences, not only during the years following World War II but from the time of the Meiji Restoration almost one hundred years ago.

I have elsewhere described in Japanese youth a *sense of historical dis-location*[2] accompanying the rapid social change their country has experi-

Reprinted from *Comparative Studies in Society and History*, Vol. 6, 1963/4, pp. 369–83, with permission of the author and the editors of *Comparative Studies in Society and History*. Footnotes abridged for this printing. Original reference numbers have been retained.

[2] Robert J. Lifton, "Youth and History: Individual Change in Postwar Japan," *Daedalus, Proceedings of the American Academy of Arts and Sciences* (1962), 91:172–197.

enced: the feeling that traditional ideologies, styles of group and family life, and patterns of communication are irrelevant and inadequate for contemporary life, a tendency which I have also called a *break in the sense of connection*. I suggested that this break is only partial, and that lingering influences of the past have a way of making themselves felt persistently within the individual character structure, creating a series of psychological conflicts which in turn add both pain and zest to their lives. Now I wish to carry this analysis further by delineating three more or less specific patterns of imagery[3] characteristic for Japanese youth in their efforts to break out of their historical dislocation and re-establish a sense of connection with viable ideas and human groups. This imagery includes emotionally charged convictions about one's relationship to his world (ideology) as well as a sense of personal development within the psychological idiom of these convictions (self-process). I shall focus upon the relationship of this imagery to the individual's sense of time: that is, his means of symbolizing past, present, and future, both in his conscious beliefs and in that part of his emotional life which is inaccessible to, and often in direct conflict with, conscious beliefs.

MODE OF TRANSFORMATION

The first of these three patterns may be called the *mode of transformation*, by which I mean a vision of remaking social and individual existence into something that is fundamentally, if not totally, new. This pattern is best represented by the political revolutionary; but it also includes diverse groups of youth and intellectuals who insist upon a radical political and cultural criticism of Japanese society.

Among those I interviewed, the youth who falls into this category tends to hold complex but readily identifiable imagery concerning the element of time in the historical process. His quest for human betterment and self-realization attaches itself strongly to a sense of the future. For he sees in the future man's only hope for overcoming the sordid and demeaning elements of existence which he associates with the present and the recent past. Perhaps the most forceful expression of this transformationist image of the future can be found in the ideology of the student movement, particularly the "mainstream" of the *Zengakuren* (All Japan Federation of Student Self-Governing Societies): a vision of "pure communism" which would transcend and eliminate the evils of both the "monopoly capitalism" held to characterize Japanese and Western society, and the "stagnant bureaucratism" seen to dominate most of the Communist nations.

A student leader vividly described these sentiments to me, referring to

---

[3] These patterns of imagery are, of course, by no means absolute or exclusive. They can and do overlap, and appear in various combinations. They may thus be regarded as "ideal types."

the goals he and his followers were seeking to achieve by means of their militant behavior during the mass demonstrations of 1960 (including the violence which took place within the Diet grounds):

> We are seeking something new through our own efforts. . . . Our ideal, according to what we have learned from Marx, is that all human beings are equal . . . and that all are entitled to full realization of their capacities. Our ideal is like that of the Renaissance in which human beings reach the highest possible development. . . . Yet what we do does not simply come from an ideal, but rather is for the purpose of changing the present society . . . and to do this we must somehow destroy its foundation. This is our task now, and the society which will be created in the future — well, I do not think that we ourselves will be able to see it in its magnificence. . . .

In this imagery, the future has a near-absolute purity. And in sharp contrast to this purity is the decided impurity of the present. The young transformationist, acutely sensitive to inauthenticity and corruption of any kind, finds much in the contemporary Japanese social scene that grates upon these sensitivities. Combinations of power, wealth, and easy sensuality can trigger off a strong reaction in a youth struggling to integrate his austere ideology, his quest for authenticity, and his own compelling sexual urges. And he may also, with the special intensity Japanese have derived from their recent history, deplore another impurity in the world around him — the threat of war — and seek out, however theoretically, a universal symbol of peace.

The transformationist applies similar judgments of impurity to his own individual life, especially to his vision of his own future. The ambivalent symbol here is that of the *sarariman* (salaried man) — on the one hand, as the Japanese version of the American Organization Man, the personification of impure self-betrayal, of rote, purposeless subservience both to his immediate superiors and to the overall social and economic system; and on the other hand, by no means without attraction, partly because of these very qualities, and partly because of the security, status, and even power the *sarariman* may achieve.

The transformationist sees these impurities of the present as having strong roots in the "feudalism" of the past. Under attack here is the complex pattern of human relationships originating in ancient Japanese rural life, and still of great importance for contemporary social behavior and individual psychology. Known as *giri-ninjō*, it involves an interplay of obligation and dependency,[4] in which, beginning with family relationships

---

[4] Ruth Benedict (*The Chrysanthemum and the Sword*, Boston: Houghton Mifflin Co., 1946) tended to stress the element of obligation in *giri-ninjō*; while L. Takeo Doi ("*Giri-Ninjō*; An Interpretation," unpublished manuscript) has stressed the underlying element of dependency which he feels was neglected by Benedict in her general approach to Japanese culture.

but extending into all human contacts, there is an unspoken understanding that one will be loved, nourished, or at least taken care of — if one "plays the game." But the young transformationist expresses disdain for the rules of the game, for the endless rituals of reciprocity, and looks upon *giri-ninjō* as a form of hypocrisy and betrayal of self.

Many have described to me highly unpleasant — even suffocating — sensations they experience at the very mention of the words *giri* or *ninjō*. Some simply attempt to ignore these concepts, dismissing them as anachronistic holdovers which have no call upon them; others make them the focus of elaborate ideological condemnation. And this ideological attack may extend to every perceived manifestation of *giri* and *ninjō*, including its appearance in relationships between parent and child, teacher and pupil, superior and subordinate, and political boss and local electorate. For transformationists, these traditional rhythms of obligation and dependency — and especially their often-distorted contemporary remnants — become rhythms of master and slave, which must be abolished if society and the individual are to be liberated. They nonetheless, as Japanese, retain these emotions to a significant degree within themselves, as evidenced by the complex *giri-ninjō* relationships (although they may be called something else) within transformationist political and cultural groups. If, however, these tendencies are recognized, they in turn may be condemned as undesirable remnants of the past. For the past remains the ultimate source of evil, the transformationist's ultimate negative symbol.

Yet I gained the strong impression that these same transformationist youth, more than any other group among those I interviewed, had a profound underlying nostalgia for old cultural symbols. In their more relaxed moments, and in their dreams and associations — frequently coming in direct relationship to discussions of ideology — they would repeatedly describe to me sentiments like these:

> There is a big stream in our village — it is really a river where you swim and fish for *ayu* (a sweetfish). . . . People in our village have a very strong attachment to that river, though it is not especially beautiful. . . . I have memories of its current dashing against the rocks, and it gives me the feeling of a true river — not like those rivers we so often see with strongly artificial beauty. . . . In the old days the water was very abundant . . . and there was a castle of a feudal lord. . . . On the site of the ruins of his castle, there are two hills of similar height, and the river flows just between them. In the old days the river was wide and there was a suspension bridge over it . . . and when the water level rose boats would often appear. But now we can no longer see such a scene . . . and the water has greatly decreased. . . .

This is a student leader, not only expressing nostalgic childhood memories, but also speaking symbolically of the beauty, authenticity, and lushness of the past, in contrast to the "dried up" world of the present. And he goes on to reinforce these sentiments in his contrast between new ways of celebrating Christmas (a Western import which has become something of a pagan festival in postwar Japan) and old ways of celebrating the Japanese New Year:

> Of course I celebrate Christmas but I don't necessarily find it pleasant. It is just an excuse to go out and drink *sake* — and during the Christmas season you pay 1,000 yen for the same cup of coffee that usually cost you 100 yen. . . . Christmas doesn't matter much to me. . . . But the last night of the year, when people eat what we call *toshikoshi soba* (New Year's noodles), some of the real feelings of the old days come out. . . . I used to go to the shrine on that night together with my family, with a solemn feeling. . . . There would be a priest, and it would be very quiet around the shrine grounds. Then at the time of the night when the moon hovered above us, when the frost made the ground transparent, the priest would offer us sacred wine (*omiki*). I would clap my hands and, standing in the dark in dim candlelight, I would ring the bell and throw offerings. . . . Only after finishing all of this could I feel relieved and go to bed. . . . These mystical feelings I had during my childhood I no longer feel toward the New Year, but when I look at my mother and father I have the impression that they feel them still. . . .

Here we get a sense of an Ultimate Past in which childhood memory blends with the earliest and most fundamental religious ritual of rebirth from the Japanese cultural past. All is in perfect spiritual and aesthetic harmony. The strength of emotional content gives us the sense that this Past (both individual and cultural) predates, and is symbolically more powerful than, the negatively tinged past we have previously heard about. It has some of the same awesome — one might say "oceanic" [5] — feeling which transformationist youth also express toward the future, and my impression is that it comes from the same psychological stuff. That is, the transformationist youth embraces a vision of the future intimately related to, if not indeed a part of, his longing for a return to an imagined golden age of the past. Or to put it another way, the transformationist's longing for a golden age of the past — a longing intensified during periods of inner dislocation caused by rapid historical change — supplies a basic stimulus for his future-oriented utopian quest.

MODE OF RESTORATION

When we turn to the second of these individual patterns in historical change, the *mode of restoration*, we encounter what appears to be the

---

[5] Sigmund Freud quoted Romain Rolland as looking upon religion as "a feeling which he would like to call a sensation of 'eternity,' a feeling as of something limitless, unbounded — as it were, 'oceanic' . . ." (*Civilization and Its Discontents*, Standard Edition, London: The Hogarth Press (1961), 64–5). The feeling need not, of course, be limited to specifically religious experience, and its emphasis upon the loss of time boundaries is especially relevant to us here.

very opposite situation. The restorationist youth repeatedly expresses a strong urge to return to the past, to draw upon great and ennobling symbols of the Japanese heritage as a source of sustenance for the present and of direction for the future. Falling into this category are the so-called rightist youth, including at their most extreme those willing to assassinate (and die) for their beliefs, as well as many others less fanatical in their actions but sharing the same passionate vision of restoring a past of divine brilliance.

A twenty-one-year-old leader of a religious youth group with strong rightist tendencies (among the relatively few intellectual youth sharing this vision) told me how, during a visit he made to a sacred shrine area said to be the place where Japan's first Emperor assumed the throne in 660 B.C., "I felt the Emperor Jimmu alive inside myself . . . and the blood of Japanese history running through my veins." And this same young man goes on to describe the absolute purity of the Japanese past, as embodied in the ostensibly unbroken line of Emperors following upon the heavenly origins of this founder:

> The great periods in Japanese history have always been those when the Emperor governed the country himself . . . the time of Prince Shotoku . . . then later on with the Emperor Meiji. . . . We cannot say that the blood of Emperors has never been mixed with that of others . . . but the descent from heaven of the Imperial Family of Japan is the fundamental spiritual idea of our nation . . . so that our *kokutai* (national polity or essence)[6] must always have the Emperor at its center. . . . Since the nation of Japan was descended from gods we call ourselves the nation of truth (*shinri kokka*). . . . I can say that in our history no Emperor has ever governed wrongly, or ever will in the future. . . , It is sometimes said that the Kojiki and the Nihonshoki [the two earliest, and partly-mythological, historical chronicles] do not describe actual history. But even if they are not historical truth, what is important is that they were written by Japanese. The thoughts of the writers are Japanese. . . . They contain the Japanese spirit. . . .

This East Asian form of fundamentalist imagery characteristically stresses a *sense of organic connection* with the past. The Japanese version expressed here focuses upon a mystical racial identity so pervasive that individuals are perceived as being more or less fused with one another in the pure (unadulterated) racial essence.

Concerning the present, the imagery of the restorationist youth in many ways resembles that of the transformationist. He too sees impurity, cor-

---

[6] *Kokutai* is a mystical-ideological concept which is impossible to define precisely, but which also contains the sense of "national body" or "national substance" — and could be translated as "national identity." See Lifton, "Youth and History," 179–180, and 196, reference note 6.

ruption, and inauthenticity everywhere around him. But he differs in his vision of the source of these contemporary impurities. Rather than attributing them to the past, he sees them as the result of evil new influences from the outside which contaminate the older Japanese essence. The young rightist we have already quoted, for instance, condemned the American Occupation for "weakening the Japanese nation" by destroying its family system, for causing the perfect harmony of *giri-ninjō* to break down. And he criticized the overall "materialism" of Western patterns of thought brought to bear upon Japan during its recent history, including the stress upon equality, socialism, self-realization, and scientific analysis. Indeed, he felt that he himself had been contaminated by these ideas, that his persistent tendency to raise questions about historical and archeological evidence for the existence of early Japanese Emperors was an unfortunate legacy of his own postwar exposure to Western ways of thinking, and that literal scientific findings in these matters were of much less importance than truths derived from the Japanese emphasis upon intuition and spirit. For him, as for Asian restorationists in general, it was less a matter of science versus faith than of science versus feeling.

The young Japanese restorationist's view of the future is compounded of anxiety and a strange form of utopianism. His anxiety is related to the general forces of change he sees around him, and aggravated by his inner awareness that these "impurities" — molded as they are to the whole apparatus of contemporary society — are becoming increasingly ineradicable. He frequently looks upon transformationist groups (radical youth and intellectuals) as threatening embodiments of evil, and vents his anxious hostility upon them. But as a fundamentalist he derives his vision of the future of Japan — and in this case of all mankind — from the words and prophecies of the sacred chronicles of the past, as again expressed by the same young rightist.

> In the Kojiki there is a prophecy of a time of purification (*misogi*) for removing the filth from all of us. This is the time we are in now, a period of struggle, of pain before the birth of something new — just like that of a mother before delivering her child. . . . We have to undergo this birth pain, which is the coming of the third world war. . . . Then, after that, there can be a world state, having the whole world as one family with the Emperor of Japan at its center. . . . Just as Christ claimed to be the King of Kings, we think of the Emperor as the King of Kings. . . . Of course we must try to avoid World War III . . . and to defend Japan's *kokutai* is to contribute to world peace, because the defense of our *kokutai* means the love of mankind. . . . But if World War III comes, Japan's Imperial House will in some way survive . . . by some power of God . . . just as the Imperial House survived after the last war, although Japan was defeated and many royal families in other countries were abolished . . . because truth and righteousness endure

always. . . . This is the meaning of our Movement for the enlightenment of mankind, for we believe that world peace can only come when the Emperor is in the center of the world. . . .

Yet even in the expression of these extreme sentiments, or perhaps particularly in such expression, the restorationist's attitude toward new historical elements is by no means as simple as it might appear. One finds that underneath his antagonism toward "new" Western principles of social equality, selfhood, and science lies considerable fascination and even attraction. We have seen our young rightist make use of Christian analogies to his ideological claims, and concern himself with the problem of scientific versus mythological historical claims. More significant was his tendency during discussions with me, to bring up frequently the names of Marx, Einstein, and Freud. Marx he mostly condemned, but he expressed a certain amount of agreement with Marxian economics, and he and his rightist teachers spoke of their anticipated world federation as a form of "Emperor-system socialism." Einstein he approvingly quoted as having favored a world federation (this much was true) with the Japanese Emperor at its center (this was a good deal less true, and apparently stemmed from a false quotation circulated among rightists). And Freud he sought to embrace as a "scientific investigator of the human spirit." He in fact organized a "Spiritual Science Study Group" for the purpose of strengthening the students' spiritual lives and opposing Zengakuren (that is, transformationist) influence; the Group was to take up the writings of Freud as its first topic of study, but as it turned out (much to my disappointment) these were postponed in favor of a reconsideration of Japan's *kokutai*.

The point here is that, however the restorationist seeks refuge in his mystical sense of connection with an undifferentiated past, he at the same time feels himself confronted by the powerful Western cultural and technological tradition which asserts itself so forcefully throughout the world. This tradition is symbolized for him by the frightening and alluring image of Science, which he perceives to be the West's most fundamental cultural intrusion — on the one hand a formidable threat to the whole structure of his thought and identity, on the other a beckoning source of unlimited power.

The restorationist thus calls forth his imagery of the past as a means of not only combating threatening new influences, but also of coming to terms with these influences — and, however tortuously and ambivalently, of absorbing them and being changed by them. I believe that Japanese history bears out this interpretation. At times of historical dislocation due to strong cultural influences from the outside, there has been a powerfully recurrent theme of restoration of old Imperial power and virtue, and this restoration has itself been a means of bringing about revolutionary changes

in both Japan's national experience and the inner lives of individual
Japanese: notably during the period of the Meiji Restoration of 1868,[7] but
also at the time of the introduction of Buddhism and Chinese learning in
the seventh century. Restorationism (like transformationism) always carries within it the seeds of totalism — of an all-or-none psychological
plunge into a pseudo-religious ideology.[8] Restorationist movements can,
and at various junctures of Japanese history have, become belligerently
fanatical — most recently in Japan's prewar and wartime militarism, and
in certain postwar demands for a "Showa Restoration" (meaning the
reassertion of the Imperial mystique through the person of the present
Showa Emperor) much like that expressed by the young rightist we have
quoted. But beyond these extreme examples, restorationism must be seen
as a general psychological tendency inherent in the historical process. For
it is his ambivalent attraction to the symbols of historical change which
drives the restorationist back into the past, and this very backward plunge
facilitates his partial absorption of these new elements by enabling him
to meet them on what is, so to speak, his own psychological ground. He
too ends up promoting historical change.

MODE OF ACCOMMODATION

The last of these patterns, that of cultural and psychological *accommodation*, is by far the most common of the three. More than the other two,
it has set the tone of historical change in postwar Japan, though at moments of crisis it has been temporarily superseded by each of them.
Accommodation is a wide category of compromise. It includes muted elements of transformation and restoration, and is the category encompass-
ing all those who do not fit into either of these two modes. In relationship
to the symbols of time, it tends toward an inner *modus vivendi* for blend-
ing imagery of past, present, and future. Rather than the zealous focus
upon either past or future which we have so far encountered, the young
Japanese accommodationist places greatest relative stress upon time im-

---

[7] Historians have made analogous observations in relation to the Meiji Restoration. Thus Albert M. Craig concludes his book, *Chōshū in the Meiji Restoration*
(Cambridge, Massachusetts: Harvard University Press, 1961) with the observation:
"It was because Japan possessed such [traditional] characteristics when first confronted by the West that it was able so early to achieve a part of the transformation
which is the goal of other nations in Asia today. In Japan . . . it is in a large measure
to the strength and not to the weaknesses of the traditional society that we must
turn to comprehend its modern history." Marius B. Jansen comes to similar conclusions in his *Sakamoto Ryoma and the Meiji Restoration*, Princeton: Princeton
University Press, 1961. See also the review article on both of these books by Thomas
C. Smith, *The Journal of Asian Studies* (1962), 21:215–219.

[8] Robert J. Lifton, *Thought Reform and the Psychology of Totalism*, New York:
W. W. Norton & Co., 1961. See especially chapter 22.

agery closest to his own life — upon the present, the immediate future, and perhaps the recent past.

Like all Japanese youth, he is thrust into a social environment dazzling in its side-by-side diversity of cultural elements: ideological admixtures of Communism, socialism, liberal democracy, existentialism, nihilism, and many versions of Emperor-centered traditionalism; religious influences related to Buddhism, Christianity, Shintoism, and the spate of new religions which combine elements of all of these in highly idiosyncratic ways; recreational disciplines of baseball, *sumō* (traditional wrestling), golf, *karate* (an old art, something like boxing, originally imported from Okinawa), tennis, flower arrangement, secular Zen, Noh and Kabuki drama, games of bridge, go, mahjong, and the incomparable *pachinko*.[9] Surely there is no other culture in which a young person finds the need to accommodate such an imposing variety of influences. But while the transformationist or restorationist can protect himself from this onslaught with a structured ideological image through which all in turn can be ordered, the accommodationist must face it more or less nakedly. And his psychological equipment for doing so is faulty, since he has been molded by a culture laying heavy stress upon the achievement of inner harmony through following closely prescribed emotional paths within a carefully regulated group structure. No wonder, then, that he places great stress upon ideas of self-realization and personal autonomy as well as group commitment — precisely the things so difficult for him to achieve.

Concerning the past, the accommodationist's imagery lacks the intensity of the transformationist's or restorationist's, but it can be nonetheless painful. He does not escape a sense of historical dislocation, and the feeling that Japan's recent past (and, to some extent, distant past as well) has been dishonored. He feels this way both because of concrete embarrassment at Japan's disastrous military adventures (and the Japanese emotions that went into these adventures), and because this sense of a dishonored past is likely to be present, particularly among the young, in any culture which has been overwhelmed, psychologically or militarily (or, as in Japan's case, both) by outside influences and is undergoing rapid change.

Similarly, his approach to the future includes a concerted effort to make

[9] *Pachinko* is a uniquely Japanese creation, a postwar slot-machine game which is a good deal more than a slot-machine game. It involves shooting metal balls in circular trajectories, so that they land, or do not land, in small round holes. It is utterly simple and repetitious. Played in large, crowded *pachinko* parlors, against a background of loud music and the constant clang of the metal balls, it has a strange fascination — to the point of addiction — for its enormous numbers of devotees. It has been called everything from a contemporary expression of Buddhist mysticism to a sign of Japan's postwar moral deterioration, though more often the latter. It is, in the very least, an interesting invention of a culture in transition.

his own way in society and at the same time maintain a sense of moral and psychological integrity, rather than envisage a radical transformation of that society or a radical restoration of the past.

We can appreciate the conflicts involved in this process of psychological and cultural accommodation by turning to an individual example — in this case a very brief dream, and the associations to that dream, of a brilliant student of American history who also happened to be devoted to the traditional art of *karate*, but had temporarily withdrawn from the *karate* group of his university, ostensibly because of the pressure of his academic work:

> I was studying *karate* with a certain teacher who is the head of one of the schools of *karate*, and is also a rightist boss. . . . I asked another student there, "Why does the *karate* spirit become associated with ultra-nationalism? Why are we asked to demonstrate *karate* in front of a shrine?" I said that *karate* should not be like this. Then the master said, "What was it that this youngster was trying to say?" . . . I didn't talk back to him then, but returned to my place and decided to practice more and become more skillful . . . so that I could defeat that master, a master such as that. . . .

The student's sequence of associations to the dream reveals the uncomfortable symbolism represented by *karate*, and particularly by the *karate* master:

> Since I quit *karate*, it seems that there are *karate* problems even in my dreams. . . . My real master, fortunately, is a very understanding person of a high intellectual level, suitable, I believe, for our university. . . . And the master who appeared in the dream has no connection with me in actuality. . . . Recently I came across a book with a very silly article about a man who practiced *karate* during the Meiji era, telling about all sorts of silly things such as spying for rightists and bragging about eating snakes. . . . I was surprised that this kind of book is still sold in the postwar period. . . . Somehow, there seems to be the tendency in Japanese society that once the heat around our throats is gone, we forget about that heat. . . . I feel that studious people should express themselves about these problems. . . . We should continue to recognize Japanese culture, not just forget about it and praise only American culture and Americans. . . . But we should not become intoxicated in doing this and decide that fine things are to be found only in Japanese culture, and that Japanese culture must be separated from all others. . . . There are people who do *karate* or *judo* or the like without considering these spiritual disciplines. . . . They are only interested in breaking roof tiles [which one does with the side of one's hand in *karate* practice]. We, as young people should be progressive and create our own society. . . . But too often we indulge ourselves in mood . . . especially a mood of helplessness. . . . Hope is not easily realized in any society . . . and this society is unsteady. . . . But desperation should not be the way of youth. . . .

We may look upon this dream as the student's embarrassed confrontation with undesirable elements in traditional Japanese culture, symbolized here by *karate*. He cannot yet defeat or even talk back to this "bad master," this tainted element of his personal and historical past. But he dedicates himself to an effort to improve his skills — skills related to the various forms of cultural and psychological accommodation he tells us about — so that he might eventually defeat the "bad master" and thus, so to speak, *purify and rescue his own past*. He is troubled, however, by a suggestion of despair, by the fear that this rescue by purification might not after all be possible, that he might not be able to reintegrate the past into his own present and future life experience.[10]

Thus the psychological tasks of the cultural accommodationist can be overwhelmingly difficult. During periods of great historical dislocation, he may readily find that the cultural symbols around him communicate everything and nothing; he may encounter an unending series of messages, none of which convey adequate meaning or lead to the kind of imagery which would enable him to re-establish a meaningful sense of connection with his symbolic world. His ever-present prospect, as we observed in the case of the young *karate* practitioner, is that of despair — despair which may take the form of nihilism, of experimental plunges into various cults of feeling and sensation; which may lead one to a rote, increasingly constricted journey along the path of social convention; or which may drive one into the more extreme forms of transformationism or restorationism.

But it is also a despair from which one can awaken with much benefit. There is nothing more stimulating to individual and cultural creativity than this struggle for accommodation in the face of profound historical dislocation. Most young Japanese resolve the struggle with at least a measure of success, and in the process of doing so gradually shape new cultural forms — artistic, ideational, or institutional. For in the struggle itself, in the effort to make disparate cultural elements into a meaningful psychological whole, lies the accommodationist's special motor of historical change.

PATTERNS OF IMAGERY: GENERAL PRINCIPLES

What further conclusions are we to draw concerning these elusive individual patterns in historical change?

First, they are wed to one another in paradox. Those who focus their imagery most strongly upon the symbolism of the future are, to a signifi-

[10] This dream could, of course, be interpreted in other ways. One could, in a more conventional fashion, look upon the "bad master" as representing parental authority; and such a symbol of parental authority can then also be equated with the authority of the cultural past. I shall pursue these symbolic relationships in later publications, but here wish to stress (however one-sidedly) the historical elements of the dream.

cant degree, driven toward change by their less apparent nostalgia for the past. Those who feel compelled to reach back into the past for the symbols with which to fight off historical change end up by using the same symbols as a means of enhancing such change. And those who are thrown into despair by their seeming inability to integrate symbols of past, present, and future, may emerge from it by "rescuing" their past and creating new cultural forms, so that the despair itself becomes a vehicle of historical change.

Such paradox exists because it is native to the individual psychological equipment. And in this cursory exploration, we have been observing the fundamentally paradoxical operation of the individual emotional life in the area of historically significant ideas and imagery. I have approached this difficult area by stressing patterns and themes — concepts which unify the individual relationship to historical forces — since I believe this the best way to attempt to extend the insights of depth psychology into a wider historical frame. And if this analysis is to be carried further, indeed to its logical conclusion, it leads us to the ultimate historical experience of death itself. The varying efforts men make to master historical time — to integrate in immediate experience both remote past and distant future — derive ultimately from the ceaseless human effort to transcend death. This effort, carried over from formal religion, perhaps underlies all historical change, and, in a sense, history itself.

Second, these patterns of imagery are, to a surprising degree, interchangeable; young people in particular can readily switch from one to the other. Thus, one of the transformationist youth I quoted had made a sudden shift from a more or less restorationist position; and the restorationist student with the extreme Emperor-system ideology had been converted to this pattern from a near-Communist transformationist stance. I have, moreover, frequently encountered conversions from a transformationist position (and occasionally from a restorationist one) to a pattern of accommodation, particularly at the time of graduation from the university, when most young people feel compelled to find a way of life within the existing social framework.

These shifts in imagery — whether polar and dramatic or gradual and invisible — defy easy psychological evaluation. They can often combine the most radical change in world-view, group affiliation, and style of psychological functioning on the one hand, with relatively unchanged underlying character structure on the other. I would suggest that this seeming contradiction is explained by the existence of an emotional substrate and a set of symbols common to all three patterns of imagery, which can be shaped or reshaped into any of the three distinctively different forms we have observed. A significant element in this substrate was expressed (particularly vividly by transformationists and restorationists) in what I have referred to as the quest for an Ultimate Past and Ultimate Future. The "ultimate" element sought here is that of ultimate unity — a state of existence in which men and ideas are so harmoniously blended that conflict and strife cease. The individual model for this unity is the original psychobiological unity of the mother-child relationship, prior to the child's sense of differentiation into a separate individual. The cultural model (clearly evident in Japanese thought and in most non-Western tradition, but also in early Western cultural history) is the stress upon a near-mystical social and racial harmony, a harmony felt to transcend historical time. This emotional-symbolic substrate (or at least the portion of it we have been discussing) tends to take on a maternal coloring which communicates a sense of the perpetuation of life itself, to the point, as already suggested, of transcending the always-threatening fact of biological death.

It is precisely this commonly-held and enduring emotional-symbolic substrate — so enduring that we may well look upon it as a major psychobiological universal underlying all historical change — that makes possible the dramatic shifts from one mode to another. But we must still account for the choice of imagery, whether in conversions or in the establishment of the modes themselves. Here I would stress the interplay of three general factors: historical influences of the kind I have presented in this paper, which not only supply imagery to the individual but create within him, and within his culture, varying degrees of readiness for that imagery; institutions and organizations, particularly those of youth, which mediate the imagery and supply the group identities necessary for its expression; and variations in individual-psychological background experience, which (although neglected in this paper in favor of other emphases) significantly influence the choice of imagery from among available alternatives, and the manner in which the chosen imagery is held and expressed.

Thus, for young Japanese, transformationist ideology is encouraged by a combination of its general strength, particularly in the non-Western world, and by the existence of historical dislocation; restorationism has been largely dishonored, but still holds considerable underlying emotional appeal; a vision of ultimate unity (transformationist or restorationist) is encouraged by an extraordinary cultural emphasis upon the undifferentiated intimacy of the mother-child relationship; but accommodation is demanded by an advanced industrial society, encouraged by economic rewards, and reinforced by a long-standing utilitarianism within Japanese character structure.

No matter what the combination, historical change cannot be generated without making use of the individual and cultural past. But in this view of history as "a forward moving *recherche du temps perdu*,"[11] I do not speak either of "regression" or even of "repetition-compulsion" in the classical psychoanalytic sense (though the latter is closer to what I mean). I refer to the continuous process of fusion of symbols and reshaping of imagery, to the symbolic constellation that comes to exist, in restless equilibrium, within individual minds as a fluctuating self-process; and which may, in significant degree, become the shared symbols of large groups of people to the extent of dominating an entire era.[12]

Finally, a beginning knowledge of these patterns of imagery may shed some light on forces now evolving in various parts of the world, particularly in the underdeveloped areas of Africa and Asia, but also in the industrialized West, including our own country (here too Japan is a particularly valuable laboratory, because it has one historical foot in the underdeveloped Afro-Asian world and another in the "developed" West). These patterns of imagery may appear more or less spontaneously, as in Japan (the three modes described), in France (the transformationism of intellectuals and the restorationism of *colons*), and the United States (the accommodationism of most segments of the population and the restorationism of the Radical Right). They may be manipulated by mass media, as, for instance, in the Middle East (a mixture of transformationist and restorationist imagery). Or they may be stimulated through an organized national program of "re-education" or "thought reform" as in Communist China (mostly transformationist, but with restorationist flashes).[13] In the latter case, and in fact in most manipulated efforts, transformationist images are stressed, since these forms of imagery stimulate passions most useful — perhaps indispensible — for bringing about social change.[14]

The dilemma presented here is that these same passionate modes neces-

[11] Norman O. Brown, *Life Against Death*, Middletown, Connecticut: Wesleyan University Press (1959), 93. While I strongly concur with Brown's focus upon the past (he stresses the individual past) as a prime mover of history, I would emphasize the interplay of time symbols, rather than his principle that "repression and the repetition-compulsion generate historical time."

[12] See Erik H. Erikson's *Young Man Luther* (New York, W. W. Norton & Co., 1958) for a brilliant exposition of the interplay between individual psychology (in this case the psychological struggles of a great man) and historical change.

[13] Lifton, *Thought Reform . . . , op. cit.*

[14] If we turn to more primitive cultures, we can see even more vividly the intimate interplay of the three modes in bringing about historical change — the combination of extremist "cargo cults" (consisting of both transformationist and restorationist elements) with more or less rationalized (accommodationist) techniques for modernization. See Margaret Mead and Theodore Schwartz, "The Cult as a Condensed Social Process," in *Group Processes* (Transactions of the Fifth Conference), edited by Bertram Schaffner, New York; Josiah Macy, Jr. Foundation, 1958; Margaret Mead, *New Lives for Old*, New York, William Morrow Co., 1956; and Peter Worsley, *The Trumpet Shall Sound: a Study of "Cargo" Cults in Melanesia*, London, MacGibbon and Kee, 1957.

sary to historical change are most prone to excess, or to totalism. But whatever their dangers, transformationism and restorationism, no less than accommodationism, are inevitable elements in the historical process, because they reflect fundamental individual psychological tendencies. The great historical problems then — from the standpoint of this psychological perspective — are to attenuate, or at least make creative use of, the despair of accommodationism, and at the same time moderate the despair-relieving excesses of transformationism and restorationism. While one can hardly approach these problems with optimism, much hope lies in the constant reshaping of imagery of which men are capable. For just as the full range of human emotional potential seems to be necessary for the assimilation of historical change, so might this richness and diversity lead to new combinations of thought and feeling, and to new possibilities for applying change to man's benefit rather than to his destruction.

Notes for
Further Reading

For analyses of the basic relations between personal and collective identity, see:

Benedict, R., *Patterns of Culture*. London: Routledge and Kegan Paul, 1945.

Erikson, E.H., *Childhood and Society*. London: Pelican, 1966.

————, *Youth, Change and Challenge*. New York: Basic Books. 1963.

Hallowell, A.I., *Culture and Experience*. Philadelphia: University of Pennsylvania Press, 1955.

Wallace, A.F., *Culture and Personality*. New York: Random House, 1962.

For those relations in situations of change and modernization, see:

Bettleheim, B., "Individual and Mass Behavior in Extreme Situations," *Journal of Abnormal Psychology*, Vol. 38, No. 4, October 1943, pp. 417–452.

Eisenstadt, S.N., *The Absorption of Immigrants*. London: Routledge and Kegan Paul, 1954.

Henry, J., "Culture, Personality, and Evolution," *American Anthropologist*, Vol. 61, 1959, pp. 221–226.

Inkeles, A., "Industrial Man: The Relation of Status to Experience, Perception, and Value," *American Journal of Sociology*, Vol. 66, No. 1, July 1960, pp. 1–31.

————, "The Modernization of Man," in Myron Weiner (ed.), *Modernization*. New York: Basic Books, 1966, pp. 138–150.

Mead, M., "Cultural Discontinuities and Personality Transformation," *Journal of Social Issues*, Supplement Series, No. 8, 1954, pp. 3–16.

Rappaport, D., "Technological Growth and the Psychology of Man," *Psychiatry*, Vol. 10 (3), 1947, pp. 253–259.

Seeman, M., "On the Meaning of Alienation," *American Sociological Review*, Vol. 24, 1959, pp. 783–791.

IX

Movements of Change

The following articles analyze two responses to change on a macro-societal level. The first, by Barber, discusses one very common response that develops during acculturation: the development of messianic, charismatic religious movements, which aim at recreating a glorious past and forging out of it a new collective future. But the religious-charismatic movement is only one of a wider range of such movements which arise in situations of change and modernization. Social and national movements are obvious additional cases. But whatever the exact nature of such movements, their concrete structure as well as their ability to transform society depends to no small degree on the nature of the élites or leaders which develop from within them and which are able to guide them.

The second article, by Benda, analyzes the social composition of the nationalist élites in Southeast Asia which developed in the colonial situation, and discerns two major subtypes within them — the more rigid, purely intellectual élite which was alienated from its background, and the more flexible élite, composed not solely of intellectuals and which had more solidary relations with its environment. The major focus of his analysis is the extent to which the social background or composition of these élites influences their perception of the problems of modernization and their ability to forge out new institutional patterns.

11   BERNARD BARBER

Acculturation and Messianic Movements

Robert H. Lowie has recently called our attention again to the problem of messianic movements among the American aborigines.[1] Among the North American Indians, one of the fundamental myths was the belief that a culture-hero would one day appear and lead them to a terrestrial paradise.[2] Under certain conditions, which this paper will describe and analyze, these myths have become the ideological basis for messianic movements. In the messianic movement, the ushering in of the "golden age" by the messiah is announced for the *immediate* future. Twenty such movements had been recorded in the United States alone prior to 1890.[3]

The messianic doctrine is essentially a statement of hope. Through the intervention of the Great Spirit or of his emissary, the earth will shortly be transformed into a paradise, enjoyed by both the living and the resurrected dead. In anticipation of the happy return of the golden age, believers must immediately return to the aboriginal mode of life. Traits and customs which are symbolic of foreign influence must be put aside. All members of the community — men, women, and children — must participate. Besides reverting to the early folkways, believers must adopt special ritual practices until the millennium arrives. Thus, in the American Ghost Dance movements ceremonial bathing and an elaborate dance were the chief ritual innovations.[4] The doctrine always envisages a restoration of

Reprinted from *Americal Sociological Review*, Vol. 6, 1941, pp. 663–668, with permission of the author and The American Sociological Association. Footnote abridged for this printing.

[1] Lowie (1940).

[2] Fletcher (1891), 58.

[3] Chamberlain (1913). Here may be found also accounts of five new religions for Mexico and Central America, and four for South America. The best detailed summary of the early American movements is in Mooney (1892). Macleod (1928), 507, says that messianic movements among the American Indians have been "more numerous . . . than among any other race or people or culture save the Jews." See also, Wallis (1918), 150 ff.

[4] These elements, and other ritual practices as well, varied from tribe to tribe in accordance with divergent cultural backgrounds. For a detailed description of the ritual of the Ghost Dance, see Mooney, chapter 15, *et passim*. There are other descriptions in the sources cited herein in other connections.

earthly values. These values will be enjoyed, however, in a transcendental setting, for in the age which is foretold there will be no sickness or death; there will be only eternal happiness. The messianic doctrine is peaceful. The exclusion of the whites from the golden age is not so much a reflection of hostility toward them as a symbolization of the fulfillment of the former way of life. The millennium is to be established through divine agency; believers need only watch and pray.[5]

The general sociocultural situation that precipitates a messianic movement has been loosely described as one of "harsh times." Its specific characteristic is the widespread experience of "deprivation" — the despair caused by inability to obtain what the culture has defined as the ordinary satisfactions of life.[6] The fantasy-situation pictured in the messianic doctrine attracts adherents chiefly because it includes those things which formerly provided pleasure in life, the loss of which constitutes deprivation. The pervasiveness of the precipitating cultural crisis may be inferred from the broad range of sociocultural items to be restored in the golden age. For example, one of the Sioux participants in the Ghost Dance experienced a vision of an old-fashioned buffalo hunt, genuine in all details. He said that he had beheld the scouts dashing back to proclaim the sighting of a herd.[7] Now, the killing off of the buffalo was probably the greatest blow to the Plains Indians. Another bitter grievance was the expropriation of the Indian lands and the segregation of the tribes on reservations; removal to a new geographical setting had more or less direct repercussions on every phase of the culture. For example, the prophet Smohalla promised, among other things, the restoration of the original tribal lands.[8]

Deprivation may arise from the destruction not only of physical objects but also of sociocultural activities. In the aboriginal Sioux culture, millions of buffalo furnished an unlimited supply of food. Buffaloes and their by-products were perhaps the most important commodity in the Sioux economy, being employed as articles of exchange, as material for tepees, bedding, war shields, and the like. In addition, the buffalo was the focal point of many ritual and social activities of the Sioux. When the buffaloes were destroyed, therefore, the Sioux were deprived not only of food, but also of culturally significant activities. The tribal societies concerned with

[5] Sometimes, however, messianic movements passed over into physical violence. The preachings of the Delaware Prophet, for example, were used by Pontiac in his war against the whites. See Parkman (1886). On the Sioux outbreak of 1890, see Mooney, chapters 12–14.

[6] See Nash (1937). As used by Nash, "deprivation" is the complementary term to "indulgence." Nash borrowed the concepts from Lasswell (1935).

[7] Lowie (1925), 188 ff.

[8] Mooney, chapter 6.

war and hunting lost their function and atrophied. The arts and techniques surrounding the buffalo hunt, arts and techniques which had once been sources of social status and of pride in "workmanship," were now rendered useless.[9]

The impact of the white culture, besides depriving the Indians of their customary satisfactions, adds to their suffering by introducing the effects of new diseases and intoxicating liquor. In 1889, the Sioux suffered decimating epidemics of measles, grippe, and whooping cough.[10] It is significant that Tenskwatawa prophesied that there would be no smallpox in the golden age.[11] Complaints about the evil influences of firewater were expressed by "Open Door"; by "Handsome Lake," the Iroquois Prophet; by the Delaware Prophet; and by Känakuk, among others.[12]

The messianic movement served to "articulate the spiritual depression" [13] of the Indians. Those groups which faced a cultural impasse were predisposed to accept a doctrine of hope. Correlatively, the tribes that rejected the doctrine were in a state in which the values of their old life still functioned.[14] In a condition of anomie, where there is a disorganization of the "controlling normative structure," [15] most of the members of the group are thrown out of adjustment with significant features of their social environment. The old set of social and cultural norms is undermined by the civilized culture. Expectations are frustrated, there is a "sense of confusion, a loss of orientation," [16] there is no longer a foundation for security. At such a time, messianic prophecies are most likely to be accepted and made the basis of action. Messiahs preach the return to the old order, or rather, to a new order in which the old will be revived. Essentially, their function is to proclaim a *stable order*, one which will define the ends of action. Their doctrines describe men's former life, meaningful and satisfactory.

The stabilizing function of the messianic movement may be illustrated in specific cases.[17] Investigation of the 1870 and 1890 North American Ghost Dance movements shows that they are correlated with widespread

[9] See Lesser (A), 45–49; also, Lesser (B).

[10] Mooney, 820 ff.

[11] Macleod, 519.

[12] On "Open Door," see Macleod, 517; on "Handsome Lake," see Hodge (1907), 309.

[13] Macleod, 505.

[14] Lesser (A), 58.

[15] Parsons (1937), 377.

[16] *Idem*, 334.

[17] Messianic movements which have occurred elsewhere than in North America are outside the scope of the present paper. The following literature, however, may be consulted: Métraux (1928), 217; Moszkowski (1911); Nimuendaju (1914); Williams (1923); Chinnery and Haddon (1917); Driberg (1931); and MacDonald (1890).

deprivation. The two movements, though they originated in the same tribe, the North Paiute of Nevada, spread over different areas, depending upon the presence or absence of a deprivation situation. A comparison of the two movements makes the relationship clear-cut. The Ghost Dance of 1870 spread only through northern California;[18] the tribes in that area had "suffered as great a disintegration by 1870 . . . as the average tribe of the central United States had undergone by 1890." [19] In 1890, the Ghost Dance once again spread from the North Paiute, but this time not to California. By 1875, the movement there had exhausted itself and was abandoned.[20] All the dancing and adherence to the rules of conduct had failed to bring the golden age. Disillusionment supervened upon the discovery that the movement was an inadequate response. The alternative response seems to have been a despondent and relatively amorphous adaptation. The Indians "had long since given up all hope and wish of the old life and adapted themselves as best they might to the new civilization that engulfed them." [21] The 1890 movement did spread to the Plains tribes because by 1890 their old life had virtually disappeared, and the doctrine of the Ghost Dance was eagerly adopted for the hope that it offered. The radical changes among the Plains tribes in the twenty-year period, 1870–90, may best be traced by examining the history of the Teton Sioux. Up to 1868, they were the least affected by white contact of all the tribes of the Plains area. By 1890, however, they were experiencing an intense deprivation situation, the climax of a trend which had begun twenty years before. Especially severe were the years between 1885–90, when crops failed, many cattle died of disease, and a large part of the population was carried off by epidemics.[22]

Further corroboration of the positive correlation of the messianic movement with extended deprivation has been presented by Nash. In 1870, the Ghost Dance doctrine was presented to three tribes which had been brought together on the Klamath reservation six years before, the Klamath, the Modoc, and the Paviotso. Of the three tribes, the Modoc, who had experienced the greatest amount of deprivation, participated most intensely. The Paviotso, who had experienced minimal cultural changes,

18 Gayton (1930).
19 Kroeber (1925), 868; see also Kroeber (1904), 32–35.
20 All the California tribes were not affected in the same fashion. The Karok and the Tolowa participated more intensely than did the Yurok. Moreover, none of the tribes in the mission area took part. The Hupa, leading a stable reservation life, and the mission tribes, whose life had definitively been made over, had passed beyond a deprivation situation and had made an adequate substitution, in terms of derived satisfactions, for the aboriginal culture.
21 Kroeber (1925), 583.
22 Mooney, 824 ff. A detailed account of their vicissitudes may also be found in Lowie (1925), 188 ff.

participated least of all. Moreover, Nash found that within the tribes the members participated differentially, in rough proportion to the deprivation experienced.[23]

A case study of the Navaho furnishes still further support for our thesis. Until quite recently, the Navaho territory was relatively isolated; few roads crossed it and there were not more than two thousand white inhabitants.[24] The Navaho had managed to maintain the essentials of their own culture; their economic life had remained favorable; and, from 1869 to 1931, they increased in numbers from less than 10,000 to 45,000.[25] In 1864, in retaliation for their marauding, the United States Government rounded up the Navaho and banished them to the Bosque Redondo on the Pecos River. This exile was an exception to the fact that in general they had not suffered deprivation. They could not adapt to the agricultural life imposed on them and begged for permission to go home. Many died during epidemics of smallpox, whooping cough, chicken pox, and pneumonia. After four years, they were given sheep, goats, and clothing by the Government and allowed to return to their own country.[26]

The equilibrium of the Navaho culture was quickly restored. The tribe grew rich in herds and silver. The old way of life was resumed in its essentials, despite the greater emphasis on a pastoral economy. The deprivation situation of 1864–68 was left behind; life was integrated around a stable culture pattern. In the winter of 1889–90, when Paiute runners tried to spread the belief in the coming of the Ghost Dance Messiah, their mission was fruitless. "They preached and prophesied for a considerable time, but the Navaho were skeptical, laughed at the prophets, and paid but little attention to their prophecies." [27] There was no social need of a redeemer.

Within the last fifteen years, however, the entire situation of the Navaho tribe has changed. There has been constantly increasing contact with the white culture. Automobiles and railroads have brought tourists. The number of trading stores has increased. The discovery of oil on the reservation has produced rapid changes. Children have been sent to Government schools, far from their homes. Since 1929, the depression has reduced the income from the sale of blankets and silver jewelry. By far the most important difficulty now confronting the Navaho is the problem of overgrazing and soil erosion. To avert disaster, a basic reorganization of the economic activities of the tribe is necessary.[28] Therefore, the Government

[23] Nash (1937).
[24] Lindquist (1923), 275–85.
[25] Woehlke (1933), 2.
[26] Amsden (1933).
[27] Mooney, 809.
[28] Woehlke, 4.

to meet this *objective* condition, has introduced a soil-erosion and stock-reduction program but it has been completely unsatisfactory to the Navaho. Stock-reduction not only threatens their economic interests, *as they see them*, but undermines the basis of important sentiments and activities in the Navaho society. To destroy in a wanton fashion the focus of so many of their day-to-day interests cuts the cultural ground from under them.

Thus at present the Navaho are experiencing widespread deprivation. Significantly enough, within the past few years there has been a marked emergence of anti-white sentiment. Revivalistic cults have appeared.[29] There has also been a great increase in recourse to aboriginal ceremonials on all occasions.[30] Long reports of Navaho revivalistic activities were carried recently in *The Farmington Times Hustler*, a weekly published in Farmington, New Mexico. These activities bear a detailed similarity to the Ghost Dance and other American Indian messianic doctrines.

Despite the positive correlation of the messianic movement and deprivation, there is no one-to-one relation between these variables. It is here suggested that the messianic movement is *only one of several alternative responses*.[31] In the other direction, the relationship is more determinate; the messianic movement is comprehensible only as a response to widespread deprivation. The alternative response of armed rebellion and physical violence has already been suggested. The depopulation among the natives of the South Pacific Islands may be viewed as still another response. The moral depression which, it often has been held,[32] is one of the "causes" of the decline of the native races may be construed as a mode of reaction to the loss of an overwhelming number of satisfactions.

The theory of alternative responses may be tentatively checked against another set of data. The Ghost Dance among the Plains tribes lasted little more than a year or two, coming to a sharp end as a result of the suppression of the so-called "Sioux outbreak" with which it adventitiously had become connected in the minds of the whites. The Government agents on the Indian reservations successfully complied with their instructions to exterminate the movement. However, the deprivation of the tribes remained as acute as ever. It is in this context that the Peyote cult emerged

[29] This statement is verified by data in an unpublished paper by Clyde Kluckhohn.

[30] Kluckhohn (1938), 359.

[31] See Lasswell for a modified psychoanalytic categorization of the possible alternative responses to deprivation. In Lasswell's terms, if we shift from the individual to the group level, the messianic movement is an "autistic" response.

[32] See Rivers (1922) and Pitt-Rivers (1927); LeFevre (1931) argues the thesis that a certain minimum of liberty is necessary for continued interest in life. For a discussion of this point, see Sorokin (1937), III:174–76.

and spread among the Indians *as an alternative response*. It became the focus of a marked increase of attention and activity after 1890, thus coming in approximate temporal succession to the Ghost Dance. Completely nonviolent and nonthreatening to the White culture, the Peyote cult has been able to survive in an environment which was radically opposed to the messianic movements.

The general and specific sociocultural matrices of the Peyote cult are the same as those of the messianic movements. The Indians

> Fifty years ago, when Peyote first became known to them[33] . . . were experiencing . . . despair and hopelessness over their vanishing culture, over their defeats, over the past grandeur that could not be regained. They were facing a spiritual crisis. . . . Some turned to Peyotism, and as time has but intensified the antagonistic forces, more and more have become converted to the new religion which offers a means of escape. . . .[34]

The Peyote cult, like the messianic movement, was an "autistic" response, in Lasswell's terms, but the essential element of its doctrine was different. Whereas the Ghost Dance doctrine had graphically described a reversion to the aboriginal state, the Peyote cult crystallized around passive acceptance and resignation in the face of the existing deprivation. It is an alternative response which seems to be better adapted to the existing phase of acculturation.[35]

Thus we have tested the hypotheses that the primitive messianic movement is correlated with the occurrence of widespread deprivation and that it is only one of several alternative responses. There is a need for further studies, especially in regard to the specific sociocultural conditions which produce each of the possible responses.

---

[33] Actually, the use of peyote among the natives of Mexico was reported as early as 1569, but until 1890, "peyote spread at most to only five or six tribes north of the Rio Grande; . . . since 1890 it has been carried to some thirty additional tribes." See Shonle (1925), 54. The most complete bibliography on peyote may be found in LaBarre (1938).

[34] Petrullo (1934), 27.

[35] A more extended discussion of the Peyote Cult by Mr. Barber [appears] in the *American Anthropologist*. . . .

Political Elites in Colonial Southeast
Asia: An Historical Analysis

I

Present-day political systems in the nation states of Southeast Asia can be classified in accordance with various criteria; they can, for example, be politically grouped on a spectrum ranging from parliamentary democracy to totalitarian dictatorship.[1] The focus of the present inquiry is the sociology of political elites rather than the forms of polity which these elites have created or helped to create. It deals exclusively with the ruling "national" elites, leaving out of consideration secondary groups, such as territorially- or ethnically-based local and regional elites, religious leaders, and other traditional elites. Two kinds of "national" elite can be discerned in contemporary Southeast Asia, which we shall call "intelligentsia elites" and "modernizing traditional elites." Disregarding for the time being the constitutional frameworks and the degree of popular participation of each individual state, it may be said that both elites are in many respects oligarchies. Their oligarchic nature stems from the fact, first, that they are by and large the only exponents and representatives of the modern national states of Southeast Asia whose populations are only gradually undergoing the transition from "primordial" to "civil" allegiances.[2] Second, they are also oligarchies in the sense that core members are predominantly recruited from among limited segments of society.

Intelligentsia regimes, as used in this essay, are polities governed by groups of Southeast Asians whose major, if not sole, claim to the exercise

Reprinted from *Comparative Studies in Society and History*, Vol. VII, No. 3, April 1965, pp. 233–251, with permission of the author and the editors of *Comparative Studies in Society and History*. Footnotes abridged for this printing. Original reference numbers have been retained.

[1] Such classifications have i.a. been attempted by Gabriel A. Almond and James S. Coleman (eds.), *The Politics of the Developing Areas* (Princeton, 1960), 532 ff., and Edward Shils, "Political Development in the New States," *Comparative Studies in Society and History*, II (1960), 265–92 and 293–411. (Separately published, Mouton and Co., 1962.)

[2] This terminology is borrowed from Clifford Geertz, "Primordial Sentiments and Civil Politics in the New States," in Geertz (ed.), *Old Societies and New States: The Quest for Modernity in Asia and Africa* (Glencoe, 1963), 105–57.

of political power stems from their Western-style education and consequent orientation. In other words, it is not their social background — the group or class of their birth — that is the most significant datum about such intelligentsias (in fact, they usually represent a rather heterogeneous grouping from that point of view), but their commonly experienced training and outlook.[3] Equally important, these intelligentsias are in our definition ruling classes proper: they rule *because* they are the intelligentsia and not because they are educated members of other ruling groups in society; they correspond rather closely to Karl Mannheim's *freischwebende Intelligenz*[4] or, for that matter, to Platonic philosopher-kings.[5] Their emergence as a ruling class will be historically traced in this essay; suffice it to say now that their existence is predicated on a present-day social order in which there are no other viable groups able to exercise political power, or where such (usually traditional) groups have been so weakened as to leave the intelligentsia as virtually the sole successful claimant to power.

Modernizing traditional regimes, by contrast, consist of elite groups predominantly recruited on an ascriptive basis, from among established, not to say vested, social classes, strata or groups. It is true, of course, that the modernizing segments of these groups derive their contemporary political pre-eminence also from a Western-style education and outlook, and that they therefore constitute a fairly distinct minority within the traditional classes of their origin. Both elites thus may be said to belong to a modern Southeast Asian intelligentsia in the broadest sense of the term. But the intrinsic differences between them are of greater significance than the basic similarity of their educational experiences: where in the first type of polity intelligentsias act as ruling classes in their own right, the other is ruled by Westernized, "intellectualized" branches, so to speak, of traditionally-established ruling classes or groups. Reserving a closer historical investigation of modernizing traditional regimes for subsequent parts of this essay, we may briefly note that their existence depends on a greater or lesser degree of continuity in the social order, which has permitted traditional holders of power (economic, social and political) to adapt themselves to historical change, and to make some of them at least active participants and, indeed, leaders in the processes of modernization. It does not necessarily follow that in such regimes the Westernized elite is

---

[3] This shared experience and outlook is important for both civilian and military intelligentsias.

[4] See Karl Mannheim, *Ideology and Utopia* (London, 1948), esp. ch. 3.

[5] I have discussed this concept in two earlier essays, "Non-Western Intelligentsias as Political Elites," *The Australian Journal of Politics and History*, VI (1960), 205–18, reprinted in John H. Kautsky (ed.), *Political Change in Underdeveloped Countries: Nationalism and Communism* (New York and London, 1962), 235–51; and "Intellectuals and Politics in Western History," *Bucknell Review*, X (1961), 1–14.

coterminous with the (broadly defined) intelligentsia. Insofar as there exist intellectuals outside the educated traditional oligarchy, they may in fact form oppositional nuclei, as often as not vegetating on the (barely) tolerated fringes of political life.[6]

In accordance with the above set of criteria, Indonesia, Burma and North (and perhaps also South) Viet Nam may be classified as intelligentsia regimes, while Laos, Cambodia, Thailand, Malaya (Malaysia) and the Philippines belong to the category of modernizing traditional regimes. It should be stressed once again that these categories are sociological rather than political, and that they refer to the composition of the respective elites (i.e., to the question of who they are) rather than to the policies they adopt (i.e., to what they actually do). Such a classification need not *ipso facto* imply differences in, or even degrees of, "progressiveness," "modernity," "democratization," and such like. Either kind of regime can be progressive, modern or democratic to various extents, just as both can be the obverse to various extents.

II

The existence of these two types of contemporary Southeast Asian political elites is the result of a variety of historical developments. Two sets of such developments will receive detailed attention in this analysis, one rooted in premodern times, the other resulting from the imposition of modern colonial rule in the nineteenth and twentieth centuries. The first concerns the formative influences affecting the basic social and political structures of the various Southeast Asian societies, and the second, the effects of alien overlordship on these structures. The selection of these two sets of historical phenomena is, of course, arbitrary; they are not necessarily the only significant nodal points in Southeast Asian history.[7] Similarly, the emphasis on foreign, "imported" factors in Southeast Asian history is largely dictated by the focus of the inquiry itself. Whatever the proper balance between imported superstructure and indigenous substructure may be in each part of Southeast Asia, there seems little doubt that socially and politically the region's core areas of developed civilizations have been profoundly and more or less lastingly affected from the outside.[8] This is particularly true of the premodern era, but to some extent also holds for the colonial period.

According to the early formative influences, Southeast Asia can be

[6] See Edward Shils, "The Intellectuals in the Political Development of the New States," in Kautsky, *op. cit.*, 195–234.

[7] Cf. Harry J. Benda, "The Structure of Southeast Asian History: Some Preliminary Observations," *Journal of Southeast Asian History*, III (1952), 106–38 (*Yale University Southeast Asia Studies, Reprint Series, #5*).

[8] Cf. Georges Coedès, *Les peuples de la péninsule indochinoise: histoire — civilisations* (Paris, 1962), 58–60 and 204 ff.

divided into three distinct sectors, the Indianized, Sinicized and Hispanized. Using contemporary national boundaries we would place Burma, Thailand, Laos, Cambodia, Malaya and Indonesia in the first group; North and South Viet Nam in the second, and the Philippines in the third. Obviously, such a simple tripartite division does inadequate justice to the region's complexity, variety and history. First, though the effects of the three foreign influences on social and political structures were significant and profound, they were the result of quite different, and chronologically disparate, developments. Indianization proceeded gradually and apparently pacifically, the impetus for this acculturation very likely coming from within the area rather than from without; by contrast, Sinicization and Hispanization originated in military conquest and subjugation. It must, second, be borne in mind that all of these foreign elements impinged to varying degrees of intensity upon the different regions of their respective orbits, some parts having to all intents and purposes remained virtually free of their influences. As a rule, it was lowland areas favored by geographic and economic factors that experienced the fullest extent of alien influence and thus developed into core areas of civilization. And within each of these three orbits — and, *mutatis mutandis*, within most of the modern national states — we find a wide variety of cultures and subcultures exhibiting different levels of "imported" structural elements. Third, the boundaries between the various orbits, especially between the Indianized and Sinicized, were not historically static; not only do we sometimes find them side by side in what has become a single national entity in modern times,[9] but we also know of examples, notably Champa, where a formerly Indianized polity has been supplanted by a Sinicized one. In the subsequent analysis these highly important qualifications will be ignored, the names of present-day national entities being used as convenient shorthand symbols.

Indianized Southeast Asia. The most significant socio-political characteristic of the polities in the Indianized sector was, that all power and, effectively, all right to land, were vested in the kingly office. Accession to kingship was not directly a function of either wealth or ancestry, but rather of possession of the royal regalia.[10] In Indianized societies possession of these regalia gave power not only to the king, but also to his kin, and it became normal to parcel out the more important offices of state — particularly those involving the governance of a region — to the close kin of the monarch. If offices were given to a commoner, one of

[9] Cf. Edmund Leach, "The Frontiers of 'Burma'," *Comparative Studies in Society and History*, III (1960), 49–68.
[10] Cf. Robert Heine-Geldern's classic study, *Conceptions of State and Kingship in Southeast Asia* (Ithaca, 1956).

his female kin would often be taken as a royal concubine, thus creating a quasi-affinal relationship between king and official.[11]

With such extreme emphasis on the royal power the distinction between "royal" and "non-royal" became crucial. Royalty was a sacral force, *sui generis*, and the social and political division between those in contact with such a force (those of the sacred sphere) and those not in such contact (those of the profane sphere) became absolute.

Since the possession of the symbols of royalty — the capital city, the palace, the throne, the tiered umbrella, the lingam, etc. — was the essential prerequisite of royal power, and far outweighed the family status of any particular claimant, cases of disputed succession were not only frequent but virtually the rule. While succession rules theoretically provided that the ruler's eldest son should succeed him, in fact whoever managed, by guile, personal prestige, or main force to possess himself of the symbols of royalty at the end of a reign automatically became heir to the power of the throne. Most successions were fought over by members of established royal families or nobilities, but there are many instances of successful usurpation of the royal power by commoners. Thus in spite of the gulf separating the royal and nonroyal "segments" of society, the vacuum created by the demise of a monarch made it possible for an individual to cross the dividing line and become royal and sacred, and hence possessor of political power.[12]

Kingly power was, then, largely personal, not dynastically institutional. It was also virtually absolute or "despotic," though not necessarily only or primarily because of the "hydraulic" nature of many Indianized polities (a characteristic they shared with others) but rather because the realm was not intrinsically conceived of in terms of a functionally controlled and administratively demarcated territory so much as in terms of the radiation, so to speak, of royal charisma, itself a reflection of the sacral, rather than secular, nature of the polity.[13] The "patrimonial" realm proper was unstable and almost invariably of limited geographic size; Indianized

[11] See, for example, a contemporary Chinese report on Angkor: "Usually princes are chosen for office, and if not, those chosen offer their daughters as royal concubines." Paul Pelliot, *Mémoires sur les coutumes du Cambodge de Tcheou Ta-Kuan* (Paris, 1951), 14.

[12] Kevin O'Sullivan has traced royal successions in Angkor in his illuminating essay, "Concentric Conformity in Ancient Khmer Kinship Organization," *The Bulletin of the Institute of Ethnology, Academia Sinica*, 13 (1962), 87–96.

[13] The question of the supremacy of royal power vis-à-vis the Brahman priests in India has recently been critically examined by Ludo and Rosanne Rocher, "La sacralité du pouvoir dans l'Inde ancienne d'après les textes de Dharma," in *Le Pouvoir et le Sacré* (Brussels, n.d.), 123–37. In the Southeast Asian context, this problem still requires attention. Coedès (*op. cit.*, 206) observes that in Cambodia and Champa the Brahmans did not occupy as pre-eminent a position as in India, but apparently a position inferior to that of the king.

"empires" (insofar as they were primarily agricultural) were very likely not stable administrative entities so much as at best loose confederacies recognizing the temporary charismatic suzerainty of an outstanding *primus inter pares*. The key to this kind of polity lay in the combination of sparse populations and the absence of landed property. All land (with some specific exceptions[14]) "belonged" to the king and was farmed, so to speak, in usufruct, whether by individual peasants or corporate villages. Indianized Southeast Asia had no landowning classes, such as gentries or feudal nobilities. Royal officials were appointed by the ruler; they were, it is true, rewarded by tax farming privileges, but not only were these privileges by definition revocable at the whim of the king, they applied — as e.g. in the Javanese *tjatjah*[15] — to at times disparately located groups of human beings rather than to contiguous territorial entities.[16] This concentration of power thus precluded the existence of "countervailing" power stemming from more or less independently-wielded administrative, territorial control. The bilateral kinship system prevailing in Burma, Thailand, Cambodia and Java may have further tended toward the dispersal rather than the conservation of landed wealth, prestige and power.[17] In any case, official tenure was non-hereditary, as often as not tenuous and brief, and frequently entailing dismissal and even loss of life.[18] Last but not least, the rule of decreasing descent precluded the perpetuation *sine die* of ascriptive charisma.

If we disregard the complex problems of village autonomy and of the "countervailing" power at times available to religious, notably Theravada Buddhist and Muslim, elites in later centuries, we may say that basically the "sacral" Indianized polities were characterized by dualism, a division into two social compartments, the royal and the non-royal, and that the

[14] The exceptions were lands — at times entire villages — granted to religious personnel, usually in perpetuity.

[15] For good descriptions of the *tjatjah* as "tax unit," see G. P. Rouffaer, "Vorstenlanden," in *Adatrechtbundels*, XXIV (1931), 245, 289, 303–304.

[16] Cf. Leslie H. Palmier, "The Javanese Nobility under the Dutch," *Comparative Studies in Society and History*, II (1960), 200, and literature cited there. John S. Furnivall acutely observed that the Javanese system constituted "the direct contrary of feudalism." *Netherlands India: A Study of Plural Economy* (Cambridge and New York, 1944), 13–14. For the same writer's comment on the similarities between Java and Burma, see his *Colonial Policy and Practice: A Comparative Study of Burma and Netherlands India* (Cambridge, 1948), 37.

[17] Cf. Lauriston Sharp, "Cultural Continuities and Discontinuities in Southeast Asia," *The Journal of Asian Studies*, XXII (1962), 9.

[18] Cf. Rouffaer, *op. cit.*, 277–78 and 309–10, and also B. Schrieke, *Indonesian Sociological Studies: Selected Writings of B. Schrieke*, Part Two (The Hague, 1957), 200. On the modes of royal control over officialdom in Cambodia and Thailand, respectively, see Lawrence P. Briggs, *The Ancient Khmer Empire* (Philadelphia, 1951), 151 and H. G. Quaritch-Wales, *Siamese State Ceremonies* (London, 1931), 196.

political gap between these two compartments was not spanned by an institutionalized system of graded power based on landownership or other socio-economic criteria.[19]

Sinicized Southeast Asia. In contrast to this dualistic, sacral Indianized polity the Sinicized and Hispanized polities both could be termed structurally hierarchical and "secular" (or territorial). Both possessed social groups spanning the gap between royal (albeit ideologically absolute) power and peasant society. These groups as a rule had direct access to, and command over, landed wealth — and hence over segments of the population living on these lands — which provided them with "countervailing" power. It is these groups that, in turn, supplied the personnel for what was essentially functional, territorial administration.

The Sinicization of Vietnam (with the exception of its Southern "Cochinchinese" part, a late colonization territory) which occurred during the first millennium of the Christian era was structurally so profound that it survived the end of Chinese political control in 939 A.D. by several centuries. Whatever the causal relationship between "hydraulic" agriculture and political authoritarianism, the Sino-Vietnamese polity was primarily differentiated from its Indianized counterparts by the absence of absolute, "despotic" political power. Certainly the Vietnamese state *par excellence* was the centralized monarchy.[20] The emperor was thus far more than mere *primus inter pares*, and the charisma of the imperial office was of crucial importance; but the emperor was the guardian rather than the owner of the realm: though the Son of Heaven, he was not a *devaraja*. The imperial throne as such was open to usurpation, but more than possession of the charismatic paraphernalia of emperorship was involved in successful usurpation of the intrinsically secular power at the apex of the polity. Compared to the Indianized polities, power in the Sinicized state was institutional rather than personal, and dynasties were relatively long-lived. More important still, continuity was embedded in a hier-

[19] This kind of polity was limited to profoundly Indianized areas only where, as Coedès says (*op. cit.*, 204), "plusieurs facteurs ont contribué à briser les barrières entre groupes fermés les uns aux autres, et à les fondre dans une organisation plus ou moins centralisée." Elsewhere, as e.g. in Western Malaya but also in parts of Sumatra, royal power, though it used the panoply of the Indianized monarchy, was restricted and circumscribed by the existence of the "countervailing" power — whether landed or mercantile — of territorial or kin chiefs. See e.g. J. M. Gullick, *Indigenous Political Systems of Western Malaya* (London, 1958), 49.

[20] Remnants of feudalism and powerful nobilities in fact continued to obstruct monarchical centralization in Vietnam for several centuries. For a survey of the successive efforts to create a centralized state modelled on Imperial China see Lê Thánh Khôi, *Le Viêt-Nam — Histoire et Civilisation* (Paris, 1955), 170–74, 222–24, 251–53, 263–64, 323–26. On the Sinicization process, see Hisayuki Miyakawa, "The Confucianization of South China," in Arthur F. Wright (ed.), *The Confucian Persuasion* (Stanford, 1960), 21–46.

archically structured officialdom, the Confucian-trained bureaucracy. It was, it is true, appointed by, and responsible to, the emperor, but it was — ideally, at least — recruited on merit, not on the basis of ascriptive criteria, let alone at the whim of the emperor. Indeed, though the scholar-officials were dependent on the emperor, the emperor was almost equally dependent on a cohesive, institutional group which could and did survive not only individual rulers but even changing dynasties.[21]

The key to the Vietnamese polity was not only the centralized monarchy, but also a "gentry," which to a large extent derived its status from a system of land tenure that permitted patrilineages to accumulate lands (though individual tenure could, partly due to the absence of primogeniture, vary a great deal from generation to generation). This gentry could exercise independent, "countervailing" social power, whether as *notables* in the Vietnamese *commune* (in French administrative parlance) determining local and regional affairs by virtue of the example they set of Confucian civic morality,[22] or as members of the central bureaucracy, the "mandarinate." While it is true that this meritocracy was open to candidates from all social classes, the social outsider was very likely at most times in a small minority; in any case, the Confucian school-tie made him into an assimilated member of what in essence was a gentry-dominated group of literati-officials; very likely, too, accession to political office may have helped to accumulate landed wealth.[23] Thus, whereas a great social and

[21] Unfortunately no institutional study on the Vietnamese bureaucracy has to my knowledge yet appeared. While it was obviously very closely modelled on the Chinese bureaucracy, on which the analysis in the text is largely based, the parallel may have to be qualified in the light of specific data at a later date. Dr. Truong Buu Lam, Director of the Institute of Historical Research in the University of Saigon, currently at Harvard University, has been kind enough to read the sections on Vietnam. On the Chinese gentry, I have drawn on Fei Hsiao-tung, *China's Gentry: Essays in Rural-Urban Relations* (Chicago, 1953), esp. Chs. I and II; Hsiao Kung-chuan, *Rural China: Imperial Control in the Nineteenth Century* (Seattle, 1960); and on Chang Chung-li, *The Chinese Gentry: Studies on Their Role in Nineteenth-Century Chinese Society* (Seattle, 1955), according to whose tabulations landownership played a relatively insignificant role in gentry recruitment.

[22] A "Council of Notables" administered village affairs. It was recruited, writes Paul Mus, by co-option among "la petite oligarchie des villages, en y associant un certain taux de lettrés ou de fonctionnaires en retraite." *Viet-Nam: Sociologie d'une guerre* (Paris, 1952), 23. The position of *notables* thus seemingly paralleled that of the local gentry in China. On the latter, cf. Fei, *op. cit.*, Ch. IV, and Hsiao, *op. cit.*, esp. 263–65, 289–97, and *passim*.

[23] The social origins and composition of the Vietnamese "mandarinate" has, once again, not yet been systematically investigated. Lê Thánh Khôi (*op. cit.*, 328) stresses the "democratic" recruitment through open examinations as one of the great reforms of the Nguyên dynasty in the 19th century, but his assessment appears legalistic, devoid of sociological insights. Ch. Gosselin, *L'Empire d'Annam* (Paris, 1904), 39, observed that "tous les lettrés du pays, organisés depuis des

political gap existed between the royal and non-royal in the societies of Indianized Southeast Asia, in the Sinicized polity of Vietnam that gap was bridged by powerful lineages (often of landowners) able to exercise independent economic, social and — to some extent — political power.

Hispanized Southeast Asia. If India and China had brought new systems of political organization to the greater part of Southeast Asia, in the Philippines this task fell to medieval European Spain. Indian influences had apparently at best only been of peripheral and even then isolated significance in the islands; with the exception of Muslim strongholds in the south.[24] Preconquest Philippine social organization was limited to the *barangay*, a territorially circumscribed village group largely bound together by kinship ties and led by *datus*. Competition for leadership was a constant feature of these geographically small entities, which moreover feuded with each other without ever attaining even a limited measure of political consolidation into larger, more viable political units. In the areas where the Spaniards came to exercise control from the late sixteenth century onward, a new and centralized political super-structure emerged. But the Hispanization of the Philippines did not lead to a replica of the Hispanic-American societies based on *latifundia* and a numerically and socially significant Spanish-Filipino *mestizo* class.[25] Rather, due to the limited number of Spaniards (the result in part of geographic distance and in part of the relative economic, especially mineral, poverty of the islands), the new order to a large extent involved the gradual transformation of the preconquest Filipino ruling group of *datus* into a privileged, landed class of *principales*, the major beneficiaries of the new social, economic, and legal order introduced by the Spaniards. Though political — and ecclesiastic — control remained firmly in European hands, and though commercial wealth until the end of the eighteenth century was likewise primarily a Spanish — and to a lesser extent a Chinese — monopoly, land continued to be predominantly owned by a segment of the native population.

Not too dissimilar to the Vietnamese social structure, Filipino society

---

siècles en une espèce de franc-maçonnerie [*sic*], se prêtent mainforte les uns les autres. . . ." Cited in Paul Isoart, *Le phénomène national viêtnamien* (Paris, 1961), 61. Cf. also Jean Chesneaux, *Contribution à l'histoire de la nation vietnamienne* (Paris, 1955), 85–86. For China, see *i.a.* Hsiao, *op. cit.*, 382–83, 390–91, and for an earlier period, E. A. Kracke, Jr., *Civil Service in Early Sung China, 960–1067* (Cambridge, Mass., 1953), 69–70.

24 Muslim power actually extended to Luzon in the 16th century, but the Spanish conquest pushed it Southward. . . .

25 John L. Phelan, *The Hispanization of the Philippines: Spanish Aims and Filipino Responses, 1565–1700* (Madison, 1959), 118–20. See also the same writer's "Free versus Compulsory Labor: Mexico and the Philippines," *Comparative Studies in Society and History,* I (1959), 189–201.

thus possessed a native class with access to an increasing measure of social power, and it was from that class that the alien rulers recruited the subordinate officialdom on whose existence and loyalty their political hegemony ultimately depended. For our present, limited purposes of comparison, the major structural difference between Vietnam and the Philippines was, that in the former, political power at the apex had been wrested from foreign rulers in the middle of the tenth century, whereas in the latter, the process of merging socio-economic with national political power only took place under American aegis during the first half of the twentieth century.

III

Though European maritime and commercial influence in Southeast Asia commenced in the early sixteenth century, the Western impact on, and interference with, the native social structure remained for long limited to parts of the Philippines and to Java. It was only in the second half of the nineteenth century that European colonialism came to embrace all of Southeast Asia — with the exception of Thailand — and to affect the area more or less profoundly. According to the incidence and type of colonial rule and its impact on the indigenous elite structure, we shall now superimpose on our original tripartite division of Southeast Asia into Indianized, Sinicized and Hispanized regions an additional division into areas under direct and those under indirect colonial control. Quite briefly, in terms of "ideal types" direct rule implies the abrogation or destruction of the existing political system — the elimination of the traditional political elite *qua* elite — and its substitution by a Western administrative apparatus staffed by non-ascriptive personnel, Western as well as indigenous. Indirect rule, by contrast, indicates the continuation of the precolonial system, and the maintenance of traditional political elite groups as at least *de jure* rulers; in such systems, the Western element operates "indirectly," i.e., it technically restricts itself to an outside, advisory function, without introducing a separate, modern administrative apparatus.

Important as this typological distinction is, colonial practice here and there resulted in what might be called "mixed" systems.[26] More than that,

26 The outstanding example is Java which, though technically under direct rule, was administered by a dual hierarchy, one Dutch, the other native. Thus Furnivall (*Netherlands India*, 258) claimed that "the distinction between Direct and Indirect Rule was of legal rather than practical interest, for in the parts under Direct Rule it was Dutch policy to leave the people as far as possible under their own heads. . . ." But the important fact of this dual system was that native officialdom had developed into a bureaucratic hierarchy subordinate to its European counterpart, so that, though ethnically separate, it progressively ceased to function in its own right, as a truly indigenous administrative apparatus.

several colonies comprised both directly and indirectly ruled territories: thus the hill peoples of Burma were ruled indirectly, Burma proper directly; in the Netherlands Indies, most of the so-called Outer Islands were under indirect, Java to all intents and purposes under direct, rule; in French Indochina, Laos, Cambodia, Tonkin and Annam were indirectly ruled protectorates, Cochinchina a colony under direct rule; finally, the Straits Settlements fell within the orbit of direct rule, the Federated and Unfederated Malay States that of indirect rule. Spanish as well as later American colonial control in the Philippines can be classified as direct rule. The coexistence of the two administrative systems within a given colony led to diverse configurations which cannot be examined in detail here; but two major aspects deserve brief attention. In the first place, in Burma and the Netherlands Indies direct rule prevailed in the most heavily Indianized areas, leaving the peripherally Indianized peoples under indirect rule. A contrasting pattern emerged in Vietnam, where the Sinicized heartland remained under indirect rule, with the southern frontier-land falling under direct rule. In Malaya, the directly ruled areas were in fact restricted to small, newly-created, European enclaves, known as the Straits Settlements. Second, in Indonesia and Vietnam the directly ruled areas acted as social "magnets" which attracted, or siphoned off, potential elite members from the indirectly ruled territories within the same colony.[27] In Burma, Laos, Cambodia and Malaya, on the other hand, this phenomenon was apparently far more limited on account of the ethnic, cultural and religious barriers separating the populations of indirectly and directly ruled territories.[28]

We shall now briefly examine the impact of the two colonial administrative systems on the various polities in Southeast Asia, with special attention to political and economic modernization. As we already observed in passing, direct rule led to the virtual destruction of the political precolonial *status quo*. In the case of Burma, the last incumbent of the throne

[27] This "magnet effect" needs a great deal of careful research. One typical example is that of Sumatrans drawn to Java in colonial times. A study of Indonesian "political decision makers" in the mid-1950's shows that Sumatrans, who in 1930 accounted for 8% of the total population of the Netherlands Indies, supplied 20% of cabinet members and 18% of top-level civil servants. See Soelaeman Soemardi, "Some Aspects of the Social Origin of Indonesian Political Decision Makers," *Transactions of the Third World Congress of Sociology* (London, 1956), 340; on the coincidence of such high offices with university training, see *ibid.*, 342.

[28] Educational statistics for French Indochina indicate that of a total of 525 students enrolled in the University of Hanoi in 1921–22, 265 came from Tonkin, 133 from Cochinchina (both in effect directly ruled), the protectorates of Annam, Cambodia and Laos supplying 70, 19 and 5 students, resp.; in 1929–30, the corresponding figures were 298 and 84, 98, 6 and 7 (breakdowns for the intervening years were apparently not published). See Joanne Marie Coyle, "Indochinese Administration and Education — French Policy and Practice, 1917–1945" (Unpubl. doctoral diss., Fletcher School of Diplomacy, 1963), 187–90.

and his immediate entourage were forcefully removed from the country after the third Anglo-Burmese War in 1886. The case of Java is more complex. The territory of the realm of Mataram was continually reduced in size, in addition to being divided, during the 18th and 19th centuries; while the rump principalities were preserved as autonomous, indirectly ruled territories, they lost all political significance after 1830. In modern times, then, practically the entire island was directly administered. Sudden or gradual, the imposition of direct rule in both Burma and Java resulted in the actual or virtual disappearance of the sacral, charismatic, despotic Indianized monarchy, though of course not in the destruction of the old elite groups as such. Alien, modern (and in a sense modern and efficiently despotic) colonial states took their place, geographically symbolized by the new seaboard capital cities of Rangoon and Batavia. Since sacral kingship and the court had been coterminous with the Indianized realm, the decapitation of the royal segment" actually amounted to the destruction of these polities. Deprived of their apex, and without entrenched hierarchies of social classes, Burmese and Javanese societies were in effect rendered politically elite-less, reduced to undifferentiated peasantries. The new polities were alien, the new political elites composed of foreigners; though the traditional sub-elite could, as in Java, continue a vestigial administrative existence, it could at best exist on the periphery, and in the service of, the modern colonial-bureaucratic apparatus without affecting its political destiny.[29]

Increasingly, the supra-village vacuum came to be filled with new social elements, recruited — largely through the medium of Western-style education — into the modern colonial social order. The process of modernization, then, *inter alia*, called forth an intelligentsia — in the widest sense of the term — whose members staffed posts in the modern bureaucracy, especially its technical services, the school systems, clerical posts in Western enterprise, and ultimately also the modern indigenous organizations, social and political, of the 20th century. Obviously, traditional elite families in Burma and Java supplied a large, perhaps even a predominant, percentage of the first generation of this intelligentsia; but the social origin of its individual members became progressively far less significant than its social function as a more or less distinct group in these directly-ruled colonial dependencies. Membership in the modern intelligentsias of Burma and Java was not based on ascriptive but primarily on educational and functional criteria. Equally important, the intelligentsia's social and political abode was the Westernized cities, its social, and in a sense even its

---

[29] See Note 26, above. On the modernization of the administration, coupled with the disintegration of the traditional system of Burma, see Furnivall, *Colonial Policy and Practice, op. cit.,* 73-75. On the extent of "Anglicization" among Burmese colonial officials, see the case studies in Lucian W. Pye, *Politics, Personality, and Nation Building: Burma's Search for Identity* (New Haven, 1962), 211–44.

political, loyalty lay not with the *ancien régimes* but with the modern
order: For all its anticolonialism, intelligentsia-led nationalism avowedly
aimed at the creation of a modern state, not at the restoration of the
Indianized monarchy.[30] At the same time, however, these intelligentsias
only had a limited "stake" in colonial Burma and Java as such. In part,
this was doubtless due to the colonial relationship itself; but to a perhaps
even greater extent their aloofness from the colonial order stemmed from
the fact that, as a group (and in many instances also as individuals) the
intelligentsias did not "own" anything but their educationally-acquired
proficiency. Just as the aristocracies in Indianized polities had derived
their status from royal appointment rather than from territorial control,
so the modern intelligentsias, regardless of their social origin, derived
their status directly or indirectly from the colonial order, without "representing" a vested corporate or personal interest rooted in economic or
other power.

To phrase this somewhat differently we might say that the new elites
were the socially unattached, *freischwebende* beneficiaries of (largely un-
planned) political modernization, without being holders of traditional
power, such as landed wealth. Indeed, the lack of such a secular power
base may to some extent at least account for the insignificant role played
in economic life by modern as well as traditional elites in the Indianized
orbit.[31] Doubtless colonial policies favoring Western capitalism, no less
than traditional religious-ideological orientations, both had their share in
continuing this disability into the realm of economic modernization. The
result was an economic dualism[32] expressed in ethnic pluralism, in which,
in addition to a European leading element, Asian minorities represented
the main intermediate layer in the modern economic sector. It is true that
the "ubiquitous" Chinese became the artisans and retailers *par excellence*
throughout colonial Southeast Asia. But only in Indianized Southeast Asia
did they — or, less frequently, Indian *chettyars*,[33] Arabs or even Vietnam-

[30] On this point, see Shils, *loc. cit.*, and the same author's "The Intellectuals in
the Political Development of the New States," in Kautsky, *op. cit.*, 195–234.

[31] In the peripherally Indianized societies — as e.g., in parts of Sumatra — the
response to economic innovation was far less passive. This contrast requires a good
deal of careful investigation. In Clifford Geertz's *Agricultural Involution: The
Process of Ecological Change in Indonesia* (Berkeley and Los Angeles, 1963), it is
explained in terms of different "eco-systems" and in relation to Dutch economic
activities in Indonesia.

[32] The term is here used descriptively to denote the existence, side by side, of a
capitalist and a subsistence economy. I am not here concerned with the inferences
drawn from this co-existence by such scholars as H. Boeke, which have given rise
to a voluminous and controversial literature.

[33] On the Indian *chettyars* in colonial Burma and Malaya, see Usha Mahajani,
The Role of Indian Minorities in Burma and Malaya (Bombay, 1960), 16–22,
98–101.

ese[34] — also become the major purveyors of ready cash, the moneylenders linking the modern and traditional sectors of the dual economy.[35] Little wonder that the politically conscious Burmese and Javanese intelligentsias, condemned to the oppositionist fringe of colonial political life and aloof from modern economic life, could only envisage independence in terms of the elimination of alien overlordship together with that of the alien, capitalist economy. Sociologically and ideologically *étatisme* if not socialism provided the intelligentsias with a logical, perhaps the only logical, prescription for national salvation; and, though inspired by conscious visions of modernity, such "national socialism" could in fact be nourished by long, often hidden, traditional roots.[36]

Indirect rule was variously applied and covered a wide variety of societies with differing degrees of Indianization.[37] Without investigating the historical reasons for its introduction or the varieties of its application in the orbit of Indianized Southeast Asia, we shall limit ourselves to a few generic observations. It is above all of paramount importance not to confuse the political aspects of indirect rule with its sociological consequences. While there has been some recent controversy regarding the residual legal sovereignty retained by native rulers, especially by Indonesian potentates under Dutch indirect rule in the 19th century,[38] the intrinsic political im-

---

[34] On the Vietnamese in Cambodia, see David J. Steinberg, *Cambodia: Its People, Its Society, Its Culture* (New Haven, 1959), 40–42.

[35] In Vietnam (especially in French Cochinchina), moneylenders were not primarily Chinese, as a reading of Victor Purcell's *The Chinese in Southeast Asia* (London, New York & Toronto, 1951), 236 ff. would suggest, but also Vietnamese landlords. See Charles Robequain, *The Economic Development of French Indo-China*, tr. by Isabel A. Ward (London, New York & Toronto, 1944), 40n., 85–86, 192–93, and Pierre Gourou, *L'utilisation du sol en Indochine française* (Paris, n.d.), 276–80. In the Philippines, Purcell (*op. cit.*, 635) writes, "that the Filipino is always in debt to the Chinese is undoubtedly true, but the evidence is all to the effect that the Filipino *cacique* is even more oppressive and usurious."

[36] The interplay between traditional religious or ideological and modern socialist, especially Marxist thought, has as yet received inadequate attention. A penetrating analysis of Confucianism and Marxism can be found in Mus, *op. cit.*, Chs. XIV, XVIII and XIX. Cf. also Emanuel Sarkisyanz, *Russland und der Messianismus des Orients: Sendungsbewusstsein und politischer Chiliasmus des Ostens* (Tübingen, 1955), and the same author's "Marxism and Asian Cultural Traditions," *Survey* 43 (1962), 55–64 and 129, and "Kommunismus und Geisteskrise Asiens: Marxismus und orientalische Weltanschauungen," in Dieter Oberndörfer (ed.), *Wissenschaftliche Politik: Eine Einführung in Grundfragen ihrer Tradition und Theorie* (Freiburg, n.d.), 335–64.

[37] For a careful analysis of indirect rule in British Malaya and the Netherlands Indies, see Rupert Emerson, *Malaysia: A Study in Direct and Indirect Rule* (New York, 1937).

[38] Cf. G. J. Reesink, "Inlandsche Staten in den Oosterschen Archipel (1873–1915)," *B.K.I.*, 116 (1960), 313–49, and Justus M. van der Kroef, "On the Sovereignty of Indonesian States: A Rejoinder," *ibid.*, 117 (1961), 238–66.

198   HARRY J. BENDA

potence imposed upon traditional indigenous elites by the "protective umbrella" of indirect rule seems to be reasonably well established. To be sure, the degree of European control varied considerably from area to area, as for example between the Federated and Unfederated Malay States,[39] but all native rulers under Western suzerainty *ipso facto* forfeited some essential attributes of sovereignty, notably in the realm of foreign affairs. Yet, however circumscribed in matters martial and political, the native elites were not only permitted to survive as a social group, but, thanks to the *pax occidentalis*, they were in effect given greater stability and internal cohesion. If the policing power of the colonial regimes removed the perennial strife endemic among Indianized polities, the introduction and stabilization of the principle of hereditary monarchy, with more or less orderly succession, virtually terminated their equally perennial internal instability.

Positive as well as negative consequences accrued from these innovations. Undeniably indirect rule, in its arbitrary support of the representatives of the socio-political *status quo*, tended to inhibit the growth of competing elite groups, particularly in areas subject to intensive economic modernization through Western enterprise. It is similarly true that the new, artificially protected, colonial security, combined with political impotence, could and did lead to what we might term social and cultural involution. The carefully preserved Indianized "Establishment," that is to say, could succumb to stagnation, it could withdraw from reality and narcissistically contemplate its traditional grandeur; and it could give birth to a tropically luxuriant profusion of offices and office holders, usually at the expense of the taxpaying, non-royal component of Indianized Southeast Asian polities.[40] On the credit side of the ledger, however, stand continuity, or rather the possibility of gradual modernization, of change within continuity. For sure, this is the very virtue which the most eloquent (though not invariably the most Machiavellian) colonial administrators read into the necessity of indirect rule. But one need not share their apologetic romanticism in order to admit the sociologically significant fact that indirect rule at least obviated the social and political vacuum which was the concomitant of direct rule, and that it allowed (even though it did not necessarily encourage) the modernization of members of the traditional elites in Indianized principalities. It could even

[39] See Emerson, *op. cit.*, 24 ff., 248 ff., 351 ff. For a brief but clear analysis, see Phyllis M. Kaberry, *The Development of Self-Government in Malaya* (London, 1945).

[40] This process is well demonstrated in the Javanese princely states of Mataram from the eighteenth century onward. In Malaya, a new religious officialdom was created in the late nineteenth century. Cf. William R. Roff, "Kaum Muda-Kaum Tua: Innovation and Reaction amongst the Malays, 1900–1941," in K. G. Tregonning (ed.), *Papers on Malayan History* (Singapore, 1962), 162–92.

be argued that some Indianized monarchies under indirect rule, shorn of responsibility for the conduct of political affairs proper, may have gained in charismatic lustre and stature, developing with the aid of modern media of communications into symbols of traditional-modern grandeur.

Just as in Burma and Java, Western education constituted by far the most prominent avenue to modernization in indirectly ruled territories. But whereas we saw that in these directly ruled colonial dependencies education took the place of ascription, in Malaya, Cambodia and also in Laos perhaps education in a sense enhanced ascription. The younger generation of the traditional Malayan, Cambodian and Laotian elites thus became the beneficiaries, first, of an increasingly institutionalized charisma, and, second, of Western education.[41] These (potentially) modernizing traditional elites, then, were socially a far more homogeneous group than the intelligentsias in directly ruled colonies. And, unlike their often radical counterparts, they could, individually and corporately, afford to espouse a more conservative approach to social and political problems. It would be a mistake to assume that the colonial *status quo* as such inspired true loyalty, but aloofness from the foreigner rather than radical nationalism — let alone socialism — may have been prevalent; in any case, the social order of things was not a primary target of attack for the modernized members of the traditional elites, as it certainly was for the intelligentsias.[42] Both kinds of elite, we should add, partook of political modernization far more widely and avidly than of economic modernization; we have already suggested that this imbalance may have been the result of the essentially non-economic base of the Indianized polities, as well as of the traditional value systems and of colonial policies.[43]

The distinctions between direct and indirect rule which we have so far examined in the Indianized orbit are in several respects less applicable to Vietnam. Although theoretically only Cochinchina was directly ruled, in fact Tonkin's virtual removal from the jurisdiction of the Vietnamese court from 1886 onward brought the North under more or less direct French control. Even in Annam itself, the Protectorate progressively turned into a legal fiction, relegating court and mandarinate to a shadowy

[41] Since this essay deals with colonial Southeast Asia, the special case of Thailand has been omitted from this discussion, even though important parallels do exist. Cf. David A. Wilson, *Politics in Thailand* (Ithaca, 1962), Ch. I, and Lauriston Sharp (ed.), *Thailand* (New Haven, 1956), Ch. 6.

[42] Cf. Raden Soenarno, "Malay Nationalism, 1900–1945," *Journal of Southeast Asian History*, I (1960), 1–33, esp. his comparison between Malay and Indonesian nationalism, 27–33.

[43] Since the traditional Thai elite demonstrated a negative response to economic modernization quite similar to that of elites in colonial, Indianized Southeast Asia, the importance of the colonial factor must not be exaggerated. Cf. Sharp, *op. cit.*, 160–67. Geertz (*op. cit.*, 130 ff.) draws parallels between Java and Japan which would seem less relevant than comparisons within Indianized Southeast Asia.

existence.[44] The artificial colonial dismemberment of the Vietnamese realm went hand-in-hand with the creation of the no less artificial Indochinese Union (embracing Laos and Cambodia in addition to the three Vietnamese "*pays*"). To all intents and purposes, direct rule was of far greater significance than indirect rule, and the coexistence of the two in such close proximity inevitably led to the supremacy of the directly ruled areas. Like its counterparts in some of the Indianized states, Hué, the traditional capital city of Vietnam, had to cede pride of place to modern urban centers: to Hanoi intellectually and to Saigon commercially.

Nonetheless, the sociological consequences of French rule differed in the three parts of Vietnam. Its most important concomitants occurred in thinly-populated Cochinchina, where Vietnamese rule had only been established in the 18th century and where French hydraulic technology created one of Southeast Asia's most fertile rice granaries in modern times. While the commercial wealth resulting from this agricultural revolution primarily benefited French (and Chinese) capital, ownership of the newly opened lands was predominantly Vietnamese.[45] The origins of this new and increasingly "Gallicized" class of landowners are not yet clear; but very likely some, perhaps most, of its members belonged to lower-rank Vietnamese mandarinal officialdom (the higher mandarins having left the area after the French conquest). Whatever its origin, the new class showed an easy adaptability to economic change: significantly, moneylenders in Vietnam were primarily Vietnamese, not Indians or Chinese. In Tonkin, where — as in Annam — the elite pattern was far less profoundly affected than in Cochinchina, we even find some few but significant, positive Vietnamese responses to economic modernization (banks, trading houses, factories, etc.). These positive reactions stand in marked contrast to the on the whole negative responses to economic change in the Indianized polities, and are very likely anchored in the presence of an intrinsically "secular" indigenous social structure.

Political modernization in Vietnam — largely again the result of Western education — must be primarily viewed in the context of direct colonial rule. The predominance of direct over indirect rule in contiguous territories, combined with the rapid weakening of the traditional political structure, greatly inhibited a systematic modernization of the court and

----

[44] For a brief summary of French colonial policies towards the three *pays*, see Philippe Devillers, *Historie du Viêt-Nam de 1940 à 1952* (Paris, 1952), 28–29. Cf. also Isoart, *op. cit.*, Ch. IV, and Lê Thánh Khôi, *op. cit.*, 394–406. Of Cochinchina one French historian observed that it possessed "une tonalité française, caracteristique de cette portion d'Indochine," Georges Taboulet, *La geste française en Indochine*, I (Paris, 1956), 522.

[45] Cf. Devillers, *op. cit.*, 39–40, Mus, *op. cit.*, 240–41, Chesneaux, *op. cit.*, 166, Isoart, *op. cit.*, 255–58.

mandarinate as a cohesive elite. In the twentieth century, most of the beneficiaries of Westernization thus came to be oriented towards French metropolitan culture and modern administrative and political forms. Though Western-educated members of the traditional elite in Annam here and there doubtless played important roles, the modern history of Vietnam was apparently made in Tonkin and Cochinchina. Socially, a large segment of the modernized elite very likely came from the mandarinate (in the North) and the landowning class (in the South), rather than from the "unattached" intelligentsias we observed in directly-ruled Indianized Southeast Asia. But this social anchorage did not preclude the emergence of a radical wing, side by side with a moderate wing, in Vietnamese nationalism. The latter — notably strong in Cochinchina — primarily aimed at political emancipation from foreign rule, the former, Tonkin-centered, at complete independence and, indeed, at social revolution.[46]

Philippine social evolution can be dealt with more briefly on account of its basic continuity. We saw that Spanish colonialism had called into being a class of native *principales* deriving its status from landed wealth. Increasing exploitation of the islands' resources, accompanied by commercialization of Philippine agriculture from about the middle of the eighteenth century on, initiated a period of accelerating social change. Above all else, new opportunities for capital accumulation came into existence. Recent research indicates that the main beneficiaries of this economic modernization were, in addition to Filipino *caciques* and Chinese, the numerically strong group of Chinese *mestizos*.[47] After the mid-nineteenth century immigrant Chinese started to supplant these Chinese *mestizos* as a commercial, urban middle class, but they retained status and prestige derived from landed wealth and from Hispanization. As in Vietnam, the moneylender in Luzon and other islands was a native (and *mestizo*) rather than a foreigner. Towards the close of Spanish rule, there thus existed a specifically Philippine ruling class composed of native and *mestizo* members. While the colonial power had created the preconditions for economic modernization in the Philippines, Europeans actually played a less important part in it than did Chinese and Chinese *mestizos*, in sharp contrast to the colonial empires of the capitalist Western nations in Southeast Asia. Philippine nationalism was thus primarily political, not socially radical: its leaders strove for political equality within the Spanish empire, and also the "nationalization" of Spanish, notably Church, landholdings; but they did not aim at destroying the social *status quo* as such. American

[46] Cf. Chesneaux, *op. cit.*, Ch. X, and I. Milton Sacks, "Marxism in Viet Nam," in Frank N. Trager (ed.), *Marxism in Southeast Asia* (Stanford, 1959), 102–70.

[47] See Edgar Wickberg, "The Chinese Mestizo in Philippine History," *Journal of Southeast Asian History*, V (1964), 62–100.

colonial rule, though it commenced with the destruction of the short-lived
Philippine Republic, almost immediately turned into preparation for
autonomy and independence. It thus helped to consolidate the Philippine
elite and to increase its landholdings; it also offered new commerical, and
far-reaching educational and administrative opportunities. The politically
active elite members were thus firmly rooted in a class that had enjoyed,
and continued to enjoy, the privileges of acculturation, education and
wealth.

                                     IV

The foregoing analysis of Southeast Asian elites in terms, first, of pre-
modern social structures and, second, of the variegated influences of different European colonial regimes, may provide a useful tool for the understanding of the emergence of what we have called intelligentsia-ruled
polities and polities governed by modernizing traditional elites in postwar Southeast Asia. Like all selective investigations, structural elite analysis, however embedded in historical data, only deals with some aspects of
social and political history, without seeking to explain all its ramifications. Obviously such a schematic presentation must appear misleadingly
rigorous; it neither can nor does in fact fully explain or account for the
existence, let alone the operational modes, of present-day political systems.
More particularly, it cannot possibly do justice to the significant regional
and local variations which of necessity modify the generic classifications
here attempted. Thus for example the problem of economic modernization
of indigenous elites, especially in the Indianized orbit, has only been
peripherally touched upon; if the case of Malaya deserves separate treatment on account of very large non-indigenous Asian groups, Bali presents
an interesting case study of economic modernization on the whole un-
hampered by such alien competition.[48] The brief analysis of the Vietnamese elites is similarly inadequate to account for the emergence of extreme
radicalism.

While we may have succeeded in showing how various national elites
came into existence in colonial Southeast Asia, we have not attempted to
trace their actual rise to power in the often turbulent era of decoloniza-
tion, as well as their performance as ruling classes in independent nation
states. For such purposes our social and historical scaffolding would have
to be amplified along lines which we can only briefly suggest, without
developing them in this essay. First, the emergence, during the Japanese
occupation era, of military elites — in part an adjunct to the modern
intelligentsias, though not necessarily coterminous with them — and that

[48] Cf. Clifford Geertz, *Peddlers and Princes: Social Change and Economic
Modernization in Two Indonesian Towns* (Chicago and London, 1963), esp.
Ch. 4.

of younger echelons of potential leaders has obviously profoundly affected the elite structure, and with it contemporary politics, in such countries as Burma and Indonesia. Second, the interplay between different social systems within the same political boundaries has likewise provided some of the most noteworthy dynamics in modern political history, most notably perhaps again in Indonesia (with the occurrence of "social revolutions" in several, previously indirectly-ruled territories, as well as with the tug-of-war between Indianized Java and some of the peripherally Indianized Outer Islands), in Burma (with a similar tug-of-war between Indianized Burma proper and non-Indianized minority groups) and in Vietnam (where the struggle in part revolves around the dichotomy between Sinicized Vietnamese and non-Sinicized *montagnard* minorities). Third, though rarely prime actors, religious elites have nonetheless also helped to shape the recent national histories of several Southeast Asian countries. In the fourth place, the picture must be supplemented by close study of the role of Communist leadership, ranging all the way from gaining political power in part of Vietnam to launching unsuccessful revolts, e.g., in the Philippines and Malaya. The social roots and character of that leadership differ from country to country; where in Vietnam, Burma and Indonesia it formed part of the general intelligentsia elite reared in directly-ruled colonial areas, in Malaya it originated among the Chinese urban middle class, and in the Philippines among the marginal intellectual sub-elite.

Finally, an examination of both the internal policies pursued by each individual ruling elite and its external or international orientations may yield significant insights and perhaps correlations. It is probably true that on the whole intelligentsias have embarked on wholesale social transformation while modernizing traditional elites have tended towards social and political conservatism; but exceptions to this rule can be found. It is, again, possible to detect a preponderance of "pro-Western" international orientations among such elites and "neutralist" ones among intelligentsias, but this generalization is even more questionable, less relevant, and, indeed, subject to change, depending upon international rather than domestic configurations.

Notes for
Further Reading

For analysis of several general types of social movements which arise in situations of change, see:

Brinton, C., *The Anatomy of Revolution*. New York: Prentice-Hall, 1952.
Cohn, N., *The Pursuit of the Millennium*. Fairlawn: Essential Books, 1957.

De Tocqueville, A., *The Old Regime and the French Revolution*. Garden City: Doubleday, 1955.
Heberle, R., *Social Movements*. New York: Appleton-Century-Crofts, 1951.
Talmon, Y., "Millenarian Movements," *Archives Européennes de Sociologie* (forthcoming).
Wallace, A.F., "Revitalization Movements," *American Anthropologist*, Vol. 58, 1956.

For analysis of specific types of social movements which arise in situations of change in modern and modernizing societies, see:

Coleman, J.S., "Current Political Movements in Africa," *The Annals of the American Academy of Political and Social Science*, Vol. 298, March, 1955, pp. 95–108.
————, "The Problem of Political Integration in Emergent Africa," *Western Political Quarterly*, Vol. VIII, No. 1, 1955, pp. 44–57.
Dunbabin, J.P.D., "The 'Revolt of the Field': The Agricultural Labourers' Movement in the 1870s," *Past and Present*, No. 23, 1963, pp. 68–97.
Friedrich, C.J., "The Agricultural Basis of Emotional Nationalism," *Public Opinion Quarterly*, VI, 1937, pp. 50–61.
Hodgkin, T., *Nationalism in Colonial Africa*. New York: New York University Press, 1957.
Kaplan, M. (ed.), *The Revolution in World Politics*. New York: John Wiley & Sons, Inc., 1962.
Kautsky, J.N. (ed.), *Political Change in Underdeveloped Countries: Nationalism and Communism*. New York: John Wiley & Sons, Inc., 1962.
Lipset, S.M., "The Source of the Radical Right," in Daniel Bell (ed.), *The New American Right*. New York: Criterion Books, 1955, pp. 166–233.
Lorwin, V., "Working Class Politics and Economic Development in Western Europe," *American Historical Review*, LXIII, 1958, pp. 338–357.

For the analysis of the development of some types of élite groups, and especially of so-called modernizing élites, see, in addition to material presented in the preceding bibliography:

Kerr, C., *Industrialism and Industrial Man*. Cambridge, Mass.: Harvard University Press, 1960.
Nahirny, V.C., "The Russian Intelligentsia: From Men of Ideas to Men of Convictions," *Comparative Studies in Society and History*, Vol. IV, No. 4, July 1962.
Namier, L.B., *The Revolution of the Intellectuals*. Garden City, N.Y.: Doubleday Anchor Books, 1964.
Shils, E., *Political Development in New States*. The Hague: Mouton, 1963.

SECTION THREE

Patterns of Transformation
of Total Societies

It is within the context of the transformation of total societies that most of the processions of change culminate. Such transformations are among the most dramatic types of social changes — most fully represented in the records of history. These records depict changes from one type of society to another, the rise and fall of different regimes — be they primitive political tribe regimes, patrimonial regimes, city states, great historical Empires or modern societies.

This does not mean of course that all the processes of change in the various institutional spheres analyzed in the previous sections cannot develop in relatively separate or autonomous ways: or that many economic, family or community patterns cannot also persist through changes in the central frameworks of socio-political regimes. On the contrary, all the materials presented above attest to the possibility of some such relatively autonomous developments.

205

*And yet there can be no doubt that within the
limits of autonomy of the different institutional
spheres there does exist a focal point in which
institutional and personal dimensions of change
are most clearly brought together, such focus can
be found in the transformation of total societies.*

X

Transformation
of Total Societies:
A Premodern Pattern

Wolf's article discusses the transformation of a total historical society —
the rise of Islam under Mohammed. The excerpts from Wolf's article
constitute in a way a continuation of the studies of movements and elites
in the framework of one society. He analyzes the problem which arose in
the Arab community in Mecca through the impingement on it of various
processes of change which predisposed the community to accept new
ideas of social order. The specific response to the problems was provided
by the revelation of Islam to Mohammed which enabled Mohammed to
establish the new cultural and socio-political order.

This analysis raises interesting problems about which little is known.
First, can some over-all response develop in all situations of change?
Second, are several different solutions possible in any given situation of
change? The elucidation of these questions constitutes one of the basic
problems of a comparative study of social change.

207

13   ERIC R. WOLF

The Social Organization of Mecca
and the Origins of Islam

INTRODUCTION

The present paper attempts to analyze some aspects of the early development of Islam in terms of certain anthropological concepts. It would like to take issue with the popular view best expressed in the words of Harrison[1] that "Mohammedanism is little more than the Bedouin mind projected into the realm of religion." It is concerned primarily with the change from a type of society organized on the basis of kin relationships to a type of society possessed of an organized, if rudimentary, state. It will attempt to show that this change took place in an urban environment and was causally connected with the spread of trade. No cross-cultural comparisons will be attempted, though it is hoped that the material presented may have applicability elsewhere, especially in the study of areas in which settled populations and pastoral peoples interact.

Many writers have dealt with the rise of Islam primarily in terms of diffusion. Thus Torrey analyzed "the Jewish foundations of Islam." [2] Bell dealt with "the origin of Islam in its Christian environment." [3] Hirschberg discussed Jewish and Christian teaching in pre-Islamic Arabia and early Islamic times.[4] Grimme, Nielsen, and Philby have traced Islamic elements to southern Arabia as the principal source of diffusion.[5] Kroeber has included Islam in the "exclusive-monotheistic pattern" which is said to characterize Judaism, Christianity, and Mohammedanism and serves as an instance of his concept of "systemic patterns" of diffusion.[6] The work of these writers is aimed at an understanding of the derivation of some

Reprinted from *Southwestern Journal of Anthropology*, Vol. 7, Winter, 1951, pp. 329–332, 334–338, 340–343, 344–347, 352–353, with permission of the publisher. Article abridged for this printing. Original footnote numbers have been retained.

[1] Harrison, 1924, p. 42.
[2] Torrey, 1933.
[3] Bell, 1926.
[4] Hirschberg, 1939.
[5] Grimme, 1892; Nielsen, 1927; Philby, 1947.
[6] Kroeber, 1948, p. 314.

of the culture elements utilized by Islam, or has pointed to the existence of elements analogous to Islam in other religious traditions developed within the same general area.

Our present emphasis is somewhat different. We are interested primarily in the way in which people relate themselves to each other in terms of the material culturally available to them, and how such systems of relationship change due to the impact of internal and external factors. The present approach is thus functional and historical. It is also evolutionary. The writer is interested in one case history, to show up certain changes in social organization which appear to occur at the threshold of transition from one level of organization to another.

THE ECONOMIC BASIS OF MECCAN SOCIETY

During the first century AD, the discovery of the regular change of the monsoon made possible the rise of regular coastwise trade around the Arabian peninsula. This lowered freight rates sufficiently to cause the main overland route from Yemen to Syria to lose much of its importance. While most of the coastwise trade passed into non-Arab hands, the Arab inhabitants of the Hejaz seized what was left of the carrying trade along the main caravan route. This marginal economic development led to the establishment of a permanent settlement in the valley of Mecca, around the year 400 AD.[7]

This permanent settlement was founded by members of the tribe of Koreish, an impoverished subdivision of the larger pastoral tribe Kinana. Before settling at Mecca, the Koreish lived as pastoral nomads in scattered migratory kin groups which added to their livelihood by selling protection to passing caravans.[8] The social organization of these groups appears to have followed the general pattern of such organization among the Bedouins of the pre-Islamic period. They were "local groups habitually moving together," [9] composed of a chief and his family, free families, protected strangers who were not blood relatives, and slaves.[10] The chief, usually the oldest or most respected male of the group, was responsible for the care of poor, widows, and orphans, for hospitality to strangers, for payments of blood money,[11] and for the maintenance of order within the group.[12] Yet, then as now, "it is only in war, or on the march, which is conducted with all the precautions of war, that the sheikh of a tribe exercises an active authority." [13] Chief and free families were linked to-

[7] Lammens, 1926, p. 13.
[8] Lammens, 1928, p. 239.
[9] Smith, 1903, p. 43.
[10] Levy, 1933, vol. 1, p. 278.
[11] Procksch, 1899, pp. 7–9.
[12] Ashkenazi, 1946–49, p. 665.
[13] Smith, 1903, p. 68.

gether by bonds of kinship. Those individuals who travelled with the group but were not blood relatives of the rest were tied to them by a number of ritual kin relationships which we shall have occasion to discuss more fully at a later point. These relationships enabled the component elements of the group to "combine on the model or principle of an association of kindred," [14] and made it possible for outsiders to "feign themselves to be descended from the same stock as the people on whom they were engrafted. . . ." [15]

The settled character of their life set them off from the pastoral nomads of the desert, those who "stayed on the heights of the Hedjaz." [19] "They have lived in towns, when only the heads of the Benu Amr lived in them, and others still led an unsettled existence. They have built many habitations in them, and dug wells," sang one pre-Islamic poet.[20] Another said that if he had chosen to stay with the Koreish, he would not have had to wander about the desert in search of pasture, spending the night 'at "brackish water . . . in an evil lodging." [21] The Koreish themselves set up

> a set of arbitrary regulations of the following kind; they declared themselves exempt from the obligation which required that they make sour milk, turn milk into butter, and live in tents made of camel hair, thus renouncing all the customs of the Bedouin desert nomads, from whom they wanted to distinguish themselves completely. [22]

The permanent settlement at Mecca existed solely for the purposes of commerce. A pre-Islamic poet testified to this:

> If Mecca had any attractions to offer, Himyarite princes at the head of their armies would long since have hurried there. There winter and summer are equally desolate. No bird flies over Mecca, no grass grows. There are no wild beasts to be hunted. Only the most miserable of all occupations flourishes there, trade.[23]

When Mohammed attempted to ruin Mecca by destroying its Syrian trade, after his flight from Mecca to Medina, a merchant of the Koreish clan of Umaiya said:

> Mohammed has stopped up our trade, his men do not leave the coast clear, and the inhabitants have a pact with them and are largely in understanding with them, so we don't know where to go; but if we remain at home, we shall eat up our capital and cannot maintain our-

[14] Maine, 1888, p. 127.
[15] *Idem*, p. 126.
[19] Ibn Hishām, 1864, p. 85.
[20] *Ibid*.
[21] Mufaḍḍalīyāt, 1918, p. 254.
[22] Caetani, 1905, p. 148.
[23] Essad Bey, 1936, p. 44.

selves in Mecca over a long period of time, because it is only a settlement for the purpose of carrying on trade, with Syria in the summer time and with Abyssinia in winter.[24]

Without trade, the Meccans would have perished in their "unfruitful valley." [25]

The Koreish appear to have become the dominant traders in western Arabia by stages. First, they sold protection to caravans. Then they began to offer wares "for sale along the overland routes leading through their territory." [26] Finally, they entered the large markets located outside their area, coming into direct trade contacts with Syria and Abyssinia[27] and with Persia.[28] The Koreish

> skimmed the fat off the fairs of the neighboring places. Mina, Maganna, Dhul Magaz and not least Ukaz were like outposts of Meccan trade. In all these places we find the Koreish; they concentrated business in their hands. The esteem in which they were held can be seen from the fact that the weapons which had to be surrendered for the duration of the markets and the pilgrimage were deposited with a Koreish.[29]

The Koreish thus played an important part in centralizing the economy of the peninsula. Their trading ventures turned Mecca into "a city, secure and at ease, to which supplies came from every side," [30] into a "place of crowding," [31] filled with "their movements, their comings and goings," [32] into "the mother city. . . ." [33]

Money in this society had not yet reached the stage of the universal commodity. Yet precious metals served as a means by which the value of other commodities could be measured. Byzantine and Persian coins were in use,[44] and gold was mined in the Hejaz.[45] As yet, however, "it was not customary to buy and sell with them [coins] except by considering the coins as bullion," [46] i.e., by weighing rather than by counting them. This may perhaps be attributed to the lack of a central political power whose imprint might have served to standardize the value of the different coins in

[24] Wākidī, 1882, p. 100.
[25] Koran 14, 40; p. 229.
[26] Wüstenfeld, 1864, p. 35.
[27] *Ibid.*
[28] *Idem*, p. 38.
[29] Wellhausen, 1884–99, vol. 3, p. 88.
[30] Koran 16, 113; p. 208.
[31] *Idem*, 3, 90; p. 395.
[32] *Idem*, 3, 196; p. 405.
[33] *Idem*, 42, 5; p. 271.
[44] Balādhurī, 1916–24, p. 233.
[45] Buhy, 1930, p. 51.
[46] Balādhurī, 1916–24.

circulation. At any rate, commodities like food, milk, and wine were sold.[47] Bad harvests around Mecca are said to have caused the prices of bread to rise. [48] Clothing was sold.[49] Abū Sufyān is said to have sold a house for 400 dinars, with 100 dinars for down-payment, and the rest payable in installments.[50] Slaves were sold in what was Arabia's largest slave market.[51] Camels obtained in raids were sold in the open market in Mecca,[52] and the price of horses is said to have been determined by market conditions.[53] Camels were hired out for caravan duty.[54] Ransom was calculated in money terms on certain occasions.[55] Certain occupations, such as sheepherding, guiding caravans, wall building, leeching, etc., were paid in wages.[56] While wages in Medina were usually paid in kind, in Mecca they were usually paid in money.[57]

Credit, pricing, and wages set up relationships between individuals and groups of individuals which were not comprised within the preceding system of kin relationships. Under the impact of commercial development, Meccan society changed from a social order determined primarily by kinship and characterized by considerable homogeneity of ethnic origin into a social order in which the fiction of kinship served to mask a developing division of society into classes, possessed of considerable ethnic diversity.

Accumulation of wealth and power in some clans of the Koreish tribe divided the Koreish into rich and poor. To some extent, this was mirrored in the pattern of settlement.[58] The two dominant Koreish clans, Makhzum and Umaiya, occupied the "inner city" around the central sanctuary of the Ka'ba, and were called "Koreish of the center." The other eight and poorer Koreish clans occupied the "outer city" and were called "Koreish of the outskirts." The real functional units of Meccan society, however, were no longer clans as such, nor localized groups of kin, but clusters of rich merchants, their families, and their dependents. The dependent population was made up of several groups. Differentiation of status, minor among the pastoral nomads, assumed major importance in Mecca. First, there were the slaves. Secondly, there existed a group of mercenaries, many of whom were of slave origin.[59] Thirdly, merchants maintained the

[47] Ibn Hishām, 1864, vol. 2, pp. 3, 7; Mufaḍḍalīyāt, 1918, p. 34.
[48] Wüstenfeld, 1864, p. 36.
[49] Ibn Hishām, 1864, p. 9.
[50] Wākidī, 1882, p. 340.
[51] Lammens, 1928, p. 12.
[52] Ibn Hishām, 1864, pp. 21–22.
[53] Mufaḍḍalīyāt, 1918, p. 308.
[54] Idem, p. 318.
[55] Wākidī, 1882, p. 76.
[56] Bukhārī, 1903–14, vol. 2, pp. 62–64; Sprenger, 1869, vol. 1, p. 275.
[57] Sprenger, 1869, vol. 3, p. 141.
[58] Wüstenfeld, 1864, pp. 58–75, passim.
[59] Lammens, 1928, p. 244.

necessary personnel for their caravans. Fourthly, there were middlemen, like the future Caliph Omar. Fifthly, there were people who had come under the domination of the wealthy through debts, like the dependents of al-'Abbās who had brought them under his sway through usury.[60] Sixthly, there existed a group of people who worked for wages. Finally, there were the clients or protected persons, called *mawālī* (sing. *mawlā*).

This group of clients deserves special consideration. A client stood in a relation of dependency, called *jiwār*, to a patron or protector. The word for client is derived from a root signifying "closeness." Two kinds of closeness were distinguished. A pre-Islamic poet speaks of "cousins of our cousins, of the same stock by birth, and a cousin knit to us by an oath." [61] Clients, called cousins by oath, are contrasted with cousins by birth.[62] The client-patron relationship in its pure form involved a tie of ritual kinship, sealed by commingling of blood and by an oath sworn at the central religious sanctuary, the Ka'ba.[63]

Within Mecca, there were thirteen major groups of clients, each affiliated to a patron family or patron clan.[64] The clients were of diverse origins. Some were freed slaves.[65] Others were outlaws from tribal groups who sought refuge. Some were individuals who had moved into the protection of the group through matri-local marriage. Some were adopted persons.[66]

Just as settlement in Mecca was nominally organized on a genealogical basis, with two clans at the center and eight clans at the outskirts, so the functioning social groups within Meccan society tended to be formally organized on the principle of the fiction of kinship by blood. This fiction was the only means by which, apart from slavery, individuals could be related to each other. Within the social clusters, the clients represented a group not linked by birth but through ritual kin arrangements.

Due to the commercial orientation of Meccan society, this patron-client tie, formally based on a fictional relation of kin, actually took on more and more the guise of an exploitative relation between members of different class groups. This relationship was reinforced by the prevalence of wage-payment and by the institution of debt slavery.[67] It has been pointed out repeatedly that the bulk of Mohammed's first converts came from this group of clients and from the slaves of the city.[68] Caetani has even argued that Mohammed himself was a client of the Koreish, rather than a blood

[60] Buhl, 1930, p. 109.
[61] Mufaddalīyāt, 1918, p. 34.
[62] Goldziher, 1889, vol. 1, p. 105.
[63] Smith, 1903, pp. 50–51.
[64] Wüstenfeld, 1864, pp. 59–75, *passim*.
[65] Smith, 1903, p. 51.
[66] *Idem*, pp. 49–52, *passim*.
[67] Lammens, 1924, pp. 236–237.
[68] Caetani, 1905, p. 240; Procksch, 1899, pp. 81–82.

relative,[69] and in this he is supported by a curious remark by Mohammed: "And they say, 'Had but this Koran been sent down to some great one of the two cities . . . !' " [70] as well as by other evidence.[71] When Mohammed first embarked on his career, the excitement among the slaves of Mecca was so intense that a leading slave owner who had one hundred slaves removed them from the city because he feared that they might become converts.[72] When Mohammed besieged Taif, he called on the slaves of the town to desert to his camp where they would receive their freedom.[73]

The mechanism of kinship between patron and client provided backing for the individual who was poor or powerless. It put the weight of a powerful group of ritual kin behind him. The isolated individual without such backing was exposed to attack or to unobstructed killing in a blood feud.[74] Yet the same mechanism was also potentially disruptive of social stability. If a client was attacked, the protecting group had to make a show of force. This demonstration of force, in turn, involved the protecting group in every-widening circles of conflict. For example, during an encounter between Mohammed and the Koreish, the client of a leading Koreish merchant was killed by the Muslims. His brother demanded that the dead man's patron exercise the duty of blood revenge. The merchant tried to avoid this duty, fully cognizant of the fact that its exercise would only involve Mecca more deeply in war with the Muslims, but was forced to give in.[75] Like the relationship between sworn allies (hilf) which involved mutual aid between two equal parties and which we shall touch on more fully later, the relations between patron and client acted as a double-edged sword. The extension of kinship bonds to the individual merely increased the possibility of conflict between groups organized on the kinship model.

As Mecca came to be characterized by growing heterogeneity of status, its population also became more heterogeneous ethnically. Mention is made of Syrian caravan leaders; of travelling monks and curers; of Syrian merchants; foreign smiths and healers; Copt carpenters; Negro idol sculptors; Christian doctors, surgeons, dentists and scribes; Christian women married into a Koreish clan; Abyssinian sailors and mercenaries.[76] Abyssinian, Mesopotamian, Egyptian, Syrian, and Byzantine slaves were sold in the market place.[77] The market center of Mecca exercised an at-

[69] Caetani, 1905, pp. 68–69.
[70] Koran 43, 30; p. 136.
[71] Caetani, 1905, pp. 233–234, note 1 to p. 225.
[72] Sprenger, 1851, p. 159.
[73] Encyclopedia of Islam, vol. 1, p. 80.
[74] Buhl, 1930, pp. 36–37.
[75] Procksch, 1899, p. 38.
[76] Lammens, 1928, pp. 12–32, passim.
[77] Idem, pp. 18–19.

traction on groups and individuals beyond the Arabian periphery, as well as within the confines of the peninsula itself.

RELIGIOUS DEVELOPMENT IN MECCAN SOCIETY

Economic development set off related tendencies in the field of religion. Gibb has spoken of "the abandonment of local shrines and the growing practice of pilgrimage to central shrines venerated by groups of tribes (of which the Ka'ba in Mecca was one of the most important)." [78]

The leading Koreish held the ranking positions in the Meccan religious hierarchy as well as the dominant positions in the economic system. The Umaiya clan, especially, appears to have owed its predominance, at least in part, to its possession of special religious prerogatives in the past. One pre-Islamic poet swears "by the holy month of the sons of Umaiya" and another is quoted as saying that the Banu Umaiya in Koreish were like the [priestly] family of the Banu Khafajah in the tribe of 'Uqail.[79] At any rate, the strongly monopolistic character of this Koreish religious oligarchy is evident in their attempt to pass their religious offices down to their first born in the direct line of descent.[80] The major offices, that of the priesthood, the presidency of the council house, and the offices concerned with the distribution of food and water to the pilgrims, were apparently developed by the Koreish themselves, and were preëmpted by them. Three minor offices which seem to have been traditional in the worship of the Ka'ba[81] were held by three minor tribal groups. The religious society of the *Hums*, again headed by the Koreish, further served to reinforce their dominance in the religious sphere.[82]

Like other Arabian sanctuaries, the Ka'ba was surrounded by a sacred area, called the *harām*. Within this precinct no blood could be shed. As the economic importance of Mecca grew, the Koreish self-consciously sought to extend the sacred precinct as a means for increasing the stability of social relations in their trading territory. They sought to "put their warehouses, their strong boxes, at greater distance from their turbulent neighbors." [83] The story of Amr b. Luhaiy illustrates the secular interest involved in this effort. It shows that the Meccan traders ringed the Ka'ba with the idols of other tribal groups, in order to increase the importance of the sanctuary and to attract more visitors to the growing city.[84]

The extension of the concept of an inviolable zone in which blood feuds

---

[78] Gibb, 1948, p. 113.
[79] Mufaḍḍalīyāt, 1918, pp. 125–126.
[80] Wüstenfeld, 1864, p. 34.
[81] Caetani, 1905, p. 105; Wellhausen, 1884–99, vol. 3, p. 77.
[82] Caetani, 1905, p. 148.
[83] Lammens, 1928, p. 239.
[84] Ibn Hishām, 1864, vol. 1, p. 39.

were outlawed, and new fights could not develop, appears to have resulted from the development of trade and to have fostered a further development of it. Wellhausen writes:

> Within the tumultuous confusion which fills the desert, the festivities at the beginning of each season represent the only enjoyable periods of rest. A peace of God at this time interrupts the continuous feuds for a fair period of time. The most diverse tribes which otherwise did not trust each other at all, make common pilgrimage to the same holy places without fear, through the land of friend and foe. Trade raises its head, and general and lively exchange results. . . . The exchange of commodities is followed by an exchange of ideas. A community of ideological interest develops that comprises all of Arabia. . . .[85]

The Koreish developed a special pact with other tribal groups to guarantee the inviolability or pilgrims on their journeys to the religious center.[86] Their attempts to maintain peace earned them the scorn of the more war-like desert tribes. "No one has yet lived through a terror [raid] by them," said a Hudail poet.[87] "They are people who do not know how to fight," said a Jew of Medina.[88] "Your courage fails you in battle," sneered another poet, "at best, you are [only] good at figuring in the ranks of the processions!"[89]

In stressing the Ka'ba as the center of their power, the Koreish broke with the traditional notion of a territory belonging to a certain kin group, and representing its inviolable property. . . .

THE ORGANIZATION OF POWER IN MECCAN SOCIETY

The way in which power organized in a given society must be considered both in terms of internal, or endogenous, and in terms of external or exogenous factors.[97]

In terms of internal development, the lines of political power in Mecca tended to coincide with the lines of economic power. In theory, power in Mecca was located in a town council, made up of adult males. In actuality, however, the council was dominated by the same wealthy merchants who ruled over the clusters of kin and dependents, and who held the main religious offices. They decided general policy and made alliances. They represented the "union of the Koreish" and their representatives made formal trade agreements with the Abyssinian and the Persian

[85] Wellhausen, 1884–99, vol. 3, p. 183.
[86] Caetani, 1905, p. 165.
[87] Hell, 1933, p. 10.
[88] Ibn Hishām, 1864, vol. 2, p. 2.
[89] Lammens, 1928, p. 145.
[97] Wittfogel, 1932, pp. 542–551.

courts.[98] They permitted foreigners to address the town council on specific matters; and received the taxes which all foreigners who were not kin or ritual kin had to pay if they wanted to trade in the area. Despite its oligarchic character, the council had no direct legislative power and lacked a central executive organ. In a society which was rapidly moving away from primary reliance on kinship ties, its power was still largely kin-based. It lay in the council's ability to break a recalcitrant by refusing to grant him protection. The mechanism for enforcing such decisions was the blood feud, and law was maintained only by the unwillingness of potential culprits to risk the dangers of an encounter with the powerful "Koreish of the center." The limitations of this negative power as a means of effective social control are shown clearly in the story of the supposed boycott against Mohammed at the end of his Meccan period. Whether apocryphal or not[99] the story demonstrates that

> the ideological movement created by the prophet tore apart the ancient Arab order which was based on kinship. Most members of the boycotted lineage did not believe in Mohammed . . . and on the other hand, some of Mohammed's most fervent adherents like Abu Bekr and Umar were left untouched by this rule of conduct, since they did not belong to his lineage.[100]

Just as the blood feud as a means of social control in a class-divided society could not govern internal friction, so kin-based mechanisms used to ensure security against the outside world failed of their purpose. We have already seen that the patron-client relation, extending protection to individuals or groups, at the same time extended the possibility of intertribal conflict. The same may be said of the so-called *hilf* relationship. The *hilf* generally designates a relation of coöperation between roughly equal partners, in contrast to the patron-client relation which involves a stronger and a weaker party.[101] Such a pact of coöperation could be entered into temporarily for a specific purpose like joint action in war or for the purpose of protecting a caravan. Or it could develop into a permanent tie between tribes and tribal groups.[102] The tie was sanctified by a ceremony in which both parties mixed their blood,[103] and might be surrounded by a mythology of common descent.[104] Wellhausen has spoken of the Arab genealogy as a statistical device,[105] and both he and Caetani[106] have stressed

[98] Wüstenfeld, 1864, pp. 35, 38.
[99] Caetani, 1905, pp. 290–291; Buhl, 1930, p. 175.
[100] Buhl, 1930, p. 176.
[101] Pedersen, 1914, p. 29; Bräunlich, 1934, p. 191.
[102] Bräunlich, 1934, p. 194.
[103] Pedersen, 1914, p. 21; Smith, 1903, pp. 60–61.
[104] Nallino, 1941, pp. 77–78.
[105] Wellhausen, 1884–99, vol. 4, p. 27.
[106] Caetani, 1905, p. 59.

the fictional character of descent in Arabia in general. The Koreish maintained such pacts, for example, with many members of the tribe Sulaim who possessed mineral resources and commanded the road from Medina as well as access to Nejd and the Persian Gulf;[107] with individual Syrian merchants;[108] with a Bedouin marauder like al-Barrad; and others. . . .

If interaction with the tribal groups near Mecca could be phrased in terms of ritual kin relations, interaction with societies beyond the Arabian periphery meant contact with developed state organizations. These were, first, the satellite states of the greater powers, like the Himyarite Kinda, the Persian Hira, and the Byzantine Ghassan; secondly, the great powers themselves: Byzantium and Persia in the north and first Himyar and later Abyssinia in the south. Hira and Ghassan were outposts which kept the pastoral nomads in check. Built up by nomads themselves, they were used "as barriers against their brothers who pushed after them." [113] They also set the "terms of trade" against the pastoral nomads in the exchange of products between desert and agricultural area. The cultivated zone furnishes the nomads with cereals and handicraft products, permitting them free access to pasture, meadowland, and watering places after harvest. The nomads in turn supply the settled area with livestock and livestock products. When the nomads are strong, they rig the terms of exchange against the settlers, by adding tribute in kind to their other demands. Sometimes they may be compensated by outright payment by a larger power. When the settled area is strongly organized politically, it can exploit the need of the nomads for pasture to exact tribute from them in turn.[114] Thus the kings of Hira received leather, truffles, and horses from the nomads,[115] in exchange for pasturing rights in Iraq. Ghassan and Hira even fought each other over the right to exact tribute from a certain area.[116]

These satellites had certain characteristics in common. They maintained armed "Praetorian guards" consisting of detribalized elements[117] and a system of taxation.[118] Their very existence constituted a dilemma for the larger dominant power. If they grew too strong politically, they had to be incorporated into the domain of the dominant power.[119] When they were incorporated, the lack of an independent buffer was immediately felt in new exactions and incursions on the part of the nomads. . . .

[107] *Encyclopedia of Islam*, vol. 4, p. 518.
[108] Lammens, 1914, p. 79.
[113] Rothstein, 1899, p. 130.
[114] Dussaud, 1907, pp. 3–4.
[115] Fraenkel, 1886, p. 178.
[116] Rothstein, 1899, pp. 130–131.
[117] *Idem*, pp. 136–137.
[118] *Ibid.*
[119] *Idem*, pp. 117–120; Nöldeke, 1887, p. 31.

THE EMERGENCE OF THE ISLAMIC STATE

The religious revolution associated with the name of Mohammed made possible the transition from Meccan society as we have described it to a society possessed of the elements which permit state organization. The success of Mohammed's prophetic mission permitted these elements to crystallize out of the preceding social network in which kin relationships had become increasingly fictional and disruptive.

The emergence of Islam completed the centralization of worship by making Mecca the sole religious center. It completed the trend towards worship of the deity governing non-kin relations by making this deity the supreme and only god, "the personification of state supremacy." [130] In Islam — "voluntary surrender" or "self-surrender" to a supreme deity[131] — all men were to be clients of God, the only patron. "And warn those who dread being gathered to their Lord, that patron or intercessor they shall have none but Him," says the Koran.[132] "God is the patron of believers." [133]

"There are no genealogies in Islam," states a traditional saying.[134] The very act of adherence to Islam implied an individual decision into which considerations of kin did not enter. The story of the boycott of the Prophet's lineage shows how completely the principles of kin relationships failed to cope with the new force. "Truly, the most worthy of honor in the sight of God is he who fears Him most," [135] not the individual whose lineage is the most famous or the most powerful. When Mohammed entered Mecca, he declared: "God has put an end to the pride in noble ancestry, you are all descended from Adam and Adam from dust, the noblest among you is the man who is most pious." [136] Adherence to Islam was not a matter of kin relationships: "Mohammed is not the father of any man among you, but he is the Apostle of God." [137] Islam set kinsman against kinsman. "The swords of the sons of his father were drawn against him," mourns a song about the battle of Badr, "oh God! Love among relatives was deeply injured there!" [138] A son turned Muslim could approve the death of his father who had fought with the Koreish against the new faith.[139]

---

[130] Wellhausen, 1927, p. 8.
[131] Smith, 1927, p. 80; Lyall, 1903, p. 784.
[132] Koran 6, 51; p. 321.
[133] *Idem*, 2, 258; p. 367.
[134] Levy, 1933, vol. 2, p. 79.
[135] Koran 49, 13; p. 470.
[136] Wākidī, 1882, p. 338.
[137] Koran 33, 40; p. 438.
[138] Ibn Hishām, 1864, vol. 1, p. 390.
[139] *Idem*, p. 340.

As Islam built on ties other than those of kinship, it had to put a limit on the disruptive exercise of power and protection implicit in the blood feud. On the occasion of his entrance into Mecca, Mohammed "declared all demands for interest payments, for blood revenge or blood money stemming from pagan times as null and void." [140] The same demand was expressed in a letter to the people of Najran: "There are no interest payments and no demands for blood revenge from pagan times.[141] God permits a relaxation of the *lex talionis*.[142]

> A believer killeth not a believer but by mischance: and whoso killeth a believer by mischance shall be bound to free a believer from slavery; and the blood money shall be paid to the family of the slain, unless they convert it into alms. But if the slain believer be of a hostile people, then let him confer freedom on a slave who is a believer; and if he be of a people between whom and yourselves there is an alliance, then let the blood-money be paid to his family, and let him set free a slave who is a believer: and let him who hath not the means, fast two consecutive months. This is the penance enjoined by God; and God is Knowing, Wise! [143]

The passage cited shows that the incipient Islamic state did not suppress the *talio* as such. It even left the settlement of such disputes to the families concerned. It did, however, insist that the manner in which they were settled conformed to the "penance enjoined by God," and attempted to convert the demand for blood into a demand for wergild. In pre-Islamic times, the duty of carrying on the blood feud passed from father to son in direct inheritance.[144] Islam demanded early and peaceful settlement. The moratorium on blood feud was so much part of the new creed that certain tribes postponed their affiliation with Mohammed, until they had settled all questions of blood revenge.[145]

Another set of kin-like relations superseded by Islam were the relations involving past allies. There was to be "no *hilf* in Islam. . . ." [146]

The core of the new society was the militant brotherhood of Muhajjirin and Ansār. The Muhjjirin were the Muslims who fled with Mohammed from Mecca to Medina. The Ansār were their Medinese hosts. Armed, and without ties of kin to bind them, they resembled the "Praetorian guard" of the kings of Hira and Kinda. They were the storm troops of Islam. A Hudail poet compared them to his own tribes. The Hudail were called

140 Wākidī, 1882, p. 338.
141 Sperber, 1916, p. 91.
142 Koran 2, 173–174; p. 356.
143 Koran, 4, 94; p. 421.
144 Lammens, 1928, p. 202.
145 *Idem*, p. 197.
146 *Encyclopedia of Islam*, vol. 2, p. 308.

"a luxurious people of [many] subdivisions." The Muslims were "a multitude drawn together from many sources of [warriors] clad in iron." [148] They rent the ties of kinship which had bound them in the past. The Ansar were commanded to inform on those "who have been forbidden secret talk, and return to what they have been forbidden, and talk privately together with wickedness, and hate and disobedience towards the Apostle." [149] "The foundations of society, faithful coöperation of kin, were so undermined that they were not safe from espionage on the part of their closest relatives. [150] Disaffected individuals were threatened with use of force. . . .[151]

The new society which arose in Medina and was given organized form by means of a town charter promulgated by Mohammed,[155] was called *umma*, i.e. community. The community included not only Muslims, but non-Muslims as well. The *umma* comprised the whole territory of Medina, embracing all who lived within it.[156] These were all included in the incipient Islamic state, "one community over against mankind." The core of the new community were the Muslims, "a unit with its own laws within the whole society, destined of necessity to disrupt the ties of the whole." [157]

The elements of state power developed gradually. In his deportment as a prophet, Mohammed followed pre-Islamic precedents.

> The mantic knowledge [of the pagan seer, called *kahin*] is based on ecstatic inspiration. . . . They are interrogated in all important tribal and state occasions . . . in private the *kahins* especially act as judges. . . . They interpret dreams, find lost camels, establish adulteries, clear up other crimes. . . . The prophet Mohammed disclaimed being a *kahin*. But . . . his earliest appearance as a prophet reminds us strongly of the manner of the soothsayer. He was an ecstatic and had "true dreams" like them. . . . Even the forms which he was still using for administering justice and settling disputes in Medina during the early years of his stay there correspond in their main features to those of the pagan *kahin* and *hakam*.[158]

Mohammed himself acted as judge in a few known cases only.[159] Yet his very word, said to be the word of God, acted as law in the new state. During his life-time, the prophet himself was the final judicial authority. He deposed lineage chiefs and replaced them with his own candidates.[160]

[148] Hell, 1933, p. 6.
[149] Koran 58, 9; p. 451.
[150] Sprenger, 1869, vol. 3, p. 27.
[151] Ibn Hishām, 1864, vol. 1, pp. 266–267.
[155] Wellhausen, 1884–99, vol. 4, pp. 68–73.
[156] *Idem*, p. 74.
[157] Buhl, 1930, p. 210.
[158] *Encyclopedia of Islam*, vol. 2, pp. 625–626.
[159] Caetani, 1905, pp. 645–646.
[160] Margoliouth, 1905, p. 216.

He appointed officials, in the majority of cases apparently on a temporary basis.[161] The incipient state did not take on itself direct governing power over groups which became affiliated with it. Usually, its "emissaries exercised a sort of supervision and collected taxes." [162] In many cases, local authorities continued, themselves becoming officials of the new state.[163] In one case, a Christian chief became collector of the Islamic tax from his own people. . . .[164]

CONCLUSION

Our brief historical survey has shown that the tendencies which Mohammed brought to fruition were reaching their peak of development in pre-Islamic times. Commercial development in urban settlements had caused the emergence of class groupings from the preceding network of kin relations. Centralization of worship and the emergence of a deity specifically linked with the regulation of non-kin relations as the chief deity went hand in hand with the centralization of trade and the disintegration of the kinship structure. Yet in the political sphere, the use of kinship mechanisms in situations which increasingly exposed their non-functional character in the new setting led to disruption and conflict, rather than to further organization and consolidation.

The religious revolution associated with the name of Mohammed permitted the establishment of an incipient state structure. It replaced allegiance to the kinship unit with allegiance to a state structure, an allegiance phrased in religious terms. It limited the disruptive exercise of the kin-based mechanism of the blood feud. It put an end to the extension of ritual kin ties to serve as links between tribes. It based itself instead on the armed force of the faithful as the core of a social order which included both believers and unbelievers. It evolved a rudimentary judicial authority, patterned after the role of the pre-Islamic soothsayer, but possessed of new significance. The limitation of the blood feud permitted war to emerge as a special prerogative of the state power. The state taxed both Muslims and non-Muslims, in ways patterned after pre-Islamic models, but to new ends. Finally, it located the center of the state in urban settlements, surrounding the town with a set of religious symbols that served functionally to increase its prestige and role.

The revolution accomplished, power quickly passed out of the hands of the armed brotherhood of the faithful into the hands of the Koreish who had fought against them. It may be said that Mohammed accom-

[161] 'Abdurraziq, 1934, p. 168.
[162] Wellhausen, 1884–99, vol. 3, p. 29.
[163] Wellhausen, idem, p. 30.
[164] Husain, 1938, pp. 126–127.

plished for the Meccan traders that which they could not accomplish themselves: the organization of state power.

Notes for
Further Reading

The processes of transformation of great historical societies have constituted one of the major foci of comparative historical and sociological studies of which the following are illustrations:

Balazs, E., *Chinese Civilization and Bureaucracy*. New Haven: Yale University Press, 1964.

Beloff, N., *The Age of Absolutism, 1660–1815*. London: Hutchinson's University Library, 1954.

Eisenstadt, S.N., "The Causes of Disintegration and Fall of Empires: Sociological and Historical Analysis," *Diogenes*, No. 34, Summer, 1961, pp. 82–107.

————, *The Political Systems of Empires*. Glencoe, Ill.: The Free Press, 1963.

Fairbank, J.K., O. Reischauer, A. Craig, *East Asia, The Moslem Transformation*. Boston: Houghton Mifflin Co., 1965.

Grunebaum, E. (ed.), *Unity and Variety in Muslim Civilization*. Chicago: University of Chicago Press, 1955.

Parsons, T., *Societies, Evolutionary and Comparative Perspectives*. Englewood Cliffs: Prentice-Hall, 1966.

Walbank, F.W., *The Decline of the Roman Empire in the West*. London: Cobett Press, 1946.

Weber, M., *Ancient Judaism*, translated and edited by H.H. Gerth and D. Martindale. Glencoe, Ill.: The Free Press, 1952.

————, *The Protestant Ethic and the Spirit of Capitalism*, translated by Talcott Parsons, New York, 1930.

————, *The Religion of China: Confucianism and Taoism*, translated and edited by H.H. Gerth. Glencoe, Ill.: The Free Press, 1951.

————, *The Religion of India: The Sociology of Hinduism and Buddhism*, translated and edited by H.H. Gerth and D. Martindale. Glencoe, Ill.: The Free Press, 1952.

————, *The Sociology of Religion*, translated by Ephraim Fischoff (mostly from Wirtschaft u. Gesellschaft). Boston: Beacon Press, 1962.

Wittek, P., *The Rise of the Ottoman Empire*. London: Royal Asiatic Society, 1938.

XI

Transformation
of Total Societies:
Patterns of Modernization

In this chapter three articles are presented which illustrate some of the major problems of comparative studies of modernization.

Huntington's article analyzes the different responses to the problem of modernization in the United States and England in terms of the development of different institutional patterns, and Dore compares the process of modernization in Japan and Latin America.

Eisenstadt's article attempts to analyze the transformation of the major Asian civilization in terms of the influence of their preceding social structure on the processes of change and especially in terms of the autonomy of their institutional and cultural spheres. He briefly compares the processes of transformation of Asian civilizations to the first patterns of modernization in Europe.

224

Political Modernization: America vs. Europe

DIFFERENTIATION OF STRUCTURE

In comparing European and American development, a distinction must be made between "functions" and "power." In this article, "power" (in the singular) means influence or control over the actions of others, and "function" refers to particular types of activity, which may be defined in various ways. "Powers" (in the plural) will not be used, since most authors use it to mean "functions." It is thus possible to speak with the Founding Fathers of legislative, executive, and judicial functions, and, with Bagehot, of dignified and efficient functions — and also to speak of legal and political functions, military and civil functions, domestic and foreign functions. Governmental institutions may be equal or unequal in power and specialized or overlapping in function.

In Europe the rationalization of authority and the centralization of power were accompanied by functional differentiation and the emergence of more specialized governmental institutions and bodies. These developments were, of course, a response to the growing complexity of society and the increasing demands upon government. Administrative, legal, judicial, and military institutions developed as semi-autonomous but subordinate bodies in one way or another responsible to the political bodies (monarch or parliament) which exercised sovereignty. The dispersion of functions among relatively specialized institutions, in turn, encouraged inequalities in power among the institutions. The legislative or law-making function carried with it more power than did the administrative or law-enforcement function.

In medieval government and in Tudor government the differentiation of functions was not very far advanced. A single institution often exercised many functions, and a single function was often dispersed among several institutions. This tended to equalize power among institutions. The government of Tudor England was a "government of *fused* power"

Reprinted from *World Politics*, Vol. XVIII, No. 3, April, 1966, Parts III and IV, pp. 391–408, with permission of the author and the publisher. Article abridged for this printing. Original footnote reference numbers have been retained.

(functions) — that is, Parliament, Crown, and other institutions each performed many functions.[38] In the seventeenth and eighteenth centuries British government evolved toward a concentration of power and a differentiation of function. In Great Britain, as Pollard argues, "Executive, legislature, and judicature have been evolved from a common origin, and have adapted themselves to specific purposes, because without that specialization of functions English government would have remained rudimentary and inefficient. But there has been no division of sovereignty and no separation of powers." [39]

In America, in contrast, sovereignty was divided, power was separated, and functions were combined in many different institutions. This result was achieved despite rather than because of the theory of the separation of powers (i.e., functions) which was prevalent in the eighteenth century. In its pure form, the assignment of legislative, executive, and judicial functions to separate institutions would give one institution a monopoly of the dominant law-making function and thus would centralize power. This was in part what Locke wanted and even more what Jefferson wanted. The theory was also, of course, found in Montesquieu, but Montesquieu recognized the inequality of power that would result from the strict separation of functions. The "judiciary," he said, "is in some measure next to nothing." Consequently, to obtain a real division of power, Montesquieu divided the legislative function among three institutions representing the three traditional estates of the realm. In practice in America, as in Tudor England, not only was power divided by dividing the legislative function but other functions were also shared among several institutions, thus creating a system of "checks and balances" which equalized power. "The constitutional convention of 1787," as Neustadt has said, "is supposed to have created a government of 'separated powers' [i.e., functions]. It did nothing of the sort. Rather, it created a government of separated institutions *sharing* powers [functions]." [40] Thus America perpetuated a fusion of functions and a division of power, while Europe developed a differentiation of functions and a centralization of power.

In medieval government no distinction existed between legislation and adjudication. On the Continent such institutions as the *Justiza* of Aragon and the French *parlements* exercised important political functions into the sixteenth century. In England, Parliament, an essentially political body, was viewed primarily as a court down to the seventeenth century. The courts of law, as Holdsworth observes, "were, in the days before the functions of government had become specialized, very much more than

---

[38] McIlwain, *High Court*, xi.

[39] Pollard, *Evolution of Parliament*, 257.

[40] Richard E. Neustadt, *Presidential Power: The Politics of Leadership* (New York 1960), 33.

merely judicial tribunals. In England and elsewhere they were regarded as possessing functions which we may call political, to distinguish them from those purely judicial functions which nowadays are their exclusive functions on the continent, and their principal functions everywhere. That the courts continued to exercise these larger functions, even after departments of government had begun to be differentiated, was due to the continuance of that belief in the supremacy of the law which was the dominant characteristic of the political theory of the Middle Ages." [41]

In England, the supremacy of the law disappeared in the civil wars of the seventeenth century and with it disappeared the mixture of judicial and political functions. English judges followed Bacon rather than Coke and became "lions under the throne" who could not "check or oppose any points of sovereignty." In the eighteenth century, Blackstone could flatly state that no court could declare invalid an act of Parliament, however unreasonable it might be. To admit such a power, he said, "were to set the judicial power above that of the legislature, which would be subversive of all government." [42] Parliament had evolved from high court to supreme legislature.

In America, on the other hand, the mixture of judicial and political functions remained. The judicial power to declare what the law is became the mixed judicial-legislative power to tell the legislature what the law cannot be. The American doctrine and practice of judicial review were undoubtedly known only in very attenuated form in late sixteenth-century and early seventeenth-century England. Indeed, the whole concept of judicial review implies a distinction between legislative and judicial functions which was not explicitly recognized at that time. It is, nonetheless, clear that Tudor and early Stuart courts did use the common law to "controul" acts of Parliament at least to the point of redefining rather sweepingly the purposes of Parliament. These actions did not represent a conscious doctrine of judicial review so much as they represented the still "undifferentiated fusion of judicial and legislative functions." [43] This fusion of legislative and judicial functions was retained by American courts and was eventually formulated into the doctrine and practice of judicial review. The legislative functions of courts in America, as McIlwain argues, are far greater than those in England, "because the like tendency was there checked by the growth in the seventeenth century of a new doctrine of parliamentary supremacy." Unlike English courts, "American courts still retain much of their Tudor indefiniteness, notwithstanding our

[41] P. 169.

[42] Sir William Blackstone, *Commentaries on the Laws of England*, ed. Thomas M. Cooley (Chicago 1876), 1, 90.

[43] See J. W. Gough, *Fundamental Law in English Constitutional History* (Oxford 1955), 27.

separation of departments. They are guided to an extent unknown now in England by questions of policy and expediency." [44] Foreign observers since De Tocqueville have identified the "immense political influence" of the courts as one of the most astonishing and unique characteristics of American government.

The mixing of legal and political functions in American government can also be seen in the consistently prominent role of lawyers in American politics. In fourteenth- and fifteenth-century England lawyers played an important role in the development of parliamentary proceedings, and the alliance between Parliament and the law, in contrast to the separation between the Estates General and the French *parlement*, helped to sustain parliamentary authority.[45] In Elizabethan England, lawyers played an increasingly important role in Parliament. In 1593, for instance, forty-three percent of the members of the House of Commons possessed a legal education. The Speaker and the other leading figures in the House were usually lawyers. Subsequently, the role of lawyers in the British Parliament declined in significance, reaching a low in the nineteenth century. In the twentieth century only about twenty percent of the M.P.'s have been lawyers. In America, on the other hand, in the colonial governments, in the state governments, and in the national government, the Tudor heritage of lawyer-legislators has continued, with lawyers usually being a majority of the members of American legislative bodies.[46]

Every political system, as Bagehot pointed out, must gain authority and then use authority. In the modern British system these functions are performed by the dignified and efficient parts of the constitution. The assignment of each function to separate institutions is one aspect of the functional differentiation that is part of modernization. It can be seen most clearly, of course, in the case of the so-called constitutional monarchies, but in some degree it is found in almost all modern governments.[47] The American political system, however, like the older European political sys-

[44] McIlwain, *High Court*, ix, 385–86.
[45] Holdsworth, 174, 184–85, 188–89.
[46] See J. E. Neale, *The Elizabethan House of Commons* (London 1949), 290–95; Rowse, 307; Thompson, 169–73; Donald R. Matthews, *The Social Background of Political Decision-Makers* (New York 1954), 28–31; J. F. S. Ross, *Elections and Electors* (London 1955), 444; W. L. Guttsman, *The British Political Elite* (New York 1963), 82, 90, 105; D. E. Butler and Richard Rose, *The British General Election of 1959* (London 1960), 127.
[47] Walter Bagehot, *The English Constitution* (London 1949), 3–4. See also Francis X. Sutton, "Representation and the Nature of Political Systems," *Comparative Studies in Society and History*, 11 (October 1959), 7: ". . . the kind of distinction Bagehot made when he talked of the 'dignified' and 'efficient' parts of the English constitution is observed clearly in many states. . . . The discrimination of functions here rests, of course, on an analytical distinction relevant in any political system. It is that between symbolic representation and executive control."

tems, does not assign dignified and efficient functions to different institutions. All major institutions of the American government — President, Supreme Court, House, Senate, and their state counterparts — combine in varying degrees both types of functions. This combination is, of course, most notable in the Presidency. Almost every other modern political system from the so-called constitutional monarchies of Great Britain and Scandinavia to the parliamentary republics of Italy, Germany, and France before De Gaulle, to the Communist dictatorships of Eastern Europe separates the chief of state from the head of government. In the Soviet system, the differentiation is carried still further to distinguish chief of state from head of government from party chief. In the United States, however, the President unites all three functions, this combination being both a major source of his power and a major limitation on that power, since the requirements of one role often conflict with the demands of another. The combination of roles perpetuates ancient practice. The Presidency was created, as Jefferson declared in 1787, as an "elective monarchy"; the office was designed to embody much of the power of the British king; and the politics that surround it are court politics.[48]

The Presidency is, indeed, the only survival in the contemporary world of the constitutional monarchy once prevalent throughout medieval Europe. In the sixteenth century a constitutional monarch was one who reigned and ruled, but who ruled under law ("non sub homine sed sub Deo et lege") with due regard to the rights and liberties of his subjects, the type of monarch that Fortescue had in mind when he distinguished *dominium politicum et regale* from *dominium regale*. In the seventeenth century this old-style constitutional monarch was supplanted by the new-style absolute monarch who placed himself above the law. Subsequently, the eighteenth and nineteenth centuries saw the emergence of a new so-called "constitutional monarchy" in which a "dignified" monarch reigned but did not rule. Like the absolute monarch he is a modern invention created in response to the need to fix supreme power in a single organ. The American Presidency, on the other hand, continues the original type of constitutional monarchy. In functions and power, American Presidents are Tudor kings. In institutional role, as well as in personality and talents, Lyndon Johnson far more closely resembles Elizabeth I than does Eliza-

---

[48] Thomas Jefferson, Letter to James Madison, December 20, 1787, *Writing* (Washington, 1903–05), vi, 389–90; Ford, 293. For an elegant — and eloquent — essay on the President as king, see D. W. Brogan, "The Presidency," *Encounter* (January 1964), 3–7. I am in debt to Richard E. Neustadt for insights into the nature of the American monarchy and into the similarities between White House politics and Palace politics. See also, Pollard, *Factors in American History*, 72–73: "Down to this day the Executive in the United States is far more monarchical and monarchy far more personal than in the United Kingdom. 'He' is a single person there, but 'it' is a composite entity in Great Britain."

beth II. Britain preserved the form of the old monarchy, but America preserved the substance. Today America still has a king, Britain only a Crown.

In most modern states the legislative function is in theory in the hands of a large representative assembly, parliament, or supreme soviet. In practice, however, it is performed by a relatively small body of men — a cabinet or presidium — which exercises its power in all fields of governmental activity. In America, however, the legislative function remains divided among three distinct institutions and their subdivisions, much as it was once divided among the different estates and other constituted bodies in late medieval Europe. On the national level this arrangement derives not from the ideas of any European theorist but rather from the "institutional history of the colonies between 1606 and 1776." [49] The relations among burgesses, councils, and governors in the colonies, in turn, reflected the relations among Crown, Lords, and Commons in the late sixteenth century.

In modern politics, the division of power between two bodies in a legislative assembly generally varies inversely with the effective power of the assembly as a whole. The Supreme Soviet has little power but is truly bicameral; the British Parliament has more power but is effectively unicameral. America, however, is unique in preserving a working bicameralism directly inherited from the sixteenth century. Only in Tudor times did the two houses of Parliament become formally and effectively distinguished, one from the other, on an institutional basis. "The century started with Parliament a unitary institution, truly bicameral only in prospect." When it ended, the growth in "the power, position, and prestige of the House of Commons" had made Parliament "a political force with which the Crown and government had to reckon." [50] The sixteenth century represented a peak of bicameralism in English parliamentary history. Each house often quashed bills that had passed the other house, and to resolve their differences the houses resorted to conference committees. Originally used as an "occasional procedure," in 1571 the conference committee was transformed into "a normal habit." In Elizabethan Parliaments, conferences were requested by one or the other house on most bills; the conference delegations were at times instructed not to yield on particular items; and when there were substantial differences between the versions approved by the two houses, the conference committee might substantially rewrite the entire bill, at times at the urging and with the advice of the Queen and her councillors. Although all this sounds very contemporary, it is, in fact, very Tudor, and it is this conference com-

[49] Benjamin F. Wright, "The Origins of the Separation of Powers in America," *Economics*, XIII (May 1933), 169ff.

[50] Neale, *Elizabeth I and Her Parliaments* (New York 1958), 1, 16–17.

mittee procedure that was carried over into the colonial legislatures and then extended to the national level. In Great Britain, however, the practice died out with the rise of cabinet responsibility to the Commons. The last real use of "Free Conferences," where discussion and hence politics were permitted, occurred about 1740.[51]

The participation of two assemblies and the chief executive in the legislative process caused the continuation in America of many other legislative methods familiar to Tudor government. An assembly that legislates must delegate some of its work to subordinate bodies or committees. Committees made their appearance in the Tudor Parliament in the 1560's and 1570's. The practice of referring bills to committees soon became almost universal, and the committees, as they assumed more and more of the functions of the House, became larger and more often permanent. The committees were also frequently dominated by those with a special interest in the legislation that they considered. Bills concerned with local and regional problems went to committees composed of members from those regions and localities.[52] By the turn of the century the larger committees had evolved into standing committees which considered all matters coming up within a general sphere of business. This procedure reflected the active role of the Commons in the legislative process. The procedure was, in turn, exported to the colonies in the early seventeenth century — particularly to the Virginia House of Burgesses — where it also met a real need, and 150 years later was duplicated in the early sessions of the national Congress. At the same time in England, however, the rise of the cabinet undermined the committee system that had earlier existed in Parliament; the old standing committees of the House of Commons became empty formalities, indistinguishable from Committees of the Whole House, long before they were officially discontinued in 1832.

The division of the legislative function imposed similar duties upon the Speaker in the Tudor House of Commons and in subsequent American legislatures. The Tudor Speaker was a political leader, with a dual allegiance to the Crown and to the House. His success in large measure depended upon how well he could balance and integrate these often conflicting responsibilities. He was the "manager of the King's business" in the House, but he was also the spokesman for the House to the Crown and the defender of its rights and privileges. He could exercise much influence in the House by his control, subject to veto by the House, over the order in which bills were called up for debate and by his influence on the "timing and framing of questions." The struggle between Crown and

[51] *Ibid.*, 235, 287, 387–88, 412–13; G.F.M. Campion, *An Introduction to the Procedure of the House of Commons* (London 1929), 199; Ada C. McCown, *The Congressional Conference Committee* (New York 1927), 23–37.

[52] Rowse, 307.

Parliament in the seventeenth century, however, made it impossible for the Speaker to continue his loyalties to both. His overriding duty was now to the House, and, in due course, the impartiality of Onslow in the eighteenth century (1727–1761) became the norm for Speakers in the nineteenth and twentieth centuries. Thus in Britain an office that had once been weighted with politics, efficient as well as dignified, radically changed its character and became that of a depoliticized, impartial presiding officer. In America, on the other hand, the political character of the Tudor Speakership was perpetuated in the colonial assemblies and eventually in the national House of Representatives.[53]

The sharing of the legislative function among two assemblies and the chief executive gives a strikingly Tudor character to the contemporary American law-making process. In Elizabethan England, Rowse observes, the "relations between Crown and Parliament were more like those between President and Congress than those that subsist in England today." [54] The Tudor monarchs had to badger, wheedle, cajole, and persuade the Commons to give them the legislation they wanted. At times they were confronted by unruly Parliaments which pushed measures the monarch did not want, or debated issues the monarch wished to silence. Generally, of course, the monarch's "legislative program," consisting primarily of requests for funds, was approved. At other times, however, the Commons would rear up and the monarch would have to withdraw or reshape his demands. Burghley, who was in charge of Parliamentary relations for Elizabeth, "kept a close eye on proceedings and received from the Clerks during the session lists showing the stages of all bills in both Houses." [55] Elizabeth regularly attempted to win support in the Commons for her proposals by sending messages and "rumours" to the House, by exhorting and instructing the Speaker on how to handle the business of the House, by "receiving or summoning deputations from the Houses to Whitehall and there rating them in person," and by "descending magnificently upon Parliament in her coach or open chariot and addressing them" personally or through the Lord Keeper.[56]

Although the sovereign did not "lack means of blocking obnoxious bills during their progress through the two Houses," almost every session of Parliament passed some bills that the Crown did not want, and the royal veto was exercised. Although the veto was used more frequently against private bills than against public ones, important public measures might also be stopped by the Crown. During her reign Elizabeth I apparently

[53] Neale, *House of Commons*, 381 and *passim*; Holdsworth, 177; Campion, 11, 52–54.
[54] P. 294.
[55] Neale, *House of Commons*, 411.
[56] Rowse, 294–95.

approved 429 bills and vetoed approximately 71. The veto, however, was not a weapon that the Crown could use without weighing costs and gains: ". . . politics — the art of the possible — were not entirely divorced from Tudor monarchy. Too drastic or ill-considered a use of the royal veto might have stirred up trouble." [57] The tactics of Henry VIII or Elizabeth I in relation to their Parliaments thus differed little from those of Kennedy or Johnson in relation to their Congresses. A similar distribution of power imposed similar patterns of executive-legislative behavior.

The differentiation of specialized administrative structures also took place much more rapidly in Europe than it did in America. The contrast can be strikingly seen in the case of military institutions. A modern military establishment consists of a standing army recruited voluntarily or through conscription and commanded by a professional officer corps. In Europe a professional officer corps emerged during the first half of the nineteenth century. By 1870 the major continental states had developed most of the principal institutions of professional officership. England, however, lagged behind the Continent in developing military professionalism, and the United States lagged behind Great Britain. Not until the turn of the century did the United States have many of the institutions of professional officership which the European states had acquired many decades earlier. The division of power among governmental institutions perpetuated the mixing of politics and military affairs, and enormously complicated the emergence of a modern system of objective civilian control. Even after World War II, many Americans still adhered to a "fusionist" approach to civil-military relations and believed that military leadership and military institutions should mirror the attitudes and characteristics of civil society.[58]

American reluctance to accept a standing army also contrasts with the much more rapid modernization in Europe. In the sixteenth century European military forces consisted of feudal levies, mercenaries, and local militia. In England the militia was an ancient institution, and the Tudors formally organized it on a county basis under the Lord Lieutenants to take the place of the private retinues of the feudal lords. This development was a step toward "domestic tranquility and military incompetence,"

---

[57] Neale, *House of Commons*, 410–12, and *Elizabeth I and Her Parliament*, *passim*. Until the eighteenth century, Privy Councillors, of course, functioned as advisers to the King much as cabinet members now do to the President. Perhaps reflecting both this similarity and the later drastic change that took place in the British cabinet is the fact that in the United States the executive leadership is still called "the Administration," as it was in eighteenth-century Britain, while in Britain itself, it is now termed "the Government."

[58] See, in general, Huntington, *The Soldier and the State* (Cambridge, Mass., 1957), *passim*.

and in 1600, "not a single western country had a standing army: the only
one in Europe was that of the Turks." [59] By the end of the century, however, all the major European powers had standing armies. Discipline was
greatly improved, uniforms introduced, regulations formalized, weapons
standardized, and effective state control extended over the military forces.
The French standing army dates from Richelieu; the Prussian from the
actions of the Great Elector in 1655; the English from the Restoration
of 1660. In England the county militia continued in existence after 1660,
but steadily declined in importance.

In America, on the other hand, the militia became the crucial military
force at the same time that it was decaying in Europe. It was the natural
military system for societies whose needs were defensive rather than of-
fensive and intermittent rather than constant. The seventeenth-century
colonists continued, adapted, and improved upon the militia system that
had existed in Tudor England. In the next century, they identified militia
with popular government and standing armies with monarchical tyranny.
"On the military side," as Vagts says, "the war of the American Revolution was in part a revolt against the British standing army. . . ." [60] But
in terms of military institutions, it was a reactionary revolt. The standing
armies of George III represented modernity; the colonial militias embodied traditionalism. The American commitment to this military traditionalism, however, became all the more complete as a result of the War
of Independence. Hostility to standing armies and reliance on the militia
as the first line of defense of a free people became popular dogma and
constitutional doctrine, even though these were often departed from in
practice. Fortunately, however, the threats to security in the nineteenth
century were few, and hence the American people were able to go through
that century with a happy confidence in an ineffective force protecting
them from a nonexistent danger. The militia legacy, however, remained
a continuing element in American military affairs far into the much more
tumultuous twentieth century. It is concretely manifest today in the political influence and military strength of the National Guard. The idea that
an expert military force is better than a citizen-soldier force has yet to
win wholehearted acceptance on this side of the Atlantic.

TUDOR POLITY AND MODERN SOCIETY

The rationalization of authority and the differentiation of structure were
thus slower and less complete in America than they were in Europe. Such

[59] J. H. Hexter, *Reappraisals in History* (Evanston 1962), 147; and Clark, 84.
On the fundamental changes in European military practice, see Michael Roberts,
The Military Revolution: 1560–1660 (Belfast n.d.).
[60] Alfred Vagts, A *History of Militarism*, rev. ed. (New York 1959), 92. See
generally Louis Morton, "The Origins of American Military Policy," *Military
Affairs*, XXII (Summer 1958), 75–82.

was not the case with the third aspect of political modernization: the broadening of political participation. Here, if anything, America led Europe, although the differences in timing in the expansion of participation were less significant than the differences in the way in which that expansion took place. These contrasts in political evolution were directly related to the prevalence of foreign war and social conflict in Europe as contrasted with America.

On the Continent, the late sixteenth and the seventeenth centuries were periods of intense struggle and conflict. For only three years during the entire seventeenth century was there a complete absence of fighting on the European Continent. Several of the larger states were more often at war during the century than they were at peace. The wars were usually complex affairs involving many states tied together in dynastic and political alliances. War reached an intensity in the seventeenth century which it had never reached previously and which was exceeded later only in the twentieth century.[61] The prevalence of war directly promoted political modernization. Competition forced the monarchs to build their military strength. The creation of military strength required national unity, the suppression of regional and religious dissidents, the expansion of armies and bureaucracies, and a major increase in state revenues. "The most striking fact" in the history of seventeenth-century conflict, Clark observes, "is the great increase in the size of armies, in the scale of warfare. . . . Just as the modern state was needed to create the standing army, so the army created the modern state, for the influence of the two causes was reciprocal. . . . The growth of the administrative machine and of the arts of government was directed and conditioned by the desire to turn the national and human resources of the country into military power. The general development of European institutions was governed by the fact that the continent was becoming more military, or, we may say, more militaristic." [62] War was the great stimulus to state-building.

In recent years much has been written about "defensive modernization" by the ruling groups in non-Western societies, such as Egypt Under Mohammed Ali, the eighteenth- and nineteenth-century Ottoman Empire, and Meiji Japan. In all these cases, intense early efforts at modernization

---

[61] Clark, 98; Quincy Wright, *A Study of War* (Chicago 1942), 1, 235–40. See also Clark, *War and Society in the Seventeenth Century* (Cambridge 1958), *passim*.

[62] *Seventeenth Century*, 99, 101–2. See also Wright, 256: ". . . it would appear that the political order of Europe changed most radically and rapidly in the seventeenth and twentieth centuries when war reached greatest intensity. The seventeenth century witnessed the supersession of feudalism and the Holy Roman Empire by the secular sovereign states of Europe. The twentieth century appears to be witnessing the supersession of the secular sovereign states by something else. Exactly what cannot yet be said."

occurred in the military field, and the attempts to adopt European weapons, tactics, and organization led to the modernization of other institutions in society. What was true of these societies was also true of seventeenth-century Europe. The need for security and the desire for expansion prompted the monarchs to develop their military establishments, and the achievement of this goal required them to centralize and to rationalize their political machinery.

Largely because of its insular position, Great Britain was a partial exception to this pattern of war and insecurity. Even so, one major impetus to the centralization of authority in English government came from the efforts of the Stuart kings to collect more taxes to build and man more ships to compete with the French and other continental powers. If it were not for the English Channel, the Stuart centralization probably would have succeeded. In America in the seventeenth century, however, continuing threats came only from the Indians. The nature of this threat, plus the dispersion of the settlements, meant that the principal defense force had to be the settlers themselves organized into militia units. There was little incentive to develop European-type military forces and a European-type state to support and control them.

Civil harmony also contributed significantly to the preservation of Tudor political institutions in America. Those institutions reflected the relative unity and harmony of English society during the sixteenth century. English society, which had been racked by the Wars of the Roses in the fifteenth century, welcomed the opportunity for civil peace that the Tudors afforded. Social conflict was minor during the sixteenth century. The aristocracy had been almost eliminated during the civil wars of the previous century. England was not perhaps a middle-class society but the differences between social classes were less then than they had been earlier and much less than they were to become later. Individual mobility rather than class struggle was the keynote of the Tudor years. "The England of the Tudors was an 'organic state' to a degree unknown before Tudor times, and forgotten almost immediately afterward." [63] Harmony and unity made it unnecessary to fix sovereignty in any particular institution; it could remain dispersed so long as social conflict was minimal.

The only major issue that disrupted the Tudor consensus was, of course, religion. Significantly, in sixteenth-century English history the Act of Supremacy meant the supremacy of the state over the church, not the supremacy of one governmental institution over another or one class over another. After the brief interlude of the Marian struggles, however, the shrewd politicking and popular appeal of Elizabeth restored a peace among religious groups which was virtually unique in Europe at that time.

[63] McIlwain, High Court, 336; Rowse, 223ff.

The balance between Crown and Parliament and the combination of an active monarchy and common law depended upon this social harmony. Meanwhile on the Continent, civil strife had already reached a new intensity before the end of the sixteenth century. France alone had eight civil wars during the thirty-six years between 1562 and 1598, a period roughly comprising the peaceful reign of Elizabeth in England. The following fifty years saw Richelieu's struggles with the Huguenots and the wars of the Fronde. Spain was racked by civil strife, particularly between 1640 and 1652 when Philip IV and Olivares attempted to subdue Catalonia. In Germany, princes and parliaments fought each other. Where, as frequently happened, estates and princes espoused different religions, the controversy over religion inevitably broke the medieval balance of powers between princes and parliaments.[64]

English harmony ended with the sixteenth century. Whether the gentry were rising, falling, or doing both in seventeenth-century England, forces were at work in society disrupting Tudor social peace. The efforts to reestablish something like the Tudor balance broke down before the intensity of social and religious conflict. The brief period of Crown power between 1630 and 1640, for instance, gave way "to a short-lived restoration of something like the Tudor balance of powers during the first year of the Long Parliament (1641). This balance might perhaps have been sustained indefinitely, but for the rise of acute religious differences between the Crown and the militant Puritan party in the Commons." [65] In England, as in France, civil strife led to the demand for strong centralized power to reestablish public order. The breakdown of unity in society gave rise to irresistible forces to reestablish that unity through government.

Both Puritan and Cavalier emigrants to America escaped from English civil strife. The process of fragmentation in turn, encouraged homogeneity, and homogeneity encouraged "a kind of immobility." [66] In America, environment reinforced heredity, as the common challenges of the frontier combined with the abundance of land to help perpetuate the egalitarian characteristics of Tudor society and the complexity of Tudor political institutions. And paradoxically, as Hartz has pointed out, the framers of the Constitution of 1787 reproduced these institutions on the federal level in the belief that the social divisions and conflict within American society made necessary a complex system of checks and balances. In reality,

[64] Friedrich, 20–21; Sabine, 372–73.
[65] Chrimes, 138.
[66] Louis Hartz, *The Founding of New Societies* (New York 1964), 3, 4, 6, 23. Hartz's theory of fragmentation furnishes an excellent general framework for the analysis of the atrophy of settlement colonies, while his concept of the American liberal consensus in large part explains the preservation of Tudor political institutions.

however, their Constitution was successful only because their view of American society was erroneous. So also, only the absence of significant social divisions permitted the continued transformation of political issues into legal ones through the peculiar institution of judicial review.[67] Divided societies cannot exist without centralized power; consensual societies cannot exist with it.

In continental Europe, as in most contemporary modernizing countries, rationalized authority and centralized power were necessary not only for unity but also for progress. The opposition to modernization came from traditional interests: religious, aristocratic, regional, and local. The centralization of power was necessary to smash the old order, break down the privileges and restraints of feudalism, and free the way for the rise of new social groups and the development of new economic activities. In some degree a coincidence of interest did exist between the absolute monarchs and the rising middle classes. Hence European liberals often viewed favorably the concentration of authority in an absolute monarch, just as modernizers today frequently view favorably the concentration of authority in a single "mass" party.

In America, on the other hand, the absence of feudal social institutions made the centralization of power unnecessary. Since there was no aristocracy to dislodge, there was no need to call into existence a governmental power capable of dislodging it.[68] This great European impetus to political modernization was missing. Society could develop and change without having to overcome the opposition of social classes with a vested interest in the social and economic status quo. The combination of an egalitarian social inheritance plus the plenitude of land and other resources enabled social and economic development to take place more or less spontaneously. Government often helped to promote economic development, but (apart from the abolition of slavery) it played only a minor role in changing social customs and social structure. In modernizing societies, the centralization of power varies directly with the resistance to social change. In the United States, where the resistance was little, so also was the centralization.

The differences in social consensus between Europe and America also account for the differences in the manner in which political participation expanded. In Europe this expansion was marked by discontinuities on two levels. On the institutional level, democratization meant the shift of power from monarchical ruler to popular assembly. This shift began in England in the seventeenth century, in France in the eighteenth century, and in Germany in the nineteenth century. On the electoral level, democratization meant the extension of the suffrage for this assembly from aristocracy to upper bourgeoisie, lower bourgeoisie, peasants, and urban workers. The

[67] Hartz, The Liberal Tradition in America (New York 1955), 9–10, 45–46, 85–86, 133–34, 281–82.
[68] Ibid., 43.

process is clearly seen in the English reform acts of 1832, 1867, 1884, and 1918. In America, on the other hand, no such class differences existed as in England. Suffrage was already widespread in most colonies by independence, and universal white manhood suffrage was a fact in most states by 1830. The unity of society and the division of government meant that the latter was the principal focus of democratization. The American equivalent of the Reform Act of 1832 was the change in the nature of the Electoral College produced by the rise of political parties, and the resulting transformation of the Presidency from an indirectly elected, semi-oligarchical office to a popular one. The other major steps in the expansion of popular participation in the United States involved the extension of the electoral principal to all the state governors, to both houses of the state legislatures, to many state administrative offices and boards, to the judiciary in many states, and to the United States Senate. Thus, in Europe the broadening of participation meant the extension of the suffrage for one institution to all classes of society, while in America it meant the extension of the suffrage by the one class in society to all (or almost all) institutions of government.

In Europe the opposition to modernization within society forced the modernization of the political system. In America, the ease of modernization within society precluded the modernization of the political system. The United States thus combines the world's most modern society with one of the world's most antique polities. The American political experience is distinguished by frequent acts of creation but few, if any, of innovation. Since the Revolution, constitutions have been drafted for thirty-eight new political systems, but the same pattern of government has been repeated over and over again. The new constitutions of Alaska and Hawaii differ only in detail from the constitution of Massachusetts, originally drafted by John Adams in 1780. When else in history has such a unique series of opportunities for political experiment and innovation been so almost totally wasted?

This static quality of the political system contrasts with the prevalence of change elsewhere in American society. A distinguishing feature of American culture, Robin Williams has argued, is its positive orientation toward change. In a similar vein, two observers have noted, "In the United States change itself is valued. The new is good; the old is unsatisfactory. Americans gain prestige by being among the first to own next year's automobile; in England, much effort is devoted to keeping twenty-five-year-old cars in operating condition." [69] In three centuries, a few pitifully small and poor rural settlements strung along the Atlantic seaboard and

[69] Williams, *American Society*, 2nd ed., rev. (New York 1961), 571; Eli Ginzberg and Ewing W. Reilley, *Effecting Change in Large Organizations* (New York 1957), 18–19.

populated in large part by religious exiles were transformed into a huge, urbanized, continental republic, the world's leading economic and military power. America has given the world its most modern and efficient economic organizations. It has pioneered social benefits for the masses: mass production, mass education, mass culture. Economically and socially, everything has been movement and change. Politically, however, the only significant institutional innovation has been federalism, and this, in itself, of course, was made possible only by the traditional hostility to the centralization of authority. Fundamental social and economic change has been combined with political stability and continuity. In a society dedicated to what is shiny new, the polity remains quaintly old.

Modernity is thus not all of a piece. The American experience demonstrates conclusively that some institutions and some aspects of a society may become highly modern while other institutions and other aspects retain much of their traditional form and substance. Indeed, this may be a natural state of affairs. In any system some sort of equilibrium or balance must be maintained between change and continuity. Change in some spheres renders unnecessary or impossible change in others. In America the continuity and stability of government has permitted the rapid change of society, and the rapid change in society has encouraged continuity and stability in government. The relation between polity and society may well be dialectical rather than complementary. In other societies, such as Latin America, a rigid social structure and the absence of social and economic change have been combined with political instability and the weakness of political institutions. A good case can be made, moreover, that the latter is the result of the former.[70]

This combination of modern society and Tudor polity explains much that is otherwise perplexing about political ideas in America. In Europe the conservative is the defender of traditional institutions and values, particularly those in society rather than in government. Conservatism is associated with the church, the aristocracy, social customs, the established social order. The attitude of conservatives toward government is ambivalent: Government is viewed as the guarantor of social order, but it also is viewed as the generator of social change. Society rather than government has been the principal conservative concern. European liberals, on the other hand, have had a much more positive attitude toward government. Like Turgot, Price, and Godwin, they have viewed the centralization of power as the precondition of social reform. They have supported the gathering of power into a single place — first the absolute monarch, then the sovereign assembly — where it can then be used to change society.

[70] Merle Kling, "Toward a Theory of Power and Political Instability in Latin America," *Western Political Quarterly*, IX (March 1956), 21–31.

In America, on the other hand, these liberal and conservative attitudes have been thoroughly confused and partly reversed. Conservatism has seldom flourished because it has lacked social institutions to conserve. Society is changing and modern, while government, which the conservative views with suspicion, has been relatively unchanging and antique. With a few exceptions, such as a handful of colleges and churches, the oldest institutions in American society are governmental institutions. The absence of established social institutions, in turn, has made it unnecessary for American liberals to espouse the centralization of power as did European liberals. John Adams could combine Montesquieu's polity with Turgot's society much to the bafflement of Turgot. Nineteenth-century Europeans had every reason to be fascinated by America: It united a liberal society which they were yet to experience with a conservative politics which they had in large part forgotten.

15   RONALD P. DORE

Some Comparisons of Latin American
and Asian Studies with Special
Reference to Research on Japan

It is not easy to generalize meaningfully about differences in the approaches of American social scientists to the study of Latin America and of Japan; there is approximately the same diversity in assumptions and preoccupations and theoretical frameworks. One meets the same fashionable jargon metaphors of thrusts and drives and mixes and inputs; there is the same evidence of terminological confusion, the same fondness for those protean words like "modernization," "development," "nationalism,"

From *Items*, Social Science Research Council, Vol. 17, No. 2, June 1963, pp. 13–20, adapted from "Latin America and Japan Compared," by R.P. Dore, from *Continuity and Change in Latin America*, edited by John J. Johnson. Reprinted with the permission of the author and the publishers, Stanford University Press. © 1964 by the Board of Trustees of the Leland Stanford Junior University. Footnote abridged for this printing. Original reference numbers have been retained.

which can mean all things to all men and consequently nothing precise
to anyone; and in conference discussions there are the same occasional
bouts of linguistic self-consciousness when the confusion becomes plain
and attempts are made to define (though I have never heard Asian
scholars reach such an advanced stage of terminological agnosticism that
they questioned the proper use of words like "writer" and "peasant," as
happened during this conference). In these respects the differences seem
greater between disciplines than between students of different areas.
Economists more often know what they are talking about than do other
social scientists because more of the economist's terms are clearly related
to quantitative measures. The economist can define economic growth in
terms of an increase in per capita Gross National Product at constant
prices, and discussion can proceed with a clear idea of the issues at stake.
Sociologists and political scientists are much less certain of the connota-
tions of social or political "development" and sometimes they can even
be heard arguing in fruitlessly essentialist terms about what such words
really mean.

CONTRASTS BETWEEN STUDENTS
OF THE TWO AREAS

Some differences between the students of the two areas are largely determined by the nature of the areas studied. In the first place, students of
Asia tend to be more narrowly specialized. There are a few who take
Southeast Asia as their oyster, some who bestraddle China and Japan,
but most confine their research to only one society. By contrast, one hears
of Latin Americanists, but not of Bolivianists or Peruvianists.

The advantages of such a global, or at least semi-hemispherical, approach are not immediately obvious. It is not easy for any one man to
know enough about so many different societies, and the attempt to be
comprehensive may lead to a diffusion of energy — to the quick survey of
formal structure rather than the detailed analysis of process. The attempt
to arrive at *descriptive* generalizations seems in any case to be of dubious
value. The predicate of any sentence beginning, say, "Students in Latin
America . . ." is likely to be so general, so vague, and so hedged about
with qualifications as to be neither informative nor useful.

On the other hand, Latin America does provide excellent opportunities
for the kind of comparative sociology that seeks to arrive at generalizations about *causal* connections of the type: "X is likely to lead to Y,
other things being equal." It is obvious that one has a better chance of
arriving at such generalizations with fair confidence if other things *are* as
equal as possible. It is in this respect that Latin America offers a promis-
ing field. Its societies do have so many points of similarity that an examination of their differences might yield new information about the way

those differences are interrelated. Thus, for instance, Latin America is an excellent place to study, say, the relation between levels of literacy and the political role of labor unions; between the size of the professional middle-class and the strength of liberal democratic parties; between the real extent of racial or cultural differences and the political or social importance attached to such differences; between the type of land tenure and the political involvement of peasants, and so on. Economists have used such methods in a purely statistical way, for instance, in seeking a correlation between inflation and the rate of economic growth; but there is still not enough systematic collection of data to enable sociologists or political scientists to use the same technique effectively.

A second difference between students of Latin America and students of Japan is, I think, that the latter are better informed. This is not a sign of any particular virtue in themselves. It derives in part from the fact that Japan has had a strong central government for the last century, dominated by a bureaucracy which saw no part of life as falling outside its purview and sometimes displayed a veritable mania for recording and tabulating every bit of possibly useful information it could lay hands on. It derives also from the development of Japanese scholarship. There was a time when Westerners led the field in the academic study of Japan. The first professor of Japanese philology at Tokyo in the 1890's was an Englishman. At the beginning of this century Western students of Japanese history were still more acutely critical of their sources, less easily content with mere chronicling, and more sophisticated in their analysis of motive than their Confucian-trained Japanese counterparts. In the newer social science fields Western superiority persisted (thanks partly to the handicaps imposed by Japanese militarism) until much more recently. There is, for instance, no prewar Japanese village study with quite the breadth and sophistication of Embree's *Japanese Village*.[1]

The situation today is very different. The Japanese themselves have acquired the same attitudes toward research, the same canons of evidence, and the same comparative knowledge of other societies as their Western colleagues, and Japan has become rich enough to maintain a very large number of professional scholars in all the social science fields. This means that the Western student of Japanese history now has a vast body of secondary Japanese sources to draw on; that the Western anthropologist who studies a village in Japan is wasting his time unless he first works through the substantial production of Japanese rural sociologists.

The similarity of styles and standards makes more painfully obvious, therefore, the one major disadvantage under which the foreigner labors —

---

[1] John F. Embree, *Suye Mura: A Japanese Village,* Chicago: University of Chicago Press, 1939.

that he rarely starts to learn Japanese young enough to acquire a real fluency in the language. I know of no Western historian who can handle Japanese historical documents with anything like the speed and accuracy of his professional Japanese colleagues. Consequently the Western scholar is perhaps best employed as a synthesizer for Western audiences of the results of Japanese scholarship, though his synthesis may in itself make original contributions to the subject, inasmuch as his position outside the tangled web of personal relations in the Japanese academic world does enable him to challenge accepted shibboleths and suggest new lines of inquiry more easily than can those inside.

This is not altogether a popular role, however, and relations between Japanese and foreign scholars are not wholly free from strain. The linguistic handicaps of the foreign scholar combine with a long tradition of cultural isolation to convince many Japanese that the foreigner can never "really understand" Japan. They therefore may be reluctant to take the writings of foreign scholars very seriously. This tendency to deprecate their work may further be exacerbated by a more specific *anti-yanquismo* of various kinds — either political, as in the Japanese Marxist's scorn for the naive bourgeois interpretations of the American historian; or personal, as when ill-paid Japanese scholars are induced by the lure of better research facilities, extra income, or the opportunity for foreign travel to become involved in American research projects and accept the direction of American scholars whose scholarship they cannot respect as much as their financial resources.

My impressions of how this compares with the situation in the Latin American field are uncertain, but it does seem safe to assert that much less reliable information about Latin American societies is available from their own governmental sources, and that the development of the social sciences in Latin American universities has been quantitatively much inferior to that in recent Japan. Given, further, that Spanish and Portuguese pose lesser obstacles for the English speaker, it follows that there remain greater opportunities for foreign scholars to do useful fundamental research in the Latin American field. Secondly, the initial gap between native and foreign scholarly approaches and critical standards was undoubtedly smaller in the case of Latin America. The Mediterranean academic style may be different from the Anglo-Saxon, but the differences are within the European cultural tradition, all elements of which have been constantly interacting over the whole course of their development. As such, the differences are of lesser magnitude than the gulf that separated the Chinese from the European traditions developing for millennia in mutual isolation. It would seem easier, therefore, for Latin American and North American scholars to work together, but it is not altogether clear that this is the case. In the first place, the smaller initial gap between the predominantly philosophical and normative bias of Latin American academism and the more pragmatic and scientific bias of its North American counterpart may prove even more difficult to bridge — partly because subtler differences of style and orientation are not always consciously appreciated and allowed for, partly because the closing of the gap in the Japanese case was made entirely by the Japanese themselves. It was *their* historians and social scientists who abandoned their own intellectual heritage and consciously assimilated Western — predominantly German, British, and American — academic traditions. Latin Americans are not disposed to make the same kind of capitulation; they are more likely to look on their intellectual heritage as a cause for pride than for self-disciplinary correction. And it is perhaps harder for two parties to meet in the middle of a stream than for one to leap over it. The other irritants noted in the Japanese case are also relevant. The American scholar cannot escape the consequences of his greater affluence, or of the political and economic involvement of his country in Latin American affairs.

This closer political involvement suggests a third difference between North American students of Latin America and of Japan. It could be argued that by a process either of selective recruitment or of acculturation the students of an area tend to take on something of the characteristics of its people: that students of Japan tend to form an integrated group, harmonious, industrious, circumspect, and serious-minded, while the students of Latin America are personalists, irresponsible, disorganized, ideological, and preoccupied with demonstrating their *machismo*. This would be a gross exaggeration, but it does seem that Latin American studies give rise to sharper divisions of opinion, for the reason that Latin America does have very serious problems of poverty, political oppression and economic stagnation, the competing solutions for which evoke strong political emotions. Should labor unions be encouraged to play a leading political role? Should there be land reforms? Should the state play a leading part in industrial development? Can the military be a benign source of national leadership? North American students of North American politics may celebrate, with Daniel Bell, the *End of Ideology*,[2] but the political battles which enlivened the 'thirties have contemporary relevance to Latin America. By contrast, Japan, economically a going concern, politically relatively stable, has fewer social problems that do not seem to be on the way to gradual solution. Consequently there is today (though this was not the case 15 years ago) a lesser tendency for American students of modern Japan to look on Japan as a society about which something should be done. If this means that Latin America is a more exciting field in which to work, it also means that it is potentially a more difficult one,

[2] *The End of Ideology*, Glencoe: Free Press, 1960.

for Latin America, besides having problems of welfare, is a sensitive area
in the cold war. Students of Japan are fortunate in being free of the
particular kind of pressure involved in studying an area that is a problem
in cold-war terms.

COMPARISONS BETWEEN THE TWO AREAS

In the mid-nineteenth century both Japan and Latin America were underdeveloped areas: predominantly rural, lacking all but the rudimentary
beginnings of a modern industry or transport system, lacking a rationalized bureaucracy or judiciary, lacking even, as cellular societies knit together by authoritarian personal bonds, a coherent society-wide polity. In
both areas there were individuals who preached the need for a drive to
modernity, to emulate the industrial and political systems of the Western
powers and equal, if possible, their economic and military strength. In
Japan that drive was successful in terms of values that most of us share
today — successful, that is, in achieving a highly developed industrial
potential, a level of living already approximating that of the original industrial countries, and a rapidly rising level of living at that; a high level
of universal education; an impartial system of justice; a relatively impartial bureaucracy and a political system that imposes minimal restraints
on freedom of expression, permits wide popular participation, and appears to have a good chance of proving stable. By contrast, no single
Latin American country could be described in quite such terms, although
Latin America started with a more favorable endowment of natural resources in proportion to population and with a much longer acquaintance
with those intellectual traditions that had produced modern Western industrialism and the variety of modern Western political forms.

One ought perhaps to pause at this point to recall something of the
cost of Japan's "success," the cost so obvious to a Western observer in the
'thirties or 'forties that he would have been reluctant to apply the word
"success" to any aspect of Japan's transformation. And one has to remember that the cost of Japan's foreign wars in human lives and resources
was not an incidental aberration in Japan's development but an integral
part of it. Aggressive nationalism and an expansionist foreign policy
helped to maintain the internal unity which enabled the state to mobilize
resources for industrial development and even conditioned the disciplined
acceptance of the recent postwar reforms; military objectives dictated a
great deal of the investment in heavy industry; the expansion of technical
education for military purposes before and during the war was a precondition for the industrial growth since; and so on. The present concern,
however, is not with over-all appraisals but with the attempt to account
for differences, and although war may be a partial explanation of how

Japan achieved her present status a lot more needs to be said if one is to explain why.

INITIAL ADVANTAGES

Japan at the beginning of her transformation enjoyed a number of advantages which offset her disadvantages in terms of natural resources and the alienness of the Western culture from which industrialism had sprung. The very density of population, perhaps, was one such advantage. It meant that Japan was already a much more closely "governed" country. Her peasant agriculture was already quite productive and operated in a framework of village-wide cooperation which required responsible behavior and some "public spirit" from a sizable proportion of the population. The mass of the people was by no means wholly sunk in misery and ignorance, as witness that other major advantage of nineteenth-century Japan, the relatively wide spread of education. The schools for the masses were mostly small private establishments supported by parents; the governmental authorities gave only moral encouragement, but at least they did not actively discourage. In the version of Confucianism which dominated Tokugawa Japan, man was not the repository of original sin but a being capable of infinite improvement. The more he improved himself, however humble his status, the better society became, and the most important method of improving himself was by learning to read the moral classics of ancient China, or at least the summary versions of their message written in simple Japanese. It was this tradition, catalyzed by the discovery of Northern European educational systems, that prompted the new central government in the early 1870's to decree the institution of compulsory education as one of its first acts of reform, and it was the existence of numerous private schools and of a widespread popular demand for education that ensured that the decree was eventually translated into reality.

The attempt to build a system of universal education well before industrialization got under way suggests another important difference between Japan and Latin America. The leaders of Meiji Japan felt a responsibility for the mass of Japanese peasantry, and held an assessment of its importance, which argues a sense of common Japaneseness far deeper than any sense of common nationality binding, say, the Montevidean lawyer with the *gauchos* of the *pampas*. There are numerous obvious reasons why this sense of a nationality which embraced *all* the population should have been stronger in Japan than in Latin America: the absence of internal racial divisions and of anything comparable to the cultural and linguistic gulf that, conceptually at least, divides the Indian from the *mestizo*; the absence of the immigration that made nationalism when it came in Latin

America often an internally divisive rather than a unifying factor; the geographical isolation of Japan; the fact that nationalism in the nineteenth century was given a powerful initial stimulus by the very real threat of direct military colonization. It was, in Rostow's terms, largely a reactive nationalism and, as such, sharper and stronger in proportion to the dramatic suddenness and clarity of the threat it reacted against. In Latin America, under the shelter of the Monroe Doctrine, there was only the more elusive threat of economic domination, or the frontier wars, to provide anything like the same kind of stimulus.

Most important of all, perhaps, is the fact that Japan was not only culturally homogeneous but also culturally distinct from the outside world. The boundaries of Japanese culture and of the Japanese nation-state were coterminous. It is a familiar observation that there is little in, say, the Chilean cultural tradition to distinguish it from the Argentinian. The Venezuelan writer defines himself only partially as a Venezuelan; he is also a Latin American, and beyond that he belongs to European, or at least to Western, culture. But the Japanese was not at the center of widening circles of loyalty and cultural identity; he dwelt on a cultural island. Only with China did he feel any sense of cultural kinship and this was a tenuous bond, much weaker, probably, than the bond between a Portuguese-speaking Brazilian and a Spanish-speaking Argentinian. And beyond that there was the West — to be approached in books only over a difficult linguistic gap or through the medium of often barbarous translations; to be approached in personal intercourse only through a barrier of awkwardness and confusion of the cues of etiquette. Even when he got over those barriers, the ideas and values which he absorbed came to him with the label *Western* culture firmly attached.

Even today the tendency of the Japanese to analyze their modern culture into its indigenous and Western components has survived the *de facto* coalescence of these cultural streams. Universities do not have history departments, but departments of Japanese, of Chinese, and of "Western" history. Houses have rooms and "Western rooms." Clothes are *kimono* or "Western clothes." Translators of Western academic works normally do not even attempt a style that would make the translation indistinguishable from an original Japanese work. The everyday experience of the Japanese, and especially the educational experience of the Japanese intellectual, has constantly served to remind him of his Japaneseness, particularly when he was absorbing or using elements of Western culture. Such an enhanced sense of the separateness of Japanese culture could hardly have failed to reinforce his sense of membership in the Japanese nation and his commitment to its goals.

The contrast with the cosmopolitanism of urban and intellectual Latin America is very marked and had, I would suggest, important political and economic consequences. In the first place, it set rigid boundaries to the possibilities of political opposition. The absence of easy opportunities for tolerable exile was a powerful teacher of the virtues of compromise. The Argentinian newspaper editor in danger of arrest or assassination could slip across the river to Montevideo and still find himself at home, amid familiar things, able easily to find friends and a new job. But to all but a tiny fraction of Japanese only one place has ever been home.

The sense of cultural separateness meant, secondly, that Japanese nationalism was not just an occasionally useful political weapon to channel frustrations into harmless xenophobia, but a real motivating force on the part of Japanese political leaders and intellectuals, with roots in history and contemporary culture strong enough for these leaders to make of it a coherent ideology which could be diffused to the whole Japanese nation. The great entrepreneurs of the nineteenth century who founded the biggest concerns may not have been so overwhelmingly inspired by patriotic motives as they often said they were in their speeches and autobiographies, but if only as a marginal element patriotism, it seems, did enter into their calculations. The real desire to see Japan develop economically and expand militarily did on occasion prompt a willingness to sacrifice sectional interests for the sake of the overriding national interests, to accept taxation or protective tariffs which might seriously inflate their costs.

Another aspect of the sense of separateness and of the sharpened awareness of the alien nature of Western importations is relevant to economic development. Modern technology came to Latin America piecemeal and simply as technology. It came to Japan as part of a package deal with the whole of Western civilization. It has been rather neatly said, and with some truth, that the greatest innovation is the idea of innovation itself. If enough people can be induced to make enough new departures from traditional habits with what seem to them beneficial consequences, they may finally acquire the disposition to regard novelty in itself as desirable, and when this happens the psychological preconditions for technological take-off are fulfilled. In Japan in the 1870's and 1880's the tempo and impact of innovation were extremely great. Moreover, all the new things that invaded Japan came bearing the same label of newness and foreignness. Because they all came together, the acceptance of one element of the package helped to create the psychological predisposition to accept other elements. The farmer who had taken to cigarettes and soap would look more favorably on a new plough which came from the same certified source. In Latin America, which had no period of seclusion followed by a sudden opening of the floodgates and which had always been a part (albeit peripheral) of Western culture, there was no such supporting reinforcement of the predisposition to accept technological innovation. What is suggested here, of course, is a variant of the psychological aspects of the "big push" theory of economic development. The snowballing growth of proneness to innovation can be accelerated if there are cultural and ideological elements to be added to the technological ones.

Nationalism, of course, is a two-edged weapon. It can provide those anxious for change with a charter for innovation (innovation in the national interest) and with a powerful argument for cajoling the recalcitrant. It can also provide those anxious to preserve the *status quo* with a charter for resisting change — in order to protect the national essence. The innovators may be attacked as traitors to all that is sacred in the national life. The intellectual and even the political history of modern Japan can plausibly be interpreted as an oscillation between the dominance of these two types of nationalism, a succession of periods in which first the innovators and then the traditionalists have held dominant command of the ideological airspace.

The common metaphor of the swinging pendulum, however, is less apt than that of the zigzag forward movement. At each change of direction accommodations were reached between the traditionalists and the innovators which allowed the strengthening, or the preservative embalmment, of elements of the national tradition which hardly impeded, and even sometimes helped, the process of economic growth. In the "largely irrelevant but no impediment" category, one might include the preservation of elements of Japanese material culture. Japanese dress and domestic architecture, Japanese food and wine, government grants for the protection of ancient shrines and temples, the vigorous continuation of certain Japanese arts and crafts, all helped to reassure conservative Japanese that in some respects at least Japan was still Japan. Perhaps only the Mexicans in Latin America have anything like a similar symbolic base for this kind of assured sense of national self-identity.

In the field of social relations, the role of the preserved traditional elements was more subtle. They were modified and mobilized, not simply preserved. The Emperor, restored to nominal power by the Restoration in 1868, provided a legitimation for the new innovating government and offered a personal focus of loyalty which helped to make the new nationalism intelligible to the people. Without the sanctioning authority of the Imperial tradition further fortified by the mystique of a reconstructed Shinto religion, it is doubtful that nineteenth-century governments would ever have had the strength and stability to impose high taxation and otherwise mobilize resources for state-sponsored economic development. Other traditional elements were similarly utilized. The Confucian ethic of personal relations was reformulated as the uniquely *Japanese* family system. It served to preserve an image of society as properly hierarchical and based on personal loyalties, and thus to strengthen authoritarian tendencies in general, enhance the docility of the labor force, and hold in check the erosion of the government's traditionally sanctioned authority. It also rationalized family aggrandizement as a proper and laudable motive for entrepreneurial activity. It provided a rationale for, and thereby made a more consciously planned policy out of, the new impersonal and bureaucratized paternalism of the large corporations — the so-called enterprise-family ideal — which developed in the 'twenties.

It can be fairly justly argued that this conscious reincorporation of traditional elements in Japan not only satisfied the sentiments of the traditionalists, but also aided at least the economic development of the country. It can equally be argued that it impeded political and social change toward a more liberal and egalitarian structure. But again one can make out a case for saying that this, too, was in the long run beneficial. By acting as a damper on social and political change, this authoritarian use of tradition postponed the establishment of the institutions of liberal democracy until such time as industrialization and the development of education had sufficiently transformed the social base to give these institutions a good chance of stability. Latin America, by contrast, abounds with examples of what one could call "premature" political development: the establishment, under pressure of ideas originating outside the national boundaries, of political institutions which assume a degree of sophistication on the part of voters; a sense of responsibility in the exercise of power and the practice of opposition; and a minimum degree of consensus about national goals which simply does not exist and which the new institutions themselves cannot succeed in creating before they are perverted beyond redemption.

Similarly, welfare state ideologies, which were originally the product of an advanced stage of capitalism, have combined with traditions of the paternalistic state in many much poorer and unindustrialized countries of Latin America to produce political demands so potent that the State is forced to accept responsibilities which, however admirable in themselves, divert into consumption resources that are needed for economic development. Again Japanese governments could resist such demands until the economy could easily afford them.

These are but particular aspects of a general characteristic of the situation of the late developer. Economists can demonstrate with a good deal of plausibility that industrialization is a process which takes more or less the same length of time anywhere; take-off to maturity requires 60 years whenever the society chooses to start. But in certain things there is only one time scale — a world time scale. Ideas, ideals, consumer tastes, and the reverberations of revolutions slip across boundaries. In the first decade of this century Japanese, as well as Chilean, mines were the scene of violently suppressed strikes, and Japan, too, had the beginnings of a more permanently organized labor movement by the end of World War I. Like many Latin American countries she had social realist novelists writing "proletarian novels" in the 'thirties. It was just that isolation and the strength of tradition served until 1945 to keep the effects of these worldwide currents to a minimum.

Nor was this Japan's only advantage in the matter of timing. Another was that her industrialization began *early* enough and proceeded rapidly enough so that by 1945 Japan *was* prepared for a version of liberal democracy and *could* begin to afford extensive welfare services.

The same point can be made in demographic terms. Drugs are one of the things, like ideas, that can cross frontiers easily. The dramatic fall in the death rate came simultaneously in Japan and Latin America in the late 'forties. But in Japan the industrial and educational revolution and the revolution in mobility aspirations had by then reached the point at which a simple legislative act permitting abortion could reduce the birth rate with equally dramatic suddenness and so cut population growth back to manageable proportions.

Another aspect of the demographic problem is that Japan was relatively free of "premature urbanization" — through the push of rural poverty rather than the pull of urban opportunity — and its social and political consequences. For this, however, something more than the manageable rate of population growth and Japan's launching into machine industry in the days before the automatic factory are responsible. It is also relevant that her agriculture was based on the peasant family holding, and the institution of the landholding peasant family was strong enough to give rural areas a far more elastic capacity to absorb population than in a plantation economy. If an urban job was not easily to be found, the younger son could more easily stay at home. If he found a job and was dismissed at a time of recession, he could return home and make himself marginally useful on the farm. If unemployment one must have, there is much to be said for taking it in the concealed form of underemployment in agriculture — as the Chinese, too, seem recently to have concluded, to judge by their policy of returning population from the cities.

To return from this digression into timing and agriculture to the role of tradition, the contrast between Latin America and Japan in this regard would seem clear enough. When a conscious nationalistic urge for modernization began in the nineteenth century, little in the Hispanic American tradition could serve the dual functions of so emphasizing the specific differentiae of, say, Chilean or Brazilian society as to satisfy the traditionalists, and of in some way facilitating change. The *indigenista* movement, it seems, nowhere succeeded in making a substantial impact except perhaps in Mexico where the ideal of the ancient corporate Indian community combined with more modern forms of collectivism to produce the *ejido*. Cuauhtemoc may have proved an integrating symbol for the Mexicans, but a much weaker one than the ancient Emperors of Japan whose living descendant still resided in Tokyo. There was no continuity with the Aztec tradition sufficient for anything comparable to, say, the Japanese family system to be carried over into modern times; and although the solidarity of the upper-class family does seem to have been a distinctive Latin American characteristic, this was still a class and not a national phenomenon.

There is another economic aspect of this search for traditions. When seeking to define a national self-image in a nationalistic frame of mind, one is most likely to seize on those features that supposedly differentiate one from one's major international antagonist. For Japan this point of counterreference has been the West generally and in the twentieth century America more particularly; for Latin America, since the beginning of this century at least, it has been almost exclusively America. But in differentiating themselves from Americans, the Japanese could point to the beauties of their tight family system, their patriotic loyalty to the Emperor contrasting with American selfish individualism and so on. It was not so easy for a Latin American to establish the Latin American differentiae in terms of family, political, or legal institutions. He had to fall back on "spirit" and attitudes and, since the most visible American was the businessman, tended (cf. *arielismo*) to make comparisons in materialist-spiritual terms. Thus, by scorning devotion to technology and profit, the Latin American made something of a virtue out of the stark fact of economic backwardness. The Japanese had enough other arguments with which to fortify themselves without resorting to this one, with its inhibiting effect on indigenous economic growth.

There is also, presumably, in *arielismo* an element which can only be explained by the continued existence of a traditional landed upper-class. And here there is a powerful and important difference between Japan and almost any country in Latin America. In Japan the attenuation of the ties that had bound the feudal aristocracy and gentry to their lands began at the end of the sixteenth century and was completed in 1870. During the latter feudal period the samurai gentry left their small subfiefs to live in the castle town of their feudal lords. Each of these larger fiefs was controlled from the castle town by an administration, staffed by the samurai gentry, which as time went on became increasingly bureaucratized. There were no longer any manors, no land-based knights. The exploitation of these large fiefs took the form of a standardized impersonal produce tax levied on the peasant producers, the proceeds from which were doled out to the samurai as hereditary rice stipends. When the new central government took over in 1868, this system was fairly easily dismantled over a few years. The fiefs were turned into prefectures; the feudal lords, compensated with titles and government bonds, were forced to break their ties with their former territories. The samurai gentry were also compensated for their hereditary feudal revenues, though on a lesser scale; some were absorbed into the new centralized bureaucracy; some went into the new national army; others became teachers, lawyers, policemen, and businessmen.

The old aristocratic fiefholders, the 300 noble families who formed the new peerage, had little effective power in modern Japan. One reason was that they had already been effectively separated from the exercise of power by the development of fief bureaucracies; another, that they had lost the power and the prestige that direct ownership of land can give. This did not mean that there were no landlords in rural Japan. There were; and a few of them were rich; but the majority were members of the peasant class who had accumulated extra land through the improvidence or the misfortunes of their fellow peasants. They did manage to predominate in the early political parties and they retained some power as a veto group until the postwar land reform. But they never exercised effective political leadership because they could not rival the prestige of the bureaucracy, recruited predominantly from the samurai — their former feudal superiors.

The important difference between Japan and the Latin American countries is the difference between a society in which a new professional administrative structure and the values of the former regime; and only in trial transition begins, and a society in which the new professional groups, including the bureaucracy, which are created as a *result* of economic and social change, gradually share power with an existing landed upper-class and in the process merge with it and take over many of its values. Even in Mexico, the postrevolutionary administrators took over much of the administrative structure and the values of the former regime; and only in the recent revolutions of Bolivia and Cuba have really sharp breaks occurred. In contrast, the new samurai bureaucracy which took power in 1868 was building from the ground up; and in eliminating the landed upper-class from the scene, Japan gained great advantages for the industrializing process. The salaried bureaucracy was not bound by landed ties to competing economic interests which might make it lukewarm toward industry. Its very nature as a bureaucracy inclined it toward rationalizing legalistic procedures and the creation of predictable formal structures, rather than toward reliance on the more arbitrary wisdom and judgment of those who exercise authority by right of lineage. Unquestionably of highest rank, its members were free from the temptation to improve their social standing by buying land or by imitating the manners of a landed aristocracy.

SOME TENTATIVE CONCLUSIONS

I have referred to the fashion for studying Japan as a model of successful industrial transformation. Models should have "lessons," and one who has succumbed to that fashion is perhaps obliged to hazard a few conclusions concerning whether Japan does offer any lessons for modern Latin America. The last point concerning the advantages of discontinuity and revolutionary change, particularly in the composition of the governing class, *before* industrialization begins can hardly be generalized into a prescription for revolution in countries where these processes are already under way and much of the apparatus of the modern state is already built. Similarly, the use of traditional channels and modes of authority in Japan's development again shows only that they can be used to promote industrial and even political change if the commanding heights of authority are firmly grasped by innovating leaders *before* they are eroded away by economic and social change and the influence of egalitarian ideologies. It is probably too late to try to capture such traditional channels of authority when that process of erosion is already well-advanced. Again, many of the factors differentiating Japan from Latin America — the Confucian tradition of education, the sense of cultural separateness and the coincidence of cultural and political boundaries, the timing of industrialization with respect to world-wide ideological and demographic trends — are advantages, inherent in Japan's situation, that cannot be reproduced by an act of political will.

The only plausibly generalizable aspect is the strong identification with the nation and awareness of national purpose which in Japan undoubtedly played a part in creating the cohesion needed to induce change and subordinate short-term sectional to long-run majority interests. Although Latin American countries are so much less favored in those factors that naturally create such sentiments, they can nevertheless be induced and utilized for development. But it must be remembered that the national purposes of which the Japanese were aware and for which they unitedly strove were for most of her modern history predominantly military in character. It remains to be demonstrated that a sense of national purpose can prove as effective and as compelling when defined in terms of economic growth rates and social welfare, rather than in terms of the seizure of territory or defense against a threatening enemy.

Transformation of Social, Political, and Cultural Orders in Modernization

The institutionalization of change, or the development and crystallization of new institutional settings requires the internal transformation of the societies or groups within which it occurs. The capacity for such internal transformation is manifest in structural frameworks or cultural symbols that enable some groups to mobilize new forces and resources without necessarily destroying the existing structure.[1] In modernizing societies, internal transformation is especially critical because modernization requires not only a relatively stable new structure but one capable of adapting to continuously changing conditions and problems.[2]

Modernization, of course, does not imply a "smooth" process of "balanced" or "equilibrated" growth. It has always been a revolutionary process of undermining and changing the existing institutional structure. But the possibility of successful institutionalization of an innovating or revolutionary process is never inherent in the revolutionary act itself. It depends on other conditions, primarily the society's capacity for internal transformation.

A society can be forced to modernize under the impact of external forces, and indeed 19th- and 20th-century modernization has meant, to a very large extent, the impingement of Western European institutions on new countries in the Americas, in Eastern and Southern Europe, and in Asia and Africa. Some of these societies have never — or not yet — gone beyond adaptation to these external impingements. Lacking a high degree of internal adaptability, many become stagnant after having started on the road to modernity, or their modern frameworks have tended to break

Reprinted from *American Sociological Review*, Vol. 30, October, 1965, pp. 659–673, with permission from the American Sociological Association.

[1] See Shmuel N. Eisenstadt, "Institutionalization and Change," *American Sociological Review*, 29 (1964), pp. 235–248.

[2] On the concept of modernization see Shmuel N. Eisenstadt, *Modernization, Growth and Diversity*, Bloomington, Ind.: Indiana University Press, 1963, and Manfred Halpern, "Toward Further Modernization of the Study of New Nations," *World Politics*, 17 (1964), pp. 157–181.

down.[3] Moreover, different societies necessarily develop different institutional patterns, so that the spread of modernization has entailed a great deal of structural diversity.

Modernization, however, is associated with some definite structural characteristics. Among these the most important are a high level of structural differentiation, and of so-called "social mobilization," and a relatively large-scale, unified and centralized institutional framework. Beyond this basic core, the aforementioned structural diversity may develop. These structural characteristics are not to be regarded as simple indices of successful modernization, and their development does not necessarily assure successful modernization. Rather they are necessary but not sufficient conditions for the development and continuity of a modern institutional structure sufficiently capable of dealing with continuously changing problems to assure sustained growth.[4]

Among these conditions, of special importance is the establishment of viable, flexible and yet effective symbolic and organizational centers, responsive to the continuous problems of modernization and able to regulate them. At the same time, a more flexible orientation with new goals and a commitment to the new centers and their needs must be developed among the more active social groups. Here some aspects of the pre-modern structure of modernizing societies are especially important. With the exception of the African and to some extent the Latin American ones, most pre-industrial societies began modernizing, or were pushed into it, with a relatively complex, differentiated institutional structure. Within the great historical and Imperial civilizations for example, centralized and differentiated structures and organizations already existed, together with *relatively* autonomous basic institutional spheres — political, religious or ideological, and social organization and stratification.[5]

The centralized frameworks and the relatively autonomous institutional spheres were crucial to the transformative capacities of these societies, for they facilitated the initial modernization and helped make the new modern centers and frameworks work efficiently. Different constellations of

[3] The concept and conditions of such breakdowns are analyzed in Shmuel N. Eisenstadt, "Breakdowns of Modernization," *Economic Development and Cultural Change*, 12 (1964), pp. 345–367.

[4] See Shmuel N. Eisenstadt, "Modernization and Conditions of Sustained Growth," *World Politics*, 16 (1964), pp. 576–594.

[5] See Shmuel N. Eisenstadt, *The Political Systems of Empires*, New York: The Free Press of Glencoe, 1963, and "Religious Organizations and Political Process in Centralized Empires," *Journal of Asian Studies*, 21 (1962), pp. 271–294. On the importance of the concept of center see Edward A. Shils, "Centre and Periphery in the Logic of Personal Knowledge," *Essays Presented to Michael Polani*, London: Routledge & Kegan Paul, pp. 117–131, and "Charisma, Order, and Status," *American Sociological Review*, 30 (1965), pp. 199–213.

these characteristics, however, greatly influence transformative capacity in general, as well as the particular institutional form that modernization may take in a given case.

In the following analysis I shall point out some of the constellations that facilitate — or impede — modernization, focusing on three aspects of the relations among the various institutional spheres in pre-modern societies. The first of these aspects is the relation between the dominant value-system and political institutions; the second is the place of the political system in the stratification system; and the third is the degree of internal cohesion and social autonomy in the major social groups and strata within these societies. I shall attempt to test the fruitfulness of this approach first by analyzing the major Asian societies — China, Japan, and India — coming only later to a brief analysis of modern European societies.

CHINA [6]

China has had a long tradition of centralization, and a degree of social, political, and cultural continuity probably unparalleled in the history of mankind. Under the Imperial system Chinese society could absorb many changes brought about by conquests, changes of dynasties and rebellions, yet this great civilization was relatively unable to modernize itself from within, either through reformation of the Imperial system or through the initial revolution that developed against it. True, many reform movements did develop within the Chinese Imperial system, ranging from relatively "conservative," "traditional" attempts to preserve the Confucian ethic and its cultural primacy, to the more radical movements attempting to transform dominant value orientations and to establish a system independent of Confucian orientations and symbols. But as Levenson and others[7] have shown, these reforms were not very successful either in changing the ideology and institutions of the Imperial system or in creating new, viable frameworks.

Similarly, the first modern revolution against the Imperial system did not establish a viable, modern political system. Many external factors no doubt contributed to this failure, but it is still worthwhile to analyze the influence of some internal factors.

[6] See Etienne Balazs, *Chinese Civilization and Bureaucracy*, New Haven: Yale University Press, 1964, esp. Chs. 1 and 2, and Eisenstadt, *Political Systems of Empires, op. cit.*, which includes additional bibliography on all the societies analyzed here (except Japan).

[7] Joseph Levenson, *Modern China and Its Confucian Past*, New York: Doubleday Anchor Books, 1964, and the documents in Ssu-Yu Teng and John K. Fairbank, *China's Response to the West: A Documentary Survey, 1839–1923*, New York: Atheneum, 1963. See also Mary Wright, *The Last Stand of Chinese Conservatism: The T'ung-Chih Restoration, 1862–1874*, Stanford: Stanford University Press, 1957.

The first such factor is the nature of the legitimation of the Imperial system — the relation between Imperial political institutions and the major cultural centers, ideology and symbols. Here we find, among the great historic Imperial civilizations, the closest interweaving, almost identity, of cultural with political centers. Although in principle many universalistic ethical elements in the dominant Confucian ideology transcended any given territory or community, in actuality this ideology was very closely tied to the specific political framework of the Chinese Empire. The Empire was legitimized by the Confucian symbols but the Confucian symbols and Confucian ethical orientation found their "natural" place and framework, their major "referrent," within the Empire.[8]

This, of course, was also related to the fact that no church or cultural organization in China existed independently of the state. The Confucian élite was a relatively cohesive group, sharing a cultural background which was enhanced by the examination system and by adherence to Confucian rituals and classics. But its organization was almost identical with that of the state bureaucracy, and except for some schools and academies it had no organization of its own. Moreover, political activity within the Imperial-bureaucratic framework was a basic referrent of the Confucian ethical orientation, which was strongly particularistic and confined to the existing cultural-political setting.[9]

The relation between Chinese political and cultural orders is parallel to that between the political system and social stratification. The most interesting point here is that the total societal system of stratification was entirely focused on the political center. The Imperial center, with its strong Confucian orientation and legitimation, was the sole distributor of prestige and honor. Various social groups or strata did not develop autonomous, independent, status orientations, except on the purely local level; the major, almost the only wider orientations were bound to this monolithic political-religious center. Of crucial importance here is the structure of the major stratum linking the Imperial center of the broader society — the literati. This stratum was a source of recruitment to the bureaucracy and also maintained close relations with the gentry. Their double status orientation enabled the literati to fulfil certain crucial integrative functions in the Imperial system.[10] Their special position enabled them to influence the political activities of the rulers and of the leading strata of the population. But they exerted this influence by upholding the ideal of a hierarchical social-political-cultural order binding on the rulers

---

[8] See Eisenstadt, "Religious Organizations and Political Process in Centralized Empires," *op. cit.*, and Balazs, *op. cit.*
[9] Balazs, *op. cit.*
[10] *Ibid.*

and these strata. The very existence of the literati as an élite group was contingent on the persistence of the ideal of a unified Empire.

These characteristics of the literati were among the most important stabilizing mechanisms in the Imperial system, helping it to regulate and absorb changes throughout its long history. But these same characteristics have also severely inhibited development of a reformative or transformative capacity in China's culturally and politically most articulate groups.

Capacity for reform or transformation in the broader groups of Chinese society is also affected by their strong "familism" — the basis of their internal cohesion and self-identity. Familism has often been designated as one cause of China's relatively unsuccessful modernization. But as Levy has shown in his later analysis, it is not the familism as such that was important but rather the nature of the family's internal cohesion and its links with other institutional spheres.[11] The family was a relatively autonomous, self-enclosed group, with but few broader criteria or orientations. Beyond the commitment to the bureaucracy of those who attained positions within it, the primary duty of individuals was to increase family strength and resources, not to represent the family's worth according to external goals and commitments.

In combination, these various aspects of Chinese social structure go far toward explaining the weakness of the initial stages of China's modernization. The identity between the cultural and the political orders and the specific characteristics of the literati tended to maintain the dominance of a stagnative neo-traditionalism that continuously reinforced the non-transformative orientations in Chinese culture.

Under the first impact of modernization, Chinese intellectuals and bureaucrats faced certain problems stemming from the fact that their basic cultural symbols were embedded in the existing political structure. Any political revolution or reformation necessarily entailed rejecting or destroying the cultural order. Similarly, the strong ideological emphasis on upholding the social-political status quo inhibited the emergence of new symbols to legitimize new social institutions relatively independently of the preceding order.[12] Hence there developed little capacity for viable, flexible institution building, especially in the legal, legislative or administrative fields. Many such institutions were formally initiated, but they

[11] For the first analysis of Chinese familism from the point of view of modernization see Marion J. Levy, Jr., *The Family Revolution in Modern China*, Cambridge: Harvard University Press, 1952. Levy has further elaborated and to some extent modified the point of view expressed there in his "Contrasting Factors in the Modernization of China and Japan," in Simon Kuznets, Wilbert E. Moore and Joseph J. Spengler (eds.), *Economic Growth: Brazil, India, Japan,* Durham, N.C.: Duke University Press, 1955, pp. 496–537.

[12] Levenson, *op. cit.*, and Ssu-Yu Teng and Fairbank, *op. cit.*

lacked both "pre-contractual" bases of legitimation and the broader societal conditions and resources for effective functioning.[13]

But this weakness of initial reform and revolutionary movements in Imperial and post-Imperial China was only partly due to the ideological identity between the cultural and the political orders. No less important were the relations between political institutions and the system of social stratification. In the social sphere as in the ideological or cultural sphere, there were few points of internal strength, cohesion and self-identity on which new institutional frameworks could be founded or which could support institutional changes.

This weakness was reinforced by the limited reformative capacities of the family. When the Empire crumbled and processes of change swept over it, disorganizing and dislocating the traditional structure, and especially the major links to the center — the literati and the bueaucracy — family groups were largely dissociated from the center, but they lacked the strength to create new autonomous links. These family groups tended also to develop neo-traditional orientations, but because they were "closed" groups they could not regulate such demands effectively. In the more modern setting, they became highly politicized, making demands on the new, and for them not fully legitimate center, which sapped the resources available for internal redistribution and thus undermined the new institutional frameworks.

ISLAM

Throughout its history Islam has emphasized the identity between the religious and political communities, seeking to fuse these two institutional spheres in a manner almost unique in the history of the great universalistic religions.[14] This identity between political and religious communities represents a very important similarity between the Chinese and Islamic societies, though its religious or ideological bases are very different.

The Islamic states, especially the early Caliphates, developed out of a conquest in which a new universal religion was created and borne by conquering tribes. This identity between tribe and religion became weaker in later stages when the more centralized-bureaucratic empires (the Abbasides and Fatimides) developed and ethnically heterogeneous ele-

---

[13] For the institutional development of modern pre-Communist China see George M. Beckman, *The Modernization of China and Japan*, New York: Harper, 1962, especially Chs. 23 and 24, and William L. Tung, *The Political Institutions of Modern China*, The Hague: Martinus Nijhoff, 1964. For some of the problems of legal reform see Franz Michael, "The Role of Law in Traditional, Nationalist and Communist China," *The China Quarterly*, 9 (1962), pp. 124–148.

[14] Claude Cahen, "The Body Politic," in E. von Grunebaum (ed.), *Unity and Variety in Muslim Civilization*, Chicago: University of Chicago Press, 1955, pp. 132–163.

ments were welded together through a common religion and a new political framework, but political and the religious communities were united throughout the history of Islamic states.[15] Moreover, political issues (e.g., succession, and the scope of the political community) initially constituted the main theological problems of Islam.[16]

This political-religious unity had specific ideological and structural consequences. Within the Caliphate there developed, on the one hand, a very strong universalistic-missionary orientation and a strong emphasis on the state as the framework of the religious community but subordinate to it. On the other hand, religious functionaries and groups did not develop an overall, independent and cohesive organization. This combination limited political participation mostly to court cliques and the bureaucracy, but it also gave rise to extreme sectarian movements, some seeking to destroy the existing regime and establish a new, religiously pure and true one, others politically passive. Thus, strong reform movements based on universalistic and transcendental orientations did develop under Islam.[17] But it is very significant that these movements were successful only so far as they were not politically oriented and did not have to establish new central political institutions within the framework of Islamic tradition.

Islam reform movements were more successful in colonial situations, as in Indonesia or in Malaysia, where there were active minorities or where their political objective was to attain independence, and in cultural, educational and economic activities, than they were in the independent Muslim states where they had to try to establish a new Islamic polity. Islamic reform movements in India in the early 20th century, for instance, evinced a relatively strong emphasis on educational and cultural innovation. Subsequently, these movements were transformed into more populist, political ones during the immediate pre-partition period and especially in Pakistan after independence.[18]

[15] Bernard Lewis, *The Arabs in History*, London: Hutchinson, 1960, and Hamilton A. R. Gibb, "The Evolution of Government in Early Islam," in *Studies on the Civilisation of Islam*, Boston: Beacon Press, 1962, pp. 34–47.

[16] Erwin I. J. Rosenthal, *Political Thought in Mediaeval Islam*, Cambridge: Cambridge University Press, 1962.

[17] The first overall exposition of modernization in Islam is probably Hamilton A. R. Gibb, *Modern Trends in Islam*, Chicago: University of Chicago Press, 1947. For further elaboration see Muhsin Mahdi, "Modernity and Islam," in Joseph M. Kitagawa (ed.), *Modern Trends in World Religions*, La Salle, Ill.: Open Court, 1959, and Marshall G. S. Hodgson, "Modernity and the Islamic Heritage," *Islamic Studies*, 1 (1962), Karachi.

[18] Justus van der Kroef, "Recent Trends in Indonesian Islam," *The Muslim World*, 3 (1962), and "The Role of Islam in Indonesian Nationalism and Politics," *The Western Political Quarterly*, 11 (1958), pp. 33–54; Jan Prins, "Some Notes About Islam and Politics in Indonesia," *The World of Islam*, 6 (1959), pp. 124–126; Clifford Geertz, "Modernization in a Muslim Society: The Indonesian

Close identity between the political and the religious communities inhibited Islamic reform movements in ways somewhat similar to, but not identical with those in China. In the Islamic states as in China the identity between cultural and political institutions severely limited possibilities for the innovations necessary to develop viable modern legislative and juridical institutions;[19] nor did traditional Islamic prescriptions for appropriate political behavior facilitate legal innovations.[20]

Attempts to build modern nation-states on an Islamic base faced tremendous obstacles. The Islamic tradition was challenged by various new secular-national symbols, and efforts to legitimize national identities in terms of Islamic tradition intensified conflicts among various units.[21] The history of the attempt to establish an Islamic polity in Pakistan, for example, and similar experiences in various Middle Eastern countries, illustrate some of these difficulties.[22] Among the older Muslim states, only Tunisia — through a variety of circumstances I cannot go into here — seems to have succeeded, to some extent at least, in overcoming them.[23] (In Turkey — at the very core of the older Ottoman Empire — new institution building was attempted only through the complete negation of the Islamic tradition at the central political and symbolic level.[24])

With regard to the relations between political institutions and social

---

Case," in Robert N. Bellah (ed.), *Religion and Progress in Modern Asia*, New York: The Free Press, 1965; C. A. O. van Nieuwenhuize, *Aspects of Islam in Post Colonial Indonesia*, The Hague: W. van Hoeve, 1958, esp. Chs. 1, 2 and 5.

[19] See F. Rahman, "Muslim Modernism in the Indo-Pakistan Subcontinent," in *Bulletin of the School of Oriental and African Studies*, 21 (1958), pp. 82–99; Louis Dumont, "Nationalism and Communism," *Contributions to Indian Sociology*, 7 (1964), pp. 30–70; Hafez Malik, *Moslem Nationalism in India and Pakistan*, Washington, D.C.: Public Affairs Press, 1963.

[20] On problems of legal reform in modern Islam see James N. D. Anderson, *Islamic Law in the Modern World*, New York and London: Stevens, 1959; Joseph Schacht, "Problems of Modern Islamic Legislation," in Richard H. Nolte (ed.), *The Modern Middle East*, New York: Atherton Press, 1963, pp. 172–201; N. J. Coulson, *A History of Islamic Law*, Edinburgh: Edinburgh University Press, 1964.

[21] See Leonard Binder, *The Ideological Revolution in the Middle East*, New York: John Wiley, 1964, and Nadav Safran, *Egypt in Search of Political Community*, Cambridge: Harvard University Press, 1961.

[22] Leonard Binder, *Religion and Politics in Pakistan*, Los Angeles: University of California Press, 1961, and "Problems of Islamic Political Thought in the Light of Recent Development in Pakistan," *Journal of Politics*, 20 (1958), pp. 675–685.

[23] See Clement H. Moore, "The Neo-Destour Party of Tunisia: A Structure for Democracy?" *World Politics*, 14 (1962), pp. 461–482; Charles A. Micaud, Leonard C. Brown and Clement H. Moore, *Tunisia: The Politics of Modernization*, New York: Praeger, 1964; Gabriel Ardant, *La Tunisie d'Aujourdhui et de Demain*, Paris: Calman-Levy, 1961.

[24] Bernard Lewis, *The Emergence of Modern Turkey*, London: Oxford University Press, 1961.

stratification, Islamic patterns are less similar to the Chinese. The system of stratification in many Islamic societies was not focused to the same extent on the state, though in some extreme cases, as in the core of the Ottoman Empire, similar tendencies did develop. But on the whole, various social and cultural groups — e.g., the religious groups, the ulemas — evinced a higher degree of organizational and social autonomy. True, these same groups often became centers of reaction and traditionalism, but their autonomy did create possibilities for intellectual ferment and social change.

Moreover, in many Islamic societies a tradition of local, especially urban, community autonomy existed, even if it was only latent. Although the martial Ottoman rule weakened this tradition, on the whole, it persisted at the peripheries of the Empire, enhancing receptivity to modern intellectual and organizational trends and facilitating the concomitant development of various professional, entrepreneurial, administrative and intellectual groups.[25] But the inability of these groups to develop new, more effective links with the center, or to develop adequate self-regulative mechanisms, gave rise here also to a relatively high degree of politicization. Nevertheless, the major potential for reform and modernization must be sought within these groups.

JAPAN

The Japanese case is at a different pole of comparison with the Chinese one: here the importance of structural differences exceeds that of ideological or value orientations.

On the purely ideological level one may, at first sight, perceive a strong similarity between the Japanese and Chinese experiences. Indeed, an even more closed, particularistic orientation and collective identity existed in Japan. The identity between cultural and political orders was even closer, and universalistic elements or orientations beyond the existing political and national framework weaker,[26] so that emphasis on the Confucian ethic (though mixed with Buddhist and Shinto elements) created an even stronger identification with the particular polity than in China.

But paradoxically enough these elements did not greatly impede the internal transformation and modernization of Japanese society, although they influenced the directions and limits of modernization. On the value-

[25] Claude Cahen, "L'Histoire Economique et Sociale de l'Orient Musulman Médiéval," *Studia Islamica*, 111 (1955), pp. 93–116, and "Les Facteurs Economiques et Socieaux dans l'Ankyklose Culturelle de l'Islam," in R. Brunschwig and G. E. von Grunebaum (ed.), *Actes du Symposium International d'Historie de la Civilisation Musulmane*, Paris: Besson and Chautenerle, pp. 195–217.

[26] Robert N. Bellah, *Tokugawa Religion*, Glencoe, Ill.: The Free Press, 1956, and "Values and Social Change in Modern Japan," *Asian Cultural Studies*, 3 (1962), pp. 13–56; David M. Earl, *Emperor and Nation in Japan — Political Themes of the Tokugawa Period*, Seattle: University of Washington Press, 1964.

orientation level, as well as on that of the structural location of the central symbols of the society, several points of flexibility developed. First the structure of the center in the Tokugawa period differed in several crucial and important aspects from the Chinese or any other centralized Imperial system. The Japanese centralization took place under a special form of feudalism, and although the various autonomous feudal traditions were weakened or frozen they did not entirely lose their vitality.[27] Even more important, the arrangement of Tokugawa political institutions was such that the center was less monolithic than the strong ideological identity between cultural and the political orders might suggest.

The dissociation between the symbolic center, represented by the politically ineffective Emperor, and the politically effective center of the Shogunate obviated several of the potential consequences of a close identity between the polity and the cultural order.[28] In some ways this organizational duality was equivalent to a dissociation — on the substantive level — between the cultural and the political orders. This has facilitated a political revolution anchored in the ancient Imperial political symbolism and created an almost uniquely successful initial modernization based on neo-traditional orientations and symbols.[29] (Some of the traditional Kingdoms like Morocco, Buganda, or Ethiopia, may also attempt to modernize in this way, though they are handicapped by the absence of a similar dissociation between the traditional symbols and the effective political centers. But Professor Inkeles has drawn my attention to the fact that a development very similar to the Japanese one has lately been taking place in Nepal.)

The revival of the older symbolic center greatly facilitated and supported the overthrow, by an oligarchic revolution, of the political center of the Shogunate. This continuity of the Imperial tradition was not purely "decorative," but constituted the major focus of the new value orientations and the new national identity, and it greatly helped to mobilize the loyalties of the broader strata.[30] Such a transformation could not have been so easily attained in China or the Islamic states, where over-

[27] See Marius B. Jansen, *Sakamoto Ryoma and the Meiji Restoration*, Princeton: Princeton University Press, 1961; Albert M. Craig, *Chossu in the Meiji Restoration*, Cambridge: Harvard University Press, 1961.

[28] Ronald P. Dore, *Education in Tokugawa Japan*, Berkeley: University of California Press, 1964.

[29] See on this, among others, Marius B. Jansen, "Changing Japanese Attitude Toward Modernization," in Marius B. Jansen (ed.), *Changing Japanese Attitudes Toward Modernization*, Princeton: Princeton University Press, 1965; Robert N. Bellah, "Values and Social Change in Modern Japan," *op. cit.*, and "Epilogue," in his *Religion and Progress in Modern Asia*, *op. cit.*; Herbert Passin, "Modernization and the Japanese Intellectual, Some Comparative Observations," in Jansen (ed.), *op. cit.*

[30] Ronald P. Dore, "The Legacy of Tokugawa Education," in Jansen (ed.), *op. cit.*

throw of the political center would undermine the cultural order, and the mobilization of older traditional loyalties would diminish possibilities for developing a modern, effective political center.

Several aspects of Japanese religion enhanced the transformation. First, the syncretic nature of Japanese religion, and the relative lack of rigid orthodoxy, facilitated the absorption of new contents. Second, strong transcendental orientations, evinced in different ways in some Buddhist and Confucian circles, became more pronounced in the late Tokugawa period, which facilitated the development of independent standards under which various groups of individuals formulated legitimate collective goals.[31] The combination of religious syncretism with this transcendental emphasis facilitated both the redefinition of collective goals according to the more modern orientation of the Meiji oligarchs and the mobilization of wider loyalties in their implementation.

Other aspects of Japanese feudalism were also of great importance in the relatively successful initial modernization of the society. The hierarchically interlocked groups comprising the feudal system of stratification were strongly committed to collective obligations.[32] In their criteria of status and self-identity these groups evinced a relatively high degree of autonomy, but unlike the Chinese groups, these were not closed. Their identity, and the mutual obligations it entailed, were not entirely dependent on the political center. Nor were there homogeneous high-status political-cultural groups like the literati to monopolize the central political and elite positions. The major strata were much more dispersed and heterogeneous: there were clusters of feudal landlords, merchant and intellectual groups, each with some autonomy. Moreover, these groups were structurally linked to each other and to the center. All of these characteristics facilitated either self-transformation or a high degree of adaptability to any changes initiated by the center.

This structural aspect of the status system was reinforced by the transcendental elements of the religious orientation, permitting the transfer of loyalties from the old feudal-Shogunate-centered hierarchy to the new center.[33]

Certain aspects of Japanese family structure were also important here.[34] Although the family was a basic focus of solidarity and loyalty in Japan

[31] Bellah, *Tokugawa Religion*, *op. cit.*, and Dore, *Education in Tokugawa Japan*, *op. cit.*

[32] Herbert Norman, *Japan's Emergence as a Modern State*, New York: Institute of Pacific Relations, 1940; Levy, "Contrasting Factors in the Modernization of China and Japan," *op. cit.*; Craig, *Chossu in the Meiji Restoration*, *op. cit.*

[33] Dore, "The Legacy of Tokugawa Education," *op. cit.*, and *Education in Tokugawa Japan*, *op. cit.*

[34] Levy, "Contrasting Factors in the Modernization of China and Japan," *op. cit.*

as in China, its place depended to a large extent on its ability to further collective interests. Hence family units could develop semi-autonomous mechanisms to regulate their own activities and problems, minimizing initial demands on the center and conferring upon it the loyalties and resources of family groups.[35]

Because the older political and feudal regimes contained these seeds of autonomy and self-transformation, Japanese modernization proceeded rapidly. Industrialization, promulgated from the center, mobilized broad groups and strata. A new system of stratification emerged, as the Meiji oligarchs, themselves stemming from secondary aristocratic groups, abolished not only the political power of the older aristocracy but also its status symbols and economic (agrarian) bases. The Meiji monopolized the symbolic and political center, but they often used renovated traditional Imperial symbols to legitimize a much greater status flexibility. Although the status symbols and hierarchy they developed were close to the political center and to the oligarchs in power, emphasizing bureaucratic positions, the monolithic political forms that developed in China did not appear. In rural as well as urban sectors of Japanese society, the Meiji created more flexible, relatively autonomous new criteria for status, making it possible for new groups to crystallize their status.[36]

Some of the more specific structural characteristics of Japanese modernization can also be related to specific points of flexibility in the Tokugawa period. Among these the most important was the combination of universalistic and particularistic criteria regulating and channelling social mobility and mobilization. In the educational system, and on the "entry" to occupational statuses, universalistic criteria were applied, especially in the various periods or stages of examinations. But beyond this entrance stage, on almost all levels of the social and occupational structure, various particularistic units, such as school cliques, company and bureaucratic cliques and groups, small labor groups, etc., tended to crystallize. Within these units many traditional forms and attitudes persisted, and little mobility occurred between them. At the same time, however, the extent of overlapping between different particularistic units was relatively small, with few ecological crystallizations of such overlapping, so that particularistic developments did not impede and may even have facilitated status flexibility and recrystallization in certain social groups.[37]

This flexibility enabled Japan to deal with many of the problems of modernization, though not with all of them. She could not avoid various breakdowns, the most important of which took place in the late 1920's

[35] *Ibid.*
[36] Ezra Vogel, *Japan's New Middle Classes*, Berkeley: University of California Press, 1963.
[37] *Ibid.*

and early 1930's.[38] During that period various new élites — the more modern and independent middle classes, professional, and intellectual groups,
as well as some workers' organizations — attempted to enlarge the scope
of their political participation. Failing to absorb these new elements, the
modern system broke down and this gave rise to the militarist regimes of
the thirities. This development was mostly due to the rulers' attempt to
stifle new demands, and to control these new groups and their demands
through bureaucratic and military factions under the aegis of Imperial
symbols. The initial incorporation of new demands in the early Meiji
period was also done through such factions, but because the system was
not fully institutionalized it could not cope with the growing dissociation
among the modern business and intellectual élites and working-class leaders on the one hand, and the more traditional and oligarchic élites on the
other.

Here several weaknesses in the process of Japanese modernization stand
out. The first was in the nature of the symbolic transformation of the
center. The new, organizationally flexible center established by the Meiji
oligarchs embodied no internal transformation of values. The new national identity was couched mostly in terms of particularistic loyalty to
the Emperor as Son of Heaven rather than in terms of his representation
of any wider (transcendental) or universalistic values. While this Imperial
symbolism was flexible enough to absorb many new political orientations,
the basic legitimation of the new political community and its activities
did not transcend particularistic collective symbols. Hence value orientations through which various new social forces could be legitimated and
impinge on the center in autonomous terms, and through which support
for various autonomous regulative mechanisms and frameworks could be
provided, did not develop.[39]

Similarly, although the central groups possessed a relatively high degree of status flexibility at a relatively early stage of modernization, this
flexibility was not bolstered by an antonomous basis for legitimation and

---

[38] Some of the basic data on this period in Japanese history are collected in
Ivan Morris (ed.), *Problems in Asian Civilisations: Japan 1931–1945*, Boston:
D. C. Heath, 1963. For analyses of the Japanese situation in that period see Talcott
Parsons, "Population and the Social Structure of Japan," in his *Essays in Socio-
logical Theory* (rev. ed.), Glencoe, Ill.: Free Press, 1959, pp. 275–298; Masao
Maruyama, *Thought and Behaviour in Japanese Politics*, London: Oxford Univer-
sity Press, 1963; Dore, "The Legacy of Tokugawa Education," *op. cit.*; Passin,
op. cit.

[39] Masao Maruyama, "Patterns of Individuation and the Case of Japan: A
Conceptual Scheme," in Jansen (ed.), *op. cit.*, pp. 489–533; Bellah, "Epilogue,"
op. cit., and "Values and Social Change in Modern Japan," *op. cit.*; Herbert Passin,
"Stratigraphy of Protest in Japan," in Morton Kaplan (ed.), *The Revolution in
World Politics*, New York: John Wiley, 1963, pp. 12–113.

self-perception. The heavy neo-traditionalism of the center did not foster the development of autonomous value orientations and hence limited the ability of various social groups to develop institutional frameworks for mediating among the interests of various groups and evolving a broad base of consensus.[40]

Only under the impact of.external forces (i.e., military defeat) did Japanese modernization make a new start. This new phase is also, as yet, overshadowed by problems from the past, especially the absence of an internal value transformation at the time of Japan's initial modernization.

INDIA

India is probably the only complex and highly differentiated historical civilization that has maintained its cultural integrity without being tied to any particular political framework.[41] This is true not only of the last centuries under Muslim and later English rule but even before that. In India there were small and large states and Imperial centers, but no single state with which the cultural tradition was identified. Classical Indian religious thought did, of course, refer to political issues, and to the behavior of princes and the duties and rights of subjects.[42] But to a much higher degree than in many other historical Imperial civilizations, politics were conceived in secular terms. The basic religious and cultural orientations, the specific cultural identity of Indian civilization, were not necessarily associated with any particular political or imperial framework; whatever partial identity of such kind might have existed during the period before Muslim domination has been greatly diminished since then. The strength and survival of Indian civilization under alien rule is rooted in the very fact that it was not identified with any political framework.

This basic characteristic of Indian civilization had a very important influence on the initial modernization processes, which began under the

[40] Dore, "Education in Tokugawa Japan," *op. cit.*, and "The Legacy of Tokugawa Education," *op. cit.*; Parsons, *op. cit.*

[41] See Percival Spear, *India: A Modern History*, Ann Arbor: University of Michigan Press, 1961; Louis Renou, Jean Filliozet *et al.*, *L'Inde Classique* (2 vols.), Paris: Presses Universitaires, 1947, 1953; H. N. Sinha, *The Development of Indian Polity*, Bombay: India Publishing House, 1963.

[42] This aspect of Indian political thought is elaborated from different points of view, in V. P. Varma, *Studies in Hindu Political Thought and Its Metaphysical Background*, Benares: 1954; Louis Dumont, *La Civilisation Indienne et Nous*, Paris: Libraire Armand Colin, 1964, and "The Conception of Kingship in Ancient India," *Contributions to Indian Sociology*, 6 (1962), pp. 46–76; Charles Drekmeier, *Kingship and Community in Early India*, Stanford: Stanford University Press, 1962. The best known classical text is the Arthashastra: see Rudrapatna Shammasastry (ed.), *Kautilya's Arthashastra* (5th ed.), Mysore Printing and Publishing House, 1960. Some additional texts can be found in William T. de Bary, Stephen N. Hay, Rayal Weiler and Andrew Yarrow, *Sources of Indian Tradition*, New York: Columbia University Press, 1958, pp. 236–258.

aegis of the British and continued during the nationalist movement. Because the cultural and political orders were more or less dissociated, modernization was relatively free of specific traditional-cultural orientations toward the political sphere. The modern center was first established in terms of western symbols and was to some extent detached from the great Indian cultural tradition.[43] In the Gandhian phase, the political aspirations of the Indian national movement were to some extent couched in traditional symbols or at least were legitimized by some interpretation of such symbols, but this did not create (as it did in Islam) too specific or intensive demands on the institutional structure.[44]

This dissociation was itself at least partially legitimized in terms of traditional ideological orientations. Some of the symbols or values of the new center, expressed mostly in terms of such Western values as political and social justice, could be legitimized in older, classical Indian political terms. This was reinforced by reformist tendencies among the upper strata of Hindu society after 1850, for, significantly enough, the new political-ideological center was to a large extent developed and borne by people coming from the strata — especially the Brahmanic groups — who were the bearers of the historical tradition in its non-political aspects and emphases.[45]

The second relevant aspect of Indian society has to do with the place of the political system in the system of stratification and the internal cohesion of broader social groups and strata. In their identity and in their relation to the political order, these groups evinced a very high degree of autonomy. Parallel to the relative independence of cultural traditions from the political center, castes, villages, and the various networks of communication were highly autonomous, self-regulating in terms of their own cultural and social identity, with but limited access to the political center or centers.[46]

[43] Spear, op. cit.

[44] See, for instance, Lala Lajpat Rai, "The Remedy for Revolution," Jawaharlal Nehru, "Satyagrapha," and Mohandras Karamchand Gandhi, "Face to Face with Ahimsa," all in D. M. Brown (ed.), Indian Political Thought from Ranade to Bhave, Berkeley: University of California Press, 1961; and Stanley A. Wolfert, Tilak and Gohale in Revolution and Reform in the Making of Modern India, Berkeley: University of California Press, 1962.

[45] See the first chapter of the forthcoming work by Gopal Krishna, "The Development of the Organization of Indian National Congress, 1918–1932" (mimeo.). On the reforming potential of Hinduism see Joseph W. Elder, "Industrialism in Hindu Society: A Case Study in Social Change," unpublished Ph.D. thesis, Harvard University, 1959; and Milton Singer, et al., "India's Cultural Values and Economic Development: A Discussion," Economic Development and Cultural Change, 7 (1958), pp. 1–12.

[46] See Milton Singer (ed.), Traditional India: Structure and Change, Philadelphia: American Folklore Society, 1959, and Myron Weiner, "India's Two

For the process of modernization, this autonomy meant that the new political center could develop without intensive demands immediately impinging on it. The broader strata had their own mechanisms for coping with some of the problems of modernization, without becoming disorganized or making excessive demands on the political center. By comparison, the situation in many new states is that broader groups depend on the center so heavily that it cannot crystallize. That this did not happen in India has greatly facilitated the development, first under British influence and then in the nationalist movement through the Congress, of a central, stable institutional structure which maintained order, established a modern framework, and is gradually expanding to incorporate broader groups.

Consequently, a concrete structural feature of modernization has been the continuous recrystallization of traditional fameworks, and especially of the various networks of caste relations. The configuration of castes has been transformed; caste groups have assumed new tasks and adapted readily to new economic and political frameworks.[47] Patterns of traditional caste-mobility persist: i.e., existing subcaste groups assume some new economic, political or ritual tasks more or less within the range set by traditional culture, or they attempt to obtain a better standing within the old, traditional ritual order. But side by side with this pattern a new one has developed, in which the older caste groups gave way to new broader, more differentiated and more flexible networks of caste associations, organized around modern economic, professional and political activities in a great variety of new organizational forms. Often though not always, these new associations crosscut the existing political, social and economic hierarchies of status.[48]

But in these developments there were points of weakness. Although the center was institutionally and organizationally strong and flexible, it did not develop common symbols in which elements of the new culture could be combined with the older traditions so as to create a relatively strong collective identity and commitments to it. This also reduced its ability to provide new symbols that would serve not only as foci of rebellion against the colonial rulers but also as flexible guidelines for institution building.[49] This weakness became especially critical when the center extended, through

---

Political Cultures," in his *Political Change in South Asia*, Calcutta: Firma K. L. Mukhopadhyay, 1965, pp. 115–153. On the development of the "modern" center see Rajni Kothari, "The Congress System in India," *Asian Survey*, 4 (1964), pp. 1161–1174.

[47] The best known analysis of these developments is M. N. Srinivas, *Caste in Modern India*, Bombay: Asia Publishing House, 1962, esp. Chs. 1, 2 and 4.

[48] See André Neteille, *Closed and Open Social Stratification in India*, New Delhi (forthcoming), 1965; and Rajni Kothari and A. Maru, *Caste and Secularism in India — A Case Study of a Caste Federation*, New Delhi (forthcoming), 1965.

[49] See Kothari, "The Congress System in India," *op. cit.*, and Weiner, *op. cit.*

universal suffrage, the scope of its activities and consequently its dependence on broader groups. Then the lack of association between the cultural traditional and political framework, which was a point of strength
in the beginning, became a point of weakness. The center must create
new, binding symbols of collective identity to overcome the more "parochial" — mostly linguistic — symbols of the different regions and states
and develop some feeling of political community. This is especially important because these parochial symbols tend to become more cystallized
and better articulated as peripheral segments of the society are modernized.
The explosive quality of the linguistic question in India today is a manifestation of this problem.[50]

A second problem has to do with the extent to which the permissiveness
of the broad Indian cultural tradition and its reforming tendencies not
only facilitates new institutional frameworks, under external influence,
and the continuous adaptation of the traditional groups, but also develops innovative forces, and common integrative frameworks to support
continuous institution building. Here the question is whether caste and
other traditional groups will develop new, more flexible frameworks,
cross-cutting different status hierarchies, and new values, orientations,
and activities within them, or whether they will mainly reinforce the neo-
traditional divisive symbols and groupings.[51]

The internal transformation of the great Asian societies, then, has been
greatly facilitated by autonomy of social, cultural and political institutions. Cultural autonomy has made possible the development of new
symbols supporting and legitimizing central institution building, while autonomy in the sphere of social organization has facilitated the crystallization of viable new organizational nuclei without disrupting the pre-existing order, thus enabling the new order to rely, at least to some extent,
on the forces of the old one. The relatively strong internal cohesion of
broader strata and of family groups, with some status autonomy and
openness toward the center, has helped to develop positive orientations
to the new centers and willingness to provide the necessary support and
resources.

The precise institutional contours of emerging modern systems, as we
have seen, depend on the concrete structural location of autonomous institutional spheres.

Conversely, so far as such autonomy is absent, and the social, cultural,

[50] See Selig S. Harrison, *India: The Most Dangerous Decades*, Princeton, N.J.:
Princeton University Press, 1960; Paul Friedrich, "Language and Politics in India,"
Daedalus, 91 (1962), pp. 543–559.

[51] On these different possibilities, see Lloyd I. Rudolph and Susanne Hoeber
Rudolph, "The Political Role of India's Caste Associations," *Pacific Affairs*, 33
(1960), pp. 5–22; Beteille, *op. cit.*, and Srinivas, *Caste in Modern India, op. cit.*

and political orders are closely identified with one another, the development of viable modern structures has been greatly impeded. And where family and other groups are closed, they are likely to undermine the new institutional centers by making intensive and unregulated demands on them or by withholding resources. As the Chinese and Islamic examples show, the weak points in emerging new structures depend to some extent on the structural location of the mutually identified institutional spheres.

PROTESTANTISM AND MODERNIZATION IN THE WEST

I have confined the preceding analysis to great Asian civilizations that were drawn into modernization from the "base" of a relatively centralized and differentiated Imperial system. In this they differ greatly from African and Latin-American societies, which modernized either from relatively undifferentiated social structures without strong centers and a great cultural tradition or which, like most Latin American countries, were mainly peripheral to such centers. But it would be beyond the scope of this paper to examine the extent to which my analysis may be applied to these cases.

Even with regard to these more differentiated and centralized Asian societies, however, structural flexibility was not in itself — as the Indian and Japanese cases indicate — enough to assure the development and continuity of modern institutional frameworks. Flexibility, or the autonomy of different institutional orders, created the conditions under which more active groups and élites could attempt to institute new principles of cultural direction and social integration. But the mere existence of structural flexibility neither assured that such groups would appear nor indicated the type of integrative orientation they would develop.

Indeed, it is the extent to which such groups do develop that has been especially in China, India, and some Islamic societies — perhaps the major problem facing these societies during their modernization. The root of the problem in these societies was that modernization was a matter of encounter with foreign forces, an encounter beset with the difficulties and ambivalences of colonial or semi-colonial relations. Modernization therefore required that the new élites create a national identity from the encounter with these foreign and often alien forces. The internal capacities of these societies for reformation or transformation may have been crucial to their adaptation to these external forces and to their success in building new institutional structures to cope with these problems. But the very nature of the modernization process in these societies was such that the sources and directions of the cultural transformation, and the potential creativity of different élite groups, were not necessarily given by the same factors that initiated their modern structural transformation.

The earliest modernization — that of Western Europe since the 18th century — permits a fuller analysis of the relative importance of structural flexibility and active cultural transformation in modernization, for here both processes were, from the very beginning, initiated mainly from within. In European — especially Western Christian European — culture the tradition of autonomous cultural, political, and social orders is strong, and here the first and most continuous impetus to modernization did indeed develop. But even in Western and Central European countries, the course of modernization was neither entirely continuous nor everywhere the same.

What requires explanation is the fact that background more or less common to all Western and Central European societies gave rise to different modern institutional frameworks, with greatly varying capacities to sustain change.

One approach to this question is to reexamine Weber's famous Protestant Ethic thesis and some recent criticisms of it. At first glance, it may seem that Weber was dealing not with the structural and cultural variables I have discussed, but mainly with the religious roots of orientations to new types of economic activity. But several recent discussions of Weber's thesis indicate that some of its broader implications may be relevant to the present discussion. Of special interest from this point of view are the comments of Luethy and Trevor-Roper.[52]

Luethy, and to some extent Trevor-Roper, deny Weber's thesis in the economic field proper, claiming that economic development in Europe was independent of the specific direct impact of Protestantism. They show, for instance, as others have before them, that the first impact of Protestantism on economic life was a restrictive one, as Calvin's Geneva demonstrates. For Luethy, however, the major impact of Protestantism on European history was in the political field. This impact was effected, according to him, through direct reference to the Bible in search of new bases to legitimate authority as well as through the new structural impetus to pluralistic politics which developed through the Counter-Reformation of the Wars of Religion.[53]

Both Luethy and Trevor-Roper admit — indeed, stress — that England and the Netherlands especially, and to some extent the Scandinavian countries, were more successful after the Counter-Reformation in devel-

[52] Herbert Luethy, "Once Again — Calvinism and Capitalism," *Encounter*, January, 1964, pp. 26–39 and his earlier exposition in *La Banque Protestante en France de la Revocation de l'Edit de Nantes à la Revolution*, Paris: S.E.V.P.E.N., 1961, Vol. I, Ch. 1, and Vol. III, pp. 749–786; Hugh Trevor-Roper, "Religion: The Reformation and Social Change," *Historical Studies*, 4 (1965), pp. 18–45.

[53] In this he is close to Michael Walzer, who stresses the Puritan's revolutionary ideology in "Puritanism as a Revolutionary Ideology," *History and Theory*, 4 (1963), pp. 59–90.

oping viable modern institutions than were most of the Catholic countries. To this they attribute the ultimate, but not the initial success and continuity of modernization in Protestant countries.

Without going into the detailed merits of these criticisms of Weber's thesis,[54] it might be worthwhile to point out that in principle the criticism Luethy directs against Weber could easily be directed against his own thesis. For instance, one could show that the original political impulse of either Lutheranism or Calvinism was not in a "liberal" or democratic direction but rather in a more "totalistic" one.

But apart from such details, both Weber's and Luethy's analyses deal not with the direct economic or political "results" of certain religious beliefs or the activities of religious groups, but rather — as Troeltsch has already seen[55] — with their more indirect impact. Initially the Reformation was not a "modernizing" movement; it aimed to establish a purer "medieval" socio-political religious order. Protestantism produced an impetus toward modernity only after this initial socio-religious impulse failed. Hence theories that attempt to evaluate this influence or impact of Protestantism necessarily deal with the transformed social orientations of Protestant religious groups after they had failed to establish their initial militant, totalistic aims restricting autonomous activities in both the economic and the political field. From a comparative point of view, the special importance of Protestantism is that the basic Protestant value orientations and social organization contained within themselves the seeds of such transformation. The exact way in which this transformation worked out in the institutional framework of any given society, however, depended not only on the internal predispositions of the Protestant groups but also on some aspects of the preceding social structure and on the *initial* interaction between this structure and the original religious groups.

Here a question not considered by Luethy and Trevor-Roper is very pertinent: the extent to which the Protestant Reformation influenced the development of the social and political flexibility to which they attach so much importance. The Protestant Reformation did indeed have an enormous impact not only on the motivational orientations of its adherents but also, through the social and status orientations of various Protestant

[54] Cf. some of the older controversies around the Weber thesis in Robert W. Green, *Protestantism and Capitalism: The Weber Thesis and Its Critics*, Boston: D. C. Heath, 1959, and Sidney A. Burrell (ed.), *The Role of Religion in Modern European History*, New York: Macmillan, 1964.

[55] Ernest Troeltsch, *Protestantism and Progress*, Boston: Beacon Press, 1958; one of the most recent critical analyses of Weber which does not take this into account is Geoffrey R. Elton, *Reformation Europe*, London: Collins, 1963, pp. 312 ff.

groups, on the central political sphere. This impact was not necessarily intended by the rulers who adopted Protestantism, yet it did facilitate the further development of a more flexible and dynamic social system. In the first Protestant societies — England, Scandinavia, the Netherlands, and later in the United States — perhaps even before the full development of a new motivational orientation, the central symbolic and political sphere, and the basic relations between the political and social spheres, were transformed through the incorporation of Protestant values and symbols. This not only reinforced the existing autonomy of these spheres but created new bases of political obligations and more flexible political institutions.[56]

Protestantism had a similar impact on the internal cohesion and autonomy of the more active social groups in these societies. Most of the Protestant groups developed a combination of two types of status orientation. First was their "openness" toward the wider social structure, rooted in the "this-worldly" orientations which were not limited to the economic sphere, but were gradually extended to demands for wider political participation and new, broader political frameworks and criteria. Second, their status orientations were characterized by a certain autonomy and self-sufficiency. Unlike countries or sectors with a more autocratic or aristocratic tradition, they were, from the point of view of the crystallization of their status symbols, virtually independent of the existing (i.e., monarchical or ecclesiastical) centers of political power.

But such orientations did not develop to the same extent among all Protestant groups in all countries. The full development and institutionalization of such orientations depended to no small degree on the flexibility or "openness" of the existing political and cultural centers, and that of broader groups and strata and their initial reaction to religious innovations. So far as this reaction was restrictive, the transformative potentialities of these orientations could not bear full fruit.

The various interactions between different transformative potentialities and existing structural flexiblity could give rise to paradoxically similar — or divergent — results. The influence of the allegedly conservative Lutheranism, for example, took a variety of forms. In the German principalities Lutheranism was indeed very restrictive, because the existing political framework was not an appropriate setting for the development of a na-

---

[56] For some of the very numerous analyses bearing on this see Enno van Gelder, *Revolutionaire Reformatie*, Amsterdam: Van Kayse, 1943; Charles H. George and Katherine George, *The Protestant Mind of the English Reformation*, Princeton: Princeton University Press, 1961; David Little, "The Logic of Order — an Examination of the Sources of Puritan-Anglican Controversy and of Their Relation to Prevailing Legal Conceptions in the Sixteenth and Seventeenth Centuries," unpublished Doctor of Theology thesis, Harvard University, 1963.

tional identity and community or for the development of more autonomous and flexible status orientations in the broader strata.[57] Here, "traditional", or autocratic rulers of the small principalities adopted the new
religious orientations, and in this context the more conservative among
these orientations became predominant, often restricting further institutional development.

But in the Scandinavian countries these religious orientations were integrated into new, wider national communities and developed on the
bases of the prior autonomy of the Estates. While they certainly did not
impede the development of an absolutist state in Sweden they did help
to make possible the subsequent development of these states in a more
pluralistic direction.[58]

Similarly paradoxical results, also demonstrating the importance of restrictive prior situations, are evident in the institutionalization of Calvinism. Of special interest here is the Prussian case, where the institutionalization of these orientations by the absolutist, autocratic Hohenzollerns did
not facilitate the development of a flexible and pluralistic political framework, though it did support development of more activist collective political goals.[59]

Thus, so far as the initial impact of the religious changes reinforced the
seeds of autonomy, which were to a high degree present in all Western
and Central European societies, it created the basis of a new political
order, not only on the structural-institutional level, but also on the level
of central values and symbols which both legitimized these institutions
and prompted their further development. Under such conditions, potentially activist religious orientations could take various institutional directions — e.g., economic, or political as in Scotland, or scientific — and become institutionalized, thus reinforcing the continuous development of

[57] See, for instance, Alfred L. Drummond, *German Protestantism Since Luther*,
London: Epworth Press, 1951; John T. McNeill, *The History and Character of
Calvinism*, New York: Oxford University Press, 1954; Gerhard Ritter, "Das 16.
Jahrhundert als weltgeschichtliche Epoche," *Archiv für Geschichte der Reforma-
tion*, 35 (1938), and *Die Neugestaltung Europas im 16. Jahrhundert*, Berlin:
Druckhaus Tempelhof, 1950, Ch. 3, esp. pp. 133–170; Alfred Adam, "Die
nationale Kirche bei Luther," *Archiv für Geschichte der Reformation*, 35 (1938),
pp. 30–62.

[58] Hajalmar Holmquist, *Kirche und Staat im Evangelischen Schweden, Festgabe
für Karl Müller*, Tübingen: J. C. B. Mohr, 1922, pp. 209–277; Heinz H. Schrey,
"Geistliches und Weltliches Regiment in der Schwedischen Reformation," *Archiv
für Geschichte der Reformation*, 42 (1951), pp. 146–159; Georg Schweiger, *Die
Reformation in den Nordischen Ländern*, München: Kozel Verlag, 1962; and
Georg Ritter, *Die Neugestaltung, op. cit.*

[59] Christine R. Kayser, "Calvinism and German Political Life," unpublished
Ph.D. thesis, Radcliffe, 1961.

these societies. But so far as some of these conditions were lacking, these religious orientations were institutionalized in partial, relatively constrictive or discontinuous ways reducing their transformative potential.

The different Catholic countries, on the other hand, demonstrate the limitations of purely structural autonomy. The first impetus of many modern developments — economic, scientific, cultural or political — occurred in Catholic countries too. But the continuity of these developments was greatly impeded by the initial response to many of their more far-reaching consequences and especially to their convergence with Protestantism, which minimized, at least initially, the possibility of continuous development of modern institutions.

The case of Spain[60] — in a way the first modern state — illustrates this pattern most clearly, but it is perhaps even more prominent in the case of France, where the potentially pluralistic impact of various modern trends, including Protestantism, was inhibited by the formation of the French state during the Counter-Reformation. This provided the background for continuous rifts in the central political symbols — between traditional and modern (revolutionary), aristocratic and republican, religious and secular orientations — rifts that persisted till the end of the Third Republic.[61]

Only through the juxtaposition of the structural aspects with processes of élite formation and creativity can the transformative potential of any pre-modern society be fully evaluated. The Asian societies with which this discussion began require still further analysis, for which this paper may, perhaps, serve as a starting point.

Notes for
Further Reading

For general analysis of processes of change attendant on modernization, see:

Almond, G.A., and Coleman, J.S. (eds.), *The Politics of the Developing Areas*. Princeton: Princeton University Press, 1960, pp. 52–55.

Apter, D., *The Politics of Modernization*. Chicago: University of Chicago Press, 1966.

Deutsch, K.A., "The Growth of Nations: Some Recurrent Patterns of Political and Social Integration," *World Politics*, Vol. 5, No. 2, Jan., 1953, pp. 168–195.

Eisenstadt, S.N., *Modernization, Protest and Change*. Englewood Cliffs: Prentice-Hall, 1966.

[60] See Americo Castro, *The Structure of Spanish History*, Princeton: Princeton University Press, 1954.

[61] See, for instance, Herbert Luethy, *France Against Herself*, New York: Frederick A. Praeger, 1955.

Lerner, D.L., *The Passing of Traditional Society*. Glencoe, Ill.: The Free Press, 1958.

Shils, E.A., *Political Developments in New States*. The Hague: Mouton, 1961.

For the analysis of specific cases of modernization see:

Cline, H.F., "Mexico: A Matured Latin American Revolution, 1910–1960.' *Annals*, Vol. 334, March 1961, pp. 84–94.

Feith, H., *The Decline of Constitutional Democracy in Indonesia*. Ithaca, N.Y.: Cornell University Press, 1962.

Hannah, W.A., *Bung Karno's Indonesia*. New York: American Universities Field Staff, 1961.

Johnson, J.J., *Political Change in Latin America*. Stanford University Press, 1958, esp. Chapter 6.

Levy, M.J., "Contrasting Factors in the Modernization of China and Japan," in Kuznets, Moore, and Spengler (eds.), *Economic Growth: Brazil, India, and Japan*. Durham, N.C.: Duke University Press, 1955.

Morris, I. (ed.), *Japan 1931–1945: Problems in Asian Civilizations*. Boston: D.C. Heath & Company, 1963.

Pye, L.W., *Politics, Personality and Nation Building*. New Haven: Yale University Press, 1962.

Silvert, K. *The Conflict Society, Reaction and Revolution in Latin America*. New Orleans: Hauser, 1961.

Ward, R. and D.A. Ruston (eds.), *Political Modernization in Japan and Turkey* Princeton: Princeton University Press, 1964.